More Than
Beards, Bellies and Biceps:
The Story of the 1993 Phillies
(And the Phillie Phanatic Too)

By Robert Gordon and Tom Burgoyne
Foreword by Larry Andersen

Sports Publising L.L.C.
www.SportsPublishingLLC.com

Director of production: Susan M. Moyer
Layout and design: Tracy Gaudreau
Dust jacket design: Christine Mohrbacher
Developmental editor: Noah Amstadter
Copy editor: Cindy McNew

ISBN: 1-58261-491-1

Sports Publishing L.L.C
www.SportsPublishingLLC.com

For our moms and dads –
for swinging us so high!

Contents

Acknowledgments

- Susan, for her patience, sagacity, and sanity in putting up with two morons. Jennifer, for letting Tom trash the living room with "book stuff" for a year and for making 1993 special. To Andrew and Daniel, Tom's two Hall of Famers. To Tom's brothers and sisters (Joe, Ellen, Steve, Mark and Kathy) who made making the climb up to the 700 level so much fun.
- Ryan and Bree—no one's going to tell me it's them; if it's anyone, it's *me*.
- Rosie Rahn for being the nicest photographer in baseball and for our photos.
- Jayson Stark, Paul Hagen, Bob Brookover, Angelo Cataldi, Bill Conlin, Stan Hochman for sharing some great insights.
- Chrissy Long for your friendship and for handling all those dogs, elephants, horses, cows, monkeys, dancing pigs…
- Chad Bowman for being a "good mate." Cheers!
- Larry Krause and my "pal," Eric Gerstel, for the Letterman tapes and the normal dose of insults.
- Mon A, JTA.
- Scruffy the grumpy cat.
- Andrea Guest for making sure I make it to my appearances on time.
- Matt Mehler and Mike Alexander for keeping the tradition alive and well.
- Bill Giles, David Montgomery, and the Baron (Larry Shenk) for your sage advice and for your love of the Phillies. To everybody on the fourth floor for helping to find phone numbers, stats and pictures, especially Christine Negley, Leigh Tobin, Greg Casterioto, Susan Ingersoll, Jay McLaughlin, Mike Pacchione, Tina Urban and Melissa Maani—you guys really *do* work up there! To all the Marketing Guys, especially Kurt Funk, Dave Buck, Scott Brandreth and John Brazer, thanks for your help in getting this book out to Phillies fans (and baseball fans) everywhere. To Debbie Nocito, the Phillies Den Mother. Christine Lynch, Christine Keller and Michele Davis for watching Tom's back(side). To Video Dan Stephenson, thanks for all your assistance and great stories…you *could* write a book!
- Philadelphia Mummers Museum, and all of Philly's Mummers.
- Philadelphia Police, especially Officer John Marynowitz—a full measure of appreciation from all of Philly's citizens for all your sacrifices and valor
- Former mayor Ed Rendell, our town's biggest sport fan.
- Dave Raymond for passing the head…er…I mean the torch to Tom.
- Larry Andersen for being so damn unique and real.
- Bonnie Erickson for giving the book your special artistic touch.
- Jen and the Rt. 363 Starbucks crew—Brendan, Chris, et al for letting me camp out and write there—oh, and for the fun and great coffee too.
- Ditto for Kevin and Marie at The Daily Grind in Hatboro
- St. Dominic's Grade School, Immaculate Conception School, Father Judge HS, St. Joe's Prep, Drexel U and Lehigh U for trying to educate us.

Foreword

By Larry Andersen

"I got players that got bad watches. They can't tell midnight from noon."
That was a quote from Casey Stengel back in the '60s, but Jim Fregosi, '93 Phils
manager, could have said the same thing. You see, that '93 club didn't always feel
the need to sleep, at least not normal hours. But then again, as you read through
these pages, you'll see this wasn't your normal club.

From spring training where Eisey (Jim Eisenreich) got his real nickname
(you'll find out later: *it's not Eisey*) and DJ (Danny Jackson) became known as
Jason, to the last game in Toronto where Mitch Williams still stood proud (and
rightly so) this book will give *you*, the fans—no, let me restate that—*our fans*,
some insight and understanding into what made the '93 Phils such a special
team.

One big reason those '93 Phils were special *was* our fans. You took us into
your hearts, you cheered us on in record numbers at the Vet, and you shared the
joy of that season with us. The 40,000-plus people who showed up that summer
for twenty consecutive home dates (still a franchise record) and the hundreds of
people who entered the stadium after last call at Delaware Valley bars the night
we played (baseball, that is) till 4:41 a.m., let us know that we were one with
you, the fans.

New York Yankees President Michael Burke testified at a New York City
Council Committee hearing in 1971 (and I quote), "A baseball club is part of
the chemistry of the city. A game isn't just an athletic contest. It's a picnic, a kind
of town meeting." I think I speak on behalf of all the players who wore Phillies
pinstripes in 1993 when I say that, yes, our team had a special chemistry with
our city. And the enthusiasm and loyalty of the fans of Philadelphia provided the
perfect ingredients for that chemistry to work. You helped us through that long,
hot summer as the '93 Phils strived to play the game in a way that typified this
beautiful blue-collar town. And *was* that summer ever fun! We had one helluva
picnic and one terrific town meeting that lasted from April to October.

Our team could not have been a better mix. We had a roster of mostly
veterans, sprinkled with some rookies and no real superstars to speak of—at least
nobody acted like one. We were all in this thing together with one common
goal, to win. Well, actually two common goals … we also wanted to have fun.
You've got to have fun. It's a prerequisite for success. As former Padres manager
Don Zimmer once said. "The game has to be fun if you're gonna be any good at
all." There will never be any doubt in my mind that, beginning in mid-February
in Clearwater, Florida, right on up to the very last day in Toronto, Canada, each

and every '93 Phillie not only lived up to, but also lived *for*, these two common goals. General Manager Lee Thomas knew he had a good nucleus of players, but after 92 losses in 1992, he also realized some changes had to be made. So what did he do? He dealt himself a poker hand. That's essentially what Bill Veeck, longtime owner of the Chicago White Sox, once likened building a ball club to. He said, "You have all winter to rummage through the deck for the best combination of cards." I think the hand Lee dealt himself was as close to a royal flush as you can get without winning the whole pot. Bringing in the likes of Westy (pitcher David West), Milt (Thompson), and Inky (Pete Incaviglia) just to name a few was probably a crapshoot for Lee Thomas and Jim Fregosi, but for the team, it was perfect. The pieces they added in '93 all fit together like the greatest jigsaw puzzle the world has ever known. In my 30-plus years (and counting) in baseball, I've never seen, been part of, or heard of a group of 25- plus guys who got along better and had more fun ... on the field, in the clubhouse, and off the field. We were a "band of throwbacks," as my colleague in the broadcast booth, Harry Kalas, described us. This book will keep you laughing with tales about a game that ended at 4:41 in the morning, about Mariano Duncan dancing in the clubhouse, and about Krukkie (John Kruk) screaming and hollering at (equipment manager) Frank Coppenbarger for pizzas. This book takes you behind the scenes into the crazy and wacky world that was the '93 Phillies.

In closing, let me remind you of what former baseball commissioner Bart Giamatti said about the lessons baseball taught him. I'm quoting from Tom Boswell's farewell column to the late former commissioner.

"The largest thing I've learned as a baseball executive is the enormous grip that this game has on people and the extent to which it really is very important. It goes way down deep. It really does bind together. It's a cliché and sounds sentimental, but I have now seen it from the inside ... I think I underestimated the depth of this historical enterprise ... baseball is an unalloyed good. Of course there are passions involved, but passion is good when it is directed toward a noble end. There's nothing bad that occurs from baseball. Realizing that has been the most rewarding part of this [his experience as commissioner]."

Take a look at this '93 team and see it from the inside. Understand the grip it had on us all—players and fans alike. Enjoy reading an entertaining story that tells why that season was so much fun and why that team became so much a part of our lives. Relive the memories and make a lot of great new ones as the Phillie Phanatic and his coauthor Bob Gordon take you back in time to a place and a team we will not soon forget. Now as my dear friend and colleague Harry the K would say, I am "outta here."

Larry Andersen

Introduction

Lads that there was no more behind
But such a day tomorrow as today
And to be a boy eternal
— William Shakespeare

At its soul, baseball remains a little boy's game. In a complicated, cynical world, we sometimes forget that simple fact. We lose touch with baseball's timeless foundation. Baseball endures because it *is* a little boy's game—a game intended to be played with a little boy's gusto and grit and giddiness and glee. The noble, the naughty, the hero and the villain team up out on the baseball diamond, where there's usually a tomorrow and there's always a next year.

Baseball was born for fun, pure summer fun—the kind of fun too many serious types chuck behind them on the sandlots of their youth. And it's supposed to make you happy. You can toss the ball around, soak in that rare day in June, smell the fresh-mowed grass, whack the ball, chase the ball, dive after it, slide after it. Forget dignity. Forget the rest of the world. Forget the real world. Play ball!

If you're Ernie Banks, play two.

In our collective soul, we want baseball to be a sport that captures carefree youth and keeps it in a bottle for us to grow old with. We don't want baseball to be an industry. Despite what some naysayers say, big money has not deflowered our national pastime. But it has changed the way fans view the game and its stars. Big money tends to filter the figures on the baseball diamond through the color green—and only the color green. Too often, modern fans glare right past the Boys of Summer. They look beyond the exuberance of youth. They ignore the gifted young athlete in the glory of his times and focus, instead, on an ungrateful millionaire earning in a single year what the average fan would kill to collect in a lifetime.

What's worse, fans see too many guys who don't really love the game, at least not the way little boys love the game. They see players who don't appreciate the game the way baseball deserves to be appreciated, the way America, in its collective soul, wants its national pastime to be appreciated. They see too many players who remind them of their own coworkers at their own workplaces, the types who don't give at the office, the types who won't go the extra mile even when the team needs it.

And they boo. Especially in Philadelphia.

So a great game has become, in many a fan's mind, a bit jaded, a bit blasé, a bit formulaic. But then, every once in a while, a team touches the man-child in all of us. A band of ballplayers comes along and recaptures the fun and little-kid thrill of hitting and catching and fielding a baseball.

Which brings us to the '93 Philadelphia Phillies, a team that brought color and fun to the national pastime. With their blazing best-in-franchise-history start in 1993, they got the hometown excited and engaged in their romp right off the bat. Their quirky, crazy, devil-may-care off-field antics and their antiestablishment on-field look soon intoxicated the fans in Philadelphia. They couldn't get enough of this crew. The Phils drew everyone into their fun with off-the-wall shenanigans, quips, hotfoots, and shaving-cream-filled pies that got shoved into everyone's faces during interviews. By season's end, the Phils had become national figures, mostly for their outlaw persona. They were dubbed "America's Most Wanted Team" when they took on Atlanta's powerhouse Braves in the National League Championship Series. A week later, America's Most Wanted Team had converted their critics and become Team America battling Team Canada in a thrilling World Series.

In an era when stars are scrubbed, buff, and *GQ*-friendly, the '93 Phils were poster boys for the beer-pretzels-backyard-horseshoes set. They offended some people along the way. They ruffled feathers. They scuffled. Modesty and manners were not their forte. They spit and scratched in all the wrong places, especially when a camera was rolling. They were Peck's Bad Boys in pinstripes—rowdy and raucous. But they were real. Ultimately, that's what spun the turnstiles.

The '93 Phils drew hordes of fans to Veteran's Stadium. The Phils exceeded the three-million mark for the first and only time in the franchise's 119-year history. In fact, the 1993 Phils bested the Quaker City's second highest year in attendance by more than 300,000 people, and that includes all the combined-team yearly totals for the half-century-plus that Philly rooted for two hometown teams. Even today, the '93 Phils remain the city's darlings, as popular in Rocky's city as a weekend beer sale.

General Manager Lee Thomas took a sagging last-place jalopy of a franchise and transformed it into a macho machine that revved through a magical season on high-grade testosterone. The roster burst with bravado and belligerence: Lenny Dykstra, John Kruk, Curt Schilling, Wes Chamberlain, Larry Andersen, Darren Daulton, Pete Incaviglia, Terry Mulholland, and Dave Hollins, to name a few.

"*We're throwbacks ... thrown back by other organizations,*" observed John Kruk of the '93 Phils. They were called the "Was Kids." And they *were* throwbacks—throwbacks with bad reps and badder attitudes. Thomas brought a crew of unkempt outcasts, medical rejects, and renegades into the City of Brotherly Love. Then he blended them in with a cast of *gentlemen* like Milt Thompson, Ricky Jordan, Kevin Stocker, and Jim Eisenreich. Or perhaps the gentlemen blended in with the renegades. Whatever the case, the mix was magical. Thomas's trades

brought better baseball through chemistry to Philly, even if people did think the
'93 squad was a little crazy.

You may be right
I may be crazy
But it just may be a lunatic
You're looking for

"You May Be Right," Billy Joel

*"Maybe we did go after the crazy guys. I always like the zany types. I think they
make the game interesting and fun for the fan. With the nucleus we had, we figured
we could bring those types into the locker room and it would all work, so I told Lee
Thomas to go ahead and bring them in,"* Phils chairman Bill Giles reminisces. So
Lee Thomas went out and put together one of the game's most unconventional
rosters, packed with, as Mitch Williams called them, "gypsies, tramps, and thieves."

*"If crazy is running out ground balls, playing hard, and getting the uniform
dirty, then, yeah, they're crazy,"* Phils Manager Jim Fregosi said that season. His
team won unconventionally. To the local and national press, they also won
unconvincingly. Not a single '93 Phil hit 30 home runs. Yet their team total of
877 runs surpassed their next closest National League rival in that category by a
whopping 69 runs. They dominated the opposition with sound, old-fashioned
baseball. They frustrated opposing pitchers with patience and maddening mind
games. They led the circuit in walks. In fact, *three* Phils topped the century mark
in free passes. They worked pitchers mercilessly, challenging the opponents' resolve, annoying them into mistakes, and disrupting their concentration. They
forced opposing hurlers to show their entire pitching repertoire early in the game
—too early in the game, from the pitchers' perspective. The Phils systematically
removed the all-important element of surprise from a pitcher's arsenal when he
really needed it. The Phillies' patience at the plate escalated pitch counts and
accelerated pitching departures. The result was that Phillie batters feasted sooner
and longer on middle relievers. "Middle relief is the Achilles' heel of most pitching staffs," emphasizes Larry Bowa, a coach on that '93 squad. "Getting those
middle relievers into the game early is so important. It's a facet of the game that's
neither understood nor valued by fans. But it's crucial to wins and losses. That
team was the greatest when it came to working a starter out of the game early."

Bowa loved the way this crew played baseball the old-fashioned way. They
moved runners, took extra bases on the basepaths, got konked by pitches for the
good of the team, and did all the little things that win games. "Whatever it
takes, Dude," as Lenny Dykstra said. They also led the league in dirty uniforms.
Ask Pete Cera, Phils locker room attendant for many years. The old Gas House
Gang could have walked into the Phils 1993 locker room and felt right at home.
They'd have been far less shocked than Marty McFly on any of his time journeys.
These Phil throwbacks played intelligent baseball, not powerhouse baseball. Sure
they were wacky, but they were wily as well. Still, the media still couldn't get by

their we-don't-give-a-damn appearance. In deference to the Phils' 1950 pennant winners and the old Gas House Gang, some of the media called them the "Diz Kids".

"They have stubble on their chins and tattoos on their arms and look a little bit like a slow-pitch softball team in town for a state championship tournament," Neil Hohlfield of the *Houston Chronicle* wrote in 1993. Maybe they did. They didn't care how they looked. They cared less what people thought. All the Diz Kids cared about was winning. That's a facile cliché that most teams lean on—a nice platitude to lob to the media in an empty clubhouse after a game. But the fact remains: staying intense and focused on nothing but winning *each and every* baseball game in a 162-game season is an act of concentration that is far beyond the ken of most people—fans included. None of us goes 5 for 5 at the office or work site every day. We fans often forget that the baseball diamond, symbol of our own long-lost, carefree summers, is the *workplace* for pro ballplayers. It's their office. We forget those ballplayers are human, like us.

It's more demanding and far more difficult to devote yourself to a team and to a cause than to your own individual statistics. Especially when your individual statistics are the things that get *you* paid. Ballplayers don't inflate their salaries by taking one for the team. At contract time, stars don't boast about moving runners or taking strikes just to tire out a pitcher. In addition, it's difficult to put your skin into a little boy's game day in and day out when there are so many big-boy temptations to distract you. In the outside world, temptation welcomes you with open arms. A 162-game season is exhausting. It's draining to live, eat, drink, and sleep baseball for that long. It's a relentless commitment. But the '93 Phils, to a man, made that commitment. What's more, they demanded that commitment from everyone else on the team. They liked fun. But they were rough and nasty if they felt anyone was reneging on his obligation to his teammates or the team. These guys came to the park every day with a clear focus and purpose. They came to win. And they loved being there, loved it like little kids love seeing a major-league ballgame. Their little-boy euphoria was the ultimate key to their success, the secret to their overachievement.

The '93 squad never gave in. They never gave up. They were as unpredictable and dangerous as they were relentless. The '24-25 Pittsburgh Pirates (who had a roster full of guys with peculiar nicknames from a peculiar era when men were "mugs" and women were "dames"—names like Kiki Cuyler, Pie Traynor, and Rabbit Maranville) set a National League record that stood for sixty-seven years till the '93 Phils smashed it. Those Pirates rumbled through 150 consecutive games without being shut out. The '92-93 Phils blew that mark away, extending the streak to 174 straight (they ended the streak two bleary-eyed days after they clinched the division, but more on that later).

That's why the Philly fans loved this team. They were on the field for one purpose: to win. They refused to be intimidated. They overachieved. These guys loved their hometown and its fans. And the hometown fans, reviled nationwide as notorious boobirds, loved them back.

"You don't shortchange fans in Philly, and you don't fool them," Curt Schilling told me, seated comfortably in Diamondback blue in the visitor's dugout at the Vet. "Look, every town claims to have intelligent fans, great fans, informed fans, etc. But in Philly, and in a few other eastern cities, like Boston, New York, and Baltimore, fans really *are* different. They have the pride and tradition that newer franchises haven't built yet, because those eastern cities are old and established. In Philly, kids are raised to be Phillies fans by their fathers, whose fathers raised them to be Phillies fans, as did their fathers before them. You are born a Phillie fan—born into a Phillie-fan family, but more importantly, you *stay* a Phillie fan for life, even if you move away from the Delaware Valley. I run into Phillie fans in every town I've ever been, no matter where I go. They're people who have moved out of Philly, but with that long tradition they come from, they remain Phillie fans forever. It's that intense back there. You don't feel that kind of intensity in many other cities."

Those intense Philly fans, the ones who come to the park to see their boys do battle, saw their city's intensity mirrored out on the playing field in 1993. They got behind the hometown boys. The fans sensed early on that they were watching something special. It took Philadelphia a long while to warm up to the great Phillie teams of the seventies and early eighties. The fans always figured those talent-laden teams *should* win, but those teams didn't show the intensity that Philly fans eat up like gloppy cheesesteaks. After the club's last-place finish in '92, few fans figured the '93 team would contend, let alone dominate. Except for one day, however, the '93 Phils were atop their division from day one. Still, it was the way this team won, and the gusto they brought to the ballpark, that endeared and continues to endear them in the Quaker City. They had fun. The fans joined in their conga line.

"They love their work. It shows in the way they behave in the clubhouse, laughing and having a good time. It shows in the way they play, leaving blood and sweat all over the basepaths," Chuck Mulling of the *Tampa Tribune* wrote in 1993.

"They're sloppy, grubby, and they're always stuffing their faces with something," Mike Downey of the *L.A. Times*. They called them the "Cheese Whiz Kids".

The '93 Phils did love their jobs. They practically lived at the ballpark. They came early and they stayed late. And they were nonstop practical jokesters. The clubhouse was their private Animal House. It was the lair of the gang that some writers called the "Merry Krucksters" because when the Phils weren't stuffing their own faces, they were stuffing somebody else's. Pies piled high with shaving cream flew around the Phillies clubhouse as profusely as insults and profanities in an atmosphere that sometimes mimicked a Three Stooges fest. Interviewers and interviewees (as well as innocent bystanders, the owner, the coaches, and the general manager) often toweled Noxema off their faces or licked their faces clear of meringue after pie-ings ended interviews abruptly. Professional pranksters, like Larry Andersen, who specialized in (though his repertoire was hardly limited to) the fine art of giving hotfoots, were afoot, so to speak, everywhere.

Until game time.

"The Phillies beat you up. They leave you for dead," Joe Torre, then manager of the St. Louis Cardinals, said in 1993. Every 1993 Phillie will tell you the same thing: "We went out on that field every day to do one thing. We wanted to kick ass." "Video Dan" Stephenson (whom you'll meet in the book) produced a dynamite video for the Phillies organization after the 1993 season. The title he chose, "Whatever It Takes, Dude," could not be more appropriate. If winning called for intimidating an opponent, brawling, giving a "bow tie" to an opposing batter, coming back from an eight-run deficit, playing hurt, playing twenty innings after blowing a four-run lead, or playing a game till 4:41 a.m., the Phillies were up to the task. Whatever it takes, Dude.

The team got their inspiration from a gritty old baseball man, Jim Fregosi, who called the shots in '93 like a sharpie reading a deck of marked cards. Fregosi and general manager Lee Thomas assembled a squad that focused more on chemistry than statistics. They sought out players they thought would fit in with the nucleus of the team, guys with fire in their guts—even if they were a little wacky. Bill Giles, club president, encouraged them. "I like zany ballplayers," Giles chuckles.

"We had an excellent nucleus in Lenny Dykstra, Dutch Daulton, Krukker, and Dave Hollins," general manager Lee Thomas explains. "Those guys were devoted to their profession. They would kill to win. We listened to those guys, sought out their opinions, when we built the rest of the team. We weren't looking for individual stars or guys with gaudy statistics. We were looking for ballplayers with the same unselfish qualities that the guys in our nucleus had. We thought we could build successfully on that."

And build they did. Fregosi saw immediately that this club had a special chemistry. In spring training, once the cast of characters he and Thomas had assembled was tossed into the same beaker, that beaker bubbled over. Like something right out of Frankenstein's lab, it bubbled with energy, potential, power, and a mesmerizing cloud of suspense. Like Dr. Frankenstein, Fregosi and Thomas had collected bodies from a lot of baseball graveyards. They managed to stitch together a monster that not many purists found pretty. But to Philadelphia baseball fans, that 1993 Phillies monster was the prettiest thing to come out of Philly since Princess Grace.

"Jim Fregosi went out and got a Prison Squad. I never saw a manager get so much from players. No other manager could ever have managed that team. Fregosi could never question anyone on that team about not trying," Mitch Williams said in 1993.

Fregosi decided to manage his team with a daring, kind of quirky, philosophy—one that not many others would have the courage to try. Fregosi deputized his hoodlums—er, veterans (we kid)—a move that backfired on the Rolling Stones at Altamont but worked like a charm on the Phils. Fregosi himself set few, if any, rules. He did nonetheless lay out two very strong, clear, and uncontestable expectations.

"You play all out, all the time, and you walk into this clubhouse ready to play baseball."

His veterans—Daulton, Thompson, Incaviglia, Dykstra, and Kruk—took care of most other things, like minor scuffles, disagreements, hurt feelings, and those types of problems. Sure, most of the time, it was a grab-ass fest in the clubhouse. But whenever anyone needed to be spoken to, whenever anyone needed to get his head put back on straight, Fregosi's veterans delivered the message in no uncertain terms.

"It's one thing for a manager to chew you out," says Larry Bowa. "Some guys are very good at tuning managers out. They figure the manager's always harassing them anyway, so why bother paying any attention at all to him? But it's another thing if a fellow player tells you you're screwing up. It's so much more effective. Guys need to push one another on a team. If that's not happening, your team's not playing up to its potential. That '93 team was one of the last teams to live with those unwritten rules, that code of conduct."

No player dared miss practice or show up late. No one sloughed off a team meeting. No one trotted out an infield grounder. If anyone screwed up, or worse, eased up, he had to face what the Philly press dubbed "Macho Row," Fregosi's clubhouse kangaroo court. The Phillies themselves called the hard-ass section of their clubhouse "the Ghetto." The Ghetto, or Macho Row, became the symbol of the team's resolve and the manifestation of its collective conscience.

The central figure in Fregosi's self-policing scheme was catcher Darren "Dutch" Daulton. He was the guy that Fregosi handpicked to be his voice, the manager's regent, the sheriff's deputy. Daulton's brilliance in embracing that role was crucial, perhaps even the keystone in the Phillies' success that year. Almost to a man, the squad cites Daulton's leadership as the primary reason the Phils won that pennant. Daulton was a medical disaster. His body was racked by the pain and marred by the scars of numerous operations and injuries. Dutch could not flash the numbers that superstars do. What he had was a natural ability to reach each and every guy, to relate to each guy, earn his trust, and make him feel like an integral part of the team.

Dutch led by example. As Phils coach John Vukovich says, "Dutch would be physically hurting, and Fregosi would try to rest him. But if the team wasn't doing well, Dutch would walk into Fregosi's office and say he was suiting up to play. Guys saw Dutch dig deep down, suck it up, and play through pain. His stature in the clubhouse just grew."

That his teammates and coaches heap fulsome praise on Daulton underscores the human side of a great sport. Darren Daulton embodies the leadership, unselfishness, dedication, guts, and determination that took the Phillies over the top in 1993. When you get down to it, it is these human qualities, displayed in one of the most comical casts of characters ever seen on a modern diamond, that makes the 1993 Phils fascinating and immortal. These 1993 Phils captivated the public because they were so damn human. They were, arguably, as diverse and unusual a lot as has ever been assembled in a single locker room.

"I think people loved the '93 squad because there was somebody on that team for everybody," Bill Giles reflects. "You had Daulton that all the women loved, Johnny [Kruk] who was the hero of every overweight guy who ever dreamed of being a ballplayer, Mitch for his whole 'Wild Thing' persona, Jim Eisenreich who was an inspiration to anyone that's trying to overcome a medical problem. There was somebody there that every fan could relate to. People looked out at that field and saw a bunch of guys who loved their jobs, who loved coming to the ballpark, and it was just infectious. It made everyone want to join the party."

So here's the story of an unlikely bunch of champs who played with the zeal of children, Philadelphia's Little Boys of Summer, a team that succeeded *because*—and not in spite of the fact that—they had so damn much fun.

"You know what I was thinking when Joe Carter's ball went over the fence and ended the World Series?" muses Phils outfielder Pete Incaviglia. "I thought, 'Damn, what do I do tomorrow? I won't be coming back to the ballpark.' That was the toughest part of that loss, just knowing that season was over. I never wanted those days to end."

B ill Lyon, an eminent Philly sportswriter, dubbed 1993 "The Enchanted Season." Our account of that Enchanted Season will not be linear—after all, the '93 Phils never did anything straight. So besides telling the story of the Enchanted Season, we interpersed the account with tales about our great city, Philadelphia, along with some Philly baseball lore, Phillie Phanatic tales, and a lot of baseball stories.

As for the '93 Phils, we're telling their story, to a great extent, in the words of the guys who wore the uniforms. Whenever you see a speaker's name in capital letters, it's a current quote from an interview for this book. Other quotes, where the speaker's name is not capitalized, were made at the time of the incident they relate to. We're also providing insight and inside stories from the guy who now wears that big green klutzy uniform and runs around the park harassing the world: the Phillie Phanatic. The Phillie Phanatic in 1993 was the irrepressible Dave Raymond. His backup that year, Tom Burgoyne, is coauthor of this book. Tom got the lobotomy (the job's only requirement) and became the full-time Phillie Phanatic in 1994. However, in 1993, Tom Burgoyne had his finger in a lot of pies. And let's face it, there were a lot of pies flying around Veteran's Stadium that year—either getting shoved in people's faces or down the gullets of a gluttonous team. Tom lends a wacky insider, behind-the-scenes perspective, so look for his "Phanatic Philes" throughout the book.

What did Tom Burgoyne do in 1993? Tom picked and played the tunes that blasted around the Vet. He worked the Phanavision screen, which is the gigantic video screen high atop the outfield. He was a creative force behind a lot of the fire-the-crowd-up stuff at the ballpark. He was a liaison with local radio stations and participated in the think tanks that dreamed up contests and promotions at the stadium and elsewhere. Tom was even the PA announcer for one of the 1993 games. Besides his duties at the Vet, he was omnipresent around the Delaware Valley or anywhere Phillie spirit was needed. He was in the catbird seat, observing how the City of Brotherly Love reeled from the worst case of Phillies Phever that ever struck.

A word about format—consistency being the hobgoblin of little minds, we were not slaves to format. Just as the Phillie Phanatic pops up unpredictably around the stadium during a game, his Phizes pop up at different times and places in the book. There's no set pattern.

Larry Andersen, relief pitcher and hitman *extraordinaire*, also shared his special perspective and wisdom, for which we are appreciative. Larry has become one of the town's most beloved sport figures. But because Larry is so damn entertaining, many people are unaware that he can be sage, intelligent, and profound on occasion. We look forward to that occasion.

In doing the book, we spent endless hours tracking down members of the team. We did not use the resources or personnel of the actual *America's Most Wanted* television team to do so (frankly, some of the '93 guys would be too slick for them). We thank the Philadelphia Phillies organization for their interest and help. The Phillies are an organization, a corporate citizen, and a Philadelphia institution our city should be proud of. The cooperation of the 1993 Phillies players themselves was terrific. Their love and enthusiasm for their team and organization, as well as their mutual appreciation and respect for each other, was inspirational. We hope that, in some measure, their enthusiasm shines through in our book.

The annals of sports are full of underachievers and failures who didn't take their sport seriously enough. The '93 Phils set that truism on its ear. No one was more serious about their profession than they were. And no one had more fun. Humor, fun, and looseness in the workplace teamed in an extraordinary and effective mix in 1993. That was the year when fun won.

Phanatic Story

"Try that new kid, Raymond. He's wacky and cocky enough.
I bet he'd be good."
—*Bill Giles, Phillies President*

Bill Giles, the Phillies' past president and current chairman, is always looking for the edge. In 1978, he became obsessed with bringing a mascot to Philadelphia. The Phillies' marketing whiz, Dennis Lehman, came back from San Diego raving about the Padres' new mascot, the San Diego Chicken. That set Giles off.

"At first, I didn't know exactly what having a mascot meant," Giles concedes. "But I did know that if we did things right, we could have some fun."

Bill Giles is the son of Warren Giles, National League president from 1951-1969. Bill was raised in baseball and took his first full-time job in 1962 as general manager of the Nashville Vols, which was the Reds' Double A affiliate. Even at an early age, Bill liked to push the envelope.

BILL GILES: "I used to run promotions with the Vols. We played a game called Baseball Bingo, where the fans at the game could win prizes. One night the umps were having a tough game, and I got on the public address system and announced that if nobody won Baseball Bingo that night, then the team would donate seeing-eye dogs to the umps. Some didn't find that too funny, and the next day there was a huge headline saying, 'Warren Giles's Son Rips Umpires.' No big deal, except my dad was president of the umpire association at the time.

"I ran promotions for the Houston Colt 45's their first year at the Astrodome. I was also involved in scoreboard operations, a brand new thing at the time. One ump, John Kibler, had ejected a different Astro player four nights in a row. The fourth time he did it, I threw up a scoreboard message, 'Kibler did it again.' My dad phoned the next day and asked who put that message up on the board. I said, 'I don't know, Dad, but I'll find out and tell him not to do it again.' He answered, 'Good, son, and when you find him, tell him his allowance is cut off.'

"But to me, baseball is entertainment. I never stop looking for ways to add interest and color to the game.

"Back in the seventies, no one in baseball had a mascot except for the San Diego Chicken, and the Chicken wasn't an official part of the Padres at first. He was actually owned by a radio station in San Diego. He did his act at the Padres games and it caught on with the fans. So there was no mascot model to follow in baseball, or in sports. When I first started thinking about it, I didn't know exactly *how* a Phillies mascot would fit into the picture, or what role he could play. But I knew a mascot opened up possibilities, and I was willing to experiment simply because it sounded like fun. We hired a company in New York to design the costume and to give me something visual, a sketch, that I could show the Phillies organization. This outfit we hired worked with Jim Henson, the guy who created the *Sesame Street* characters. I figured they knew what they were doing. Turns out they did. But when I pitched the idea to the Phillies brass, the first thing they asked me was: 'Who do you have in mind to be in the mascot costume?' I hadn't really given *that* question much thought. I just blurted out: 'Try that new Raymond kid. He's wacky and cocky enough. I bet he'd be good.'"

Dave Raymond grew up in a jock family. His dad is football coach Tubby Raymond, who coached the University of Delaware Blue Hens to 300 wins in a 36-year career. Impressive stuff, but his son Dave is a *first*, a pioneer, a creator. "I'm an idiot," Dave confesses. "Mr. Giles was right. I *was* the perfect guy for that job." Dave's job was to give the Phillies' mascot a soul, to put heart into a lifeless green costume. His job was to make Bill Giles scream, "It's alive! It's alive!" when his creation, his big green monster, started moving. Bill Giles conceived a Phillie mascot, but Dave Raymond *invented* the Phillie Phanatic, move by move and pratfall by pratfall. Raymond transported Giles's monster from an innovation to an institution. Raymond's enthusiasm and talent paved the way for his alter ego to become the longest running—make that longest waddling—most recognizable mascot in all of sports, the Phillie Phanatic.

"My dad's first love was baseball, not football" says Raymond. "He was a catcher at the University of Michigan and wound up playing in the St. Louis Cardinals' minor-league system. I didn't play football until high school. My brother Chris was three years older than me. He was a high school kicker, so I became a kicker too."

Dave wound up kicking for his dad's team, Delaware.

"I idolized those Delaware football players growing up. Playing there was like a dream come true, except for listening to gripes about the coach. They were happy days for me. I've got great memories, like the time we upset Temple at Franklin Field and I almost got killed. I was back to punt, but the play was whistled dead after the ball was snapped. I decided to tuck the ball under my arm and run to the outside anyway. Joe Klecko, who was an All-American Temple defensive lineman (and later a part of the New York Jets' Sack Exchange) was waiting for me. I guess I was a little cocky. I popped off to Klecko and he just kind of picked me up like a rag doll and threw me to the ground; no, make that *into* the ground. I felt like a goal post. I made sure he was far away before I dug myself out. I don't think I even risked catching the next snap. I punted it in midflight. I wasn't taking any chances that Klecko could get to me."

Over the summers when Dave was a student, he worked as a Phillies intern. His mentor was the club's promotions director, Frank Sullivan. Besides serving as Sullivan's Man Friday, Dave helped plan the All-Star Game activities in '76 when the Phillies hosted the midsummer classic. In December of his senior year, months after his internship had ended, the Phillies called Dave at his Delaware fraternity house. They made him an offer he almost refused.

DAVE RAYMOND: "Frank's assistant, Chrissy Long, jumped on the line, saying, 'Dave, Frank is going to ask you to do something and I want you to *just say no.*' I had no idea what Frank had in mind when he asked me to be a mascot. Mascot?! Four years of college to become a freakin' mascot! ... I had been a Snoopy at a Grant's opening once, just to earn extra cash in college. I told my fraternity brothers. They weren't really, let's say, encouraging. They were saying things like, 'With the way those fans in Philly are, they'll be hanging you in effigy. And that's when the Phillies win!'"

Dave wasn't thrilled with the proposal initially. "Put on a big green suit and act silly? I thought my parents would think the whole idea was crazy," Dave reminisces. To his surprise, his parents were all for it. "My parents are from the old school. You know, if your employer asks you to do something, you do it. You don't say no. You don't turn anything down. They were right," Dave smiles. "They usually are.

"Of course, I had no idea what I was actually going to do as the mascot," Dave adds. "The Phils sent me a drawing. That gave me some idea of what I would look like. But I didn't see the finished costume itself until the first night I wore it."

That night was April 25, 1978. Obviously, when Dave Raymond/Phillie Phanatic boogied into the hard-boiled Philly crowd for the first time, he must have followed a careful plan, choreographed as precisely as a Fosse dance number.

"No. There was no plan," Dave chuckles. The neophyte Phanatic simply relied on moxie in his debut. The young Raymond had moxie to the max.

"None of us—Bill Giles, the Phils brass, or me—had a clue about how the fans would react," he recalls. "Bill Giles told me to walk down and circulate among the crowd and sort of clown around. So I did. I had no idea what I was actually going to do once I got there. But honest, the whole act, the whole Phanatic persona, just kind of came naturally.

"I don't know if that's good or bad," he adds wryly.

Neither do the rest of us, Dave ... but that's not important right now. What is important is that Raymond's act made a hit with the tough Philly crowd, and for once, a Philly hit didn't get whisked away to New York. The green-suited Raymond displayed an outrageous knack for improvisation. His timing was brilliant, sometimes inspired, and baseball fans ate up the whole shtick.

DAVE RAYMOND: "That first night, before the gates opened, I went out onto the field as some of the players were coming out for batting practice. Tony Taylor (a long time Phillie second baseman and coach and one of the Quaker City's most beloved athletes) took one look at me and started muttering something I couldn't make out in Spanish. What does *loco* mean? Tony didn't know what to make of the whole thing.

"Long about the third inning I made my way into the 200-level area behind home plate, trying to get something started. I jumped on the railing, flailed around, and kept moving around the stadium. A while later, I tripped and fell trying to climb over another railing. The spectators really got into everything I did. I went down to the picnic area, which has since been removed, and started messing with the people having a picnic, hopping from one picnic table to another. Remember, these people had never seen me before, so when I popped up, no one had a clue who or what I was—or even what I was *supposed* to be. Neither did I! Nowadays, people are used to mascots. You see them at ballparks, theme parks, and on TV. But in 1978, a mascot was something new and outrageous. I was blown away by the way people were interacting. It was like a big party. The fans played off what I did so naturally, and I fed off the crowd reaction and made everything up as I went along. Philly people are always up for a party."

The Phillies won the night the Phanatic debuted. Phillies catcher Tim McCarver remarked after the game, "Chalk one up to our new mascot. We're 1 and 0 with the Phillie Phanatic!"

DAVE RAYMOND: "Bill Giles seemed pleased. He told me the next night I should go out with the ground crew in the fifth inning and 'see what happens.' So when the ground crew went out to clean the bases, I ran out to third base, pretending to polish it by shooting my tongue out at the bag. Then I started running around the bases, bowling the ground crew over one by one. Those guys had no idea what was going on, but they played along, and we started to ad-lib routines from then on. A guy named Froggy was the main man on the ground crew. Froggy was up for anything."

Froggy

If Bill Giles hadn't asked Dave Raymond to be the Phillie Phanatic, he probably would have asked Froggy. Froggy would have made a great Phanatic. Froggy is Mark Carfagno, a charter member of the Phillies' Veterans Stadium ground crew. I knew Froggy for ten years or so before I realized that "Froggy" wasn't his real name, though it should be, since he doesn't answer to "Mark." Mark became "Froggy" in grade school because his voice was deep, like a frog's. The name stuck.

FROGGY: "I could tell from day one that we'd have fun with the Phanatic. The *Gong Show* was a big hit in those days and the ground crew guys were all big fans of the show. So we stole a little *Gong Show* material for Phanatic routines. After the Phanatic circled the bases, knocking the ground crew over one by one, we'd all dance to that 'Gene, Gene the Dancin' Machine'—the song they played on the *Gong Show* when the 'Unknown Comic' came out. He was the guy who wore a brown bag over his head and told stupid jokes. One night, a bunch of us put brown bags over our heads and danced that number. We made those Phanatic routines up as we went along."

PHANATIC PHILE

In Froggy, the Phanatic found a friend and soul mate. Hell, the Phanatic found a playmate. Froggy was first to volunteer as a Phanatic foil. One night, Larry Anderson shaved Froggy's head bald before the game. Froggy slipped into a dress, put a long wig on, and jumped up on the Phillies dugout as a Surfer Girl to dance with the Phanatic to the song "Wipeout." During the drum solo, the Phanatic ripped off Froggy's wig, exposing his newly shorn dome. Then the Phanatic used Froggy's noggin for bongos.

Froggy, incidentally, has a thing for women's clothing. When the Phanatic needed something for guaranteed laughs, we'd just send Froggy out in a gaudy blue dress and a curly blonde women's wig, dancing to "Devil with the Blue Dress." Not exactly what Mitch Ryder had in mind, but it got laughs.

We created a monster. Froggy became a dancing fool.

There's a huge difference between Froggy and me. I put a costume *on* to make people laugh. Froggy takes his costume *off*. Let me explain what several generations of Phillie players know, or dread. Froggy is a streaker.

FROGGY: "If the team is on a losing streak, I'll run through the clubhouse wearing nothing but a pair of flip-flops. Those guys start screaming and howling. It loosens them up when they're uptight. Steve Bedrosian [who played with the Phils from '86-89] really used to egg me on. He'd be like, 'C'mon, Frog, you've got to go for it!' Bedrosian loved it."

I'm not sure if Froggy's streaking inspired Bedrock when he won his Cy Young award in 1987. Behind every great man there's a great behind—or whatever.

Froggy didn't limit his, uh, talent, to the clubhouse. He has been known to "moon" fellow ground crew members from just about every nook and fanny, er, cranny, in the Vet—including the catwalk high above the stadium or the back of his John Deere. One day, before the stadium gates opened, Froggy performed the never-to-be-duplicated "cannon moon."

Cannon moon?

"The Phillies had a big cannon hanging from the facing of the outfield upper deck," Froggy gloats. "After a Phillies home run, the cannon shot off and steam billowed out of its mouth. I was in charge of adding the water that made the steam. While I was up there checking the water, I crawled inside the cannon with my bare butt sticking out. Not a smart move. Some of the other ground crew guys were nearby changing light bulbs on the scoreboard. They used my butt for target practice."

Froggy had a special welcome-back gift for his old pal Larry Andersen when LA returned to Philadelphia wearing a Houston Astros uniform back in 1987. Larry had left Philly in 1986 after a four-year stint with the Phils.

PHANATIC PHILE

"The ground crew always stands in the stadium area behind home plate during the game," Froggy explains. "There used to be a Plexiglas window that you could look out of and watch the action. I stood up on a chair in front of the Plexiglas and mooned Larry while he was on the mound one night. I didn't know if he could see it, so we went back to Video Dan's room and played back the tape. He could see it, all right."

LARRY ANDERSEN: "I figured Froggy would do something 'special' for me. I looked in for the sign and glanced back at the Plexiglas. I realized I saw a crack, but it wasn't in the Plexiglas."

Froggy owns another dubious distinction (actually, he owns several, as you already know). He will undoubtedly be the only member of the ground crew ever ejected from a game. Don't get ahead of me here. He was fully clothed.

FROGGY: "[Umpire] Nick Colosi was calling balls and strikes. Actually, he was calling strikes balls and vice versa—know what I mean? He was pinching Dick Ruthven, our pitcher, the whole game. Ruthven threw one right down the middle that Colosi called a ball. I lost it. I screamed and pounded the glass with my fist till Colosi had enough. Colosi called time out, yanked off his mask, walked back and yelled, 'You're out of here!' He refused to resume play until I left."

Froggy is a Mummer, which explains a lot about why Froggy is Froggy. Since childhood, he's been hooked on the Mummers, an organization which goes with Philly like mustard on a soft pretzel. Every New Year's Day, the Mummers dress in extravagant costumes, and after consuming mass quantities of antifreeze to help weather Philly's sometimes harsh winter weather, they march up Broad Street, playing banjos and other instruments of destruction. Froggy strums the banjo and performs in a group called "The Ragtimers." On occasion, he'll belt out a tune over the PA system at the Vet. Yes, Froggy the mooner turns into Froggy the crooner.

FROGGY: "My dad was a bartender at a place called Cahill Café in southwest Philly. The owner of the bar asked him if he wanted to form a Mummers' group to march on New Year's Day. So my dad started the Cahill Comic Brigade that marched in the parade in 1963 for the first time. In '64, the parade was canceled because of snow. But my dad said, 'Let's march anyway for the people in the neighborhood.' They did. He caught pneumonia and died a week later. I was only eleven at the time. When I got older, I was elected captain of my dad's old brigade. My first year as captain, I decided we'd do the same music my father did the year he died. The theme was "Lazy, Hazy, Crazy Days of Summer." We wore the same pinstriped vests and straw hats they wore in '64. My dad was a helluva guy. Everybody loved him."

Like father, like son.

Philly and the Mummers

Philly loves tradition. The tradition of the Phillie Phanatic started more than 25 years ago, when a large green inhabitant of the Galapagos Islands (where Darwin came up with his *Origin of Species*) went to a Phillies game, saw how fanatic Philly fans were, and decided he never wanted to leave.

Philly's Mummer's Parade is a lot older. It started in 1902, and like most American traditions, the Mummers tradition evolved from a number of different ethnic groups. The tradition of ringing in the New Year with music, revelry and costumes comes from a blend of Northern European, British, and Black American heritages, dating back some 40 years before William Penn founded Philadelphia in 1682.

The Swedes and Finns brought with them their tradition of shooting off guns and visiting neighbors the day after Christmas. The Germans also shot off guns, but they added a twist by disguising themselves as clowns. Philly's Mummers derived from that European tradition: "shooting in" the New Year. The practice became so widespread around Philly that in 1808, legislation declaring "masquerades, masquerade balls, and mass processions to be public nuisances" threatened fines and imprisonments for violators. The edict did nothing to slow down the festivities, so in 1901, the city of Philadelphia sponsored a New Year's parade consisting of the Fancy Dress Club and Comic Clubs. Philadelphian James Bland's 1879, "Oh! Dem Golden Slippers" was officially adopted as the Mummers' theme song, and in 1902, the first string band marched and was awarded a $25 "Token of Recognition."

"Today, the city provides $250,000, from which cash prizes up to $7,000 can be won," said Palma Lucus, director of the Mummer Museum, located on 2nd Street and Washington Avenue in South Philadelphia. "The Mummers are known all over the world. Our String Bands have traveled throughout Europe and have visited China as well. The New Year's parade is picked up by affiliate TV stations all over the country and is broadcast over the internet, too. It really has grown into a global phenomenon."

No longer a small neighborhood celebration, the Mummer's Parade now includes up to 10,000 marchers. Mummers clubs meet at various locations around the city, with a strong concentration on 2nd Street in South Philly, where the rivalries are particularly fierce. The parade has moved off the traditional route along Broad Street and now travels west to east on Market Street. Then, still dressed in their outrageous feathered costumes and wench outfits, the participants pour onto 2nd Street until the wee hours of the morning. The tradition thrives. The Founding Fathers would be proud.

Dave Raymond's gift was his ability to define—yet not confine—his alter ego. The Phanatic character became the Mr. Hyde to Dave Raymond's Dr. Jekyll, the Charley McCarthy to his Edgar Bergen, except that the Phanatic was a lovable manifestation of the "dark side," that mischievous green monster inside all of us.

"The Phanatic's the guy who actually *does* the things that the devil inside us puts in our heads that we're forced to resist," Dave philosophizes. "We've all got a little bit of the 'Three Stooges' in us. It's inside, locked and loaded. We're just not allowed to fire it. The Phanatic acts out those naughty, rascally things that cross our minds but that we can't do in polite society. The Phanatic *can* go up to the guy with the bald head, polish it and kiss it, and leave the guy laughing. He *can* chase pretty girls around the park and grab them and kiss them. He *can* stomp on opposing players' hats, heckle Tommy Lasorda, mock batters in the on-deck circle, make faces at the umpire, and dance on the dugout roof."

If Max Patkin was the Clown Prince of Baseball, the Phillie Phanatic is the Clown Prince of Bait-ball. He baits the umpire, the opposition, and the people in the stands. He's a hero to the guy in the stands who's gobbling hot dogs, dribbling beer on his T-shirt, and screaming and booing—just because he can, just because he's there. Through the Phanatic, that average-Joe fan can stick his tongue out at his boss, or his annoying brother-in-law, or the guy who gets paid too much to play baseball, or the rest of the world in general. Phillie fans expect the Phanatic to embarrass someone—even if it's them. The fans want that big green ever-evolving or devolving species to be boorish and oafish. Because, like them, at heart, he's lovable.

DAVE RAYMOND: "Yeah, the Phils gave me a free ticket. Sort of. I could invent the Phanatic character the way I saw him. The Phils gave me lots of latitude. I never had to run my Phanatic routines by the brass for approval. They trusted my judgment. I figured it was my job as the Phanatic to push the envelope, to kind of test the limits. If I wasn't on the carpet at least once every couple of weeks for ruffling someone's feathers or taking my act a little too far—at least in some people's minds—I figured I wasn't doing my job. The Phanatic's act has to stay fresh and fun and a little on the edge."

After the Phanatic's debut, the phone started ringing of the hook with requests for Phanatic appearances.

DAVE RAYMOND: "It was bedlam in the beginning, particularly the first three years. And it all happened by accident. We weren't ready. Early on, five thousand people showed up for one Phanatic appearance at the Lancaster Mall! We had to cancel an appearance in Delaware because they didn't have enough security people to handle the crowds. I can't tell you how many days I spent that year at car dealerships. I was doing two outside appearances daily, even on game days. One day, Giles stopped me as I was walking down the hallway in front of his office. He told me I looked a mess. I told him that I had just gotten back from two different appearances—and we had a game that night. Mr. Giles said he wanted me fresh for the games, that he didn't want me running around doing appearances on game days. He gave me a raise right then and there."

In the disco era, the Phanatic made an appearance at a record store, helping Pete Rose promote his new record called "The Charlie Hustle." The Phanatic accidentally broke the store's front window imitating Pete's headfirst slide. "I think some people thought it was part of the act," Dave laughs. "It wasn't. When the police arrived and asked me to file a report, I signed it 'Phillie Phanatic.' I was beginning to think everyone loved the Phanatic. I thought the police would think it was funny. They didn't. I also got the star treatment at Studio 54 that year. We were in line, trying to get in, but the line was wrapped all around the block. So I went back to the van and put the Phanatic suit on. They ushered me right in. Naturally, I wasn't supposed to do that kind of thing. That's one of those stories that the Phillies never found out about."

And they never will, Dave.

The Phillie Phanatic is now one of the national pastime's institutions—a profitable institution. Wayde Harrison, one of the Phanatic's creators, reminisces about the early days. "The idea was to create a character not only to perform at games but one that could be merchandised as well. My wife, Bonnie Erickson [who was the Phanatic's artistic cocreator with Wayde], and I owned the copyright. We started creating Phillie Phanatic products like dolls, T-shirts, and pennants. After the first year, we had generated sales of two million dollars. The Phanatic stuff just took off."

"When the costume was first designed, we could have bought the copyright and the outfit for $5,200," laments Bill Giles. "I remember, at the time, thinking that was a lot of money. We had no idea whether the mascot thing would catch on or fizzle. Four years later, we bought the copyright for $250,000."

Giles adds wistfully, "That was *not* one of my better deals."

On The Road Again

I've been fortunate enough to travel all over the country and all over the world bringing the Phanatic's special brand of humor to ballparks and arenas everywhere.

Dave started doing Phanatic appearances for Phillie minor-league affiliates in the mid-eighties. Non-Phillie minor-league teams started booking the Phanatic, who started touring the country on the minor-league circuit à la Max Patkin. In fact, the "Clown Prince" and the Phanatic had a friendly rivalry for a while to see who could draw bigger crowds. We clowned to a draw.

A year after Dave Raymond's farewell to the Phanatic fur, MLB International came calling. MLB International, a division of Major League Baseball, promotes the sport of baseball worldwide. They're the main reason I've had the opportunity to travel overseas. I've been to Japan and Australia twice each. I've toured Central Mexico, Europe, Venezuela, and Puerto Rico, where the fans really party at the park.

People know how to have a good time in the Netherlands too. Organized baseball has been played there for over 50 years, and the country plays host to an international baseball tournament every year. Once, the Phanatic was invited to Rotterdam to show Europeans how we Americans have fun at the old ballpark. Turns out it was the Hollanders who taught the Phanatic about partying. By 9 in the morning, hundreds of fans with grills and coolers had lined up waiting for the gates to open—for a *quadruple* header! When the gates did open, people wheeled their grills and coolers into the stadium and started grilling their own food and chugging down Heinekens. Between innings, all the spectators got out of their seats to dance in the wide aisle that wrapped around the stadium. You can dance to remember, dance to forget, dance to keep from crying—but these people were dancing so they didn't have to listen to the music. I talked them into playing some cooking CDs of mine: The Cherry Poppin' Daddies and James Brown. Heinies and the Godfather of Soul! Man, that stadium was rockin'!

In Japan it was a different scene. The first time I traveled to Japan, I performed at the Tokyo Dome for a Yomiuri Giants game. The Yomiuri Giants were the New York Yankees of Japan, at least for one stretch when they won nine straight Japanese Series from 1964 through 1973. Home run hitter Saharaha Oh was their big star. The Japanese people take baseball seriously, especially the bleacher bums. One half of the bleachers is filled with fans from the visiting team and the other half with fans from the home team. They take turns making noise and waving flags when their team is up to bat. It's noisy out there, which was promising. I thought, "These people are crazy. Crazy is good. They're gonna love the Phanatic."

But as soon as I wandered into the crowd, I knew something was wrong. Instead of starting my act out in the bleachers where all the loonies sat, I tried interacting with the fans seated around the infield. They were much more reserved, way too reserved for somebody accustomed to Philly crowds. I think they thought I was something from a bad Godzilla movie (a redundancy, I know). It's not that they don't have mascots in Japan. It's just that their mascots never go into the crowd. I tried to get something going, stealing people's food and jumping on the backs of seats. No one cracked a smile. I felt as out of place as a weight-loss counselor at a sumo wrestling school. Finally, a very official-looking security guard in a spiffy military outfit came marching down the steps, motioning that it was time for me to leave. Sure, I've been kicked out of better places, but I had come all this distance to show the Japanese how an American mascot rocks, and now they were kicking me out!

Not to be denied. I headed straight to the outfield bleachers. "These are my kind of people," I thought, as I watched a pair of dueling trumpeters and people waving pennants. As I walked down the steps, a really agitated Japanese guy in a ceremonial red robe came at me from nowhere and tried karate-kicking me down the steps and onto the field below. He was screaming something I couldn't understand. I knew he wasn't inviting me out for a sandwich and a cup of tea, and certainly not for sushi. I got out of there as fast as I could. The last thing I saw, the guy was being restrained by some of his friends. Later, I was told that I had unwittingly wandered into a group of known Japanese mafia and they were protecting their turf.

That incident was an exception to the rule. Usually the Phanatic gets laughs everywhere. The other big exception was my friends the Cubans.

Thanks to the Cubans, the Phanatic almost caused an international incident in Australia in 2000. I was in the "land down under" for the Intercontinental Cup, an international baseball tournament hosted that year by Australia. The tournament was held immediately prior to the 2000 Summer Games in Sydney and served as a trial run to check out the logistics for the Olympics. The people in Australia love to get crazy at the Games, so they really loved the Phanatic. The players from the other participating countries seemed to enjoy the act, too. The championship game pitted the hometown Australian team against the team ranked number one in the world, the Cubans. When I walked into the ballpark for the final game, the tournament officials pulled me aside. They said the Cuban team was going to pull out of the championship tilt and file a protest that would have resulted in a $10,000 International Federation fine on the people running the tournament if the Phanatic set foot on the field. I couldn't believe it! It had seemed to me that the Cuban players were having more fun with the Phanatic than any team there. After a day of closed-door meetings between the tournament big wigs and the Cuban officials, I was granted permission to perform on the field before the game. But if I stepped on the field anytime during the game, Cuba would forfeit.

The Phanatic, of course, had a little fun with the whole fiasco.

The manager of the Cuban team was particularly annoyed with the Phanatic's act. He sat in the dugout throughout the whole pregame show, glaring at me while I did my "Rocky" routine in front of his dugout, shadow boxing and knocking out my one-armed push-ups. When the Cuban team took the field, I stood on the field, arms crossed, gesturing like I was not going to budge. I had set it up with the guys working the tournament that at the last possible minute before the game started, they would rush out and drag me off the field. They did, to a chorus of boos. The fans were oblivious to the whole brouhaha. During the game, I ran down to the front row of seats, and with the Cuban coaches looking directly at me, I pretended to climb over the railing and onto the field. They came close to protesting. Close, but no cigar. It was worth the 15-hour plane ride in the middle seat just to see that Cuban manager turn red. In the fifth inning, instead of doing the Phanatic skit on the field, I climbed a light tower in center field and danced to Aretha Franklin's "Respect." The Cubans' eyes were rolling faster than cigars in a Havana cigar factory.

There *is* justice. The Australian team pulled off a huge upset over Cuba to win the championship. The Aussies invited me to their victory party. Had Cuba won, I think I'd have declined an invitation to the Cuban party. I'm a mascot, not a piñata.

If Bill Giles misread the worth of the Phanatic, his instinct on who should be the Phanatic was unerring. Dave Raymond bundled little-boy mischief with party-animal pizzazz. The Phanatic's "Wild and Crazy Guy" persona has made the Phanatic an integral part of the stadium scene for twenty-five years.

Dave's mom, Suzanne Raymond, was deaf and extremely active in the deaf community. She was certified in sign language and a counselor at the Sterck School for the Deaf in Newark, Delaware, for which she was once honored as Deaf Person of the Year in that state. Dave's penchant for pantomime started with signing with his mother.

DAVE RAYMOND: "I was able to communicate in costume because of my experience with the deaf. I didn't really know it at the time, but my mom used to tell me that I moved and gestured the same way she taught her deaf students to communicate."

Of course, not everyone loves the Phanatic. Tommy Lasorda, never one to retreat from an opportunity to show his sweet, lovable nature, hated the big green bird. On the other hand, you'd expect the hard-boiled Phillies coach John Vukovich, cantankerous and traditionalist, to reject the Phanatic. Instead, Vuke says, "I love the Phanatic. He makes me laugh every day." Go figure.

Dave did the Phanatic gig for sixteen years. In 1994, he decided to step out on his own. He joined forces with the Phanatic's creators, Bonnie Erickson and Wayde Harrison, and launched his own enterprise, a company called Acme Mascots. He helped design and animate another furry creature, "Sport." As Sport, Dave performed all over the country for seven years, crossing paths with the Phanatic at various minor-league gigs. Eventually he started his own business, Raymond Entertainment Group. The service he offers his clients is to "create fun."

Though Dave is officially retired as a mascot, he does occasionally climb inside the body of his latest creation, "Reggie," just for kicks.

Dave retired as a Phillie all-time good-luck charm. The Phillies were 154 games above .500 in games where Dave appeared as the Phillie Phanatic.

As Dave points out to anyone who'll listen, "If I had been a pitcher, I would have been making $8 million a year!"

Phanatic Too

"What's he doing?" Jennifer, my newlywed, asked me. The two of us were watching our wedding video. Dave Raymond was being interviewed at our reception.

"He's giving us the best wedding gift we could ask for—his job!" I said.

Dave was collapsing to the ground, symbolically acting out his own death, falling on his sword, doing a "The Phanatic is dead. Long live the Phanatic!" kind of routine.

I thought he was just kidding around. You know, open bar, a few drinks, Dave being Dave. But a week later, there we were sitting at a cheesesteak joint on Broad Street. Dave told me he was moving on, starting his own mascot company.

For the previous five years, I had been the backup Phanatic and had the time of my life. I was averaging about 225 appearances a year, showing up in places all over the Delaware Valley. I made countless mall, school and banquet appearances. I showed up as a special guest to liven up weddings, bar mitzvahs, birthday parties, cow-milking contests, and dog-and-pony shows. In Philly, the Phanatic can show up at just about *any* occasion except maybe a funeral. And I'm sure someday some crazed Phillies fan will put it in his will that the Phanatic show up at his funeral. I can pantomime grief. I've seen John Kruk's face when we ran out of spareribs in the clubhouse.

I didn't let myself believe what Dave seemed to be saying. He was turning the costume over to me. I was the logical successor to the throne. But I still sat there with my mouth open and cheese whiz dripping down my hand, dumbfounded. I kept thinking about what an incredible ride the past three months had been. First there was that wonderful World Series run in October and the unforgettable charter flight with the Phillies organization to Toronto. Then in November, I got married—a huge bash followed by a twelve-day honeymoon in Maui.

And now the Phanatic job ... Two weeks after Dave told me, he went public with the news. The Phillies shot out a press release that I would be filling Dave's shoes. Like Lou Gehrig, that day I felt like the luckiest man on the face of the earth.

Since I became the Phanatic, no matter where I appear, the question always comes up: "How did you get that job?" The real story is how I got to be the Backup Phanatic. I'll tell the story once and for all. And there *will* be a test.

It started as a kid—the road that led me to the Phillie Phanatic job. Actually, the "being a kid" part never ended. The Phanatic is living proof that you're only young once but you can be immature forever. A wise *old* relief pitcher named Larry Andersen told me that. I was a twelve-year-old kid who ate, slept and breathed Philadelphia sports. Every inch of my bedroom walls was covered with posters, pennants and magazine covers of my favorite Phillies, Sixers, Flyers and Eagles. I had a collection of every magazine cover graced by Julius Erving, and about ten different posters of Dr. J. in midflight. I had a tin can for ticket stubs from each and every game I ever attended. And I went to lots of games for a suburban kid living forty-five minutes away from the South Philadelphia stadium complex. Once a year, my Dad came home from work and gave my brothers and sister and me a brand new copy of the Phillies yearbook. I treated those yearbooks like they were gold.

I played all the major sports as a kid: baseball, football, and basketball. I lived for sports (what's changed?). I played street hockey, too. The Flyers were called the Broad Street Bullies when I was growing up, and every kid in my neighborhood had a pair of roller skates and an orange-bladed hockey stick. Every winter, the Jenkintown Youth Association, which ran the baseball and football leagues I played in, had a sports banquet. The featured part of the evening for me was watching the Phillies' highlight film, an NFL Films production narrated in the God-like voice of John Facenda. I walked out every year wishing baseball season started tomorrow.

Of all the days I spent at the Vet, the most memorable was in the summer of 1978. Dad came home from work and told the whole family we were going to the Vet for a Phillies game. But this wasn't just any Phils game. *The Chicken* was coming to town.

I had heard plenty about the Chicken but never really saw much of his act. He was drawing a lot of attention clowning at the Padres games—an amazing feat, given the stiff comedic competition of the twenty-five guys wearing San Diego Padre uniforms. (Okay, so the Padres finished fourth in 1978, but that was their first winning season in franchise history. They *owned* last place from 1969-1974.)

But the big deal was that the Chicken was making his first-ever visit to the Vet for a first-ever meeting with the Phillie Phanatic. And I loved the Phanatic from the get-go. When the Chicken came to town, I was a wide-eyed seventh grader with only three things on my mind: sports, *Charlie's Angels* and making my friends laugh. And though the Phanatic didn't satisfy all three—well, two out of three isn't bad. The Phanatic wasn't Farrah Fawcett, but who is?

To me, the Phanatic had the life. He saw every Phillies game. He pumped up the crowd. My brothers and I could never do that.

Once in a while we could get the crowd to clap, but we succeeded less often than a first-pitch Mitch Williams strike. The Phanatic could mimic everyone in the Phillies' lineup, from Mike Schmidt's butt wiggle to Pete Rose's crouch. He did the things the Three Stooges did, which automatically made him a hero. My family and I always made sure we were in our seats in the fifth inning so that we didn't miss the Phanatic's shenanigans.

So the Burgoyne family was pumped that the Chicken was coming to town. No way he could upstage the Phanatic, and there was no way we were going to miss the showdown. Mom dutifully made Italian hoagies and packed plenty of chips and pretzels. Then Mom, Dad, and all six kids scrunched into our paneled station wagon and headed for the Vet.

When the Chicken made his first appearance, the hard-edged Philly crowd started stirring. Sure, the baseball purists were oblivious to these kinds of promotions, just like they were oblivious to electric scoreboards, dancing waters and cannons firing for home runs. (They were oblivious to the hot-pants girls, too, but for a different reason—they couldn't get to first base with them.) The Chicken surprised the Philly crowd by plopping down a folding chair next to Mary Sue Styles, the left-field ball girl. Mary Sue was easy on the eyes. She snapped more heads during her brief career than Ali's left jab. The Chicken edged his chair closer and closer to Mary Sue's. Then, without warning, feathers started flying. The Chicken leaped on Mary Sue and they hit the turf rolling, one on top of the other, Chicken-Mary Sue-Chicken-Mary Sue … They rolled all the way into left field.

The question was not: "Why did the Chicken cross the outfield?" The question was: "How could he be so gross?" The Chicken's act was a little too tawdry, a little too blue. The Phanatic's shtick was slapstick, a pinch of Vaudeville, a dash of Chaplin, a sprinkle of Daffy Duck—all served up family style. The Chicken seemed out of kilter to me even as a seventh grader. The Phanatic fit into the diamond scene as naturally as the traditional seventh-inning song, "Take Me Out to the Ballgame," although I've always thought it strange that people who are already at the ballgame sing, "Take me out to the ballgame." That wise *old* relief pitcher pointed this one out to me, too.

As I got older (phwew, I almost said, "As I grew up …"), that showdown, the "Thrilla in South Phila," lingered with me. For whatever reason, I identified with the Phanatic. Four years after the Phanatic-Chicken showdown, I found myself stepping inside a hawk costume that looked more like a chicken. The Hawk is the mascot for St. Joseph's Prep, a north Philadelphia institution and the satellite school for the "big" Hawks of St. Joseph's University. My class unanimously voted me into the fur and feathers at the beginning of my senior year (my selection as Hawk mascot was more lopsided than Steve Carlton's Hall of Fame selection). The Prep (when you say "Prep" in Philadelphia, everyone knows you mean St. Joe's) had ditched the traditional black-and-brown-feathered costume of yesteryear for an outfit that was part Elmo/part Perdue Oven Stuffer Roaster. My Hawk costume sported thin orange legs attached to oversized furry webbed feet. The body was as red as Santa's suit, and the head was white, with bulging eyes and a bright orange beak.

Whenever I put that suit on it was "Showtime!" I wasn't going to copy the St. Joseph University Hawk, who flaps his wings nonstop the entire game. Nor would I reduce my shtick to "flying" figure eights along the sidelines after touchdowns. I decided I'd bring a little bit of Phillie Phanatic to the character. I danced along with the cheerleaders and mimicked them on the sidelines. I stormed onto the field to join the opposing teams' marching bands. The student body passed me above their heads, from the very first row in the bleachers back to the last row. I handled every situation the way I thought the Phanatic would. Imitation is the sincerest form of flatulence. I led the cheers for the home team. And I left them all laughing.

My entire senior year at the Prep, I attended every sporting event I could, dressed in my half-hawk, half-chicken getup. I was hawking things up at swimming meets, basketball and baseball games, bowling matches, and, of course, football games. I even suited up at the Vet for a Catholic League semifinal high school football game. Little did I know that I would be dressing up in a different mascot costume at that same stadium six years later and getting paid for it.

Before graduating from the Prep and moving on to Drexel University, a freshman from the Prep's newspaper interviewed me and asked me what it was like to be the Hawk mascot. I answered with all the humor I could muster, fighting desperately to maintain my reputation as the school's number-one clown. Before the interview was through, he asked me what I thought I'd be doing in five years. "I'm going to be the Phillie Phanatic, of course!"

Okay, let's fast-forward six years. With my bachelor of science degree from Drexel stowed away in my closet somewhere and my short-lived career as a computer supplies and business forms salesman grinding to a halt, I found myself thumbing through the want ads in the *Philadelphia Inquirer*. Nothing excited me under "S" for sales. I flipped back to the "Ms" for management. Nothing. Then I saw: "Mascots Wanted." I made sure I wasn't looking in the personals under bondage. I wasn't. I checked them later on (I kid, of course). The classified ad for the mascot read: "Send resume and letter to PO Box 7575, Philadelphia, PA, 19101." I thought I might be able to earn a little extra cash on weekends dressing as a cartoon character. Or maybe McDonald's was looking for a new Ronald McDonald or Hamburglar or something. I sent a resume touting my corporate experience. I was in Drexel's co-op program in college and had worked for several different corporations. I ended my cover letter with the tag "Let me bring your costume to life."

Two weeks later, the Phillies were on the phone saying they were looking for a backup Phillie Phanatic. Dave Raymond, the regular Phanatic, needed help meeting his personal appearance schedule. His current backup was leaving to be the Dragon for the new NBA basketball franchise in Orlando. The Phillies, my Phillies, were calling me, asking me to come down and audition for the Phillie Phanatic job.

A week later I found myself seated with several other candidates in a waiting room. We were all filling out questionnaires. Everyone there had two things in common. One, we had all been mascots at one time or other, and two, we were all unemployed. One candidate had been the original Socceroo, a kangaroo mascot for the now defunct Philadelphia Fever of the professional indoor soccer league. The league was sinking fast, so to avoid becoming Sinkeroo, Socceroo was looking for an escape hatch. Socceroo appeared to be about 10-15 pounds overweight. Sucking on a cigarette, he leaned over to me and rattled off his impressive resume: "Before Socceroo, I was a clown with the circus, and before that, McGruff, the crime dog."

How could I compete with this guy? I hadn't put on a costume since high school. I only sent in my resume to break the monotony of looking for a *real* job. What the heck had I gotten myself into? Before I entered the interview room, self-doubt was galloping inside me like Dave Hollins busting from first to third.

It seemed like forever that I waited. Then it was my turn. A panel of four greeted me when I entered the room. Wayde Harrison and Bonnie Erickson—the husband-wife team that designed the Phanatic—were there. The duo had teamed up with legendary puppeteer Jim Henson to mastermind the Miss Piggy character. Chris Long of the Phillies was there. Chrissy started at the Vet as a hot-pants girl and was working in the promotions department with Frank Sullivan, dean of National League promotions gurus in those days. Dave Raymond was there, too, in the flesh rather than dressed in fur. I recognized him immediately. My hero.

The interview didn't go exactly as planned.

"What's your favorite cartoon?" Dave asked.

"Well, uh, I like so many," I stammered, my mind straining to remember the last time I even *watched* a cartoon—well, sober, at least. "Well, I've always been partial to Bugs Bunny."

Clearly this was not going to be an IBM-type interview. Most interviewers are trying to weed out the biggest clown, not hire him.

"What's your favorite comedy movie of all time?" Dave fired back.

I could feel a bead of sweat trickling past my earlobe. I've gone back and forth with this one for years. I've spent tortured, sleepless nights searching for the answer ... Animal House or Caddyshack? Caddyshack or Animal House? No time for indecision now. My career as a mascot might be riding on being decisive.

"It's got to be Animal House," I stated matter-of-factly. The panel feverishly scribbled. Maybe they were making store lists, or playing hangman, or doodling. I couldn't really see.

My mind vacillated, in Ed Grimsley fashion. "Should I have said Caddyshack? What kind of interview is this, anyway? Whatever happened to questions like: What are your aspirations? What are your greatest strengths? Greatest weaknesses?"

Chrissy fired the next volley: "What kind of music do you listen to?"

"Well, I guess I'm a classic-rock kind of guy," I stuttered. "With a heavy emphasis on Jackson Browne, Bruce Springsteen and southern rock." Then I thought, "Oh no, that's not what they wanted to hear. That's not what the Phanatic dances to. They want to hear Madonna, or the Jackson Five, or DeBarge. I'm blowing this interview big time."

"Do you like to dance?" Chrissy asked.

"Yeah, I do," I answered.

"Where do you dance?" Chrissy came back.

"Well," I said, gathering my thoughts quickly, "I like to dance at weddings, and on summer weekends, I'm a regular at the Springfield Inn down in Sea Isle City." (Note to non-Philadelphians: Philadelphians go down the shore, not to the shore.) I thought to myself, "Now I'm coming across like a barfly who only dances once he has a few beers in him. They hate me."

"Can we see some of your dance moves?" Dave jumped on my answer with speed and stealth, like the Phanatic moving in on a pair of blondes in halter tops.

"You mean right here?" I asked, my head scouring the room for a hidden camera.

"Sure, why not?" they all said in unison, reminding me of the group answering, "That's a different kind of flying altogether," in the movie *Airplane*. (Damn, I'll bet they wanted me to say *Airplane* was my favorite movie.)

"Yeah, why not?" I thought. I was getting the picture now— just go with the flow. They're not about to hire the guy who's the last one out on the dance floor. They want the life of the party! Okay, bring it on! Pass the lampshade!

"Can I take off my shoes?" I asked, getting a little braver.

"Sure, whatever you want," Chrissy winked.

Before I knew it, Sam Cooke's "Twistin' the Night Away" was blaring on the boom box and I was pulling Chrissy off her chair and cutting the rug in my stocking feet. The panel laughed, making cracks about my facial expressions, saying I'd get more laughs without the Phanatic head on. I didn't care. I was twistin' the night away for all I was worth, going head to head for my dream job against an out-of-shape, unemployed kangaroo.

When the music ended, I slipped my shoes back on and went back to the table to take my seat in front of the panel.

"Listen," I wrapped up, "I've been a diehard Phillies fan, a diehard Phanatic fan, and a certifiable Philly sports nut all my life." I fanned out several documents on the table in front of the panel. "Look," I said, "This is me on top of a statue at 15th and Market Street during the Phillies' 1980 World Series parade." The panel was now gawking at one of my prized possessions, an 8"x10" color picture that had run in a Philadelphia *Inquirer* supplement after the celebration.

"And here I am dressed in a tuxedo with a Julius Erving jersey under the coat, shaking hands with the one and only Dr. J." That picture had run in the *Inquirer* the day after Doc's last regular season game at the Spectrum, when he lit up the Pacers for his 30,000th career point.

"'Sall good," I thought. "I'm scoring here." Time to play my trump card.

"And this," I roared, "this is an interview I gave six years ago when I was my high school's mascot. They asked me what I'd be doing after I graduated from college, and I answered—well, read for yourself what I answered."

As they read the words, "I'm going to be the Phillie Phanatic, of course!" I stated with conviction, "So there you have it. This is my destiny." Melodramatic? Hokey? Whatever—they seemed to be buying it.

After a pregnant pause, Chrissy asked me to come back after lunch for the final phase of the interview—auditioning in the Phanatic costume.

I gulped down lunch. When I got back, Bonnie Erickson, one of the panelists, was with me in the dressing room. "This is going to be a little snug," she said as she pried my backside into the spandex. I started feeling queasy after she zipped up the back of the furry green rotund body and reached for the head.

Am I really doing this? Do I really have a shot at becoming the character I idolized all through my childhood? Dave Raymond does this stuff for a living. I haven't worn a costume since my brother had a toga party in college, and I went dressed in my mother's top bed sheet. I had been a failure selling computer supplies, and I was peddling water filters door to door as recently as yesterday. What did I think I was doing?

"Now, remember, as soon as I open that door, you will be the Phillie Phanatic," Bonnie instructed, starting to sound more like a hypnotist than mascotologist (no, that might not be a real word, but if it is, Bonnie qualifies).

I was a little dazed and feeling damned uncomfortable in that suit. The lacrosse helmet which supported the Phanatic's head was buckled firmly in place. The headpiece rises a good ten inches above my head. It really threw off my equilibrium. When I turned my head from side to side, it seemed that the Phanatic's head was on time delay. The roly-poly belly made me jiggle when I walked. I now had four fingers instead of five.

And the smell. The costume smelled like a rug dried out after a night in the rain. I started sweating—great, smell it up some more, Tom—the moment I headed towards the conference room.

Bonnie repeated: "Now, remember, when I open these doors, you will be the Phillie Phanatic."

What the heck is that supposed to mean? Is there some sort of Jeff Goldblum fly-transformation machine in that room? Will I walk and dance and act like the Phanatic in and out of costume now? I've seen Men in Black. She was freaking me out. And what was behind those doors? Has this all been one big gag? Will Alan Fundt be there with a microphone, shouting, "Don't look now, but you're on *Candid Camera*!"

The doors flung open. There sat the panel, and behind them, a camera. I was right! I was going to be on camera.

"Hi, Phanatic," Chrissy sing-songed.

"Is she talking to me?" I thought. "Settle down, I'm the Phanatic, not DeNiro!"

"This is Anthony," Chrissy continued, pointing to the cameraman. "He's videotaping all our Phanatics today."

"All our Phanatics?" I fumed. "But I thought *I* was the Phanatic?" Forget it. I am the Phanatic. I hustled over to the panel, hugging and high-fiving everyone. When I went to give Chrissy a big Phanatic smooch with the elongated snout, I conked her on the forehead. Like most men, I have trouble judging lengths.

"Hey, Phanatic," Dave yelled. "There's a pregnant women crossing the street!"

Chrissy had shaken off my head-butt and was walking across

the floor with a pillow under her shirt. "Okay, I can role-play," I thought. Gotta be quick on the uptake. I scampered over to Chrissy, thrusting my belly out, mimicking her delicate condition. Getting down on one knee, I pressed my ear up against her pillow/belly. I pantomimed that I could feel kicking. I kicked my own leg out and held up two furry fingers. Twins!

"Hey, Phanatic, Mike Schmidt just hit a home run," Dave Raymond barked. "Who the hell does this guy think he is, Tubby Raymond?" I thought. He kept throwing out new situations like a football coach doing grass drills.

"How do you feel?" Chrissy yelled.

"Happy," I thought. "I feel happy. I can do happy." I jumped around the room, high-fiving, hugging, and dancing a jig. Music blared from the boom box. I picked Chrissy up again and twirled her around until we were both dizzy. By this time I was gasping for breath, sweating buckets. I didn't think I could last another minute without passing out. And I'd only been at it for five minutes. I wanted to shed that shag carpet right away.

Mercifully, the audition came to an end. I staggered to the dressing room panting like a dog in heat. The Phanatic job? You can have it. I didn't want any job where suffocation was a job requirement. Where the hell was OSHA when I really needed them? What was I going to do when I put that Phanatic suit on in 100-degree weather?

Driving home, my disenchantment gave way to sheer exhilaration. I had actually worn the Phillie Phanatic costume, and, hell, I was the Phillie Phanatic, even if it was only for five minutes! But making it a career? No, thanks! Driving away that night, I kept hoping the group that watched my video was going to roar instead of wince when they saw me bonk Chrissy on the head.

Apparently they roared. A week later, Chrissy gave me the call I was hoping for.

"Hey, Phanatic," she chuckled, "You got the job."

Disbelievers

"They talked about David Cone. They delivered Danny Jackson. They negotiated with Joe Carter. They wound up with Pete Incaviglia. It was one of the Phillies' most critical off seasons in twenty years. And now that it's over, all they've produced is rampaging indifference in a city desperate for something better."
— Jayson Stark, February 7, 1993

The Roots of Disbelief

New York is the city that never sleeps—the place where the sun never goes to bed. That's why the Empire City casts long shadows. Those shadows roll north all the way to Boston and south down to Philadelphia.

That damned New York shadow. To really understand the mentality of the Philly fan (non-Philadelphians view that phrase as an oxymoron), you have to grasp one annoying fact of Philly life. Philly teams seldom bust out of that New York shadow and into the sunlight. Long ago, the gods of baseball sanctified the boroughs that Willie, Mickey, and the Duke patrolled. When the Dodgers and Giants caught the last train for the coast, the music did not die. The gods simply set up their Olympus in the House That Ruth Built.

Throughout so much of baseball's glorious history, Philadelphia and Boston have found themselves here alone on the ground while New York's in midair. So send in the clowns. In Boston, fans obsess over the Curse of the Bambino. The Red Sox were baseball's strongest team in the teen years of the last century, but their growth has been stunted since '18.

The Boston Red Sox won the World Series in 1912, leading New York by a whopping 55 games. In 1914, Boston picked up a 19-year old left-handed pitcher named Babe Ruth. With Ruth on the hill, Boston won the World Series in 1915 (against the Phillies), and again in 1917 and 1918. Ruth contributed 18, 23, and 13 victories respectively to those championship seasons. In 1918, the Red Sox lost regular left fielder Duffy Lewis to military service, and Ruth played the outfield, where he bashed 11 homers (the Babe had never hit more than four in a season up till then) to capture his first home run title. After 1918, baseball's once and forever Sultan was sold to the Yankees, and the Red Sox have never won another World Series.

There's no crying in Boston. It ruins the beans.

The Curse Moves West

The Red Sox started the 1919 season in grand style. Pitchers Carl Mays and Sad Sam Jones twirled 18 innings of goose eggs for a boffo 2-0 start. Then Boston rocked its own world by selling Babe Ruth to the Yankees. Goodbye Babe, hello Curse.

The 2001 World Champion Arizona Diamondbacks began their 2002 season just like those 1919 Bosox. Randy Johnson and Curt Schilling blanked the San Diego Padres on the first two days of the season, making Arizona the first defending champion since the 1919 Red Sox to open a season with back-to-back shutouts. Though they're not planning an exorcism at Bank One Ballpark, the Diamondbacks have to feel a little uneasy. Babe Ruth's daughter is a Phoenix area resident and a fan of the Diamondbacks.

Philadelphia doesn't have the Curse of the Bambino, but Philly definitely has its own mark of the demon. No, it's not 666. It's "1964"—a figure that symbolizes Philly's forever Freddy Krueger nightmare on Broad Street. Actually, the nightmare happened at 22nd and Lehigh, at Connie Mack Stadium. In 1964, the Phillies and the city of Philadelphia endured baseball's most monumental collapse. The Phillies blew a six-game lead with two weeks to play. Unheard of. Unparalleled. Undying. Any time that wistful, we're-gonna-win-it-all-this-year rapture starts to overtake the City of Brotherly Love, Philadelphians refuse to roll with it. When a Phillies team is leading the pack, heading down the home stretch with a comfortable lead, Philly fans lie awake at night disbelieving, refusing to get sucked into a Freddy-like netherworld of disillusionment, despondency, and despair. Philadelphia's heart got ripped open once in the Days of Wine and Rojas. Ever since, Philadelphia parents warn their children about 1964. Before Philly kids eat their first soft pretzel or first Pat's cheesesteak, parents drill into them: "Never get in a car with a stranger. Never run around the house with scissors. And *never* believe that the Phillies have a pennant locked up until the one-hundred sixty-second game has been played, all the pregnant chads have been counted, and you've heard the story confirmed by Vai Sikahema, Don Tollefson and Gary Papa." For non-Philadelphians, Vai, Don, and Gary are long-time trusted Philly sport anchors.

Yeah, meet Philadelphia's eternal killjoy—1964. Any time the Phillies are on a tear, someone is bound to throw a wet blanket on the party with the obligatory, "Yeah, well, don't get too excited. Remember 1964."

So Philly, like Boston, plays its baseball forever in New York's shadow. In the second half of the twentieth century, both Philly and Boston watched hometown baseball franchises crawl out of that New York shadow and achieve world acclaim in other cities. The Philadelphia Athletics, after finishing in the cellar nine times during the thirties and forties, relocated to Kansas City in 1955. The club wallowed there till 1967, then headed to Oakland. In 1972, '73, and '74, the Oakland A's became only the second team in baseball to three-peat as World Champs. Yes, the other was the Yankees.

Boston's Braves deserted Beantown in 1953 to became the Milwaukee Braves. From 1917 through 1945, only three times did the Boston Braves finish as high as fourth. Only once did they come within nine games of the top team. However, in their sixth season in Milwaukee, they won a World Series after assembling one of the fabled lineups of the fifties. In 1966, the franchise moved once more, this time to Atlanta. Starting in 1995, the Atlanta Braves have won their division seven straight times at this writing.

Granted, the Big Apple also lost a couple of franchises during the fifties. However, in 1962, they got a brand new team right back, the New York Mets, who promptly lost a record 120 games in one season. To benchmark how amazing that feat is, the 1961 Phillies lost 23 *games in a row* yet "managed" only 107 losses. As manager Casey Stengel put it: "They've shown me ways to lose that I never knew existed." Yet the Mets vaulted incompetence into *haute chic*, endearing and immortalizing themselves by virtue (?) of their own ineptitude. It doesn't seem fair to Philadelphia or Boston. The Mets lose and they become darlings; the Phils or Red Sox lose and they're bums. To make matters worse, only seven years after the "Amazin'" Mets' inaugural season, they nabbed their first World Championship, eleven years before the old and established Phillies won their first-ever world championship.

When it comes to baseball, time and time again, New York manages to push Philly back into the shadows. The City of Brotherly Love drew some national attention with its pennant-winning 1950 Whiz Kids. However, New York swept the Kids in four, and the shadow deepened. Philly didn't get back out into the sunlight till 1964, the year that Doubting Thomas, compared to Phillie fans, seemed like the patron saint of optimism.

Philly limped through the rest of the sixties, seldom climbing out of the second division. But in the seventies, Philly enjoyed its finest period of baseball since the '29 A's. Philadelphia fielded a superb team throughout the Seventies, fronted by Hall of Famers Mike Schmidt and Steve Carlton. In the latter part of that decade, the Phils rolled off three straight division crowns as well as two straight 101-win seasons. But they failed to win a championship till 1980. By that time, the nucleus of the seventies' juggernaut was aging. After the championship season, the club dropped in the standings, but Phillie management retooled quickly. A group of veterans, in the twilight of stellar careers, was whisked —some would say, wheeled—into town for 1983. Three ex-Reds destined for the Hall of Fame—Pete Rose, Tony Perez, and Joe Morgan—stumblingly led the "Wheeze Kids," as they were dubbed, to a National League pennant.

That year was the Wheeze Kids' last gasp. It was time for Philly to head back to the shadow.

After ten consecutive .500-or-better seasons commencing in 1975, Philadelphia tumbled. From 1985 to 1992, the Phils registered one winning season—a second-place 1986 finish under manager John Felske that was mostly aberration. They were the only team in baseball with a losing record at All-Star break every year from '84-'92.

Lee Thomas Arrives

The Phillies organization tried to halt the skid way back on June 21,1988 by hiring Lee Thomas as general manager. Thomas was a savvy, experienced baseball man who committed to a long-term plan intended to position the Phillies as perennial contenders. It was a daunting task. The Phillies clubhouse was in shambles when Thomas arrived. The new GM was appalled at the lethargy and bad attitude he observed in the locker room.

The Phils plummeted into the cellar in Thomas's first year, the unenviable spot they occupied for two of the next four years. After his rookie season as GM, Thomas started wheeling and dealing. He tapped the Minnesota Twins for second baseman Tommy Herr, a Lancaster native. (Lancaster is in the heart of Pennsylvania Dutch territory, a couple hours away from Philadelphia.) Herr batted .287 in 1988 but never emerged as the impact player the Phillies needed. He left at the end of the 1990 season, traded to the Mets for the eminently forgettable Nikco Riesgo and Rocky Ellis.

From Thomas's arrival through the end of the 1993 season, he made sixty-four player moves. None were bona fide blockbusters. However, with the seemingly ho-hum acquisition (at least, it was viewed that way at the time) of John Kruk and Randy Ready from San Diego on June 2, 1989, Thomas started packing attitude into the Phillies' locker room. He welcomed rebels. He opened Philly's doors to guys who competed with such intensity that it disturbed their laid-back teammates elsewhere. Gypsies, tramps, and thieves started finding refuge in Philadelphia.

A few weeks after the Kruk trade, Thomas dealt popular Phillie Juan Samuel to the Mets for Lenny Dykstra, Roger McDowell, and Tom Edens. Hometown fans howled. Sammy was a local hero. Sure, he had some fundamental flaws. He was an undisciplined free swinger who chased low-and-away pitches to his ultimate extinction. But Sammy was kinetic. He swiped bases—lots of them. He ran out every ball he hit. Year after year, he seemed oh-so-close to superstardom. But as the years rolled by, it was apparent that Sammy couldn't make that quantum leap. In contrast, Lee Thomas saw Dykstra as an undervalued gem, destined for greatness. Lenny was not getting a chance with the Mets, so Philly's GM plucked him away.

On the same day as the Dykstra trade, pitcher Terry Mulholland joined the fold. Mulholland, Charlie Hayes and Dennis Cook left San Francisco for Steve Bedrosian and Rick Parker. Bedrosian had won the Cy Young Award for the Phillies in 1987, but as Thomas pointed out, "You don't need a great closer when you never get a lead."

The Dykstra and Mulholland deals happened on Father's Day, a providential day in Philly history. It was on Father's Day, June 21, 1964, that Phil pitcher Jim Bunning pitched a perfect game against the New York Mets. Thomas may not have pitched perfect deals twenty-five years later, but without them, 1993's pennant would never have flown in Philly.

Despite the new blood, Kruk, Mulholland, Dykstra and their new teammates wallowed in last place in '89. In the off season, the Phils picked up Dave Hollins from San Diego, and Philadelphia climbed to fourth in 1990. In August of that year, Wes Chamberlain and Tony Longmire were plucked from the Pirates and Dale Murphy from the Braves. Atlanta was beneficent enough to toss young, unproven pitcher Tommy Greene into the deal. Unfortunately, physical problems had eroded the once great Murphy's ability. Murph never regained his two-time MVP form and was off the roster by 1993.

Although the Murph deal didn't pan out, Lenny Dykstra validated Thomas's gut feeling. Nails, as he was known in New York, became the Phils' "Start Me Up" guy, the driving wheel of the entire offensive scheme. Nails was the starting center fielder on the 1990 NL All-Star team. He led the league in on-base percentage, tied for the league lead in hits, and placed fourth in batting (.325) and walks (89).

In 1991, the Phils nabbed closer Mitch Williams from the Cubs for Chuck McElroy and Bob Scanlan. They notched up to third place, finishing 78-84. Granted, those numbers don't portend the second coming of the '27 Yankees, but Philly had reason for excitement. First of all, the Phillies were competitive even though several stars were injured most of the year. On May 6, Lenny Dykstra and Darren Daulton, returning from John Kruk's bachelor party, had a serious car crash. Dykstra broke his ribs, cheekbone, and collarbone. Daulton suffered a broken left eye socket. When Dykstra went down, he was among the league leaders in runs, hits, doubles, steals, walks, and on-base percentage. Daulton, all told, missed almost a month and a half. The Phils still managed to run off a 13-game win streak shortly after midseason. Dykstra established his role as the table-setter for the entire offense. His team was 36-27 when he was in the lineup and 42-57 when he was not. That Philadelphia's victory total would have risen dramatically had Nails played a full season was irrefutable

The 1991 campaign was the club's only first-division finish in five years. The macho nucleus of Daulton, Dykstra, Kruk, and Hollins seemed poised to contend. The Phillies and their fans anticipated big things in 1992. Their Phils had the kind of in-your-face attitude that the City of Brotherly Love loved. They had distanced themselves from their club's recent dismal past. They even changed uniforms. They were a club on a mission.

Stylin'

Is it just me, or do teams change logos and uniform design more often than the Krukker cleans his batting helmet? It seems like major-league teams do a bit of market research, figure out what colors are "hot" and what styles are "in," and bingo, they're calling a press conference to trumpet their new look.

They're also telling the public where they can buy all the new-look merchandise.

When the Phillies changed their uniform design before the 1992 season, it was a big deal. In the 109-year history of the franchise, the Phils have made only a handful of design changes. Remember that seventies/eighties vintage look—maroon pinstripes on the home uniforms and that overpowering baby blue hue on the away threads? They practically had to televise those games with a permanent "Please do not adjust your set" graphic.

Anyway, the Phillies tried a different approach with their new look in 1992. They *didn't* go public with the design.

As the backup Phanatic, I suited up for a mock press conference where team president Bill Giles announced that he was tapping the Phillie Phanatic to make sure no one got a sneak peek at the new uniforms. A picture of the Phanatic seated on a big red chain-bound trunk splashed across the front cover of the Phillies' February newsletter. With tongues planted firmly in cheek, local newspapers began speculating why the public wasn't privy to a glimpse. Radio stations screamed, "Sacrilege!" How dare the Phils mess with the team's logo and not let a sports-crazed town like Philly in on it?

Angelo Cataldi and the Morning Guys on WIP radio tried all the angles to scoop the story. They called several Delaware Valley fashion designers searching for someone—anyone—in the know. The WIP sports jocks tried to get the Phillies brass to spill the beans. They stooped so low as to send Al Morganti, one of the Morning Show's freer spirits, on a commando mission into the Phillies' clubhouse. (You know—one of those *"This is Big Brother to Little Sister. I am in the yard. Repeat. I am in the yard"* kind of missions.)

Al's mission? Break into the locked trunks and swipe the new uniform so WIP could scoop the world.

Dave Raymond, the regular Phanatic in '92, and I were part of the schtick.

Morganti went live on the air, chirping, "Angelo, I'm in,"

'furtively' reporting to Cataldi and the listening audience from manager Jim Fregosi's office.

"Great, Al—any sign of the Phanatic?" Angelo asked. (Angelo reminded me of my neighbor, Vince Johnston, when I was a kid. The neighborhood kids never wanted to play with Vince, so one Christmas, he got a walkie-talkie, thinking the kids would play with him. Didn't work, though—another kid got a Miata. We were eighteen years old at the time.)

"No, the idiot abandoned his post! Hey wait ... What's this? The Phanatic left the keys sitting on top of the trunks. What a moron!" Dave Raymond and I were sitting next to Al, cracking up.

Angelo crowed, "All right, Al. Here's the moment we've all been waiting for! Open that trunk and describe what the new uniforms look like to all the sports fans in Philadelphia!"

Al shot back, "Okay, Angelo. I'm turning the key now." Al jiggled his car keys into the mouthpiece of the telephone. It was like doing one of those pre-TV radio-days programs with sound effects, like *The Shadow*. "Now I'm opening up the trunk, and, oh my, I can see the unif-oo-oo- ... wait a minute ... Who's that? ... uh ... uh oh, Angelo ... It's the Phanatic! He's heading right for me! ... Oh no ... Look out ... AARRRRRRGGGGGGG!!!!"

Dave and I had fished some empty bottles out of Fregosi's trash can (vitamin supplements, or something that had "VO" on it) and were now smashing them, making a god-awful racket. We slammed the phone back on the hook.

"Al! Al!" Angelo was screaming into the microphone back at the studio, listening to the dead line. Sidekick Al had desecrated the inner sanctum, á la Indiana Jones. He was probably running his buns off in front of some rolling giant ball with red seams and Spalding stamped on it.

It was a great gig. I didn't have to put that hot costume on. I didn't even have to break a sweat. Maybe I could start phoning in appearances instead of putting that smelly costume on.

A week before the opener, the trunks containing the uniforms (wink, wink) were transferred to the window display in John Wanamaker's department store in Center City Philadelphia. The Phanatic pulled guard duty, sartorially resplendent (we Phanatics used to listen to Howard Cosell) in a specially made blue security guard outfit. The outfit also had a holster housing a can of silly string and a water gun. Dave Raymond and I took turns on guard duty, camping out for four days in Wanamaker's window. Since Wanamaker's is directly across from City Hall, we took "breaks" when prisoners were bussed in and out of the courtrooms. When the buses arrived, the Phanatic ran out on the street, flashed his badge, and shook his water soaker at them. The prisoners seemed to love it. At least, we hoped they did. If any of you guys took offense and are now on the outside, Dave Raymond made me do it.

When the '92 home opener arrived, the Vet was sold out. The home team was poised for a breakout season. Curiosity about the new uniforms had become a cheeky fan obsession. Before the game, Phanavision showed the Phanatic cruising down Broad Street to the stadium on top of a Phillies-red Brooks security truck, with a full police escort. Some of the Phillies' front office staff, dressed as Secret Service agents in dark suits and sunglasses, ran along side the truck. The caravan footage was taken a few days earlier but was portrayed as happening live. Immediately after the National Anthem, the Brooks truck thundered onto the field. The Phanatic jumped off and helped the ground crew unload the trunks and wheel them into the clubhouse. Next, Phanavision flashed a previously taped bit showing Darren Daulton and Mickey Morandini waiting in their underwear for the new uniforms to arrive (the women were probably hoping that Darren *was* in uniform. Oh, yeah, you too, Mickey ... Yeah, that's the ticket ...). When the Phanatic barreled into the clubhouse, Daulton and Morandini opened the trunks and tossed the uniforms up in the air like kids unwrapping Christmas toys. If it sounds hokey, it's because it was.

The Phanavision screen went blank. Suddenly, the team sprinted out on to the field wearing the new threads. The gloomy maroon pinstripes had been replaced by bright red stripes. "Phillies" was emblazed across the chest. Blue stars dotted the two I's in "Phillies." A lone blue button capped the new red hat.

You look marvelous, darling, absolutely marvelous...

Terry Mulholland sat the Cubs down one-two-three to start the game. Lenny Dykstra dug in at the plate. I was in the control room, feeling the power with a new CD player. Itchy to fire that baby up, I grabbed the Rolling Stones' "Tattoo You" disc. I punched track number one. Keith Richards's searing guitar licks in "Start Me Up" rocked the Vet. Then the Dude got plunked.

It is not *better to look good than to feel good ...*

1992 ... Kerplunk

A sellout crowd of 60,431 showed up for the opener on April 7, 1992. Philly let its guard down and forgot 1964. Silly Philly. On the second pitch of the season, the "Start Me Up" guy got plunked by Greg Maddux. The Phillies season went kerplunk.

VIDEO DAN STEPHENSON, PHILLIES VIDEO OPERATIONS: "You could actually feel the disappointment in the stadium, like a balloon bursting.

I've never seen anything like it before or since. It was as though everyone realized the season was shot right then and there. Lenny was our one indispensable guy. The season went downhill from that point on."

With Dykstra out, everything failed. The pitching was abominable. Kyle Abbot went 1-14. Only six other pitchers in the twentieth century, with fifteen or more decisions, had worse records. By midseason, Mitch Williams was barking to a San Francisco reporter, "No way we can win with the players we have. Until somebody upstairs figures that out, and gets us some players, no way."

The Phils ended an ugly season in last place. The fans felt dissed—disappointed, disheartened, and disillusioned. Many were angry. They wanted results. They demanded big fixes in 1993.

The Phillies promised those big fixes.

The term "big fixes" means different things to different people. To the fan, big fixes meant big-name players. Big fixes meant spending wads of money to land high-cost, high-profile superstars. Big fixes meant a cavalcade-of-stars approach to winning it all. But the Phillies brass had other things in mind.

LEE THOMAS: "We figured we already had a great nucleus, even if we did finish last the year before. Lenny's injury, Murph's injuries, the Krukker's—they killed us. We never got started. We knew we had some weaknesses and a few areas to shore up. Getting one big-name pitcher at great expense was not the answer. Bolstering only one position ignored our other shortcomings and needs. We didn't have unlimited funds. No one does. We needed to spend our cash wisely to patch up all our holes the best we could."

So Lee Thomas stayed the course. The National League was preparing for two new teams, the Colorado Rockies and the Florida Marlins, in 1993. Each team at the time had to provide the names of fifteen players to protect. The Rockies and the Marlins selected a roster from the players who were left unprotected. Mariano Duncan and Ricky Jordan, nonregulars with high salaries, were prime prospects for the expansion franchises. Duncan earned $2 million a year, and Ricky Jordan was preparing for arbitration with his eye on a million dollar-a-year stipend. Neither was a starter, but both were valuable. Duncan, who sported a World Championship ring from the 1990 Cincinnati Reds, was a superb role player. He started at every infield and outfield position except first base and right field during the previous two campaigns. A native of the Dominican Republic, Mariano was a happy-go-lucky character, a splashy dresser who added his own funky style to the diverse Phillies locker room. Ricky Jordan was steady, seasoned, reliable, and one of the best-liked guys on the roster. A home-grown product of the Phils' organization, he was drafted in 1983 and remained a Phil ever since. However, with Kruk's performance at first base (the Krukker batted .294 in 1991 and .323 in 1992), Ricky was relegated to bench duty.

Thomas chose to protect them both, thus walking the talk of his avowed strategy. Thomas and Fregosi insisted that the Phillies' bench had to play a key role. However, many disbelievers snickered in Philly. What's special about keeping guys who don't even start on a last-place club? Besides, how does a last-place team consider itself a contender in the first place?

Later that month, Thomas wangled a deal for Danny Jackson. Lee had heard a rumor buzzing that Jackson's 1992 employer, the Pittsburgh Pirates, was not intending to protect him in the expansion draft. The Phils' GM contacted Bob Gebhard, Colorado general manager, and suggested that Colorado draft Jackson. If they did, the Phillies promised to swap Matt Whisenant and Joel Adamson for Jackson. Whisenant and Adamson were highly regarded Phillies minor-league pitching prospects at the time.

Thomas's tender was a radical departure. Till then, he always placed more emphasis on potential than past performance, particularly with pitchers. Danny Jackson's best days seemed to be behind him. In 1988, Jackson's glittering 23-8 record earned him the second slot in the NL Cy Young voting, behind Orel Hershiser. Since '88, however, Jackson's combined record was 23-25. In '92 with the Pirates, he started game two of the National League Championship Series and was chased after 1 2/3 innings. However, his '92 ERA was a respectable 3.84.

JOHN KRUK: "Dutch [Daulton] and I were eating at Ruth's Chris Steakhouse in Philly when Lee and Jim Fregosi walked in and had dinner with us. Lee said they were looking for a left-handed pitcher. They ran a lot of names by us. One was Jason [Danny Jackson]. Dutch and I both jumped on that one, 'Yeah, get that guy. He can throw.' Fregosi always let us put our two cents in on those deals."

In December, Thomas traded Mike Hartley to Minnesota for leftie David West. The GM then inked a string of free agents: outfielders Pete Incaviglia and Milt Thompson, relief pitcher Larry Andersen, and outfielder Jim Eisenreich.

The Hot Stove League in Philly was frenetic. Those names did nothing for most fans, who contended the Phillies had done absolutely nothing. The moves they made were as baffling to the locals as Philadelphia scrapple (For non-Philadelphians, scrapple is *not* a board game, nor is it made from boards. Scrapple professes to be food, although in those rare cases when someone actually eats scrapple, that claim is disputed as well).

Even Darren Daulton was quoted in December: "We made some moves that I think are going to help because of what we had last year. But I don't think we made a major impact."

On February 7, 1993, then Philly columnist Jayson Stark wrote, "They [the Phillies] talked about David Cone. They delivered Danny Jackson. They negotiated with Joe Carter. They wound up with Pete Incaviglia. It was one of the Philles' most critical off seasons in twenty years. And now that it's over, all they've produced is rampaging indifference in a city desperate for something better."

The Phils were severely criticized for not landing that one big-name free agent guy that fans could rally around and look to for salvation.

BILL GILES: "Looking back, we did what we could to get some of those big names. I offered David Cone $16 million, but he re-signed with Kansas City. We couldn't convince him to come to Philly because he wasn't really interested. Same with Swindell. He wanted to play in Houston. We couldn't persuade him either. It wasn't the money."

After the 1992 season, free agency was careening out of control. Ninety-one players, out of 153 free agents who filed, changed clubs in 1992-93. Three of the four previous Most Valuable Players (Barry Bonds, Kevin Mitchell, and Andre Dawson) and two of the three previous Cy Young winners (Greg Maddux and Doug Drabek) shifted clubs in 1993. A whopping 34 players from the four 1992 playoff clubs switched home teams. With baseball's glory names flying around like Barry Bonds's home runs, the crew that wound up in Phillies pinstripes seemed undistinguished and humdrum. Of course, all motion is relative, as that Princeton pitcher of theorems, Albert Einstein, proposed long ago. Philly baseball fans agreed with Einstein. Relative to the rest of the baseball pack, it appeared as though their Phils had stood still.

Free Agent Statistics Between 1985-86 and 1992-93

Year	Filed	Stayed	Moved	% that Moved
85-86	62	25	3	4.8 %
86-87	80	28	13	16.3 %
87-88	76	37	19	25 %
88-89	77	38	22	28.6 %
89-90	91	28	43	47.3 %
90-91	98	28	43	43.8 %
91-92	99	32	42	42.4 %
92-93	153	32	91	59.4 %

Some of the numbers the Phils put up in 1992 don't jibe with their last-place finish. They were the only last-place team in history with a trio of players in the top three in RBIs (Daulton won the RBI title), batting (Kruk), and runs scored (Dave Hollins). On the negative side, they were the only NL team with three guys (Hollins, Daulton, and Duncan) who whiffed more than 100 times. By bringing Incaviglia into the '93 fold, they were adding a guy who had averaged 140 strikeouts a year for the seven previous years. Inky held the American League record for most whiffs in a season (185) until his Detroit teammate, Rob Deer, broke it. To make matters worse, if Dale Murphy's comeback were successful, Murph was a three-time NL leader in whiffs. Continuing, Phils pitchers were punched out 145 times in 1992. New hurlers Danny Jackson and Larry Andersen had struck out in 52.3% of their major-league at-bats. (Had pitching talent not been thinned by expansion, that percentage would be higher. It's an ugly thought, but not as ugly as the way those two swung.)

In the face of criticism about his perceived lackluster acquisitions, Lee Thomas stuck to his guns. "I'm tired of losing. I think we have a club right now that can play with anybody."

PAUL HAGEN, WRITER, *PHILADELPHIA DAILY NEWS*: "I remember sitting with Fregosi and Thomas in a bar in Montreal during the '92 season. Each of them was going on about what you had to do to win in the NL. 'You win by having a full bench. Without the designated hitter, you've got to have your guys sharp for pinch hitting. They've got to see action all season long,' Fregosi insisted. That's what he and the GM set out to do. After all their transactions, the big salaries they wound up paying role players outraged the locals. The thing was—those roles were pivotal to the big picture, to Fregosi's strategy. People didn't realize that."

The strategy was a tough sell. At the start of 1992, the Phillies' six nonstart-ers were Wally Backman, Dale Sveum, Kim Batiste, Ruben Amaro, Steve Lake, and Jim Lindeman. They batted a combined .218 with four home runs and 30 RBIs. Over the course of the '92 season, Tom Marsh, Joe Millette, Stan Javier, Julio Peguero, Steve Scarsone, Brauilio Castillo, and Jeff Grotewold joined these six. No one accused Philly of incubating baseball's next Murderer's Row with that litany. Unlike '92, as spring training 1993 approached, Fregosi was crowing, "This is the best bench I've ever had. Every guy on the bench can be an integral part of the team, and I'll try my best to keep them all sharp." Fregosi proved a man of his word.

Still, the ranks of disbelievers swelled. WIP, Philly's all-talk sports-radio sta-tion was in its infancy in 1993, according to one of the station's pioneers, Angelo Cataldi. Caterwauling about the Phils' winter transactions filled the airwaves.

ANGELO CATALDI, WIP RADIO: "We were brutal about those acquisi-tions. We jumped all over the Phillies for not spending big money. We wanted them to land big-name guys. We ended up with Incaviglia, Thompson, Eisenreich, and Jackson. Look, radio is entertainment. We kept stirring the pot for enter-tainment purposes. That's what was going on. The '93 Phils hated us because we never showed up in the locker room. They didn't understand that sports talk radio was different from newspaper journalism. As a beat writer, I had spent eighteen years in locker rooms. But when the Phillies never saw us in that club-house, the way they were used to seeing newspaper reporters, they thought we didn't have the guts to face them. It got to the point where they hated us and we hated them. A lot of those guys have never forgiven us to this day. Dutch Daulton still doesn't talk to me. I saw him at a benefit in 2001, and he hardly spoke to me. But no, to be honest, before the season, we didn't think the Phils did much to improve. They proved us wrong, and we hated to admit it! But it made for good radio, good listening, and good ratings. We never had ratings like that year."

One longtime Philly pundit, Bill Conlin, had a swift change of heart. On January 20, 1993, he expressed how unimpressive the Phillies' off-season deals were. "The Phils got Danny Jackson instead of Swindell, Drabek, and Cone, because love is never having to say you're sorry for signing a guy four years re-moved from his fifteen minutes of fame." By February 17, Bill Conlin was see-ing the team in a different light. He wrote, "My gift to you this bleak February morning is ninety Phillies victories. Maybe ninety-five. These numbers come to you without guarantee of an East Division title but with the promise of a vibrant summer, a palpable outbreak of pennant fever."

Exactly one month later, on the day that Erin Goes Braagh, Bill Conlin stepped out on the limb alone where no one else would perch. "Okay, long-winded as we Irish like to be when telling a story, let's cut to the chase. The Phils will win the NL East."

You got the feeling that it wasn't because he had downed too many pitchers of green beer that Bill Conlin converted into a believer. Bill Conlin is hardened to the realities of pro sports in Philly, sensitive to the dangers of speculative optimism. He is not prone to the mood swings of the uninitiated.

BILL CONLIN: "I've gone to more spring training camps than I'd like to admit. Whatever doubts I had about the '93 Phillies when I went to Clearwater were cleared up quickly. I saw things I never saw before. Haven't seen them since, either. Like, the last intrasquad game. Inky charged into the fence, a cinderblock wall! In an intrasquad game! When he got back to the bench, everyone was high-fiving him. These guys had an intensity you could feel. And they loved being at the ball yard like no group I ever saw. Mitch [Williams] used to hang with the ground crew after the games, drinking beer. The whole organization was like family. I knew these guys were gonna make something good happen."

Conlin's intuition proved right. Philly's season in the sun started, fittingly, in the Sunshine State.

You Gotta Believe

The Phanatic always believes. No matter how bad things are going for our boys in red, the Phanatic has that little-kid belief that the harder you cheer, the more chance your team has to win. I always think my home team will come out on top—that this is the year we go all the way. I always think that no matter what trades we make, they'll work out well. When a player puts on the Phillies uniform, I figure he's gonna have a career year. He automatically becomes someone I never stop rooting for—till he changes uniforms.

I'm a Philly sports nut. I listen to WIP radio, can't help listening. They make me laugh one minute and go ballistic the next.

Angelo and the Morning Guys make my morning commute to the Vet fun. Even when Angelo is on his soapbox ripping everything, you can tell he's doing it for laughs. Angelo has played along with many of the Phanatic's antics. One year, to promote the Phanatic's birthday, Angelo pretended to spoil the party by revealing the secret identity of the Phanatic, that the guy underneath the fur was Dave Raymond. So Dave did an interview in street clothes with Angelo in the lobby of the Franklin Plaza Hotel where they were broadcasting the show. As Angelo was grilling Dave and comparing Dave to Clark Kent, I bounded in dressed as the Phanatic. I had a birthday cake in my hands.

"I can't believe it," bellowed Angelo. "The Phillie Phanatic is real! And all this time I thought it was just Dave Raymond wearing a costume!" With that, Angelo got a face full of cake.

Angelo likes hyping the Phillies' opening day, even in lackluster years. He used to buy a block of tickets in the 700 level at the Vet in the deepest part of center field, under the Phanavision board, for his army of listeners. Of course, Angelo got creative in distributing the tickets. First he gave out a row of tickets to the most beautiful girls who called in. Behind Babe Row came Bald Fat Guy Row, followed by Gambler Row. These guys used to bet on every aspect of the game, like who would make the first out and how long the National Anthem would be. The rest of the section would be filled with the zaniest Phillies fans they could find.

One year, Angelo and his gang got into the park at 6:00 a.m. on opening day to do their show. Angelo wanted to prove that despite being athletically challenged, he could throw a ball from Section 744 in center field all the way to the pitcher's mound. Unbeknownst to the listeners, Angelo had consulted with a professor of physics, who assured him that once that ball hit the turf, it would roll all the way to the pitcher's mound. Angelo successfully made the throw and was busy congratulating himself when the WIP Sports Babe, the pinup girl for the station, wound up and heaved the ball farther than Angelo.

Going into the '93 season, however, the WIP radio jocks were big disbelievers and really vocal about it, too. Listening in on my drive back from the Vet one day, I couldn't take it anymore. I stormed into my house as soon as I got home, picked up the phone, and called the station. The hosts had no idea who I was.

"Tom from Mt. Airy, you're on 610 WIP," Steve Fredericks sang out.

"Hi, Steve and Mike," I opened. "I've been sitting here listening to you guys and some of the listeners talk about how bad the Phils were last year and how bad they're going to be this year. You're crying for the Phils to go out and throw all their money at David Cone. If the Phillies are as bad as you think, doesn't it make sense to go out and fill the holes they have rather than spend all of their money on one player?"

"They are going to be god-awful again this year. Sorry, Tom," Steve insisted.

"But I like the players they got," I continued. "Danny Jackson is a big-league pitcher. Incaviglia has hit 20 or more home runs five times in his career. You know what Milt Thompson gives you in the outfield. And they say that this guy Eisenreich can really hit."

"Tom, you don't know what you are talking about," Steve contradicted.

"But last year we were trotting out guys like Brauillo Castillo. Don't you think we've upgraded?" I emphasized.

"You're living in a fantasy world, Tom," Fredericks said abruptly. "Hello, Moon Hoverer from the Osbournes, you're on 610 WIP ..."

I had been cut off, and they were on to their next victim.

My biggest show of faith that off season came when I got engaged. My sweet, naïve fiancée had visions of a beautiful spring wedding dancing in her head. The flowers would be in bloom, the girls would wear off-pink, or purple, or some other pastel color that I couldn't identify, and the wedding pictures would be taken in a meadow, babbling brook and all.

"But remember, Honey Bunny, I'm pretty busy in the spring, what with the season getting under way and all. I'm pretty well booked with appearances and games all the way through September," I explained to my wife-to-be.

The idea of marrying a baseball mascot suddenly didn't seem quite as appealing to her. Well, she reckoned, "At the very least we'll have a lovely September wedding. The flowers will still be gorgeous, the weather is still warm, and ..."

"Whoa, hold it right there, Pumpkin," I explained. "The Fightins made some key acquisitions who are gonna plug some holes in the lineup. With everybody staying healthy and the starting rotation giving us some innings, we may be playing some meaningful games this fall."

"Okay," she conceded, "Then early October is still ..."

"The playoffs and World Series start in October, Cupcake," I said reluctantly. "How about November?"

That was my now wife Jennifer's introduction to the life of Mrs. Phillie Phanatic. I imagine Santa and the Mrs. tied the knot in January because of his schedule. The result of our discussion? We got married in November. The weather was raw and overcast, the girls wore black and white, and that babbling brook was a couple weeks away from being iced over.

Spring Training

"Getting all those characters together in one locker room—it was lightning in a bottle. It'll never happen again."
— Mitch Williams

Self-belief is the fuel that propels the complex 25-part engine that is a base-ball team. Like a car engine, a baseball team can be assembled beautifully, boast the highest quality parts, but never rev like it's designed to unless it has the proper fuel. Sure, during the regular season, a team can cruise on low-grade fuel. But fall brings the big chill.

During the late seventies, Philadelphians winced every October when some great Philly engines pinged, popped, and lost power. Their fuel, their confi-dence, couldn't overcome that chill. That fuel changed when Pete Rose arrived. He filled the Phillies' engine up with the high-octane confidence they needed to chug to the top of the hill.

Confidence is an acquired trait, shaped by reinforced successes. But confi-dence is a whimsical mistress. Her bags are always packed, next to the door. She can flit off as soon as things go sour. Some ballplayers never stop wallowing in self-doubt. They sentence themselves forever to mediocrity because of their lack of confidence. Gaining confidence is a complex enough process for an indi-vidual, let alone an entire team. Yet lack of confidence—or worse, loss of confi-dence—is a team's most insidious killer. That was the harsh lesson of 1964. Phillies manager Gene Mauch panicked with the finish line in sight. He lost confidence in his team and particularly in his pitching staff. Mauch started pitcher Jim Bunning or Chris Short day after day, ignoring the rest of his staff. The team sensed its skipper's desperation, which sealed Philly's doom.

The graveyard of also-rans teems with teams short on confidence. Even fabled teams, like the Brooklyn Boys of Summer, languished among the also-rans for several seasons, unable to consecrate their immortality with a world championship. It wasn't until 1955, eight seasons after the Boys of Summer initially banded, that they won a World Series.

Baseball and sports are microcosms of real life. In real life, we watch families fail, families that seem to have it all—wealth, status, education, health, and looks. Those families fail, crumble and fragment because individual members stop be-lieving in each another. Baseball teams are no different.

JIM FREGOSI: "To be a good team, you have to have confidence in each other's abilities. I can remember sitting at a country club in Florida and talking with Dutch and Lenny and Mitch and them telling me that the guys on that '93 squad believed in each other that way, that strongly."

The '93 Phillies adopted a different attitude from the get-go—a feisty takin'-care-of-business style on the field that belied their offhanded, unfocused off-field mien.

LENNY DYKSTRA: "Guys came to the ballpark that spring expecting to win instead of wondering what was going to happen today. It wasn't that way any other year. It's one thing to say you expect to win. It's another thing to really believe it."

TERRY MULHOLLAND: "I could tell at spring training that this team was something special. We just clicked. A lot of guys went down to Florida early that year. We couldn't wait to get started. The guys on that team really loved the game of baseball. We really got along, too, and it showed on and off the field. I've been around baseball a long time, and I've never enjoyed my daily baseball life like that before or since."

In 1992, manager Fregosi subscribed to the old baseball theory that won-lost records in spring training are meaningless. Neither Fregosi nor his charges took the preseason too seriously as far as wins were concerned. The Phillies ended the '92 Grapefruit League season with a 9-19 record. They finished the regular season in last place. Both Fregosi and Thomas thought that their lackluster spring contributed. The '92 Phils didn't cultivate any victory-lust in spring training. Fregosi resolved that spring training 1993 would be different. He resolved to win early, to start fueling his machine with some high-octane confidence. His strategy worked. The '93 gang lusted for victories like vampires lust for blood.

LEE THOMAS: "Nobody in Philadelphia believed in this team going into spring training. We were losing season ticket holders. The media was on us. So we sat down and talked about the fact that we had a little more to prove this spring."

JIM FREGOSI: "The '93 crew made a commitment to winning and a commitment to each other. When you're down in Clearwater, the starters generally don't want to take those bus trips for away games in Vero Beach or Port St. Lucy. They'd rather stay in Clearwater, relax, and conserve their energy and their hits for the regular season. These guys were a different breed. When the regulars didn't make the bus trip for an away game, they'd come back to the clubhouse and meet the bus when it returned. The whole squad would sit around with beer and pizza and talk baseball. That's very rare. So I knew immediately we had something good going on."

The Phils broke out of the gate fast in the Grapefruit League. By the tenth of March, they were 3-1. They were batting .343 as a team, with 24 runs scored. Despite the great start, the disbelievers lay all around like Florida 'gators, itching for a chance to surface and snap. When '92 Phil Wally Backman left, he chattered about how the Phils had reneged on their promises. "The Phillies organization told the players a lot of different things to convince them to sign. They told the key players they were going to make certain changes, but they didn't make those changes." Lee Thomas countered, "We didn't sign guys with a promise of what we were going to do. If Wally knows how we can promise and guarantee anything. I'd like him to tell me how."

The disbelievers grew more strident when *USA Today* released its annual report on baseball salaries. The Phils ranked seventeenth in team salary among the sport's 28 teams. The Reds, with an overall payroll of $44.3 million, topped the list; the expansion Rockies, at $9.1 million, were at the bottom.

What was not evident from the figures was the Phils' commitment to their players, despite finishing last. Dale Murphy, who had made $2.5 million in 1992 while appearing in only eighteen games, reported to Clearwater as a nonroster player at $275,000 plus incentives if he made the team. Aside from Murph, only one other 1992 Phil, Jose DeLeon, took a pay cut. DeLeon's $247,000 1992 salary was chopped to $200,000. Jose had pitched only 15 innings for the Phillies in 1992 and ended his season on the DL. All in all, the Phils' payroll—for a team that finished last the year before—jumped from $23,981,500 in 1992 to $27,491,500 in 1993. The average salary shot up from $799,383 to $916,383. The highest paid Phillie was Mitch Williams, whose wages rose from $3.2 million to $3.5 million.

ONE MORMON AND 24 MORONS

Once in a while, someone shows up in the big leagues who really is the stuff of straight-arrow, boy-next-door Americana— one of those increasingly rare, aw-shucks, strong silent types who remains noble and untainted despite the temptations of wealth, power, and fame. Dale Murphy is such a man. Murph's code of living would make Jack Armstrong start vowing to clean up his act.

Murph was headed for baseball immortality when a series of injuries rendered him mortal. He won consecutive National League MVP awards in 1982 and 1983. He played four consecutive 162-game seasons, hitting over 35 home runs and driving in more than 100 RBIs in each. Murph was such a complete ballplayer that despite being 6'5," 215 pounds, he ranked among the league's top thirty in stolen bases for three straight years.

By the time Dale came to the Phillies in 1990, health problems had put him in precipitous decline. He managed to hit 24 homers that year (only seven, however, were as a Phil) before slipping to 18 round-trippers and a .252 average in 1991. The following year, he stepped to the plate only 62 times.

Dale Murphy does not drink or smoke or curse. You'd think Murph would be as out of place in the Phillies' raucous clubhouse as a Twinkies booth at a dieter's convention. Murph was minding his own business at spring training one day when he was surrounded by Mitch Williams, Lenny Dykstra, and John Kruk, who must have looked more like Beelzebub,

Mephistopheles, and Lucifer to Murph. Lucifer—well, Kruk—spoke for the group when he announced, "Murph, you've been good too long. Now all that's gonna change."

No, "all that" didn't change. Murph, whom some teammates called the Anti-Kruk, remained a devout Mormon. As part of their religious obligation, Mormons do missionary work, causing Kruk to deduce, "Yeah, this is Murph's assignment. They sent him to the Phillies."

During the 1992 season, Kruk was told that Canada was considering tightening its restrictions on visitors, banning anyone with a shady past. Kruk thought that could cause problems on the next trip to Montreal and quipped, "I hope Murph can play all nine positions."

Surprisingly, Murph enjoyed his Philadelphia stay. He reached equilibrium with his rowdy coworkers. Not that Murph was exempt from those dicey volleys where four-letter words zoomed around like missiles, not missals.

CHRIS WHEELER, PHILLIES BROADCASTER: "Murph wore number 3 and Lenny Dykstra wore number 4. When we were on the road, they always assigned lockers numerically according to jersey numbers in the visitor's clubhouse, so those two were always right next to each other. Every time I'd walk through the clubhouse, I would here Lenny chirping and cursing. Then I'd hear Lenny say, 'Sorry, Murph,' after which Lenny would start cursing again, and turn and say 'Sorry, Murph' again."

JOHN KRUK: "I didn't treat Murph different. I was always riding him, and he was always a good sport about it. One day I went too far, though. Murph told me if I didn't shut up, he was gonna *bop me*. I didn't know what 'bop me' meant, but since that was the strongest language he ever used, I think it meant he was gonna hurt me. I looked at Murph's size and my size, and I shut up."

Nowhere in the Book of Mormon could we find the term "bop me." Nonetheless, Krukker probably interpreted Murph's phrase as well as Joseph Smith.

Kruk concluded: "I always told Murph he was the only sane one in the clubhouse. Our clubhouse had one Mormon and twenty-four morons."

DALE MURPHY: "That was my favorite line. Krukkie came up with the funniest one-liners. Everybody was fair game in that clubhouse. If you were getting razzed, you knew you belonged. I really can't compare that collection of guys with any other group I ever played with. What a bunch of characters! To win, you don't need a team of guys with the same beliefs. *You need a team of guys with the same belief in winning.* We had that. They were characters, but they took the game seriously and were as competitive as any team I've ever played on."

That spring, Terry Mulholland was prepared to go to arbitration. So was Curt Schilling. However, the Phillies avoided arbitration in each case, and each hurler got a handsome increase.

Schilling had come to Philly as a relief pitcher. Curt was just another enigmatic entry on baseball's long list of talented, powerful arms headed for mediocrity. However, in 1992, Curt led the major leagues in lowest opponents' batting average (.201). He finished second in the NL in complete games, tied for third in shutouts, and was fourth in ERA. Schilling's compensation rocketed upward 388% in one year, from $205,000 to $1,000,000.

Terry Mulholland was seeking three million dollars. No Phillie had ever asked for two million dollars in arbitration, let alone three million. At the start of negotiations, Terry and management were more than $500,000 apart. Mulholland, while unspectacular, had quietly put up some impressive numbers. He tallied 29 wins over the previous two seasons. Only one other NL left-hander, 1991 Cy Young winner Tom Glavine, had more. Mulholland's two-year win total matched Atlanta's John Smoltz, the 1992 NLCS MVP, who was considered one of the finest talents in the game. When the smoke cleared, the two sides came to terms amicably, and Terry received a $1.35 million salary increase.

The club's heftiest contract was awarded in Clearwater. Darren Daulton, who had emerged as a star in 1992, penned an $18.5 million contract, largest in Phillies history. The move and the timing of the signing were strategically perfect, a seminal event in the winning of the pennant.

VIDEO DAN STEPHENSON, PHILLIES VIDEO OPERATIONS: "The Phils made a strong statement about trust, commitment, and loyalty to the organization. Dutch had taken a long, hard road to get where he got. He endured plenty of physical hardship over the years. The fans gave him a tough time, too, as he was coming up. The rest of the team saw his contract as a message from management—that guys who were loyal to the organization would be rewarded. Dutch's teammates were impressed—maybe even moved—that the Phillies were so generous. I'll tell you a funny story about that day—well, actually the next day. I was making a video for the '93 season at the time, and Lenny [Dykstra] and Headley [Dave Hollins] kept putting me off. 'Hey, Video, catch me tomorrow for that interview ...' Turns out, I scheduled interviews for both guys for the day after Dutch signed. So that day, here come Lenny and Headly staggering my way, looking like zombies. They just got back from celebrating Dutch's new contract. They were out all night, drinking champagne in a limousine. I had to push back the video interviews a few more days till they both recovered."

JIM FREGOSI: "We established Dutch's role with that contract. I had many talks with Dutch and the other veterans, and I made Dutch the leader of that clubhouse."

"If You Build It, We Will Come"

When I first got a job with the Phillies, what made most of my friends (NOTE TO MY WIFE: I'm speaking of my friends. This thought never entered my mind) most jealous was that, as they put it, "You get to look at Lynne Austin every night!"

Lynne Austin was the first pinup girl for the Hooters restaurant chain. And as my friends could tell you, she was also a Playboy Playmate. Before Darren Daulton became "Darren Daulton—Phillies All-Star Catcher," he was known in some circles as "Darren Daulton—Lynne Austin's Husband."

A huge billboard of Lynne in her Florida-orange short-shorts and cutoff Hooters shirt slinked across the outfield wall at the Phillies' spring training home, Jack Russell Stadium. At the time Dutch signed his big $18.5 million contract, he and Lynne, unfortunately, were in the midst of a divorce. Now, divorce is generally taboo, not a laughing matter. But with this Phillies squad, not much was off limits. The day after Dutch signed, some wise guy went out and scribbled on the billboard in huge numbers: "$9.25 million" (*you* do the math) above Lynne's smiling face.

DAVE RAYMOND: "That billboard was the first thing you saw when you walked into that stadium. I think Dutch was a little embarrassed that it was out there. But I had a major crush on Lynne at the time, so there was no way the Phanatic was not going to have some fun with that sign. I would cruise onto the field in my ATV, and when I passed by Lynne's billboard, I'd stop suddenly and do a big doubletake. I'd get off the bike and start bowing down in front of her. Then I'd walk up to the billboard, get down on my knees and pretend to look up her little cutoff half shirt. At one point, Darren told me to stop. I don't think I listened. It was just too good to pass up."

PETE INCAVIGLIA: "I remember after Dutch signed that big contract, he told us, 'I feel like buying a huge house with that money. It'll have a big party room with a giant TV, bar, pool table, and a big swimming pool. Then I'd invite all you guys over and you could stay as long as you want.' Krukkie told him, 'Dutch, if you build it, we will come!'"

The disbelievers claimed, when all was said and done, that the Phillies were overpaying Dutch, that he was simply another overvalued commodity like Duncan and Jordan. They predicted that this year's club was the "same old Phillies" repackaged. There were dissenting voices. Montreal's general manager, Dan Duquette, called the Phillies the most dangerous team in the division. "They've got three guys with better pitching credentials than people think. They score a lot of runs. They've got three of the top performers at their positions in Daulton, Hollins, and Dykstra. And that Kruk isn't too bad either."

Street and Smith, one of the premier baseball magazines in the country, was not as impressed with the Phillies, picking them dead last, behind the expansion Marlins. They picked the Mets to win the East. Atlanta, the Blue Jays, and Minnesota were predicted as winners in their respective divisions.

The Phillies players were happy with the treatment and salaries they were getting. As Video Dan pointed out, that satisfaction contributed significantly to their unity, their bedrock strength in 1993.

The personalities in that clubhouse were a rare mix. "It was lightning in a bottle," said Mitch Williams. "Getting all those characters together on one team —it'll never happen again." The locker room became the Phillies' members-only fraternity house, a den of nonstop grab-ass fun. No one was off limits, no one was above or exempt from getting a hotfoot or pie pushed into his face.

The coaches were in on the act, too, never missing a zinger, as Mitch Williams, the Wild Thing, knew all too well. One day, the pitchers were doing a drill on intentional walks. When Mitch's turn came, coach Larry Bowa yelled for all at the Carpenter Complex to hear, "Just be yourself, Mitch."

JIM EISENREICH : "Everyone talked to everyone else in the clubhouse. Everyone felt equal, like they had a place, like they were accepted for who they are and what they are. Lenny Dykstra was a top player, but he wasn't one of those superstar names. On other teams, guys of Bonds's caliber intimidate everyone else. Their teammates are more or less afraid to talk to them in a lot of cases. We didn't have anybody that big and famous.

"It's the most fun I ever had in baseball. There was no tension on that team."

The humor in the '93 clubhouse never had a personal edge. The barbs were good-natured, never crippling. And they were never-ending.

EISEY ARRIVES

Jim Eisenreich is a profile in courage. Eisey, as he was called, suffers from a little understood disease, Tourette Syndrome, which causes the afflicted person to make uncontrollable tics and unintended sounds and noises. Eisenreich went through his entire childhood not knowing why he behaved the way he did—not comprehending why he was different or what caused his erratic and often mortifying behavior.

EISENREICH: "I didn't know what was wrong with me till I was 23. After my rookie season, the Twins sent me to all kinds of specialists. Till then, I thought I was the only kid in the world like that. That's the same thing I hear now from kids when I go into schools to speak to them."

Eisey hit .303 in 99 at-bats in 1982, his rookie season in the majors, despite extended stints on the disabled list between May 6-28 and June 18-September 1 for his neurological disorder. He returned in 1983 but informed his manager, Billy Gardner, that the Tourette disorder had resurfaced. He placed himself on the voluntary retired list the following year, where he remained from June 4, 1984 till September 29, 1986.

He spent those few years back home on the fields of St. Cloud, where he could perform in relative seclusion. In 1987, at the age of 28, Jim felt good enough to return to pro baseball. The Royals, under John Schuerholtz (who was largely responsible for rebuilding the Atlanta Braves' nineties juggernaut), signed Eisenreich to a minor-league contract. He played 44 games for the Royals in 1987. In 1988, he made the team's opening-day roster but spent most of the season in the minors. He returned to the majors for good in 1989, batting .290, .280, and .269 in successive seasons. He joined the Phillies as a free agent in 1993. In 1991, Eisey was the first recipient of the Tony Conigliaro Award, given to the player who overcomes adversity through the attributes of spirit, determination and courage.

Jim was uncomfortable with his situation in Kansas City. Jim Eisenreich is a rare guy. He felt he was overpriced.

EISENREICH: "I made $1.65 million with the Royals, and that was too much for what I was going to do. They never really told me what I was supposed to be doing in Kansas City. I was a guy in the middle. Teams were trying to eliminate that kind of player. It just came down to a feeling that I wasn't wanted."

So Eisey was dealt to the Phillies in 1993. The Phillies' wild and woolly—well, hairy—locker room seemed a daunting place for a guy with Tourette Syndrome.

EISENREICH: "Those guys were great. There's no other place that compares, really. No one danced around my problem, that's for sure. I took a lot of abuse, same as everyone else. But that only made me feel a part of the group. They didn't treat me different or special. What a great year!"

When Eisey first walked into the clubhouse, there was a brief, uncomfortable hush. Jim, a quiet, unassuming type, simply went to his locker and tended to his personal affairs without speaking. Dave Hollins, as he walked by, said for all to hear, "Nice talking with you, Eisey."

JOHN KRUK: "Eisey and me had lockers next to one another in spring training. Those first couple of days, he was really quiet. We didn't know what to make of him. He had this bow and arrow with him and he would sit there and fiddle with them at his locker. Finally I said, 'So what's with that bow and arrow?

Are you thinking about shooting anyone with that thing?' He looks up and starts aiming it at Darren Daulton who was across the room, and he says, 'There's a lot of meat on that one over there.' I knew we had another Phillie."

PETE INCAVIGLIA: "Kruk started calling Eisey 'Dahmer' because he said he always kept to himself and he had those little eyes and this really unusual laugh. It was hilarious. One day in spring training, we were sitting around the clubhouse drinking beers, when LA [Larry Anderson] asked Eisey why he was sitting all alone over by his locker. Krukkie chimes in, 'He's just waiting for one of us to pass out so that he can eat him.' I think it made Eisey feel welcome, in a kind of sick way, kind of typical for our crew. I roomed with Eisey that spring, and on a bus trip back from Vero Beach, we were all drinking and having a good time. Eisey was sitting up towards the front of the bus, so I yelled, 'Hey Eisey, thanks for not eating me last night.' And Eisey comes back, 'No problem ... lunch!'"

From then on, Eisey was "Dahmer," a nickname that made him chuckle rather than bristle. By midseason, Jim's wife, Leann, approached Kruk, the leader of the eponymous Merry Kruksters, and said, "I hate you, John Kruk, because this is the happiest Jim has ever been in his career. Now he keeps me up till three in the morning listening to all the crazy things you guys do."

Kruk answered, "That's 'cause he has less problems than the rest of us."

From the start of spring training, the veterans on the club—both those who were in place and the new arrivals, like Andersen and Thompson—set the tempo. The clubhouse was filled with guys who had never played a postseason game—guys whose athletic clocks were ticking. In 1993, Kansas City's Hubie Brooks, with 1,597 games under his belt, topped the list of active players who played the most major-league games without ever playing a postseason game. Don Mattingly (yes, the *Yankees'* Don Mattingly—this is not a misprint) was second, with 1,528 games. However, three Phils—Milt Thompson, John Kruk, and Pete Incaviglia—littered the next dozen. Even skipper Fregosi could relate. Fregosi played 1,602 games with nary a postseason appearance.

JIM FREGOSI: "I'll always say that the greatest thrill I ever had in baseball was watching those veterans win that pennant. All those guys who played all those years and never won before. To see the looks on their faces when they finally won was everything to me."

By the time St. Patrick's Day rolled around, the Phils were playing great, but after all, it was only spring training. Disbelievers were not about to relent based on Florida performances. Only a few Philly sportswriters saw the fire in this team's belly.

BILL CONLIN: "Even in spring training, that team just kept coming at you. I was sitting with Eddie Liberatore, the Dodgers' superscout at the time (he later went to the Orioles) at Jack Russell. He leaned over and said to me, 'I think this team's gonna be really dangerous. Every time you look up, they've got the bases loaded.'"

Daily News columnist Paul Hagan was another spring training convert when he wrote, "More and more baseball men tell me that everybody in the league fears the Phillies and their slashing Men at Work offense. No matter who Fregosi starts, his nine-inning mix seems to produce about fourteen hits."

CURT SCHILLING: "That was the most unpredictable, crazy group I've ever been associated with. When you take twenty-five guys and 80 percent of them, including me, are immature, something's gotta happen. And it did. Our guys, more than any group I ever saw, knew how to get serious between the lines. The fun in the locker room switched to intensity once the game started. It started in Clearwater. How often do you see brawls in spring training? How often do you see benches empty in Florida? Well, we emptied the benches about three times that spring. I've never seen that before. The '93 Phillies weren't willing to lose. Ever. Not even in spring training."

On March 21, the Phillies had a bench-clearing donnybrook with the Cardinals in St. Petersburg. Donovan Osbourne threw at Ricky Jordan, who charged the mound.

PETE INCAVIGLIA: "That little brawl with the Cards was a big character builder. Ricky Jordan charged the mound! Ricky, of all people! When I saw Ricky running out to Osborne, I had to get out there with him. Imagine, all us crazies on that team, and Ricky Jordan is the guy who ends up lighting the fire that set us off! Ricky was the nicest guy on the team. If you had a kid, you'd want him to be like Ricky Jordan, not like any of the rest of us! That really did something to unite this team. We stood up for each other, and we didn't ever let anyone intimidate us."

RICKY JORDAN: "That was out of character for me. The next day, I was watching the film and I said, 'Did I really do that?' I'm usually the 'silent Gemini' type, but that whole incident rubbed me the wrong way. That game started an intense rivalry with St. Louis all year. We wanted to beat Torre and the Cards so bad that season. We took *extra* pleasure sweeping them a couple times."

DAVE HOLLINS: "Intimidation was certainly a big factor in our success. We didn't have that All-Star, All-American Boy type image that teams like the Braves had. I always got the impression that some teams thought we weren't good enough for them, like they were above us. So, yeah, I was out to intimidate them. That's how I ran the bases. I thought our club had to play a little harder, show a little more determination and guts and desire. We had to prove to other teams that we were for real."

HEADLEY'S CHOICE

"**D**ave Hollins is the only guy I've ever seen who is actually capable of killing somebody on a baseball field," Curt Schilling chuckles. "I've never seen anyone as intense as Headley," as Dave is known to his teammates. "Mikey" was another of his nicknames.

MILT THOMPSON: "Dave was so focused he was scary. We were at the batting cage in Clearwater, just practicing. Dave was getting frustrated, not hitting anything solid. I said, 'Dave. Chill out. It's only BP.' Dave turned to me and said, 'This isn't Dave. It's Mikey.'"

Mikey was Dave's evil twin. When Mikey showed up, everybody gave him ten feet all around. Before a game, Hollins/Headley/Mikey sat motionless, speechless, trancelike, preparing for battle. Baseball was, literally, a battle to Headley. The opposition was the enemy. Headley would do anything, endure any pain, to defeat the opposition. That's why he set a Phillies franchise record in 1992 when he was hit by pitches 19 times.

JIM FREGOSI: "Head has this habit of crowding the plate, and he wouldn't back off when they pitched him inside. He wouldn't concede anything to the pitcher. And he would never give the pitcher the satisfaction of seeing him rub where he was hit."

Dave Hollins was not the most gifted athlete. What he lacked in ability, he made up in desire and effort. As Fregosi pointed out, "He's probably the best I've ever seen going from first to third on a single. Our whole team excelled at that, but none as much as Head." Indeed, Headley's 77 percent success rate at going from first to third, or second to home, on a single was the best in the NL and second best in the majors—flashy though incongruous figures for a guy with only *three* stolen bases.

DAVE HOLLINS: "I played football in high school. I was a quarterback and a linebacker. That's how I ran the bases, like a linebacker."

CURT SCHILLING: "Head did something really unusual but effective the year before we won the pennant. He was suspended four days for charging the mound after Bob Scanlan hit him. When he came off the suspension, he gathered the pitchers together and said, 'I'm never going to rush the mound again if a pitcher throws at me. I hurt the team when I got suspended. What I am gonna do, though, is if a pitcher throws at one of our guys, and you guys don't retaliate, then I'm gonna charge *you* when we get in the clubhouse!' We knew he meant it, so I made my choice right then and there. Besides, as Headley told me, 'With me at third, no one's ever gonna get to you at the mound before I get to them.'"

In spring training on March 21, 1993, after Hollins had issued his "Headley's Choice" manifesto to the staff, Donovan Osbourne plunked Hollins in the first inning. Tommy Greene was on the mound in the third when Osbourne stepped to the plate.

JOHN VUKOVICH: "I knew what Headley told the pitchers about retaliating. Now, of all people, Tommy Greene's out on the mound. Tommy's biggest problem was always being too nice a guy. I look out at the mound, and Tommy's just sweatin' bullets looking in at Dutch. I turn to Fregosi and say: 'Watch this.' Skip says, 'Why? Osbourne wasn't trying to hit Headley.' I say, 'Doesn't matter. Watch.' Well, Tommy nails Osbourne right in the neck, and then a few innings later, all hell breaks loose when Ricky charges the mound. That was when I knew something special was going on with this team. When I saw Tommy retaliate, I knew Tommy had it figured out, and if Tommy did, so did everybody else. I'll tell you, nobody came after us that year."

The Phillies fashioned an impressive 16-10 record, even though spring training ended on a sour note. The Phillies were no-hit by Boston on April 2 in their final dress rehearsal for the season. Disbelievers anticipated that the Boston game burst the bubble. And though the Phils came north with a load of promise, they started the season with more unanswered questions than one of Leno's Jay Walkers on *Jeopardy*. Nobody was certain how Incaviglia and Milt Thompson fit in. Starting pitching was a huge question mark. Only Mulholland was seasoned. Ben Rivera was untested and unproven. Tommy Greene had pitched a no-hitter in 1991, when he ended up 13-7, 3.38. However, Tommy missed 98 games in 1992 with tendonitis and made only six starts all season. No one knew if Curt Schilling could repeat his 1992 performance. Juan Bell, the starting shortstop, remained an enigma. Spotty and unpredictable, Bell lacked spark and seemed a square peg in a roster of round holes (Mitch and the Krukker should have fun with that reference).

Closer Mitch Williams's poor spring showing was disconcerting. Mitch closed spring training with a 10.03 ERA, giving up 22 hits and 8 walks in 11 2/3 innings. In 1992, the Phillies' bullpen ranked an abominable 24th out of 26 teams. They tied for second in blown saves and fourth in most relief losses with 28. The '93 pen had a new look now that Larry Andersen and David West were on board. But both were question marks. Andersen was forty years old; enough said. West possessed a great arm but had never converted that potential into bona fide success. West had already floundered in professional baseball for ten years, mostly in the minors. His big-league stats were not comforting: 16-20, with a 5.45 ERA. Furthermore, he was coming off a 1-3, 6.99 year at Minnesota.

Nonetheless, the Phillies brimmed with confidence when they left Florida. Their patchwork squad of middle-level professionals had adapted to their roles harmoniously and productively. Kruk called his mates throwbacks—thrown back by other organizations. They were already being called throwbacks to the old St. Louis Gas House Gang, whose manager Frankie Frisch once said, "We could end up in first—or in an asylum." Fregosi could relate to Frisch, in more than an alliterative sense.

The opening-game opponent, the Houston Astros, could not have been better selected. The match pitted two different strategies—like a boxer against a puncher. The Astros *did* spend big bucks in the off season on high-profile talent. They lured two of the sport's top free agent pitchers, Greg Swindell and Doug Drabek. The Astros were kicking off their season of hope against a team that finished last the year before. Houston had the Phillies locked up in their home corral for three games. With the eyes of Texas upon them, Houston's high-priced guys were optimistic about bringing a pennant to the Lone Star State. Disbelievers expected a Phillies collapse. But these Phillies, as Bill Conlin had seen, were hungry. They were anxious to steamroll anyone in their way.

PETE INCAVIGLIA: "Normally spring training doesn't mean a thing. But we played hard every day that spring, and that became *us*. That's who we were. When we walked out on that field every day, we had only one thing in mind. We were gonna kick your butt."

Houston, *you* have a problem.

Convincing

"We had a good offense in 1992, but we were always playing catch-up, and that was demoralizing. In '93, Mulholland, Schil, Mitch—they all went out and did their jobs. It was different all of a sudden. The whole squad was playing like they believed they were going to win."
— John Vukovich, '93 coach

Only once in a blue moon do Philadelphia teams start like a blue streak. But slow starts don't give Quaker City-ites the blues. We're used to them. They're our heritage. It took years to get our Blue Laws abolished. It took longer, or so it seemed, to get our Blue Route built.

For you non-Philadelphians (you're the ones who *do not* end both syllables of the word "wa-ter" with "r" but who *do* hold your noses when drinking Philly *warter*), here's a little Philadelphia lore. Color it blue.

Way back in 1794, Blue Laws were ordained to ban the sale of practically everything on Sundays. The Laws didn't originate in Philly or Pennsylvania, but in the Dominion of New Haven in 1656. The Blue Laws were Governor Theophilius Eaton's baby. You might not recognize the name, but he sounds like somebody who would dream up such an idea.

The Blue Laws prohibited "any worldly employment or business whatsoever on the Lord's Day, commonly called Sunday." The Blue Laws were so named because blue was the color of Eaton's printed edicts, or so it is commonly believed. The Blue Law restrictions really stunted the development of Philly sports in the early part of the twentieth century. Professional football didn't kick off till the thirties, when state government finally started to back off on the Blue Laws. Football, baseball, polo, and fishing—all of which are outdoor events—were finally made legal between 2 p.m. and 7 p.m. on Sundays. In 1935, Sunday motion pictures and orchestral exhibitions were permitted. It wasn't until 1957 that Philly allowed Sunday theatre performances, basketball, and hockey—all indoor events. Perhaps allowing outdoor sports had driven Satan indoors, or maybe it was just our Pennsylvania weather.

As for the Blue Route, it was the corridor that was *finally* chosen out of several options proposed to alleviate traffic on the Schuylkill Expressway (the *Sure-Kill*, as Philadelphians call it, is where, especially during rush hour, even rational Philadelphians curse a blue streak). I emphasize *finally* because the plan was first proposed in 1929. The Blue Route took about six decades to get from conception to completion (about the length of time a trip from the suburbs to the Vet takes when someone like Madonna is appearing at the First Union Center during a Phillies or Eagles game).

Why is it called the Blue Route? Philly lore has it that several different routes were sketched on a blueprint. Each route had a different color. The path chosen (which disproved the Robert Frost maxim by immediately becoming the path *most* traveled which has made all the difference in traffic) was the route sketched in blue—the blue route on the blueprint. Blue on blue.

Heartache on heartache. That's been the history of Phillies opening-day blues in recent years. No, neither Philly nor its Phillies start very fast. The Phillies' opening-day record for the two decades prior to 1993 was a putrid 3-17. Entering 1993, the Phillies hadn't won an opener since 1984. Terry Mulholland would again be on the hill. He had lost the previous two openers. Doug Drabek, now wearing an Astros uniform in '93, would oppose him. Drabek was 9-1 in his preceding eleven starts as a Pirate against the Phillies.

But 1993 was different. Mulholland gave up a first-inning unearned run on an error by Juan Bell, then 4-hit the Astros the rest of the way for a 3-1 victory. After the game, Mitch Williams underscored the team's new attitude. "It's always good to get off to a good start. The difference is that last year we *hoped* we would. The year before we *hoped* we would. This year, we *expect* to."

The following night, another big fish in the '93 free agent pool, Greg Swindell, took the mound against Curt Schilling. The Phillies, however, jumped out to a 4-0 lead, the big blast being Pete Incaviglia's first Phillie homer. Schilling needed no more help, winning 5-3 as Mitch Williams came on in the ninth for his first save.

For the first time since 1980, the Phillies were starting a season 2-0. In the getaway game, Pete Harnisch was no-hitting them over six innings. Darren Daulton homered in the seventh to thwart the no-hit bid. With the Astros ahead 3-1, their manager, Art Howe, opted to lift Harnisch for a pinch hitter, who hit into a double play. With the Phillies still down 3-1 in the ninth, Mickey Morandini clubbed the sixth home run of his 3-year career, a 2-run blast that tied the game and sent it into extra innings. Milt Thompson's tenth-inning, 3-run double won the contest, as Mitch earned his second save.

The Phils' 3-0 start was their best since 1970, though the comparison was not necessarily propitious. The '70 Phils ended up 73-88, in fifth place. But that was then, this was now. This sweep was a watershed event.

MITCH WILLIAMS: "I'll tell you what. I knew that we were going all the way when I saw Mickey hit that two-run home run off of Doug Jones to tie it in the eighth. I could tell right then and there that this was going to be our year."

More than their performance, the press was taking notice of the Phillies' quirky ways. Led by Lenny Dykstra, the '93 Boys were media-ready throwbacks to a less enlightened, though more enlivened, yesteryear. They were as superstitious as those old-timey teams. After the opening-day win, skipper Fregosi buckled up the same pants for three straight days. Coach Larry Bowa ordered the same Mexican breakfast three days in a row (although Larry could chug a number-10 can of jalapeños and be no more fidgety than normal). Meanwhile, Kruk and Daulton (Jake and Bubba, respectively) ate lunch three days in a row at Zucchini's in Houston.

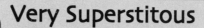

Very Superstitous

Baseball players are superstitious. But the 1993 Phillies took superstition to unheard of levels, even for ballplayers.

Being superstitious started at the top. The manager always wore his red satin Phillies jacket in the dugout, even when temperatures teetered around 100 degrees. Schil always circumnavigated the coach's box and gingerly avoided the foul line when he took the field. Inky shaved his moustache at one point in the season when hits were a little tough to come by. He said he wanted to look younger. Right, Inky. No one fretted about appearance more than the Inkman. *Not.*

John Kruk had his rituals, too. He never cleaned his batting helmet, and he'd wear the same socks and the same T-shirt under his uniform if he was in a good groove at the plate. Krukker put some long hit streaks together, too, so that's impressive. By the end of those streaks, he must have felt like he was swinging inside a suit of armor.

Announcer Harry Kalas always carried a golf tee in his pocket on the days that Tommy Greene pitched. Harry used to call Tommy "Tee the Greene," so I guess it made sense. When Greenie hit a dry spell in '93 around All-Star time, Harry tossed the tee out. Soon afterwards, Harry found a blue tee and decided that, since Tommy was from North Carolina and the University of North Carolina wore blue, Harry would carry that color for Tommy's games. Tommy proceeded to win the first but dropped the next two. Just before Harry was going to throw the tee out, Greenie stopped him.

"Don't throw it away yet, Harry," he pleaded. "Give it one more chance."

On July 21, Tee the Greene pitched a six-hit shutout against the Dodgers in L.A. Tommy thought the lucky tee had done the trick, even though he pulled a groin muscle and had to be taken out in the eighth inning. Those '93 guys only cared about winning. As for the tee...

"Outta here," Harry the K said emphatically.

Everybody rode the superstition bandwagon that year. Team president Bill Giles and other Phillies brass, watching the games from the Executive Box on the 400 level, would flip their neckties over their shoulders in the late innings to help start a rally. When I was working in the Phanavision control room that year, trying to decide on what animations and music would get the crowd fired up, I always picked the Rally Train: a locomotive with the Phanatic behind the wheel and smoke bellowing from the engine spelling

"Rally Time." The Rally Train lit up the big outfield scoreboard. I'd run over to the cart machine and pop in a locomotive and train whistle sound effect. And every time we pulled out one of those miracle come-from-behind 1993 finishes, the entire Phillies organization swore the Rally Train did it.

But the most superstitious person of all was Lenny Dykstra, the Dude.

FRANK COPPENBARGER, EQUIPMENT MANAGER: "The Dude was one of a kind, the most superstitious ballplayer I ever saw. He went through over 600 batting gloves that year. The clubhouse attendants were in charge of putting each player's initials on his equipment. Lenny wouldn't let *anyone* but me touch his equipment. He liked the way I printed his initials. If one of the other clubbies tried marking his stuff, the Dude would go ballistic. He had four different colors of batting gloves. He'd walk into the clubhouse, and if he had three hits with the red and white gloves the night before, he'd look at me and say, 'Red and white today, Dude.' If he made an out, he'd rip his gloves off, throw them in the trash, and spit tobacco juice all over them."

Coach John Vukovich is not a trash talker. But he's not above trash picking.

JOHN VUKOVICH, '93 COACH: "The Dude would throw out six pairs of gloves a game. I'd follow him around and pick them out of the trash can, at least the ones that didn't have the tobacco on them. My son supplied his whole Little League team with batting gloves that year, just from Lenny's throwaways."

Lenny once threw out an entire shipment of bats because the label was not in a straight line with where his name was signed on the barrel. The Dude swore the misalignment threw off his balance when he'd stare down the barrel of the bat. He threw out another box of bats because his name was printed, rather than autographed.

FRANK COPPENBARGER, EQUIPMENT MANAGER: "Lenny was so superstitious that he thought the tobacco he chewed made a difference. If he made an out, he'd spit out what was in his mouth, grab another handful and shove it in. The average player goes through a pack of chew every two or three games. The Dude went through two or three a *game*. His locker was very neat. That probably surprises you, but it's true. Everything was laid out just right. He had more undershirts than you've ever seen. The sleeves of his shirts all had to be cut at a certain length or he'd throw them out. I would lay out his shirts on the ground and mark his sleeves at the exact same spot. If I was so much as a quarter of an inch off, I'd hear about it. Lenny was never shy. Basically, he could have used two equipment managers all by himself."

PHIL SHERIDAN, CLUBHOUSE ATTENDANT: "Just watching him go through all those rituals was amazing. If the Dude made an out, he'd walk back to the clubhouse and strip his whole uniform off. Then he'd put another one on before taking the field again. He'd sit in the dugout during the game and say, 'Hey, Phil, last night when I got that hit, did you get me a soda? Yeah—you did? Then go back there and get me another soda.' And if he got a hit in a particular inning, I'd make sure that I was standing in the same spot the next night, ready to get him a soda. If I wasn't standing there, he'd run around the clubhouse looking all over for me."

Larry Andersen had his share of superstitions, too. Just ask Mitch Williams.

MITCH: "Let's just say that Larry was never one to quit easily on a garment. Larry'll fill you in on the rest."

LARRY ANDERSEN: "That year, I had a cap that I sort of refused to toss out cause it was bringing me good luck. By midseason, that cap could have walked to the mound on its own. Mitch couldn't stand the sight of it—well, okay, maybe it was the smell. So one day, Mitch was parading around the clubhouse in brand new shoes. He had to take them off cause they were a little tight. When he did, I casually leaned over and put my cigarette out on his new shoe, but that was retaliation for him putting a cigarette out on my shoe in the bullpen in Los Angeles earlier in the season.

"Now, I didn't think he noticed it at the time, but a few weeks later, I went back into the bathroom around the fourth inning. All of a sudden, here comes this flame under the stall. I look down and there's my hat on fire. I start jumping up and down, afraid I'm gonna make a mess in there, so I finally just kicked it out of the stall. The only good thing about being on the receiving end of something like that is that it presents an opportunity to come up with something even stupider, like cutting Mitch's tie or pants in half, or gluing his zipper down. Paybacks are a bitch."

Larry lives by his own eloquent motto: "You're only young once. But you can be immature forever."

That three-game sweep was the beginning of a journey that took the Phillies to some deeper zone of self-belief where they would reside all season. Losses, or failures of any kind, did not shake this crew of gypsies, tramps, and thieves. Their success coming out of the gate was nitro, but the rest of the world still needed convincing.

When they squared off against Houston, the Phils were like an unproved boxer who unleashes that first volley against a big-name champ and staggers him. The Phillies saw they had punch against a quality opponent. The Houston series was a moment of truth, a collective awareness. They had drawn first blood.

Like Dutch [Arnold Schwarzenegger] in *Predator,* who saw the extraterrestrial's blood on the ground and said, "If it bleeds, we can kill it," the Phillies saw an opponent's blood and became predators. As Joe Torre said, "These guys beat you up. They leave you for dead." Their unkempt hair and shoddy appearance became almost tribal, a primal way to pump up for the kill.

PAUL HAGAN: "I think they won that '93 pennant because of those first three games. They tasted success. They thought they were good, but that series made them believe in themselves. From then on, they had attitude. So many guys on that team had never won a championship before and yet *were* winners—good baseball players and gamers. Talent-laden teams, and teams that have won before, like the Yankees, can recover from a bad start. The Phillies didn't have that kind of talent or history. They needed to break out fast, and they needed the affirmation it brought."

JOHN VUKOVICH: "I knew we were going to win the pennant after the Houston series—just knew it. Pitching made me feel that way. We had a good offense in 1992, but we were always playing catch-up, and that was demoralizing. In '93, Mulholland, Schil, Mitch—they all went out and did their jobs. It was different all of a sudden. The whole squad was playing like they believed they were going to win."

The Phillies were headed to Philadelphia for the home opener. For once, at the start of the season, the sky wasn't falling, although that's not exactly true. As paratroopers say, only two things fall from the sky: bird droppings and fools. In Philly, one huge bird would soon be dropping: Philly's biggest Phool.

6

Phor Openers

"Ladies and Gentlemen, to open the 1972 season for the Fightin' Philadelphia Phillies, I present ... Kiteman!"

"BOOOOOOOOOO!"

After a pregnant pause, and no sign of life from Kiteman, Phillies PA announcer Dan Baker tries again.

"Ladies and gentlemen ... Here he is ... *Kiteman*!"

Frozen at the top of Veterans Stadium, peering down a 100-foot-long plywood ramp, Richard Johnson, aka Kiteman, is stiffer than a Jim Fregosi martini after a Mitch Williams high-wire-act save.

"BOOOOOOOOOO!"

Bill Giles, Phillies 38-year-old executive vice president and marketing whiz, lunges for his walkie talkie.

"Yo Paul! (Note to non-Philadelphians: Rocky is correct. Philadelphians *do* say Yo, but we're still wondering where Stallone came up with the "Paul-*ie*.") What's going on up there? Can't you hear the introduction? You're on! What the hell is the problem?" Giles growls.

"The guy is shaking," Phillies sales rep Paul Callahan timidly says, the words that strike fear into a GM on opening day or a vasectomy patient on operating day.

"Well, give him a little push!" says Giles, the definitive showman.

Giles's words are like spinach to Popeye. Richard Johnson suddenly transforms himself into Kiteman. Stepping into a pair of water skis and strapping a huge red hang glider to his back, Kiteman starts inching his way down the makeshift runway.

He picks up speed quickly as he wobbles by row after row of seats. Kiteman's knees begin to tremble. Halfway down, with the glider swaying back and forth, teetering on disaster, Kiteman's left foot slides out from under him. With the grace of, let's say, John Kruk, Lenny Dykstra, and Pete Incaviglia dancing *Swan Lake* in tutus (admittedly, a disturbing visual), Kiteman slips off the ramp and into the upper-level seats. He's reduced to a mangled mess of arms, legs and hang glider rubble. He lies there, waiting for a sympathetic reaction from the crowd in this hospitable metropolis renowned worldwide as the City of Brotherly Love.

"BOOOOOOOOOOO!"

Kiteman scurries to extricate himself from his tangle of kite, glider, seats, fans, and perhaps a stray hot dog vendor or two. Humiliated, he searches his pocket for the ceremonial first ball of the 1972 Phillies season. His mission is to deliver that ball to then mayor Frank Rizzo to kick off the Vet's second season. He is not going to be denied. Nor is dignity a deterrent. Bruised and battered, Kiteman limply hurls the ball onto the turf, just clearing the outfield fence as thousands of Philadelphians boo their disapproval.

"He never even practiced," Bill Giles complains later. "He had the opportunity for a test run the day before in an empty stadium. But he said, 'If I'm going to kill myself, I want more people to witness it.'"

Thus ended another unglamorous, though peculiarly entertaining, beginning to a mediocre season.

I'm telling you the story of Phillie openers out of order, so forgive me. Remember my normal *job* is to be out of order. Besides, all those years of watching Mitch Williams has taken its toll. Mitch forced us all to do things out of order. Here's what I mean. The typical sequence in Philly when a pitcher comes into a game goes like this: ball one (boo), ball two (boo), ball three (boo), ball four (*now worry*). But with Mitch, that sequence flip-flopped. Our worrying started as soon as Mitch stood up in the bullpen. That's way out of order.

So to set the table about opening-day games in the Quaker City, let me tell you a little about my boss, Bill Giles. Bill has a mania for opening-day games. Staging a boffo first-ball delivery is Bill Giles's passion, a trademark that defines him more than any trade he ever approved or any baseball decision he made later as the president of the Phillies. In fact, he brought Lee Thomas in as GM of the Phillies organization for just that reason. Bill Giles wanted to focus more on the promotions and the business aspects of his baseball franchise.

"I grew up in Cincinnati. My dad was general manager of the Reds when I was a kid. Out there, they treat opening day like a national holiday. When I came to Philadelphia in 1970, I was surprised how little fanfare there was for the opener."

Bill Giles vowed to change that.

In 1971, Philly's new sports palace, Veterans Stadium, opened in South Philadelphia. The new home of the Phillies and the Eagles featured the totally modern plastic grass called "Astroturf," dancing water fountains in the outfield, and hostesses dressed in short-shorts called hot-pants girls. There were exploding scoreboards, and oversized Colonial mascots named Phil and Phyllis paraded around in the stands.

For the Vet's first opening day in 1971, Bill arranged for the first ball to be dropped from a helicopter. Backup catcher "Irish" Mike Ryan was on the receiving end. "The highlight of my career," Irish declares these days, looking back at that blustery April day in 1972. "We only practiced once the day before, and it was windy, so I was a little nervous. When I first saw the helicopter, it was over by third base. I was standing at second. I started waving for the chopper to come closer to where I was standing. When the ball came down, it blew all over the place, hit my glove and popped out. Luckily I lunged with my other hand and caught it. All I worried about was getting booed if I dropped it!"

Irish and I recreated that ball drop to start the 1995 season, the 25th anniversary of the Vet. I had the honor of hanging out of the helicopter with my green fur flapping in the wind. You learn to stick your tongue out in the face of danger in my line of work. Actually, you learn to stick your tongue out at everything. When you're mauled daily by Cub Scout packs armed with ice cream cones, a 200-foot tumble down to Astroturf is, literally, a day at the park. Anyway, I leaned out and dropped the ball to Mike. Once again, Irish came up with the catch.

"I'm probably the only guy who is three for three catching balls thrown from a helicopter," Mike crows in retrospect (Mike also made a catch from a helicopter in 1981, the Vet's tenth anniversary. I told Mike I'd bring Guiness over for him to check it out. Mike lost interest when he found out I meant the *Guiness Book of World Records*, not the stout.

Since 1971, Bill Giles has had the first ball delivered every way imaginable. Acts like Rocketman and Cannonman did their thing. Parachutists sailed around the stadium. In 1976, in honor of the Bicentennial, Bill created a new route for Paul Revere. A trick rider dressed like a Minuteman rode from New England to the Vet to deliver the first ball. In 1998, I took matters into my own hands. For whatever reason, our promotions team decided that the Phanatic should deliver the first ball by zipping down a cable wire from the top of the stadium to the top of the Phillies dugout.

Why? Why not? We called it the Phanatic's "Slide for Life." Unlike Kiteman, I *did* practice the day before the opener. Even though it looked like I was hanging from just one small strap around my wrist, I did have a hidden safety harness attached underneath my costume. Listen, I'm a mascot. I'm supposed to be dumb, but I'm not stupid. When the moment of truth came, I grabbed hold of the strap and jumped. The folks who set the wire up had given me two rules: lift your feet up when you jump and hold on. I got half of it right. I held on for dear life (wouldn't you?) but I didn't get my feet up in time. My big Phanatic shoe hit the seat in front of me just as

I took off, and I spun like a top the whole way down. No, folks, spinning was *not* part of the act. And remember, I am a paid professional. Please do not try this at home.

But now, let's return to Kiteman.

The year is 1973. Bill Giles threw caution to the wind and gave Kiteman a shot at redemption. This time Kiteman made it to the end of the ramp, but instead of gracefully gliding into home plate, he fluttered and sputtered and crashed ingloriously in left field. Then Phillies catcher Bob Boone, who had been waiting patiently at the plate, had to run to the outfield to retrieve the ball. More boos.

Philadelphia had not seen the last of Kiteman. As the saying goes, the third time's the charm. Kiteman, like the Phillies, finally got it right in 1980 when he was the opening day act. He ditched the startup ramp. Instead, a 6' x 16' wooden platform was erected about 75 feet above field level between the 500-level and 600-level seating. This time, TJ Beatty was Kiteman. What became of the original Kiteman, Richard Johnson, I'll never know. But as TJ Beatty/Kiteman walked past the Phillies' locker room, Pete Rose called out, "I'm betting on you today, pal."

I'm not making that up.

When Kiteman III climbed to the top of that platform, he was a sight to behold—a full-grown man wearing an Evil Knevil jumpsuit with a TV camera strapped to his head and his trusty hang glider resting on his shoulders and strapped around his waist. But this was the new, improved Kiteman. Kiteman-1980 had made some other significant alterations. His glider was festooned with blinking lights, and there were flares attached to each wing. If he was going to crash, he was going to go out in a blaze of glory, literally.

"Ladies and gentlemen, do you remember Kiteman I?" Dan Baker's voice boomed.

"BOOOOOOOOOOOOOOO!"

"Do you remember Kiteman II?"

"BOOOOOOOOOOOOOOO!"

"Ladies and gentlemen, please welcome Kiteman III!"

"BOOOOOOOOOOOOOOO!"

With the wind nearly still inside the Vet ("Perfect conditions," TJ was to say later over a beer—drinking it, not gliding over it, don't be so literal), and the crowd hushed, Kiteman jumped.

In horror, Bill Giles and the fans watched Kiteman nosedive towards the center-field Astroturf. An instant later, he swooped upwards, veered left, veered right, trying vainly to gain control of his aircraft. On cue, he hit the switch to set off red smoke on either end of the glider. He coasted over the pitcher's mound and landed safely in front of home plate. But at that moment, which should have been his finest hour, one of his wings caught fire from the flare. The Phanatic had been enjoying the spectacle from the sidelines (they also serve who stay at home and wait). Seeing the fire, the Phanatic and a cadre of ground crew members rushed onto the field and lifted the burning side of the wing so it wouldn't torch the turf. The fire was extinguished while Kiteman unhooked his harness and handed the ball to mayor Bill Green, who tossed the ceremonial first pitch.

The Phillies Kiteman trilogy didn't rival *Star Wars* or *Indiana Jones* for special effects, but it did prove one thing. Opening-day stunts always need a Plan B. Most stunts rely on good weather conditions, no wind, and the like, and April weather in Philly is as erratic as a Dave Hollins throw to first.

In 1994, we planned for the Navy Leap Frog team to parachute into the stadium with the first ball. The weather forecasts predicted high winds, so we sent my Phanatic backup, Matt Mehler, to the 700-level seats—the nosebleed section. Matt hid out in the Phanatic costume underneath the Phanavision panel. If the jump did not come off for any reason, Matt was set to appear on a lift rising above the sign over the Phanavision screen with a surrogate first ball.

Plan A went off without a hitch that year. The Leap Frogs landed safely. The Phanatic rushed onto the field, high-fived all around, and ushered them off the field. Way up in his perch, Matt took the Phanatic suit off and crawled out of his hiding place. Next day, someone called the Morning Guys on WIP radio and swore that he saw a second Phillie Phanatic stumbling around the 700-level during the pregame show.

"How many beers did you drink up there?" bellowed Angelo Cataldi. "You must have been seeing double."

Two years later, the Leap Frogs were set to reprise their first-ball routine. Once again, the wind was whipping around, and we had Matt hiding out with the drunks. I was stationed in the tunnel behind home plate. Two minutes before the scheduled jump, the chopper radioed that they were aborting the jump because of the wind. Matt got the call and did his thing. Phanatic Matt stood on a platform as it ascended from the base of a huge Coke sign in front of Phanavision to a spot about midway up the Phanavision board. Phanatic Matt held the ball aloft and then heaved it to a kid from the Phillies' inner-city summer baseball program. The kid caught it and everybody cheered, oblivious to the eight disappointed Navy Leap Frogs flying off above.

In 1991, the Phanatic camped out with the first ball on the Vet Stadium rooftop for three days prior to the opener. I was the backup Phanatic to Dave Raymond at the time.

Why did we camp out? Why the roof? Not because it's there, but because *everything* sounds good at a pitch meeting. We checked our life insurance policies, scaled the heights, and pitched a four-man tent on the catwalk. This was hardly Sir Edmund Hillary stuff (more like Hilary Clinton). We had a small TV set in the tent and a port-a-pottie (which answers the question: does a mascot _____ on the roof?) as well as a cooler full of, uh, sustenance. We had live TV coverage of the "story," and all the local newspapers came up to cover it. Okay, it was a slow news week.

One night, Dave and I were both in the tent when two guys came busting in.

"Yo! Are you guys the Phanatic?" one of them yelled. I was sitting there with my oversized shoes on and the body of the costume at my feet. Dave was dressed in street clothes. Apparently that Clark-Kent-and-Superman-are-the-same-person plot twist was tricky for these guys. Actually, I wish that changing into the Phanatic were as easy as changing into Superman. Let's see—glasses on, I'm Clark. Glasses off, I'm Superman. People in Metropolis were easy to fool. Maybe these two were from Metropolis, not Philly.

"I can't believe we snuck [more Philly talk] in here!" he chuckled. "We live in the neighborhood and we wanted to deliver this cheesesteak to the Phanatic."

Dave and I were impressed ... well, more like hungry and appreciative, actually. These guys were true fans. A bit psychotic, but true fans.

They left, and Dave left with them. I was alone on the roof. I had to wake up early next morning, ready to wave to the traffic helicopters flying overhead to report on the Phanatic. So I settled in for the evening, with the wind howling and the tent flapping. I was watching the movie *Ghost* on TV, and the phone rang.

"Tom, this is Bill Giles. You better come down. They're forecasting hurricane-force winds tonight." I was down and off that roof faster than Eye-gor in *Young Frankenstein*, if you remember the scene. I left tent, costume, and courage on the roof and spent the night safe and sound in my Phanatic dressing room.

Next morning, the rooftop camp was luckily still intact. The winds had subsided and I was back, in costume, at my post on the roof. John DeBella, a popular morning DJ on Philly's WMMR radio station, telephoned. Because the Phanatic doesn't talk, I answered the phone as "the Phanatic's friend." John didn't play along. That's John. He mistook me for Dave.

"Dave, we want to come down there right now and bring you a couple of cheesesteaks. You must be starved. We'll be right there and then maybe we can talk to the man behind the green snout."

PHANATIC PHILE

We couldn't let DeBella know that the #1 Phanatic, Dave Raymond, wasn't on the roof. That would be like finding "Gone Fishing" scribbled on the Dali Lama's palace door. DeBella would have ragged us on the air forever. "Sure, John, come on down," I stammered.

After I hung up, I called Dave, who bolted from his house in Delaware. Dave and the WMMR van arrived at the stadium simultaneously. Our front office gave DeBella the run-around, stalling for time so Dave could scale the catwalk at the top of the stadium and reach the tent before DeBella and crew. Dave just finished stepping into costume as DeBella's crew made it up the catwalk. The interview went off without a hitch, and an early morning breakfast cheesesteak high atop the Vet was, literally, Philly *haute cuisine*. (Haute is French for "high"—get it?)

After all was said and done, the Phanatic christened the Phillies' 1991 season by throwing the first ball from the rooftop to the bullpen coach on the field. The bullpen coach? You guessed it ... Irish Mike Ryan. Philadelphians mistakenly think Tim McCarver was Philadelphia's only designated catcher because Carlton insisted on Tim instead of regular Bob Boone. Irish Mike was Philly's designated opening-day first-ball catcher, finishing his career with no passed balls.

Now, back to Bill Giles. Bill's passion for show biz didn't hibernate for 161 games once opening day was history. Giles used to dream up promotions all season long—like the Great Wallenda extravaganza.

Bill Hall, who has been a local promoter for decades, consults frequently with Bill Giles. Many of Hall's zany acts have wound up as Vet Stadium promotions over the years.

"I was pitching Bill Giles an idea for a circus night at the Vet," Hall says, retracing the Wallenda adventure. "There was a doubleheader scheduled in August—an ideal spot for some sort of big event. I thought Giles might go for a circus idea, so I pitched the Wallenda idea."

The Wallenda idea was for Karl Wallenda, with a forty-foot balancing pole in his hands, to walk a thousand feet across a 5/8" cable wire suspended across Veterans Stadium from foul pole to foul pole—without a net.

"Wallenda contracted to do the stunt for $3000. As the date approached, the Phils started getting a little nervous. Giles started looking for an 'out' clause in Wallenda's contract," Bill Hall recalled. Obviously, this was dangerous business. A nosedive from the high wire wouldn't be the best PR. But Wallenda wouldn't relent, and on August 13, 1972, the 67-year-old German tightrope walker became Vet Stadium's greatest high-wire act till Mitch arrived in '90.

"Wallenda was unfazed when newspapers wrote that Vet Stadium was turning into a deathtrap and that Giles was promoting the 'aura of death' at the ballpark," Hall said.

After he took a nap and downed three beers, Wallenda stood on the outside rim of Veterans Stadium's catwalk, with 30,000 pairs of eyes peering up at him.

"I was up there with him and the wind was whipping up pretty good," said Hall. "Not only did the wire have a big dip in the middle, but the wind was also blowing it from side to side, about four feet from the center. Stadium ushers were on the field holding on to guide wires, trying to keep the main wire from swaying too much.

"Wallenda's daughter, Carla, was up there too. She was a nervous wreck. Her husband had died two weeks before trying to do the same stunt in a minor-league stadium *during a hurricane*. Wallenda slipped under the guide rail, ready to go, when he suddenly pulled up with a leg cramp, with his daughter pleading, 'Oh, Papi, don't go! Please, don't go!'

"Wallenda walked out about 30 feet, sat down on the wire, and motioned the ushers to pull the guide wires tighter. I thought there was no way he'd be able to stand back up again with that heavy pole in his hands, but he was a strong little guy. He got back up, walked out to the middle of the wire and did a headstand over second base ('for the boys in Vietnam,' he said later). The crowd at that point went nuts and gave him a standing ovation."

"That was the best act I ever brought in here," Bill Giles reflects today. "What I remember best about the Great Wallenda was what happened afterwards. He came up to the press club and downed about eight martinis."

Besides the Great Wallenda, Bill Giles brought in pig shows, sea lions, African baboons and dancing poodles (it's starting to become clear why the *Gong Show* originated in Philadelphia). Giles has staged pregame mattress stacking contests, cash scrambles, three-legged races, postgame concerts, and even a toga party. And who could forget Benny the Bomb? Benny's specialty was to climb into a small box filled with enough explosives to blow open a one-ton safe. The crowd counted down from ten till bomb, box and Benny all blew up. Benny would dramatically lift himself up and stagger off the field. Benny made Martin Riggs, Mel Gibson's character in *Lethal Weapon*, look stable.

Once, the circus came to town, and the elephants tromped into the Vet to help promote the big show. "Normally with elephants, you have to worry about the little 'presents' they leave behind on the field," lectures Chris Long, the longtime Phillies pregame entertainment guru. "Not that night. They all stood up on their hind legs in front of the Phillies dugout and, seemingly on cue, relieved themselves into the dugout. And with elephants, that's a lot of relief!"

"One Easter Sunday, I promoted the highest-jumping Easter Bunny in the world," Bill Giles reflected. "We had a balloon tethered to the field. We put a guy in a bunny suit and gave him $1000. We were going to put the bunny in the balloon and fly him out of the stadium. Regardless of where the balloon came down, whoever got to the balloon first would get the money. We figured the guy would make it to New Jersey or Delaware."

He didn't get to first base.

The balloon was untied, went airborne briefly, then plummeted like Pete Incaviglia doing a cannonball off a high diving board. Only this balloon didn't make a big splash—at least not with the fans, who were so startled momentarily they did *not* boo. The total trip covered less distance than a single in tee-ball—about three feet, all told. On-field staffers tried repeatedly and vainly to get the balloon airborne.

The Easter Bunny slipped out of the balloon and out of sight. Then the boos rained down on Giles's Easter Parade. The Easter Bunny gets the same treatment as Santa. Philadelphians are equal-opportunity booers. The hot-air balloon had to be deflated and forklifted off the field.

What was the worst promotion? The unofficial unanimous choice in the Phillies organization seems to be the racing ostriches and camels. "Barnum" Bill Hall was involved in that fiasco too.

BILL HALL: "Those animals were spooked before they even made it onto the field. The problem was, there was only one handler for three ostriches, two adult camels, and two baby camels. First, some local celebrities didn't show up, so a couple of batboys took their places. When the race started, the camels went the wrong way—running and crapping all over the outfield [makes those complaints about Lenny Dystra's tobacco juice seem picayune]. The guy in charge was riding a donkey, trying to corral them all. It was a disaster.

"Then it was time for the sulky race with the ostriches. As soon as the gun went off, one of the sulkies toppled and the celebrity DJ, Rosemary Somers, went face first into the warning track. The ostrich ran out of control all around the outfield and then over to the stands, where it started pecking at people in the first row. Phillie Hall of Famer Richie Ashburn was riding the other sulky, and his ostrich got spooked, seeing what was happening with the other bird. Richie's ostrich was doing figure eights in the outfield, while Richie was screaming, 'How the hell are you supposed to get this thing straight!' It was awful."

Dave Raymond, working as an intern the year before his debut as the Phanatic, was sent down to the field to help.

DAVE RAYMOND: "There was supposed to be a Raquel Welch look-alike contest that night, so I volunteered for that. Yeah, let's see—ostriches ... or chicks who look like Raquel Welch—which one should I volunteer for? Ashburn's out riding an ostrich, I'm looking at Raquel Welch look-alikes, and I'm the moron? I ended up with the ostriches and camels anyway. I had no idea what I was doing. The handler told me not to look the ostriches in the eye or they would kick. So I tried not to look them in the eye. Didn't do any good. Everything went haywire, and I was out there with everyone else trying to round them all up. I remember Bill Hall had a suit with ostrich crap all over it. That night, when it was over, several of us who were involved in the fiasco got called on the carpet in Bill Giles's office. Mr. Giles wanted us to explain what went wrong. *The guy who was supposed to be in charge* starts pointing at me saying it was my fault because I looked the ostriches in the eye!"

Relax, Dave, what if you had been dressed as the Phanatic, and one of the ostriches found you attractive? Now *that* would be embarrassing—playing hard to get to a horny ostrich in front of 50,000 people.

That's just a sampling of some of the crazy promotions Bill Giles has engineered over the years. These days, our promotions team takes care of this aspect of the business. Every week we sit around a conference table dreaming of ways to do something totally new.

Dancing poodles? Done it.

Chrstmas in July? Been there.

Human sacrifice? Might be pushing it.

Dave and I were at the table in 1993 when we decided to merge the familiar guy-in-the-air-delivering-the-first-ball routine with the familiar Phanatic-delivering-the-first-ball routine.

Dave and I looked at each other.

Dave spoke up first. "Tom, did I ever tell you you're not only my backup, you're also my stunt double? Did I make that clear enough when we hired you?"

Fortunately, both Dave and I stayed grounded on this stunt. It was the Navy Seals' show all the way. Navy Chief Petty Officer David Jones suited up as the Phanatic. David Jones, a man trained to fight wily enemies, to risk life and limb in defense of his country, found himself, on April 9, 1993, standing in a CH-46 rotary-wing helicopter, ready to jump. CPO Jones was not dropping into scorching deserts in the Middle East, or torrid jungles in Southeast Asia, or some desolate, uninhabited coast in a land that time forgot. Still, as he prepared to jump, sweat was streaming from his forehead. He can't remember ever perspiring so much.

"That green suit was hot *and* uncomfortable," Jones laughs today. "Having only four fingers was a big problem for jumping. I went to reach for my parachute-release handle but could barely grasp it. Moments after I jumped, a green fur ball the size of a New York City cockroach blew off from that fuzzy mesh lining in front of my face and wedged in my throat. I couldn't see a thing out of that mesh screen. I don't know how you do it! That big green shnoz kept catching the wind as I dropped. It felt like somebody was trying to break my neck. Because my vision was so limited, I couldn't see the emergency handle attached to the parachute. So if something went wrong with handle #1, I didn't have too many other options. "

As CPO Jones got closer to the rim of the stadium, he could hear the roar from the 60,985 people below. The rest of his jump team was already safely on the ground. Now all eyes were on him. Drifting in from the sky over the outfield, he was lifted for a moment by the circling winds inside the Vet before being dumped down trippingly on the ground. One of his size 24-plus bubble-toed shoes caught in the Astroturf, causing him to stumble and land on all fours with a thud. The crowd stood and cheered the comic-book landing—a perfectly executed Phanatic pratfall. The players in both dugouts cheered. They loved it. To this day, Dave and I take credit for that jump. We wrestle alligators for the fun of it, too.

The Phlyin' Phanatic unhooked himself from his parachute and waddled over to Paul Owens, the former general manager of the Phillies and the architect of the great Phillies teams of the late seventies and early eighties. Taking the cherished first ball out of his pouch, the Phanatic handed it over to "the Pope" before being swarmed by the rest of his parachute team and whisked off the field.

Mission accomplished. The '93 season, the Enchanted Season, was off to a Phlyin' start.

Play ball.

FIRST BALLS AT VET STADIUM

1971 - Helicopter drop to Mike Ryan
1972 - Kiteman I
1973 - Kiteman II
1974 - Cannonball Man
1975 - High-wire motorcycle act
1976 - Paul Revere to Rocketman
1977 - Parachute from trapeze
1978 - Parachutist

1979 - Golden Knights Parachute Team
1980 - Kiteman III
1981 - Helicopter drop to Mike Ryan
1982 - Slide for Life
1983 - Parachutist Jim O'Brien
1984 - Cannonball Man
1985 - Starship III
1986 - Wondrous Winns High-wire Act
1987 - Rocketman (crashed in practice)
1988 - Lost Ball Contest
1989 - Rain out
1990 - Kiteman IV
1991 - Phanatic throws ball from the roof to Mike Ryan
1992 - Benny the Bomb
1993 - US Navy Leap Frog Parachute Team featuring the Phillie
       Phanatic
1994 - US Navy Leap Frog Parachute Team
1995 - Helicopter Drop to Mike Ryan (again) and Kiteman V
1996 - Phanatic throws ball from the lift in front of Phanavision
       (Leap Frogs couldn't jump due to wind)
1997 - Magic act with Phanatic appearing out of inflated baseball
1998 - Phanatic Slide for Life
1999 - Rocketman to Kiteman to Handman (man with hand tranplant)
2000 - Mission to Mars—Phanatic is carried in by Navy personnel
2001 - Navy Leap Frogs
2002 - Navy Leap Frogs

Convinced

"Tug McGraw said, 'You gotta believe!' about the '69 Mets. Well, the slogan for our team's gotta be: 'It's hard to believe, but you better believe.'"
— *Larry Andersen*

From Houston, the Phillies headed east to the largest home opener crowd in franchise history, 60,985. The Phillies swung the bats with gusto. Daulton hit two homers, while Kruk and Dykstra added one apiece. Unfortunately, pitcher Ben Rivera was flat, and the Cubs also orbited four out of the park. The home run fest set a Vet Stadium single-game record with eight round-trippers, but the loss backed the Phillies into second place behind the Pirates. April 9 would be the only day all season the Phillies did not occupy or share first place.

The 11-7 slugfest was anything but a sleeper, yet a *sleeper* turned out to be the biggest story of opening day. The game was scheduled to start at 3:05 p.m. The team was supposed to report to the clubhouse at 11:05 a.m. Wes Chamberlain sauntered in a few minutes before 2 o'clock. Wes said he had overslept, explaining that he had recently moved into an apartment on Columbia Avenue and had no phone.

WES CHAMBERLAIN: "I thought the game didn't start until later. All I know is that I was driving up to the stadium, and I started seeing all these cars in the lot, and I thought, 'Oh no! It's Murphy's Law. Whatever can go wrong, will.' I taped that saying up in my locker after opening day and kept it there all season."

PAUL HAGAN, *PHILADELPHIA DAILY NEWS*: "When Wes overslept, the episode turned into another character builder for the whole team. There was no talking behind backs on that team. That's unusual. The rest of the team was unhappy with Wes, and they let him know it in no uncertain terms, face to face —led by Daulton. That set the tone for the clubhouse the rest of the year. Those guys handled problems openly and frankly. They settled issues themselves, without involving management. Wes handled it well, too. He stood up and told everyone he was wrong. He apologized. The main thing is that the team got behind Daulton and addressed the incident. They didn't leave it fester. They never let anything fester. Wes and everyone else moved on. They were the most up-front group I ever saw."

The Phils put the incident to bed, with Kruk saying, "It's closed. It's over. It's done with. No pun intended, but I'm not going to lose any sleep over it."

Nobody's Safe

DAVE RAYMOND: "When I heard about Wes over-sleeping, I started licking my chops. Put it this way, I wasn't gonna put it to bed—the material was too good. The next day, when they announced Wes's name during the pregame introductions, I whipped out a giant alarm clock and sprawled out on my bike pretending to be asleep. Suddenly, I jumped up, looked at the clock, and started scurrying around the ATV in a panic. I hopped on the bike and sped off like I was late for the game. The Phillies were laughing their butts off. After the game, Wes took me aside and said, 'That was funny, Dave. I'll let you do it one more time and then that's it. Do it again after that, and I'll kick your butt.'"

Wes would have needed to get in line, and fortunately, that butt is pretty well padded. The Phanatic has victimized many a major-leaguer, and even those he has not would probably like to kick the Phanatic's butt. During pregame warmups, the Phanatic is always looking for a player to rag on. Every time Mike Piazza's in town, the Phanatic challenges him to arm wrestle in front of the dugout. The Phanatic *lets* him win —playing on absurdity, you know, it's preposterous that Piazza could put the Phanatic down if the Phanatic were trying. Some players bring their own water guns into the park because they know the Phanatic will be waiting for them with water gun locked and loaded.

The Milwaukee Brewers, the Brew Crew, are a wild bunch. They liked to mix it up with the Phanatic. One of their routines is to kidnap the Phanatic during the pregame show. They grab me, pull me into their dugout, and start tying me up with tape. Then they take my head off and spin it around so that the front, the snout, is facing backwards. When I'm all tied up, they roll me onto the field with my head on backwards. I stumble around for a minute or two. I act like I can't see a thing, but it's *not* an act. I can't. Then the good ol' boys from the Brew Crew throw balls at me and vandalize my cherished four-wheeler.

The Brew Crew aren't the only ones who like to mess with the Phanatic's bike. It seems like every visiting player for the past twenty-five years has taken the keys to the four-wheeler at one time or another. The major Phanatic-baiters have been Sammy Sosa, Mark Grace, John Franco and Andy Benes. However, I've got to give credit to all of them. Ballplayers can be creative. Sometimes they'll take the key out of the ignition, hustle it into the dugout, and play keep- away. Some guys will tape the key to a baseball and then heave it into the outfield. Not only do I have to walk all the way out there to get the key, but it's next to impossible to pry that taped-down key off the ball. Sometimes they'll crumple up a paper cup with the key inside. Then they'll crumple up twenty more cups and throw them all out in front of the dugout so that I have to rummage through the entire pile to find the key. Meanwhile, they're dousing me with water.

Ed Ott, a coach with the Astros in '93, stole the bike before a game and took a Mr. Toad's Wild Ride around the field. When Ed reached the front of the visitors' dugout, he slammed on the brakes and wound up on his backside after being thrown head first over the handlebars. Ott was embarrassed. With his face redder than a Phillies cap, he crawled back into the dugout, thinking his little incident was history. It was. *Recorded* history. Video Dan caught it all on videotape. Next day, we showed it on Phanavision in S-L-O-W motion. The Phanatic then presented Ed with a Big Wheel kid's bike, along with a crash helmet, in a formal ceremony before the game.

Postscript: Ed Ott has *never* again come within twenty feet of the Phanatic's bike. The Swedish Bikini Team could be pyramided on top of it, beckoning him, and Ed would decline.

Lonnie Smith played for the Phillies from 1978 to 1981. His nickname was "Skates" because Lonnie tripped more often than a ballerina wearing flippers. The Phanatic couldn't let Lonnie's clumsiness go unrecognized.

DAVE RAYMOND: "Every time Lonnie was introduced, I fell down, got up, fell down again—over and over. It got so bad that [manager] Dallas Green took me aside and told me to cut it out. I did cut it out … till Lonnie was traded to the Cards. Then I really got into it. One day, when Lonnie was out warming up in the outfield, I was nearby. I kept falling down flat on my face till my head hurt. His teammates loved it. But when I turned my back and started walking towards the dugout, Lonnie came after me and hit me low from behind. Damn, I didn't even see it coming! I sprained my ankle and was really ticked off. When Lonnie came out of the dugout to take the field, I went right back into the routine, falling down flat on top of the dugout. He grabbed a ball and threw it at my head. It missed and went whizzing into the crowd. Fortunately no one got hurt. After the game, Lonnie came by my dressing room and apologized. He killed me with kindness. I eased up on him after that."

PHANATIC PHILE

After losing the home opener, the Phillies rolled through five straight wins to close out the season's first home stand. For the first time since the Connie Mack Stadium days in 1968, they swept three from Cincinnati. On April 13, Lee Thomas made his customary early season deal (he had made an April deal for four straight years) when he brought Mark Davis over from the Braves in exchange for rightie Brad Hassinger, a highly touted Double A prospect from the Phillies' farm club in Reading. Davis was drawing a robust $3.25 million a year, of which Giles and the Phillies agreed to pay $625,000. That amounted to paying a $400,000-plus premium to guarantee Davis's signature on a Philadelphia contract. The Phillies could have chanced signing him. They could have waited till after Davis was released and then tried to sign him as a free agent for the league minimum of $109,000. They chose not to take that chance and incurred a hefty premium. To make room for Davis, the club demoted pitcher Tyler Green to Scranton. Lenny Dykstra expressed the sentiment of his teammates at the time. "Obviously they (the Phillies brass) know our team has a chance to win the division, and they're doing what they can to help make that happen. It's great news. There's nothing but positive noise around here."

"Positive noise" was pouring out of the Phillies clubhouse. Practical jokes and a no-holds-barred atmosphere ruled. The Phils, with a rare mixture of fun, openness, candor, and tolerance, found the right key to connect with any personality that paid his dues. They even won over crusty, no-nonsense old-timers like bullpen coach Mike Ryan.

MIKE RYAN: "Everyone we brought in that year—and I got to know them all 'cause most of them were relievers—fit in great. Mark Davis, Bobby Thigpen, Donny Pall—even Roger Mason, who was a devout Christian. Roger got a kick out of the crazies in that locker room. Myself, I was never big on fooling around. I'm all business about this game, but these guys were different, 'cause they were all business out on that field. That '93 team had more giddyup than any team I ever saw in 35 years of professional baseball. All their cutting up made them closer knit. It made it a pleasure to go to the yard every day."

"Fregosi's Prison Squad," as Mitch Williams called his mates, breezed into the Wild Thing's former haunts at Wrigley with an 8-1 record. In the series opener, however, Terry Mulholland took his first loss. Chicago is *not* Terry's kind of town. Going into the game, the leftie was 2-4 lifetime versus the Cubs, with an 11.18 ERA. The next day, Jose Guzman handed Schilling his first loss of the season. In the series finale, with a four-run lead in the ninth, Fregosi handed the ball to closer Mitch Williams. The Wild Thing struggled as the Cubs scrapped back to tie. Both the Krukker and Wes Chamberlain (who was finally waking up after an 0-11 start at the plate) hit two home runs. Fortunately, an eleventh-inning three-run blast by Dave Hollins iced the game. The Cubs still made things interesting, recouping two of those runs in their half of the frame and ultimately falling short by one.

Hollins particularly savored his game-winning home run off the Cubs' Bob Scanlan. The two had an interesting history. In the final meeting the year before, Scanlan plunked Hollins, which triggered a bench-clearing donnybrook that got Hollins ejected and suspended. When Dave returned, he issued his Headley's Choice manifesto to the Phillies pitching staff. When Dave stepped in against Scanlan in the first '93 Chicago series, he was 2-6 lifetime against him. Both hits were round-trippers. His game-winning homer made him 3-7 with 3 home runs. "Any time a guy throws a ball at your head, you never forget it. At least I don't," Hollins remarked after the game.

The Phillies' intensity was propelling them as it would all season. They took their two losses hard. After the overtime victory, Dutch Daulton observed, "We're 9-3 and we're in first place, but I don't know if we feel that good about it. The thing is we have guys here who think we should win *every game*."

RUBEN AMARO: "We had twenty-five throwback guys. Nowadays, there may be only forty in the whole league! They do things backwards nowadays. Young guys make lots of money early in their careers. Then in four or five years, they say, 'You know, it would be nice to win a championship someday.' Well, winning that pennant was the *only* thing these guys were focused on.

"I had been called up to the Phillies in '92 and the attitude then was nothing like what I found in '93. When I got called up to the Phils that September, I was eating at a restaurant called Rock Lobster when Larry Andersen and Danny Jackson came in. They kind of lectured me and told me, 'We've got something going here. You make sure you're ready every day, or you won't be happy in that clubhouse.' These guys were serious. I had to earn their acceptance, and I was proud when I did."

With their blazing start, the Phillies found themselves emerging from New York's perennial shadow and drawing an inordinate amount of national attention. *Sports Illustrated* dispatched a reporter to Chicago to write a feature on the Phillies. But after the Phillies dropped two to the Cubs, the editors cooled on the idea, adopting a wait-and-see attitude to make sure Fregosi's guys weren't just a flash in the pan. The magazine ran a piece on Joe Montana instead, predicting that Joe would return to the 49ers in 1993. As the article went to press, Joe changed his mind and became a Kansas City Chief.

Jim Fregosi was happy that *Sports Illustrated* backed off their story. "That's fine with me. I had my worst year ever after I was on the cover of *SI*," he confessed to reporters.

From Chicago, the Phillies returned to the Vet for a second straight fall-from-ahead-come-from-behind victory, this time against the Padres. After blowing a 3-1 ninth-inning lead, Kruk laced a two-out home run in the bottom of the fourteenth to eke out a 4-3 victory for reliever Bob Ayrault.

Thus far in the young season, aside from losing those two ninth-inning leads, the relief corps, a huge question mark going into the campaign, had been sensational. Jose DeLeon had allowed only one inherited runner to score. David West flaunted a 2.08 ERA, and Larry Andersen was unscored upon in five of six appearances.

LA Story

I asked Larry Andersen to name his biggest personal accomplishment in 1993. Larry hesitated for an instant and beamed: "It was my 1.000 batting average."

That was Philly's LA story for 1993. Larry batted one time in 1993 and hiked his career average to .455—at least by Larry's math. "I'm 5 for 11," Larry calculated at the time. "That's five hits in eleven years."

Harry Kalas is the Phillies' Hall of Fame announcer. Harry's been doing Phillies games since 1971. Here's what Harry put out over the airwaves after Larry's single: "Andy gets a hit every four years. So if anyone wants to see his next hit, buy your season tickets for 1997."

When baseball players talk about flat-out bad hitters, Larry Andersen's name pops up more than a claustrophobic prairie dog. As a hitter, LA gets no respect, not that he deserves any. In late February at spring training in the Carpenter Complex, LA stepped into the box for batting practice as the announcer pleaded, "Larry Andersen is now batting. He has requested that everyone please refrain from laughing." Larry is, above all else, a sensitive man.

Columnist Jayson Stark amused Philadelphia fans throughout 1993 reporting (okay, instigating) Larry's running feud with Jim Deshaies, a Houston pitcher who was Larry's former teammate and beer buddy. Deshaies, incidentally, holds a major-league record. He once started a game with eight straight strikeouts. And no, it was *not* a pitcher who broke the string. Manager Tommy Lasorda pinch hit for his pitcher in order to break the string.

Deshaies and Andersen each swung the bat with as much conviction as a myopic curler. After LA's early season hit, a disgusted disbelieving Deshaies told Jayson, "If Andersen got to bat in an official major-league game, someone should lose his job. How does that happen? Was there a work stoppage by the bench players? Were they in the twentieth inning?"

Larry knew exactly how it had happened. "I was trying to miss the ball and [Cubs pitcher] Dan Plesac was trying to hit my bat. Plesac won."

JAYSON STARK, ESPN: "To me, Larry Andersen getting a hit was the most surprising thing that happened in 1993. After he got the hit, Deshaies was ripping him pretty good. LA fired back, and on and on it went. I decided to end the argument once and for all. We ran a computer game to decide who the worst hitter alive was,

Andersen or Deshaies. I stretched the game out over about a month. People were stopping me in the 7-11, asking me who was going to win. Deshaies won the seven-game series in seven games. I don't know how accurate it was. After all, if it was a realistic simulation, nobody would ever have scored."

LARRY ANDERSEN: "That computer game was fixed. I remember Jayson bringing in a judge or something to make sure that the game was on the up and up. I don't buy it. In my mind, the fix was in."

That day, when Larry got his hit, turned out to be an unusual day for baseball. It was Boston Marathon Day, and for the first time in a decade, the Red Sox played their game faster than the Marathon took to run. A '93 Phillie who demanded anonymity (he knows where my office is in the Vet and he's devious), suggested that the slowest marathon runner in the race moved faster than LA's self-described "torrid line drive."

The Phils split the next series with the Padres and followed with four straight wins over the Dodgers. Schilling pitched his second shutout of the year in the Dodger series, striking out nine, a career high at the time. Attendance at the Dodgers series was fabulous —37,457 on Saturday and 53,030 on Sunday. Phillie success was seducing the city. For the moment, at least, the demon of 1964 was exorcised. The Quaker City had officially jumped on the Phillie bandwagon.

After the Dodgers left town, fans had even more reason to jump on the bandwagon. On April 26, San Francisco was on their way to an apparent laugher, 8-0 over the Phillies in the top of the sixth. Kruk had been taken out of the lineup when he injured himself early in the game. However, in the fifth inning, Giants pitcher Bryan Hickerson unintentionally lit a Phillie fire. Hickerson speared a line drive for a third out and spiked the ball on the mound. The Phillies were infuriated, feeling that Hickerson's little maneuver was done to show them up. The Fightins scrapped back fiercely, plating three in the sixth, four in the seventh, and another in the eighth. Within three innings, they erased an eight-run deficit and knotted the score. In the tenth, Juan Bell scooted in and scored on a wild pitch, giving the Phillies a remarkable 9-8 triumph that hoisted the club ten games over .500 for the first time since 1986. The game took four hours, 33 minutes to play and was notable for Barry Bonds's Veterans Stadium debut as a Giant. Bonds struck out four times and walked twice. Phils hurlers walked fourteen and struck out thirteen in a crazy game in which Larry Andersen picked up the win.

One of those walks to Barry Bonds taught the squad an important lesson. Down 8-3, skipper Jim Fregosi intentionally walked Bonds. "We still had a chance to win the game. It wasn't over," said the manager in a postgame interview. Obviously.

LARRY ANDERSEN: "To me as a player, that move was a message. That's what we mean about being 'old-school,' a throwback team. We were trying to beat you right up till the last out. That's why we set that record for not getting shut out. We always believed we could come back, no matter what the situation, particularly after that Giants game."

Not only did the team prove its mettle as a scrappy gang that never quit, but the players also capitalized on their depth, unleashing the power of the team's sound architecture. Kruk was leading the NL in batting at the time, yet Eisenreich, his replacement, came in and rapped out three hits, scored two, and knocked in two more. The game annealed the team's feisty character and steeled its resolve.

PETE INCAVIGLIA: "We never popped off about opponents. We never showed them up, like Hickerson did that day when he spiked that ball. We showed the Giants what we were made of that day—and we showed ourselves, too. We knew we couldn't be stopped after that comeback."

The Phillies were on their own bandwagon after that game, and that wagon was rolling.

Jumping on the Bandwagon

I was in the control room during that marathon against the Giants. It didn't wrap up till after midnight. It seemed as though we were playing a game like that every other night. Heading into the tenth inning with the score knotted at eight, we fired up the Rally Train animation for Phanavision. When Juan Bell (of all people) scored on the wild pitch, we went crazy up in the control room! I threw Bachman Turner Overdrive's "Takin' Care of Business" into the new CD player and the scoreboard flashed nonstop: 'Phils Win!' It was only April 26, but the Phils had already won four extra-inning games, staged some wild comebacks, and swept series against the Astros, Reds and Dodgers. There was a buzz around the ballpark that I hadn't heard for a long time.

After the miracle comeback against the Giants, I didn't have much time for celebration. I had a Phillie Phanatic appearance at 6:30 the next morning at Suburban Station in Center City Philadelphia.

Six-thirty in the morning is a bit early to be running around like a madman—make that loony bird—at a train station, especially on two hours' sleep (yes, do the math—we celebrated after the game).

But I had to be at the station. It was our first Business Person's Special, which means a weekday afternoon game. Our promotions department dreamed up the idea that the Phanatic could pass out little pink "excuse notes" to commuters on their way to work. The note read: *"Please excuse (person's name) from work today so (he/she) can root the Phillies on to victory at the Vet at 12:35."* The Phanatic handed these things out and high-fived the commuters while the Phillies' house string band, the Whiz Kids Band, played a medley of Jimi Hendrix and Goo Goo Dolls songs. Just kidding.

That morning, it struck me how much the city was getting fired up about the Phillies. People were grabbing handfuls of excuse notes, screaming, "See you at the game!" and asking me, "How about that game last night, Phanatic?" I saw lots of bleary eyes, drowsy from staying up through all ten innings the night before. I scooted over to the newsstand in the middle of the concourse and yanked out a *Philadelphia Daily News* with the headline "Cardiac Kids." I held it aloft to cheers in the concourse.

We repeated the drill for each of the four remaining Business Person's Specials. All four times, the Phils won the night before the Business Person's Special. Three of those four wins were dramatic, come-from-behind heart-thumpers. So the next morning, I'd end up running around bleary-eyed, handing out "excuse notes." But on each occasion, I found myself hugging more and more believers. Each time, I hustled over to that same newsstand and held up the *Daily News* with a screaming headline about a Phillies victory. It was like déjà vu all over again.

And so it went all year. People didn't just fall in love with the zany personalities on that team. They fell in love with the *way* we were winning. Everywhere I went, every carnival, bar mitzvah, car dealership, shopping mall, sports banquet, elementary school and ribbon-cutting ceremony I crashed as the Phanatic, people were wild about the Fightin' Phils.

My company car that year was a big customized van, with colorful artwork and 'Phillies Bandwagon' printed in large red letters on the side. It featured red crushed velvet seats, red carpet, and a $1400 stereo system with removable speakers. It rocked. I could pull into a shopping center, slip into costume, pop open the doors, and jump into the crowd with my stereo cranked up to the max. As the season marched on, the crowds got noisier than the stereo system. More and more, when I hopped out into that crowd, it was like Moses parting a Red Sea of Phillies caps and T-shirts that had flooded the entire Delaware Valley.

One guy caught up in Phillies spirit was the dean of Philly sports columnists, Stan Hochman of the *Philadelphia Daily News*. After Dave Hollins won that wild Wrigley Field game in Chicago with a three-run home run in the eleventh inning on April 18, Stan gassed up the proverbial Phillies Bandwagon, which, according to Stan, had to be "... large enough to hold all loyal Phillies fans and the ball club, and small enough to make the turn around City Hall when the late October parade chugs around Broad Street. If you've got a '64 World Series ticket, you're on. If you've got an autographed Tony Curry baseball card, you're on. If you're not a collector but you bleed Phillies red stripes, you've got a chance. Those not welcome include the ding-dongs who jeered Juan Bell on opening day. If you ever booed Mike Schmidt, read no further."

Stan went further. To surface the true believers, he dreamed up a test with 15 questions like: "Who made the last out in Jim Bunning's perfect game in New York?" "Which Phillies pitcher was married to Hedy Lamar's daughter?" He expanded the eligible list to include those people who, in 25 words or less, could complete this sentence: "I deserve to ride The Bandwagon because ... "

STAN HOCHMAN: "I kind of borrowed the idea from [journalist] Tony Kornheiser down in Washington, who had created a bandwagon for the Redskins. But it was pretty amazing. We got nearly two hundred entries despite that questionnaire being really difficult. People wrote in with some great stories. I convinced the people at the *Daily News* to print up certificates to make fans who responded official members of the Phillies Bandwagon. Each fan got his or her own certificate with their name hand-lettered right on it."

In the city where *American Bandstand* was born, the Phillies Bandwagon was cruising along. So were the Phils.

The Trifecta

When many of the 1993 Phillies look back on that pennant-winning season, they zero in on three early season plays that convinced them that '93 was *the* year, *their* year. The first play in the trifecta took place in San Diego. Milt Thompson had been struggling at the plate. But on April 29, he slammed three hits to help the Phillies to a 5-3 lead. His biggest moment, however, came with the glove. In the bottom of the eighth, with the bases loaded and David West on the hill, Scooter, as Milt was called, leaped high and reached over the left-field wall to rob Bob Geren of a grand slam and preserve the win. After the game, Mitch called it "the best catch I've ever seen in person. I jumped up and down ten feet in that bullpen."

The very next night after the remarkable comeback against the Giants, Mickey Morandini executed the second part of the trifecta—a defensive gem of colossal importance to Philadelphia's 1993 march. The Phillies were clinging to a wobbly 7-5 lead in the bottom of the ninth against the Dodgers. The Wild Thing came in and loaded the bases with nobody out. Forget the Great Wallenda routine. Mitch was practically break dancing on the high-wire.

FRANK COPPENBARGER, EQUIPMENT MANAGER: "Mitch was pointing down at his spikes and looking at me in the dugout, yelling, 'Spikes.' I figured he had broken a cleat off his spikes. So I went tearing into the clubhouse to get him his extra pair of spikes. But Mitch had forgotten to pack them. I went running all around looking for another pair, trying to recall his size."

BOB BROOKOVER *PHILADELPHIA INQUIRER*: "While all that was going on, Mitch decided he was going to take a little break. He just walked off the mound and went into the dugout to get his equipment cleaned up. The crowd was booing pretty loud for a Los Angeles crowd. Lasorda shot out of the dugout, arguing that Mitch shouldn't be allowed to take any warmup pitches. Naturally, when Mitch came back out, he immediately started throwing warmup pitches, sending Lasorda into a hissy fit—and this is all happening with the bases loaded. Typical Mitch."

When play resumed, Mike Sharperson scorched a laser shot up the middle. Second baseman Morandini dove, miraculously speared the ball, and turned an unassisted double play. Tommy Lasorda "Lasordaed" all around the dugout, squealing, screeching, and caterwauling as Mitch closed out the game.

MICKEY MORANDINI: "It was one of those reaction plays. I dove, and the next thing I knew the ball was in my glove. The thing I remember most was the look on Lasorda's face and the cuss words he was shouting from the dugout."

The Phillies finished April with a 17-5 record, the most successful April in club history. They also occupied first place on May 1 for the first time since—*gulp*—1964. Philadelphians were becoming convinced, as was *Sports Illustrated*. The magazine people were back, working on a Phillies feature.

After Morandini's miracle, the Phillies split the final four games of their West Coast trip before returning home for their first tilt with St. Louis. The hometowners took the first two contests. With designs on a series sweep, the Phillies fell behind 5-1 entering the eighth inning of the finale. The Phillies got one run and had the bases loaded, but the Cardinals' super closer, Lee Arthur Smith, was on the mound.

In his column the next day, *Philadelphia Inquirer* columnist Frank Dolson described what happened next: "Unbelievable. Surely the word was on the lips of the 43,648 Veterans Stadium spectators, who let out a yell that must have registered at least a four on the Richter Scale, as well as a four on the scoreboard, when Mariano Duncan sent a Lee Smith fastball soaring into the left center-field seats with the bases loaded and two outs in the bottom of the eighth inning. One swing. One majestic drive against baseball's all-time saves leader, and a 5-2 Cardinals lead became an unbelievable 6-5 Phillies victory. Except maybe it really wasn't unbelievable. The way the Phillies have been pulling out baseball games through the first five weeks of the season, why shouldn't we believe?"

Mariano's circuit clout was the Phils' *eighth* game-winning home run of the young season. Dave Hollins had hit four homers at that point. All four were game winners. Even though the Phillies weren't hitting particularly well as a team, they were getting hits in the clutch.

MILT THOMPSON: "We came up big all year every time our backs were to the wall."

HAPPY MOTHER'S DAY, MRS. DUNCAN

Perhaps Lee Thomas's most astute move as GM that year was keeping Mariano Duncan in '93. Mariano stabilized a young middle infield. Juan Bell, Mickey Morandini, and Kevin Stocker were all inexperienced. Duncan was no stranger to a pennant race. He wore a World Series ring that he earned with the 1990 Cincinnati Reds.

CHRIS WHEELER, PHILLIES ANNOUNCER: "Duncan had an awesome year. What a clutch player! Without Mariano, the Phillies don't win that '93 pennant. He had big hits all season long, plus he knew how to play the game. He was so underrated. Lenny would get on base, and Mariano would come up and line one to right and move Lenny to third. All of a sudden, the other team's in trouble again! Mariano did that so often. Then when we needed a long ball, he'd come up with one. He was a fun-loving guy, but he was ornery and tough between the lines. Fregosi gave him his role to play, and he played it superbly. He was like Lenny. He loved pressure. Mariano's winning attitude really influenced the club in a big way."

Not only that, Mariano added flash and much needed style to the motley Phillie mix.

LARRY ANDERSEN: "I never saw Mariano in the same clothes twice. I swear, the guy used to wear clothes once and throw them out. But he did teach us how to dance. Make that 'tried to teach us.'"

MARIANO: "I told those guys they should get out to a nightclub once in awhile. I never saw such bad dancers! And clothes! Man, some of those guys need to throw everything out—like Curt Schilling. He can pitch, but he needs to buy some new clothes!" Like so many of his teammates, Mariano calls 1993 his happiest days ever in baseball.

"We have such a great bunch of guys. I look around that locker room when I got there in spring training, and I say, 'These guys are crazy! I never been around such a group of crazies!' But I loved coming to the ballpark. There was always something going on, and I never played with guys who played so hard."

Mariano started the year as a part-time player but played himself into a starting role, platooning with Morandini at second. He started 61 games at second and 49 at shortstop. Mariano was so much a part of the regular lineup that only Daulton, Dykstra, Hollins, and Kruk had more at-bats.

> Duncan hit two crucial grand slams that year. The first gave the Phillies a come-from-behind miracle win over the Cardinals on Mother's Day. The second clinched the division in Pittsburgh.
>
> MARIANO: "I was happy with that home run off Lee Smith. That was a special one for me. My kids and I still watch that one on video. It was Mother's Day. I felt so good afterwards because of all the mothers in Philadelphia. I hit that home run for them! I called my mother in the Dominican Republic right after the game. She was so happy! She told me that was the best Mother's Day present I could give!"

Best-ever records were tumbling daily. The day after the Phils swept the Cardinals, Darren Daulton hit a grand slam to power a 5-1 Phillie win over Pittsburgh. That victory established 1993 as the best start in Phillies history.

The Phils were the hottest ticket in town. Bill Giles told the *Inquirer's* Frank Fitzpatrick, "Last year our over-the-air ratings [on TV channel 17]used to average a six. Now they're about 12. Cable numbers have tripled in some cases. One SportsChannel game we did drew a nine. Last year they were doing threes. We've had to add people on the phones in the ticket office. Last year when I walked down the street, people would say something about *my* team. This year they talk about *our* team."

The one guy not thrilled with his own performance was Lenny Dykstra. On May 13, writer Frank Fitzpatrick wrote, "It finally snapped. It happened when Lenny Dykstra watched a potentially important home run become another foul ball in the eighth inning. 'I really hit it. Then I stood there and watched it hook foul and I finally shouted at myself, 'What a bleepin' joke. Bleep it.' I'm sick and tired of thinking that I've hit the ball hard and not having any luck. The bleepin' people in bleepin' Idaho see a box score that says I went 1-5 and they don't know that I hit the ball hard and they don't care.

'I'm tired of feeling sorry for myself and tired of making excuses. The bottom line is results.' To date, Dykstra is in the longest funk since arriving in 1989. After 129 at-bats entering last night's game, he was at .233 and only had two hits in 25 opportunities with runners in scoring position."

After splitting a series in Pittsburgh, Philadelphia stormed into Atlanta. The Braves and the city of Atlanta were itching for a showdown. Fulton County Stadium was completely sold out in advance. The Phillies' staff and the Braves' staff had identical ERAs (3.44) at that point. The Phillies' bullpen took a jolt, however, when Larry Andersen was placed on the disabled list with inflammation in his shoulder joint.

Tomahawk-chopping Atlanta fans—145,764 strong—cheered their Braves on to two victories in the three-game set. The Phillies moved on to Florida for their first-ever tilts against the expansion Marlins. Kruk made the series memorable, slamming a career-high five hits (out of the Phillies' total of 17) in the series opener. In his final at-bat, the Krukker was brushed back by Marlins pitcher Bryan Harvey and responded by slicing a single. He raised his league-leading batting average 23 points in one day to .382.

Philadelphia returned to the Vet to face second-place Montreal. Mitch Williams was asked how it felt this year to have Montreal as the chas*er*, rather than the chas*ee*, for a change. Mitch chirped, "With the reputation we have, we're used to being chased—by the police. So we're comfortable being chased." In the series opener, Inky pounded his fifth career grand slam in the first inning as the Phillies coasted to a 9-3 triumph. It was the Phillies' twelfth game-winning home run of the season.

The Phillies went on to split with the Expos. In the second game of the series, David West surrendered his first earned run since opening day at the Vet. The pitching, both starting and relief, had been stellar. The most glaring problem remained the shortstop position. Juan Bell made three errors in the second game of the series. Mariano Duncan replaced him the next night and booted three more. The Phillies' shortstops thus far were on pace to commit 58 errors.

Still, the Phils were five and a half games up.

PICKY SHORTSTOPS

No wonder shortstop was such a tough position to play in Philly in 1993. The coaching staff had to be mighty tough to please. In the *New Bill James Historical Baseball Abstract,* three 1993 Phillie coaches were listed among the top one hundred shortstops in the history of the game. Fregosi came in at number 15, Larry Bowa at 44, and Dennis Menke at 62.

Finishing off the last home stand in May, the Phillies reeled off two straight against the Mets but then botched a sure victory that deprived them of another sweep. Danny Jackson left with a 4-1 lead after eight innings. Then he watched the bullpen yield four ninth-inning runs in a heartbreaking loss. Relief was on the way, however. After the game, Larry Andersen returned from the disabled list.

The Phillies' reckless style continued to draw a lot of national attention, especially for a Philly team. The '93 team's style was their lack of style, or indefinable style. To Philly fans and fans all over the county, these guys simply looked like they were having good old-fashioned fun playing a little boy's game.

JOHN KRUK: "We didn't know we were so popular while it was happening. We really didn't care either. I realized we were getting popular, though. Every city we went to, the crowds got bigger and bigger. We'd walk down the street, and cars would go by, and people would yell, 'Hey, Kruk, you *friggin'* guys suck!' Hell, we liked that. It brought us together, kind of like twenty-five of us against the whole city."

The Fightin' Phils had become one of the sport's premier draws. The Mets series attracted 153,424 customers to the Vet—the largest attendance for a four-games-in-four-days series since 1982. In Colorado, 171,285 showed up for a three-game series.

By the end of May, however, the Phillies front office and Fregosi had seen enough of Juan Bell. On June 1, Bell was outrighted to Milwaukee. Phillies defense, which had been so strong through April, was teetering on the edge of self-destruction because of instability at shortstop. The Phillies had begun the month of May on pace to become one of only four teams in history to commit fewer than one hundred errors in a season. By May 28, when they committed five errors in one game—a 15-9 win over the Rockies—their error total had bloated to a disturbing 54. Eighteen of those errors came from the shortstop position. Fregosi finally gave up on Juan Bell, who was picked up off irrevocable waivers by the Brewers. Bell played 38 games with Montreal in 1994 and 18 with Boston in 1995, after which Juan's bell tolled no more.

Fregosi started Kim Batiste at short for the first time after Bell departed. Kim had started 1992 as the regular shortstop but was optioned to Scranton on June 18. Fregosi said, "I'll try to keep some of the rough right-handers away from Batty. I had a long talk with him the other day about keeping himself in shape and being ready when his opportunity presented itself."

Batty, as he was known, had seen limited action prior to Bell's departure. When he saw Daulton reading the posted lineup card with "Kim Batiste" written in at shortstop, Batty approached Dutch, saying, "Hi. I'm the new guy, Kim Batiste. Nice to meet you."

As May was coming to a close, the Phillies closed out their Rockies series with an 18-1 win on May 30. Tommy Greene pitched his fourth straight complete game and became the first Phillie pitcher to homer since August 1991. He was also named Pitcher of the Month for May—the first Phillies hurler so honored since Mitch in August 1991. The Bandwagon was rolling, though May ended with a controversial loss at Cincinnati.

Cincinnati and Philadelphia were a study in contrasts. The Phils powered up on team unity. Meanwhile, the high-salaried Reds were bickering and underachieving. The Reds' rookie GM, Jim Bowden, had recently infuriated Reds fans by firing popular ex-Red and future Hall of Famer Tony Perez. Pitcher Tom Browning was bellyaching about being lifted after six innings in a recent game. The pitcher's gripe was all about the guaranteed $3.5 million he would receive if he pitched more than 200 innings. The Phillies' veterans modeled the right kind of team-first behavior for their inexperienced, impressionable mates. The Phillies were about sacrifice, about putting team ahead of self. When the Phillies won their 18-1 laugher over the Rockies, Lenny Dykstra was lifted in the seventh for a pinch runner. It was the first inning the Dude had missed all year. Daulton, despite unremitting aches and pains, had missed only twenty-one innings all year while playing one of sport's most demanding positions. Daulton had blossomed into the leadership role Fregosi thrust on him. Dutch was the undisputed authority figure among Fregosi's gang of gypsies, tramps, and thieves.

Daulton fulfilled that role after the final game of the home series against the Mets. Mitch Williams was ranting in the clubhouse about being lifted from the contest prematurely. Daulton grabbed the Wild Thing and in no uncertain terms told Mitch it didn't matter what Mitch thought. Mitch was out there for the team, not for Mitch. Winning, not Mitch's saves or Mitch's ego, mattered. Following Dutch's intervention, the Wild Thing pitched his best ball of the season. In his next seven appearances, Mitch held opponents to a .130 batting average while walking only one, striking out eight, and not giving up an earned run.

MITCH WILLIAMS: "Dutch got in our faces when we needed it. We all knew he did what he had to do to keep the team going well. In my whole career, Darren Daulton was the only real clubhouse leader I ever saw, the *only* team leader."

On Memorial Day, Dutch became furious with home plate umpire Bob Davidson. The Phillies lost the game to the Reds when Davidson made a costly balk call against Larry Andersen in the eighth. Prior to that, Davidson had told starter Curt Schilling, "Your catcher is screwing you," when Schilling complained about Davidson's balls-and-strikes calls. Schilling walked four in seven innings that night. Until that game, he was averaging a scrimpy 1.76 walks per nine innings. After the game, Daulton blasted Davidson: "He's an impact umpire. In my opinion, the game was on ESPN and he couldn't wait to suit up and make an impact. He's one of those guys that, if you go though his house, there are a lot of pictures of himself on the wall and none of his family. We call him 'Balkin' Bob' because he's always waiting to make an impact on the game."

After years of frustration, Dutch Daulton had become the spokesperson for the Philadelphia Phillies. He was the force that held Fregosi's motley crew together tighter than the spin on a Nolan Ryan slider. In a wild clubhouse that rocked to the tunes of the Spin Doctors, Dutch supplied his team with the spins that kept the Phillie top from tumbling. But Dutch Daulton was more than a spin doctor. He was the soul of a team.

Dutch

"I could tell you a lot more about Darren Daulton, but I'd bore you with superlatives. He never sought admiration, but I never saw a leader like him in baseball. Eddie Murray and Dave Winfield were good leaders, but even they couldn't match Darren Daulton for leadership."
— *Ruben Amaro*

Even today, 1993 Phillie manager Jim Fregosi will tell you Darren Daulton is his boy—because of the extraordinary leadership Daulton provided the '93 pennant winners. *Leadership.* When you ask each '93 Phillie about the Enchanted Season, what forces took them to the pennant, they fire back a variety of opinions. Some opinions are held singularly, some are communal. But one opinion is universal, one stands above the rest.

The leadership of Darren Daulton drove that team to heights they would not have scaled otherwise.

We hear that term, leadership, bandied about everywhere—in sports circles, in corporations, and in the military. Every time two or more people unite for a common purpose or a common interest, the issue of leadership rolls resolutely to the front and center. It seems that everyone looks for good leadership, yet no one can verbalize exactly what they're looking for. Everyone interprets leadership in his or her own way—like abstract art. One person's contribution to the garage-sale heap is his neighbor's priceless Jackson Pollock.

That's why the ability to lead is both exclusive and elusive. That's why 12-step leadership courses fall flat. No one is really certain what that twelfth step is supposed to produce. That's why one camp argues that leaders are born, and one camp insists they are made. The fact remains, however, that for whatever reason, some can lead, others cannot.

Leadership, by its nature, is back-end loaded. In other words, leadership is not *giving* the speech up front. Lots of pretenders will jump up on a podium, yap, and consider themselves leaders. They're not. They're *talkers*, of which the world has no dearth, and who would do best to heed Abraham Lincoln's advice that "It is better to keep your mouth shut and look like a fool than to open your mouth and prove it." No, leadership can only be claimed by what happens *after* the speech, what changes as a result of the speech. Leadership is product, not packaging. It's about influencing others. The leader's words and actions—the way he leads, the way he influences others—are referred to as *leadership style.* Effective leaders don't have a single style. They adopt and adapt to a number of different styles—styles that sweep an entire spectrum. From muted to brilliant, subtle to garish, leadership styles are as multihued as a Maui sunset.

JOHN VUKOVICH: "Dutch led that group a number of different ways. He had the personality to get along with all the different types of guys we had in that clubhouse. He had everyone's respect and trust. He understood all his teammates and took time for them. He was a nice guy, and people liked him, but when he had to get in somebody's face, he didn't hesitate. I've been around baseball for thirty-eight years. I've played with better ballplayers, but never a better leader. He was always aware of what was taking place around him. He was mentally tough. What did he have, nine surgeries? He was also physically tough. He wasn't afraid to put the gloves on when he had to, and he played the toughest position in baseball. He was quiet, but he could be vocal when the situation called for it. He just had the right feel about how to handle each person and each situation."

Darren Daulton was physically tough. He had been a 150-pound state champion wrestler from Arkansas City, Kansas. He had also quarterbacked his high school team to a championship. Oh, yeah, he played baseball, too. But no matter what the sport, Darren Daulton played hard and aggressively. He was never afraid to get physical.

VIDEO DAN STEPHENSON: "I remember how Dutch took care of a couple of pitchers on the '93 team who were focusing too much on getting picked for the All-Star game. He threw one of them up against a locker at one in the morning and started screaming at him, 'Nobody gives a *frig* about your *friggin'* All-Star game. We're out to win games for this team, and that's *all* we're about.' I watched Dutch yell at that guy that night, and I saw Dutch get in lots of other guys' faces too. But what I remember most is that Dutch would always end with, 'but we need you to win this thing, and we can't do it without you.'"

The pitchers to whom Dan refers were Curt Schilling and Tommy Greene. Both were young, both had great promise, and both had great arms. Schilling and Greene had blazed out of the '93 season like a house afire. The flame, however, started flickering out in mid-June. When it did, both guys dropped a few games and dropped down a few rungs on the confidence ladder. Dutch sensed they were focusing too much on their individual numbers and too little on the task at hand, which was to win each game, pitch by pitch. Their funk at the time was threatening to the team and to their own careers.

CURT SCHILLING: "I was young and immature at that point in my career. I had lost a few games all of a sudden, and I started to doubt myself. What Dutch did was just what I needed. He could be tough and intimidating when he had to, and, in this case, he helped me get back to where I needed to be, pitching my game."

After the incident, Schil never doubted himself again. He went on to win seven in a row that season and never looked back.

DARREN DAULTON: "I knew other things were distracting Curt, and the team couldn't afford that. We needed Curt. The guy had such talent! That year, '93, it was like watching the horse come out of the stall. You could tell he was going to be a great one, and the big guy put it all together that year."

Dutch Daulton, himself, had put it all together the year before. In 1992, he was the starting All-Star catcher, becoming only the fourth catcher in major-league history to lead his league in RBIs. He was also only the third catcher in history to hit 20 home runs, drive in 100, and steal 10 bases (in 1975, Johnny Bench was 28-110-11, and in 1985, at the age of 37, Carlton Fisk was 37-107-17). Dutch had blossomed into stardom. But he had taken a trying, circuitous route—a route where others lacking his fortitude, ambition, and determination would have fallen by the wayside.

Dutch was drafted in June 1980. Moose Johnson, a former Phil scout who was with the Blue Jays in 1993, relates that Daulton called the draft room each day, pleading with the Phils to select him. They finally did, on the third day of the draft, in the 25th round. The Phillies had chosen Lebo Powell in the first round. Lebo was a huge guy, a catcher from Pensacola, Fla., who had also been recruited by Florida State as a lineman. Johnson summarized, "For two years, Darren caddied for Leo." As Dutch recalled, "That was humbling. I was All-State in Kansas, but then everybody they drafted was an all-star from somewhere. I remember getting off the plane in Helena (Dutch's first minor-league assignment) and there's this big guy on my flight. He reaches down and picks up his bag and I see 'Lebo Powell' on the name tag, and I'm wondering what I've gotten myself into."

That was at Helena in 1980. Dutch was brought up to the Phils for two games in 1983, even though he never hit higher than .262 in the minors. He spent 1984 with Portland and batted .298. He returned to the Phillies from Portland in 1985 and suffered a strained right shoulder that landed him on the disabled list. In 1986, he spent three months on the DL after Mike Heath slid into him and shredded the cruciate ligament in his left knee, requiring surgery. In 1987, he was back again on the DL because of his left knee and hit only .194 in 129 plate appearances. His season was again shortened in 1988, when he was out for more than a month with a broken right hand. In 1989, he played his first non-injury-shortened season in the majors. He batted .201 with eight home runs and inked a three-year, $6.75 million contract. Philly fans were enraged, thinking he was far overvalued. In 1990, he batted .268 with 12 homers and 57 RBIs. He led all catchers in games played, walks, runs, doubles, on-base percentage, and assists. However, in 1991, he was injured in a car accident as a passenger in Lenny Dykstra's car. The two were on their way back from John Kruk's bachelor party. Dutch batted .196 that season in only 285 plate appearances.

DARREN DAULTON: "Baseball was my haven. I told Mr. Giles years ago not to give up on me, that I'd be a player one day. They brought in Lance Parrish when I got hurt, but the Phillies never really gave up on me."

Actually, several catchers—Bo Diaz ('82-85), Ozzie Virgil ('80-85), Lance Parrish ('87-88), and John Russell ('84-88)—paraded through the Phillies' roster during Darren's tenure.

CHRIS WHEELER: "I give Darren credit. The fans here rode him hard as a young player. He met nothing but adversity, but he overcame it. He had a hard road to get to the top."

JOHN KRUK: "When I got to Philadelphia, I saw Darren Daulton play, and I said, 'We need a catcher.' He wasn't hitting back then, but I didn't know his knees were so bad. Then I started hanging out with him after the game, and I knew that, mentally, he knew what was going on."

Going into 1992, Lee Thomas said, "I may be crazy, but I wouldn't trade Darren Daulton for any catcher in baseball." Thomas went on to say he thought Dutch could hit 20 homers with 80 RBIs. Dutch told the press, "If I stay healthy, I think those numbers are feasible. I don't see any reason why I shouldn't." Daulton bashers were quick to point out that such talk was nonsense for an eight-year vet whose best numbers up till then were 12 homers and 57 RBIs.

But Dutch, the Phillies, and Lee Thomas were vindicated. His numbers in 1992, and his emergence as a leader, were undeniable.

DARREN DAULTON: "Yeah, it was my success in 1992 that enabled me to assume a leadership role. After I led the league in RBIs, I felt comfortable that I could step up to the responsibility. I knew I was never going to put up Hall of Fame numbers because of all my injuries, so I hobbled around and made the best contribution I could for my team, and that was to assume the role of team leader. I tried to convey to everybody that for the Phillies to succeed, everybody on that squad had to go out of his way. We had talent on that team, but we couldn't sit back and wait for one big star or a few big stars to win it for us. I was the guy who kept everybody focused on that fact. Jim Fregosi told me the role would be tough and thankless, but it was needed, and I was the guy who had to do it."

JIM FREGOSI: "I talked at length to Dutch about accepting a leadership role. At first, he didn't want it. Dutch just wanted to be one of the guys. He was a Midwestern kid, and he didn't make a lot of noise. That was not his nature. But he had been with the Phillies the longest. He was born and raised in the Phillie organization, and he was the natural guy to be the leader of that club, particularly as a catcher. The catcher views the whole field, calls the game—that's the leadership position on the field. But Dutch had struggled as a young player, and earlier in his career, he would have had a problem being the leader, because his own production was not that good. His success in '92 enabled him to step up.

"There aren't a lot of players in today's game who would do what Dutch did. They just want to play the game, make the money, and go home. They don't want to accept the responsibility of being there for their teammates."

PETE INCAVIGLIA: "The bottom line is that Dutch had the rare ability to make people around him better than they were. Dutch got along with everyone as a friend. But he could separate himself from that role and motivate and get tough too. He was the only player I ever met in my career who could take an interest in every player on the team—who could sit down and talk to anyone in the clubhouse about their problems."

CURT SCHILLING: "I can tell you, specifically, one of the things that made Dutch special. He always made me feel that, whenever I was pitching, my pitching was the most important thing—*the only thing*—going on. I never once heard him talk about his hitting during the game. That's unusual. The regulars, the position players, that's *all* they ever talk about, all game long. But Dutch just kept focused on his pitcher. He devoted all his energy and attention to making the pitcher successful. That's putting the team ahead of yourself."

DARREN DAULTON: "My dad tossed me a catcher's mitt when I was six and told me, 'That's your position.' Even in the winter, we'd clear snow in the driveway to play catch. My dad worked with me. He always taught me that when you're the catcher, *catching* comes first. And catching is handling pitchers and calling a game and being in control of the field. Schil was not the pitcher he is today back in '93, but even then, he fed off being the top dog. That's why he comes up so big in those big games. I knew what Schil needed. That was my job. A catcher needs to know his staff inside out."

Dutch made it his business to know not just the pitching staff, but the whole squad inside out. He was consistent and fair in his dealings. He played no favorites. He would jump all over his buddies just as quickly as he would an unknown rookie if he saw wrong behavior.

DAVE HOLLINS: "I remember a game early in my career in Houston. We won, but I struck out all four times. I was pretty pissed and wouldn't let it go. When we got on the bus that took us to the airport after the game, Dutch came over and asked, 'Are you all right?' I kind of grunted and turned away.

"When I walked into the clubhouse the next day, I was still fuming. Everybody could see it. Dutch walked right up to me, right in my face, and said, 'You know, I couldn't sleep last night—didn't sleep a wink. I was just thinking about how I was going to come in here and hit you today.' I told him, 'You're right. Take a pop at me right now if you want to. I deserve it.' I knew right then and there who the leader of this club was."

JOHN KRUK: "Headley was always pissed about something—win or lose, he was always pissed. That's how he motivated himself. Darren could read Head well, and he knew how to handle him. He took Dave aside more than once in private, and told him he wasn't on the same page with the rest of the team. Thank God those two never got into it. Dutch and Headley would have been a pay-per-view fight.

"But it wasn't just Head. Dutch would go toe to toe with anybody who wasn't on the same page as the rest of the team. I saw him do it with Mitch many times. Mitch would get mad if he didn't get in the game. Even after a win, he'd come into the clubhouse chucking his glove and bitching that he should have gotten in the game. Bubba [Daulton] would take him aside and straighten him out. As a member of a team, you know where you stand if can air things out like that. You need a guy like Dutch on your team if you're gonna win."

The '93 Phils stress the importance of Dutch's role in keeping the guys Fregosi was platooning happy. Dutch had heart-to-heart and toe-to-toe sessions with Inky and Wes Chamberlain, two other behemoths, and was instrumental in keeping them productive and focused—and friends.

If Dutch assiduously built up his stature as leader, he did no less for his own physical stature. Dutch worked hard to beef up to major-league proportions (from 150 pounds) so that he could tackle baseball's most exhausting position.

BILL GILES: "Dutch really worked on his physique. I was closer to Dutch than any other player, ever. He called me 'Uncle Bill.' Still does. He was so valuable to that team and this organization. He worked tremendously hard to get his body in condition to play, maybe harder than any other player I've ever known."

JIM FREGOSI: "I'll tell you about Dutch Daulton's work ethic. I can remember an instance in early '92 when I pinch hit for Dutch in Pittsburgh. I sent up Ricky Jordan, and I could see the steam coming out of Dutch's ears when he came back to the dugout. Dutch came into my office after the game and said, 'I don't appreciate being pinch hit for.' And I said, 'I thought that was the best thing to do in that situation. Dutch, if you want to accept the responsibility of being a leader on this team, then you're going to have to get to work.' And he did. He was at the batting cage with Dennis Menke and me early the next day, and really, he went to work. He got his own numbers up. And he became leader of that team. Then he went to Florida in '97, and I don't believe the Florida Marlins would have won that championship if Dutch hadn't been there."

HARRRY KALAS: "Dutch was always a nice guy, but he had something about him, something that made the other guys respect and admire him. I don't think you can put enough emphasis on his leadership. Yes, he led in Philly, but he was also the leader in Florida. Jim Leyland [Florida Marlins manager in 1997] told me they would not have won that championship without Dutch."

Dutch stepped up in several other areas as well. He was the spokesman for the team. He showed great instinct in handling the press, just as he did in handling his teammates. He fielded questions and ran interference for guys who were in a dangerous frame of mind—guys who ran the risk of saying something damaging or embarrassing.

Initially, it was Daulton's toughness that made Fregosi see his leadership potential. But Dutch proved to be tactful, polite, well respected, and well liked, as well as tough. Dutch had always been strong enough to withstand the barbs and boos of fans in Philadelphia and elsewhere. In 1991 in Chicago, Daulton struck out five times in one game. After every whiff, a group of hecklers razzed him unmercifully. One woman nearby, however, kept cheering and shouting encouragement. After his fifth strikeout, the hecklers really unloaded. Dutch's female admirer stood up and yelled, "Don't worry, Dutch. Even your manager struck out five times one game!"

Yeah, Fregosi saw a lot of himself in Dutch Daulton, but sometimes he would have preferred that the apple had fallen a bit farther from the tree.

Animal House

"If John Kruk, Lenny Dykstra, Darren Daulton and Pete Incaviglia were all in the same grade school class, they wouldn't be allowed to sit together."
– George King, writer, **Trenton Times**

The Clubhouse

The '93 Phillies had a simple credo. Play your ass off all the time and you're one of us. Put the team ahead of yourself and we accept you. It doesn't matter what you look like, or how you dress, or how you comb your hair. Hell, it doesn't matter *if* you comb your hair. Religion, skin color, politics—nothing else matters. Only how you play the game. Play the game hard, convince us that you're throwing your heart and soul into winning for this team, and we'll invite you into our fun.

Fun. That's what most distinguishes the '93 bunch. More than any team in recent times, this team made their workplace a fun place to be. The whole squad says the same thing about that season: "I loved coming to work," " I loved my job," "I never had so much fun playing baseball," "I couldn't wait to get to the park every day," "It was so much fun on that team 'cause everybody was trying to do the same thing—win," and "Everyone was equal."

These guys not only loved their job, they understood their job. Their job was to help their team win baseball games. What made this particular team successful, however, where others fail, was their collective commitment to the *means* to that end. To succeed, they needed every member to contribute.

Not every team needs that. The talent-laden teams can rely on a few big guns to carry them. Fregosi and his Phils didn't have that luxury. They knew they had to create an atmosphere where everyone felt vital. The '93 Phils took responsibility for creating a positive workplace atmosphere. They didn't expect management to do it for them. They didn't sit back and hope it would happen. They understood that *they* created the atmosphere where they worked. They had the power to make their office, their workplace, either a fun place to be or just a place to work each day. They chose the former. They had fun. They cut up like a fraternity on perpetual spring break.

They talked incessantly about their job. They never stopped coordinating their efforts, never stopped trying to understand and fulfill their individual roles. They demanded the attitude that winning was cause for celebration, even if you went 0-4, and that a loss was not cause for celebration, even if you went 4-4. They pushed and challenged one another, and they did it all in a fun atmosphere, where openness and willingness to learn prevailed over closed-mindedness and ego.

The fun they had that year is what separated the men from the boys. And it was the boys who won.

Like kids on vacation, the '93 Phils made the clubhouse their refuge, their release, and their citadel. That's where they bonded. It's where they rallied behind the attitude "Us against the world—and we're going to win." The clubhouse was where they mended their combat wounds, celebrated their victories, and planned their upcoming battles. When they left the clubhouse each day— actually each night—they couldn't wait for their next workday to begin.

Pie Wars

Everybody loves a good pie fight.

Baseball players—well, some of them—got a kick out of a good pie-ing or food or water battle. For me, the number-one culprit had to be Chucky Carr. The diminutive Florida Marlins outfielder was always packing some cans of whipped cream when he came to the Vet. When the Marlins were in town, I knew Chucky would be waiting in the wings somewhere, itching to give the Phanatic a face full of Redi-Whip or shaving cream, whichever was available at the time. Getting "pied" pregame always gets a lot of laughs, particularly when the players get into the act. But getting cream out of that Phanatic costume is a real drag. The cream gets schmushed deep into the green fur and takes forever to get out. But what the heck. If it gets laughs, I guess it's worth it.

No team *ever* loved a good pie fight like the 1993 Phillies. The mania for smashing some unsuspecting victim in the face with whipped cream or shaving cream started in spring training and carried right through to the division-clinching game in Pittsburgh. The setup was always the same. Wait for a guy (who was most likely pumped up because he just played a great game) to do a TV interview out on the field. Sneak up behind him with a paper plate filled with shaving cream and let him have it. Curt and Inky were the main instigators.

CURT SCHILLING: "Inky was the enforcer. He was like a guy who was raised in the mob but then decided to play baseball."

But Schil and Inky were not alone. They had plenty of help. Larry Andersen got pied in spring training and vowed revenge—on anybody and everybody. Mitch always seemed to be waiting in the weeds, ready to spring. And the mild-mannered Terry Mulholland assisted Captain Curt in the brassy act of pie-ing general manager Lee Thomas. That incident sent shock waves throughout the organization. Lee served notice that he would find out who the instigators were, and when he did, justice would be served. It was no pie-in-the-sky declaration. Justice *was* served. Thomas hired Inky as his hit man. One night, shortly after Curt Schilling stepped out of the shower and put his shirt on, Inky snuck up behind him and let him have it, sending Schilling to the showers. Again.

Coach Larry Bowa was victimized in midseason. Let's see, the GM got pied, the coach got pied ... Would Manager Jim Fregosi be next?

JIM FREGOSI: "No, no, no [waving his finger back and forth]. I loved these guys like they were my own kids. I let these guys do what they wanted. But *there is a fine line*, and they all knew not to cross *that* line."

Larry Andersen had a different spin.

LARRY ANDERSEN: "Fregosi knew that pies were flying around everywhere. He was pretty confident he wasn't a target, but he couldn't be 100 percent certain. One day, we were playing the Cubs in Chicago. Some sportscaster was interviewing him before the game, and the next thing you know, the guy keeled over and dropped to the ground. Fregosi knew how wacky we all were, so he figured we put the guy up to it. Fregosi was looking all around, kind of waiting for the punch line. He was looking down at the guy saying, 'What's the joke?' After awhile, he noticed nobody was laughing, and he figured out it was real. The guy had just passed out. Turns out he passed out from the heat, or overwork, or it was just one of those things. He was checked out and things turned out okay. We told Fregosi his breath knocked the guy out."

Fear of getting pied ran rampant all year. Mitch told me that to play on the '93 Phils, your head needed to be on a swivel. Regan in *The Exorcist* would have felt at home, except that clubhouse probably would have freaked her out. It got to the point where players started *paying* Phillies personnel to watch their backs during interviews.

PHIL SHERIDAN, PHILLIES CLUBHOUSE ATTENDANT: "Once, Curt Schilling paid me fifty bucks to stand behind him for three minutes while he did an interview. I stood there and watched. It was a quiet night—easiest money I ever made. Of course, if Inky had come up and threatened bodily harm to me, I probably would have sold Curt down the river, especially if Inky offered me sixty bucks."

Julius Caesar had loyalty like that too.

> The pie wars concluded dramatically in Pittsburgh, after the Phillies clinched the division. In a TV interview, club president Bill Giles got nailed with a chocolate cream pie. Hey, only the best for the club president.
> "I'll remember that come contract time," Giles yelled.

To a man—or to a boy—these ballplayers loved baseball. They cheered, hustled, and dreamed with the abandon of a Little League team giving their all to win the Fourth of July game for neighborhood bragging rights. The game was the thing for them. Winning was their job—a job they wanted to do well for their coworkers and their employer. How many of us can say that? Drew Carey jokes that he's discovered a support group for people who hate their jobs. It's called Everyone.

The '93 Phillies were not qualified for Drew's support group. Don't dismiss that lightly. Don't say, "Hell, they're ballplayers. Why *wouldn't* they like their jobs?" For the same reason as you or I wouldn't like ours. Professional baseball might not seem like the Real World, but being a professional baseball player is a *real* job. And that real job was never a chore, never a drag to the '93 Phillies. It was never anything but sheer fun. They worked at making it that way. You don't find that in many workplaces, in or out of baseball.

Ballplayers are media stars. They're on the tube, in the papers, on the radio. We forget that they're people, no different from us. Their profession happens to be an escape for the rest of us. Sports are our fun or our no-risk passion. But it's their *job*. And if you hate your job—well, as John Kruk puts it so eloquently, your life sucks. Unhappiness breeds poor performance. It's a natural, human, and predictable response. Ask any middle manager in the country about that connection. Never think that high salaries by themselves wipe out unhappiness. If a ballplayer dreads walking into his workplace day after day or dreads interacting with his coworkers or management, eventually his dissatisfaction will override his high salary. Eventually his dissatisfaction will drag down performance—not only his own, but everyone else's around him.

Bonds and Big Mac and Sammy have thrilled the world with their individual exploits and record chases. But baseball remains a team sport. Baseball is about winning games and pennants and World Series—not about flashy batting averages and stingy ERAs, the numbers that get tossed around negotiating tables at contract time. Individual statistics are indicators. They measure, clinically and objectively, how well an individual hits and fields and pitches. But they don't necessarily measure how well an individual does his job, which is to coordinate with 24 other guys to win baseball games.

JIM FREGOSI: "Those '93 guys didn't care about personal stats. They dedicated themselves to doing the kinds of things that win ballgames over a 162-game season. They were the most unselfish group I ever coached. With the salaries ballplayers make, you don't see guys playing unselfishly nowadays. But that team had an unwritten code in that clubhouse—a code that the team comes first. Everybody followed that code. They knew if they broke it, everybody there was going to make their life bad till they straightened out.

"These guys took pitches they knew they could hit because the situation called for taking a pitch. They worked starting pitchers to frustrate them and to get them out of the game faster. They were happy getting walks. Walks are not what agents brag about at contract time. How many times do you see guys nowadays swinging 3-0 because they're thinking long ball for their next contract, when they should be thinking about getting on base to keep an inning going? These guys did those unselfish things, 'cause if they didn't do them, they'd hear about it from every other guy in that clubhouse. The coaches didn't have to say a word. That clubhouse atmosphere was critical to the club's success. And those guys loved coming to the park. I called them clubhouse rats. They hung around in the clubhouse. They grew to trust and believe in each other. There's not one guy on that team that wouldn't stand up for a teammate. When they came off that field, they had fun, and I never stopped them from having fun. My rules were simple. You come here every day to bust your butt to win."

The Ghetto

The 1993 clubhouse was noisy and raucous, filled with characters and character. In size, it was just a bit of walled-in space—sparse and nondescript. But the '93 clubhouse, like Manhattan, had distinct neighborhoods. And like Manhattan, the clubhouse had to be navigated with caution, respect, and perhaps a bit of awe. The neighborhoods, the scene, or the atmosphere could change drastically and quickly—in a New York minute—in that little clubhouse. Unlike Manhattan, it was a good place to live, but sometimes you might not want to visit there. At least, not if you were viewed as an outsider.

The area the Phils named the Ghetto was the heart and soul of the clubhouse. The veterans that Fregosi had deputized inhabited the Ghetto: Darren Daulton, John Kruk, Dave Hollins, Pete Incaviglia, Lenny Dykstra, and Mitch Williams. These guys formed the hard core that gave the Phillies their hard edge. The Ghetto guys were cantankerous. They hated pitchers, for instance, which begs the question, "How did Mitch Williams get in?"

JOHN KRUK: "We weren't gonna let Mitch in, but we figured he's not really a pitcher. Mitch is just a thrower."

Located in the far corner of the locker room, Ghetto vibes, on occasion, could make the clubhouse uncomfortable for visitors. Sometimes the press and the media got great stories and quotes in the Ghetto. The guys there could be funny. Kruk was a prime time comedian. He and Dykstra often entertained Letterman audiences with terrific one-liners and no-holds-barred candor. Zingers zipped around the Ghetto haphazardly. Stray zingers could hit the unwary and innocent or pierce the thin-skinned.

Sometimes the press could encounter attitude, along with anger or hostility. So could other players. They could make life miserable for newcomers till they proved themselves

WES CHAMBERLAIN: "Mickey Morandini and I had a tough time until those guys saw what we were made of. Once you convinced them you were here to win, they were great, but they could put you through it till you did."

The Ghetto adopted another member in midseason. In early July, Kevin Stocker was called up from the minors to plug the team's gaping hole at shortstop. The Ghetto decided to plunk him into their midst and keep him focused.

CHRIS WHEELER: "You can't win without a good shortstop. The Phillies got off to that great start, but they were getting hurt badly at shortstop with Juan Bell. The '93 guys were smart baseball players. They knew over the long haul they weren't going to win without a solid shortstop. When Stocker came up, those guys in the Ghetto got together and decided to go easy on the kid. They needed him. They took him under their wing. Fortunately, Kevin Stocker was a tough kid who handled the pressure like a veteran."

KEVIN STOCKER: "I was a bit apprehensive when I came up in midseason. The Phillies were leading the league, right in the middle of a pennant race. I knew the guys in that Ghetto could be pretty tough on anyone new. But they accepted you unconditionally if you played all out. That's all anybody around here wanted—all-out effort. They made that clear. I had never been in a locker room with unwritten rules, but that locker room had them. The veterans in the Ghetto set the rules and everyone had to abide by them.

"Here's an example. I thought the media was great to us that year. The beat reporters like Paul Hagan and Bob Brookover were fair, straight shooters. But one of the unwritten rules in that locker room was that you couldn't be too friendly with the media, because interviews were about you. It had to be about the team, not you. The guys in the Ghetto really rode anybody who sought the media out or got too chummy. But again, once you knew those rules and abided by them, that locker room was great, a fun place to be."

The Ghetto was dubbed Macho Row by the press. To the outside world, Macho Row was the embodiment of the Phillies' toughness.

JAYSON STARK, ESPN: "Those '93 Phils loved that Macho Row image. The more the press called them Macho Row, the more they identified with it. They liked the role of underdog and outcast. They liked not looking like the typical professional athlete. They flaunted the fact that they didn't give a damn about what people thought. They fed off the Ghetto and Macho Row and the mystique attached to them, and, most important, they drew power from those things."

The locker room was open to reporters before and after games. In good times, that's where the zany stuff that the cameras caught took place. The unwary or the unhumble were most likely to get pied in the clubhouse. It was here that you were likely to see Mariano Duncan teaching the "Two-Step," witness pregame putting contests, and listen to music cranked up to where Pete Townshend would scream for mercy. The zingers and the funny interviews took place in the locker room. It's also where guys relaxed, chilled, and talked baseball for hours on end. They ate here and drank beer here.

TERRY MULHOLLAND: "We respected each other and we disrespected each other. But we disrespected each other out of respect, because we knew nobody's feelings were going to get hurt. That crazy clubhouse atmosphere really helped bring that team together. We'd work through problems, help each other out, talk strategy, learn from one another, and straighten out how we'd handle different game situations. We had a lot of fun in that clubhouse, but the whole atmosphere changed about an hour before the game. Everybody put their game faces on and got set to kick butt. We all knew that's what we were there for. We had lots of fun when we got to the clubhouse before and after the game."

Belching for Glory

Larry Andersen spotted me one day walking in my street clothes through the press box.

"Yo, Phanatic," LA called out. That's what I like about Larry. He's deep. He sees the inner person, whether he's looking at a guy in a Phanatic costume or personnel at Hooters. He calls me Phanatic whether I'm in or out of costume. "Did I tell you that my proudest moment in '93 was my 1.000 batting average?" LA asked pensively.

"Yeah, you did, Larry," I reminded him.

"Well, I want to change my answer," Larry told me. "My proudest moment had to be the day I beat John Goodman in a burping contest."

Larry Andersen would have made a great mascot. In fact, Larry and I have a lot in common. One talent we share is being able to belch and talk at the same time. The only difference is that I stopped doing it after eighth grade. Larry, in contrast, continues to amaze baseball people from coast to coast. Even the great Nolan Ryan, who pitched seven no-hitters in his career, just might tell you that his fondest memory in baseball was hearing Larry Andersen belch the entire National Anthem.

LARRY ANDERSEN: "We were in Los Angeles for a series with the Dodgers when John Goodman walked into the clubhouse. Some of the guys were shaking hands with him and asking him questions. I was at the other end of the clubhouse getting dressed when I let out one of my customary loud belches. It stopped John Goodman in his tracks. He spun around, stared across the room at me, and with this real competitive gleam in his eyes, said, 'You're on.' He grabbed a beer, downed about half of it and let out a big burp. 'Sorry, John, you're in the bigs now,' I'm thinking. I knew I had him. I took a chug of my beer and let out a real locker rattler. John knew he was beat. He got down on his knees and started bowing. I was moved by his obvious show of respect. It was one of the proudest days of my life."

They were a gruff bunch, undeniably. Their jokes and their demeanor could often be crude and rude. But their openness and candor was liberating. They were a tight knit group because their tolerance was remarkable.

JOHN KRUK: "We had no cliques. It's the only time I've ever been on a team where that happened. There were cliques when I first came to Philly. But in '93, there was none of that. The guys that were brought in accepted people for who they were. That's really unusual. On most teams, you'd have the black guys in one corner or the Latin guys hanging out with one another and nobody would mix. Not with this team. We talked baseball, we busted on each other and we all went out together—blacks, Latins, and whites. Nobody acted above anybody else in that clubhouse. And everyone was fair game for pranks and jokes. I give credit particularly to Milt [Thompson], Ricky [Jordan], and Mariano [Duncan] for the way they brought that team together and kept it together. Everybody could take a joke when it was their turn."

RICKY JORDAN: "That team was one big happy family. Everybody had his own personality, that's for sure, but we all liked and respected each other. Krukkie's right. There were no cliques. Even when we went out to eat, there'd be eleven, twelve guys out in a group. That team—that was the most fun I ever had in baseball."

When the game was over, the Phillies drifted off into their true inner sanctum, the team's fortress of solitude, the trainer's room. The trainer's room was off limits to reporters and the rest of the outside world. Baseball, and everything that touched baseball, was a passion to this team. The Phils were like the Broadway types with show biz in their bellies—the ones with the hunger who live for the smell of the greasepaint and the roar of the crowd. The trainer's room was backstage for the '93 team. They hung around there for endless hours.

The team had a postgame ritual. They headed back to the trainer's room after a game to kick back and talk baseball for hours. At first, only the Macho Row guys went back. But as the season progressed, the whole team spent a portion of their postgame time back in the sanctum of the trainer's room

VIDEO DAN STEPHENSON: "Yeah, the trainer's room was their hideout. What I'm going to say probably sounds silly, but a lot of guys on that team agree. I don't think the '93 Phils would have won that pennant if Daulton hadn't been so banged up. That whole postgame bull session developed because Dutch had to go back to the trainer's room to get iced down. Kruk would get a pitcher of beer and join him. Eventually everybody started heading back. It was off limits to the press, so Darren became kind of the spokesperson for the whole team. Those '93 players were not media guys. They didn't like the spotlight, weren't comfortable there. They were totally focused on baseball. That's what they talked all night. They never had any personality or attitude problems, cause everybody stuck around and talked things through. You look out in the parking lot these days and the players' cars are all gone an hour after the game's over. The '93 guys hung out here for hours and hours before and after the game. That little ritual, joining Dutch in the training room, bonded the team. These guys had fun and loved baseball like no other group I ever saw. They loved coming to work, and they hated to leave."

The Trainer's Room

"Hey, Greaser! We're getting low in here! Fill 'er up with a little low test!" Orders would shoot out from behind the trainer's room door, and in a flash, one of the clubhouse attendants was heading into the players' lounge for another two pitchers of Bud Light. Low test was Bud Light. High test was regular Bud. With pitchers of beer in hand, whoever was delivering the suds would walk right past the waiting horde of media and into the trainer's room. There, a thirsty group of Phillies waited.

FRANK COPPENBARGER: "The beermeister in the players' lounge holds two kegs. We changed those kegs every three games. That's a lot of beer. I've never seen a team drink like that. Everywhere else, after the game, the players ice for a few minutes, grab a bite from the spread in the locker room, take a shower, and they're out the door within an hour. Not the '93 team. They'd come off the field, and a bunch of them would head straight for the trainer's room, where we'd always have three pitchers of beer waiting for them. My first job was with St. Louis, and I remember back in 1982, Bruce Sutter and Gene Tenace had an empty locker between them. They used to keep a cooler of beer there. But the whole team didn't hang out for hours after the game the way the '93 team did. Even the guys who didn't go directly to the trainer's room would shower and eat first but eventually go in and rehash the game for a while. At one point or another during the night, just about every guy on the team was in that trainer's room.

TERRY MULHOLLAND: "We basically turned the trainer's room into a bar. There were spittoons, beer bottles, empty pitchers, cups, ashtrays and pizza boxes lying around all over the place. Krukkie had a big leather chair in there right next to the counter so he could rest his beer and cigarettes. He'd be smokin' one heater [that team called cigarettes "heaters"] after another. Dutch would be on one of the trainer's tables with his back against the wall, with two bags of ice on his knees and a pitcher of beer by his side. Lenny would be sitting on the floor, smoke rising above his head, drinking his Crown Royals. Andy [Larry Anderson] would be in there just trying to catch his breath. Westie would be in there drinking right out of the pitcher. Tommy Greene would be in the corner flappin' his gums, with nobody listening to him. We loved Tommy. Fregosi would walk into the room in his underwear, with a scotch in his hand, just hanging out. Every once in a while, Krukkie would sneak out of the room, then walk back through the doors in his underwear, holding a scotch. We'd bust up, and he'd do a killer impersonation of Fregosi. He always started out, 'You know, you gotta believe me when I tell ya ...'"

PETE INCAVIGLIA: "I remember one time, Kruk was walking past Dave Hollins's locker on his way to the trainer's room. He had a couple of pitchers of beer in his hand. The game had been done for over an hour, yet Headley was still staring into his locker, mumbling to himself because he had a bad game. When Head got like that, you didn't go near him. Anyway, Krukkie walks into the trainer's room and is like, 'Head's out there talking to himself again.' Well, the next thing you know, Davey walks into the trainer's room, still looking pissed. The whole room gets that uncomfortable kind of quiet. Then Krukkie looks over right at Headley, shakes his head, and says, 'You really suck!' Hollins broke into a huge smile and we all laughed for ten minutes! Nobody but the Krukker could have pulled that one off! But that's what that team was all about. We always had the perfect guy for every situation."

More and more the trainer's room became the exclusive domain of the players. Eventually, the players blacked out the two windows that looked into the room so that the press and other curious eyes couldn't peer in.

GENE DIAS, PHILLIES MANAGER OF MEDIA RELATIONS: "It was my job to poke my head into the trainer's room and try to get whichever guy the press was looking for to come out into the locker room, where the press was allowed, and do an interview. Usually the players would tell me, 'I gotta ice. Tell them I'll be in here awhile.' Dutch was the spokesman. He usually ended up going out and talking to the reporters. Mitch took the heat a lot, too. The other guys took turns. But all in all, believe it or not, I think that team had a good relationship with the media because the '93 guys were real."

JAYSON STARK, ESPN: "That whole trainer's room and Macho Row thing worked. It didn't take long before the '93 guys started showing up on magazine covers. There was something about the way they looked that didn't fit the standard profile for a modern athlete. When you think about cover-boy baseball players these days, you picture the Yankees players, with their corporate button-down image and that Madison Avenue look. I mean, the '93 team looked like something right out of the circus. Sports writers know a good story when they see one. With that cast of characters and their worst-to-first-run, how could they not be a national phenomenon? They were a Saturday Night Live skit waiting to happen—and sure enough, SNL spoofed them. For me, they were nonstop entertainment. But to try to cover these guys day in and day out was tough. They hung inside that trainer's room and avoided the press a lot. To try to get Kruk out of the trainer's room after he's had about eight beers was tough. Kruk could stall with the best of them. But if you could break through and corral him, he was the funniest man who ever lived. When he was with the White Sox, I tried calling him for weeks. No reply. A friend of mine got a cab with Kruk and said, 'Hey, Jayson's been trying to get in touch with you for weeks.' Kruk said, 'I like Jayson, but I don't want to talk to him.' Krukker could care less about being a media darling, but when you put him in the spotlight, he was tremendous."

When Jayson says Krukker could stall with the best of them, he is serious. The '93 Phils were never anxious to leave the clubhouse.

FRANK COPPENBARGER: "They never got around to actually eating the postgame spread till hours after the game was over. All the clubhouse attendants would be sitting around waiting for them to eat so we could clean up and go home. But we couldn't go home. We had to wait till all the players left so we could lock up. There was only one door out of the clubhouse, and it had to be chained from the outside. Eventually I went to Lee Thomas and said, 'This is nuts. These guys stay here till all hours. I can't even get home.' They wound up cutting a whole new door into the manager's office. This way the players could be the last to leave and the door would lock automatically behind them."

RUBEN AMARO: "I know this isn't politically correct, but that team really put team first and family second. They were that serious."

The '93 guys went through eight or nine divorces that year. I guess every form of refuge has its price.

JOHN KRUK: "We all knew that this was a one-time thing, that we were getting older, and that feeling that we had in the clubhouse and for each other was something special. So we decided that we were gonna enjoy it. A lot of us went through divorces that year, and it was probably because we hung out together so much that year and had some late nights. But you know, you can take all the pennants the Braves have won or all the championships the Yankees have won and I don't know if they had what we had that year. I played 10 years and packed more fun in than somebody who played 20 years. I packed 20 years of fun in 10 years."

LARRY ANDERSEN: "I went through a divorce that year. I tried to tell my wife that drinking after the game with teammates was part of my job description. It didn't fly."

> *"The way a team plays as a whole determines its success.*
> *You may have the greatest bunch of individual stars in the*
> *world, but if they don't play together, the club won't be worth*
> *a dime."*
> *— Babe Ruth*

The Phillies had one other hideaway that year: Video Dan's video room, which was and still is tucked away in a corner of the weight room connected to the clubhhouse. The ballplayers used to run back there during the action to check out new pitchers or their previous at-bats either in the current game or against a pitcher that was entering that game. When guys were taken out of games, they often watched the rest of the game in the video room.

Video Dan

One of questions I hear most often is, "How hot does it get inside the Phanatic costume?" I've never dropped a thermometer down there, but the Astroturf on the field shoots up to 150 degrees some days, so you get the picture. Underneath all that fur, it can feel like the inside of a microwave oven. And, yes I sweat more buckets nightly than John Kruk could step into if he faced Randy Johnson in every at-bat for a full season. Many nights, I end up with a puddle swishing inside my Phanatic's sneakers, and you can hear me splashing when I walk by.

PHANATIC PHILE

At the Vet I have a dressing room where I can take off my head (and you thought only your boss, or your last blind date, could do that), drop the costume down around my knees, and drink gallons of Gatorade and water. I go through about five or six T-shirts a night, each one more saturated than the next. There's a huge floor fan in the corner that runs full blast and a TV so I don't miss any of the game action.

My dressing room is right next to the Phillies clubhouse, so I don't have to be watching the game to know if the Phillies win or not. That boom box says it all. If the noise in my room is several decibels over the OSHA limit, I knew we've won.

The players' preferred hideaway during the game is the video room. "Video" is the name that most people in the organization call Dan Stephenson, the Phillies' in-house video master. If you've seen Phillies videos like "Flashback—A Century of Phillies Highlights" and "Glory Days—The Story of the 1980 World Championship Phillies"—Dan was the guy who put them together.

Dan has kind of that same look about him as Norm from *Cheers*. It's that "What, me worry?" look that suggests he'd rather be sitting on a bar stool watching a game than doing anything useful. Actually, Dan *is* more comfortable around bar stools. In 1981, he was a bartender at Downey's, a legendary Irish bar in Philadelphia, famous for its Irish whiskey cakes. You don't need to eat a Downey's cake to get hammered. All you have to do is smell it.

Dan was a huge Phillies fan back in his Downey days. While he was tending bar, Dan always had an earplug in to catch the game. When the game got exciting, he'd yell and scream while pouring drinks. "I think the customers thought I was possessed by demons," chuckles Dan.

One Downey customer was Chris Wheeler, a young Phillies broadcaster who chatted it up with Dan for hours one night.

VIDEO DAN: "I told Wheels that I videotaped weddings and other affairs on the side. Wheels said that the Phils' video guy at the time was quitting and the club was looking for somebody to replace him. A short while after that conversation, the Phillies held a small reception at the bar for the Phillies' new owners. Club president Bill Giles came up to me and said, 'So I hear you're our new video guy.' It was amazing. They never checked my work or anything."

His first six years consisted of shooting and maintaining taped records of every player's at-bats and videotaping every pitcher in the league. Then, in 1988, he helped introduce a new annual line of Phillies highlight films called the "Home Companion." These videos, which are special year-end inside-out looks at the club narrated by a different player each year, feature lots of behind-the-scenes footage.

PHANATIC PHILE

Video Dan made plenty of videos for players, too. He became close friends with several players from the eighties. One year he went scuba diving in the Cayman Islands with Steve Carlton and a young Darren Daulton. He returned home just in time to hop on another plane to go hunting in Wyoming with Glen Wilson and Lance Parrish.

Yeah, the players know Video Dan well—perhaps too well.

VIDEO DAN: "I remember the night Terry Mulholland threw his no-hitter in '90. I'm sitting in the room with the game on TV. [The late] Jim Barniak was a play-by-play announcer for the Phillies at the time on Prism, the Phils' cable channel. All of a sudden I hear him saying, 'That Video Dan Stephenson really does a great job for the Phillies, working hard behind the scenes.' Mike Schmidt, who was a color commentator for the Phils that year, shoots back, *'No, he doesn't.* I'll tell you what he's doing right now. He's got his feet up on his desk with a beer in one hand and he's pushing a button with the other.' You know what? That's *exactly* what I was doing at that moment!"

Video has always loved the Phillies. He hung around with a lot of the eighties players, but he had a tremendous emotional attachment to the 1993 squad.

VIDEO DAN: "I've been with the Phillies now over twenty years, but there'll never be another team like that '93 squad, 'cause those guys were always hanging out with me in my room. Hell, they actually remodeled it. Mitch bought a huge sectional sofa with a pullout bed and two easy chairs. He and Krukkie bought a big-screen TV and Wally Backman bought a refrigerator back in '92. I kept dropping hints that the room could use a wet bar too, but it never happened.

"The video room was a real nerve center in '93 because there were so many extra-inning games. After the starter came out of the game, he'd head for the video room. Then a couple of relievers would join him, and before you knew it, it felt and sounded like Mardi Gras in my room.

"Back in the '80s Steve Bedrosian was another reliever who came in a lot. Bedrock would have fit in beautifully with that '93 team. He used to play a game called 'Madball.' He'd open up the door to the video room and scream 'Madball!' Then he'd take a ball and hit it as hard as he could into the room. Guys would go ducking for cover as the ball was ricocheting off the walls and video equipment. Finally, [Phils manager at the time] Lee Elia told the players that my room was off limits. Bedrock was crushed, until one day he couldn't take it anymore. He was outside knocking at my door, trying to get in. I told him, 'If I let you in, Elia will probably fire my ass.' Bedrock didn't care. He grabbed *an axe* and chopped a hole in the door. And then, just like Jack Nicholson in *The Shining*, he poked his head in and said, 'He-e-e-e-e-e-e-ere's Bedrock!'"

In '93, Larry Andersen and David West were the relievers who frequented Video's room. Night after night, with pitchers of beer in hand, they filed in to watch the rest of the game. Nightly, Video's "office" transformed into a fraternity-house party room. Half-filled cups of beer, wads of tobacco and cigarette butts on the carpet greeted Dan each morning after the night before. John Kruk slept on his couch every Saturday night.

"Krukkie figured he wouldn't get home until four or five in the morning anyway, and by the time he got up and came back to the park at 9:00, he'd get more sleep just staying the night in my office," said Dan.

The Phillies went 17-5 for a torrid .772 percentage as April closed. They blitzed through May at a 17-10 clip (.630), a winning percentage eclipsed in the final 1993 standings only by Atlanta and San Francisco. When June commenced, the Phils were still busting out all over. It was a rare day in June, at least in early June, that did not end in a Phillie victory. The club interspersed two-game, three-game, and six-game winning streaks between single losses. By Flag Day, the Phillies' lead had ballooned up to 11 games, which would be their biggest lead for the season. Their starting pitching was carrying them. Tommy Greene boasted an 8-0 record. Schilling, at 7-1, wasn't far behind. Terry Mulholland was 7-5, Danny Jackson, 6-2, and Ben Rivera, 5-3.

JOHNNY PODRES, 1993 PITCHING COACH: "Our starting pitching is what won it for us that year. Well, actually, it was three things. Our pitchers pitched like hell, our hitters hit like hell, and Fregosi managed like hell."

That's as solid a baseball trio as Tinkers-to-Evers-to-Chance. But as simple as Podres makes it sound, the Phillies started the season off with all their guns blazing. There were practically no misfires. The Phillies showed strength in many areas of predicted weakness. Going into the season, the starters, aside from Terry Muholland, were unproven. Greene and Schilling each had only one excellent major-league season under his belt. Ben Rivera was an unknown, and many considered Danny Jackson washed up. But the starters got on the same page—and it wasn't only the starters. The middle relief corps of West and Larry Andersen was reliable and steady. Furthermore, the closer, the Wild Thing, Mitch Williams, had already salvaged nineteen games.

PODS

"I give so much credit to Pods for my own success," Curt Schilling insists. "Pods really built up my confidence that year and helped that pitching staff reach its potential.

Johnny Podres, pitching coach for the '93 Phils, was no stranger to fame. His license plate, MVP 55, is a call-back to his greatest success. Pods, as he was known, won the first *Sport Magazine* World Series MVP Award back in 1955, when he won two games and pitched a 2-0 shutout in Game 7 to lock up Brooklyn's first-ever World Series title. Podres relied on guile. As one of the game's craftiest change-of-speed artists, Podres ended his 15-year major-league pitching career with a sparkling 148-116 record and a 3.68 ERA. In Brooklyn's final season, Pods hurled a league-leading six shutouts and had the league's lowest ERA, 2.68.

LARRY ANDERSEN: "Pods was the best I ever saw at instilling confidence in pitchers. No matter how bad things were going, Pods told you the same thing when he walked out to the mound, 'You're throwing good. Keep bringing it, you got good stuff.' When Doc [Mark Davis] came over, he was out there one night getting shelled. Doc had nothing that day and knew it. Pods came to the mound and gave his standard pep talk, 'You're throwing great, kid. You got great stuff.' Doc just stared at him and asked, 'Pods, what *friggin'* game are *you* lookin' at?'"

While the pitching staff was humming, Fregosi was handling his 25-man squad masterfully. He kept everybody ready, fresh, and mentally charged—just as he had vowed to do in February.

HARRY KALAS, PHILLIES BROADCASTER: "Fregosi did something no one else seems capable of pulling off successfully nowadays. Fregosi kept three different platoons going: Duncan and Morandini at second base, Chamberlain and Eisenreich in right field, and Incaviglia and Thompson in left. They all would have loved to play full-time, and most other guys would have squawked. But Fregosi kept everybody happy. The way he used those guys, they were always rested—always at the top of their game. The team kept winning, and the guys being platooned cheered their counterparts on. Everybody waited his turn and then performed great when it came up."

Fregosi had Lady Luck on his side as well. Whenever one of his charges got hurt, his replacement filled in spectacularly. Early in June, Kim Batiste pulled a hamstring after Juan Bell was released, and Mariano Duncan was summoned to replace him. Unfortunately—or not—Duncan was sick. Though he had a slight fever, the happy-go-lucky Dominican native played gamely and rapped out two hits. Next day, still woozy, he knocked out four more safeties. Coach Larry Bowa ordered both guys, "Stay sick." The point was that no matter who got hurt, the Phillies were lucky enough to have somebody step up for another Phillies win. However, as Branch Rickey once said, "Luck is the residue of success." As Jayson Stark and many '93 Phils point out, nothing succeeds like success, and the predator Phillies were in a feeding frenzy.

Batiste returned to health in time to fill in for the injured Dave Hollins, who was forced out of a 7-6 win over the Mets on June 10 with a fractured hook of the hamate bone in his wrist. Headley had been playing with a sore right wrist for almost a month. But a bad-hop grounder in infield practice at Shea that day finally forced him to the sidelines. In his absence, Batty, as Batiste was known, filled in admirably. With cleanup hitter Hollins out of action, the Phils still managed to take the next three from the Mets. They also took the following game against the Expos at Olympic Stadium.

Prior to the Expos series, John Wetteland, Montreal's superb closer, had verbalized what many baseball people expected. "Philadelphia will fold and take a skid. They're not the powerhouse they're made out to be." When asked today about Wetteland's comment, Terry Mulholland, who started and won the opener in the Expos series, explains the Phillie attitude.

TERRY MULHOLLAND: "To be honest, I don't remember anything about that incident. I may have said something, but it really doesn't matter. Wetteland wasn't my teammate, and I really wouldn't care what he said, so if he or any of the Expos had a problem, it was their problem, not ours."

After Mulholland won the series opener, the Phillies dropped the next two to the Expos. They returned to the Vet on June 17 to face the Marlins and flubbed the opener for a third straight loss. They hadn't lost more than two in a row all season. However, Philly didn't lose faith. By mid-June, the Quaker City was careening along on the Phillie bandwagon with a full dose of Phillie Phever. After the three losses, the Phillies did not disappoint their city. They took the next three from Florida. Record crowds cheered them on—185,679 fans packed into the Vet for the four-game Marlins series. On June 20 against the Marlins, the Phillies extended their Sunday win streak to eleven wins against no losses. When asked to explain their Sabbath success, Kruk chimed, "Hell, I don't know. Most people in baseball don't know what day of the week it is. I know this team doesn't." Fregosi had a different spin: "Clean living." Clean living notwithstanding, Fregosi was taking no chances. The superstitious manager continued to wear his heavy warmup jacket in the dugout on those Sunday day games, despite Philly's oppressive summer heat.

Despite the doubts of Wetteland and others, the Phillies had busted out of the perennial New York shadow by late June. Their newfound celebrity and stature surprised them. John Kruk, a fixture on *This Week in Baseball*, was number one in the All-Star balloting. Kruk's reaction? "It's exciting. I mean, Galarraga's [Colorado's first baseman who ended up leading the NL with a .370 average] hitting what? About .700 or something? So it's amazing the fans want to see me play. It's scary. What's our society coming to?"

HARRY KALAS: "People loved to come to the park and watch Kruk play. He was the idol or inspiration of every overweight slow-pitch softball player in the country. What a great character and what a plus for the sport of baseball!"

Kruk wasn't the only Phillie getting national acclaim. Dutch Daulton had copped almost double the votes that Benito Santiago had. Santiago, who was running second in the balloting, had started three of the four previous four All-Star games. Lenny Dykstra was running fourth in the NL among outfielders. All in all, things were going well in Phillieland. The Phillies organization, in late June, awarded new contracts to the chief architects of the New Phillies, Jim Fregosi and Lee Thomas.

The Phillies continued to roll, taking two of three from Atlanta to close out their home stand. Danny Jackson and Ben Rivera were the winning pitchers in those contests. Both DJ and Big Ben had identical 7-3 records at that point.

On June 25, the club headed out on a seven-game road trip. The trip would prove disastrous, striking the first sour notes of the feel-good summer. After winning the first game against Pittsburgh at Three Rivers Stadium, they dropped the next three in the Steel City before traveling to St. Louis, where Darren Daulton flexed his leadership muscles and perhaps saved the season.

The St. Louis series shaped up as a crucial matchup. The Phillies rode into the Gateway City with a seven and a half-game lead, but as Wetteland had expressed earlier, many opponents still weren't convinced the Phillies had enough pop to keep playing at the same level. "They're ripe for the taking," Cardinal catcher Tom Pagnotti was crowing after the Phillies lost the opener of the series.

DENNIS MENKE, 1993 PHILLIES COACH: "I don't think that St. Louis club respected us early that year. But as the season wore on, they gained a lot of respect. Gregg Jefferies told me later that the Cardinals were really intimidated by our team that year. We had some big, strong guys on that team. I think we had the advantage coming out of the gate. After finishing last the year before, a lot of teams kind of didn't expect us to be for real. By this point in the season, that was changing. Teams were gunning for the Phillies. We were getting a lot of national attention, and fans were showing up in every city to see guys like Kruk and Inky and Lenny. So as we got to the second half, teams were playing tougher against us."

Never one to lose his sense of humor in bad times, Larry Andersen, along with rest of the bullpen crew, figured they knew how to stop the team's downward spiral. They found the root of the team's woes.

LARRY ANDERSEN: "Mark Davis had given me a T-shirt that read, 'At 40, the first thing to go is the memory. I can't remember what's next.' I wore it under my jersey during batting practice for two nights. We lost both those games. So we had the bullpen crew soak the shirt in rubbing alcohol and burn it. We saved the ashes in a cup and scattered them over the bullpen mound when we got back home."

The bullpen's brainchild actually worked for a night. The Phillies, behind Ben Rivera (who upped his record to a glittery 8-3), outclubbed the Cards 13-10. After splitting the first two games, however, the Phillies, for the first time, appeared to lose their macho—with the same disastrous results as Austin Powers losing his mojo. The Cards drubbed them 9-3 as Tommy Greene suffered his second loss against nine wins. The following night, Schilling was shellacked 14-5. Dutch Daulton, after the game, publicly blasted his teammates. "I've been on some bad teams, and I've been a very, very bad player in the past. But tonight, that's the most embarrassed I've ever been."

In the course of a few weeks, Greene and Schilling, the two guys who had been pitching like Supermen, were suddenly pitching as though the ball were stuffed with kryptonite.

The Phillies came back to the Vet for Fourth of July weekend. They were still ahead by five games, but in only half a month, they had squandered more than half of the 11 1/2-game lead they had built by June 14. At that pace, they would tumble from atop the National League East by the All-Star break. The Ghost of 1964 started to haunt the Phillies..

MILT THOMPSON: "Sure, we heard about 1964, but most of the guys weren't even born in 1964. We never had a sense of panic, which is why we didn't go through long losing streaks. We didn't really have long winning streaks either. We had what I call a veteran mentality. That means so much to a team over the long haul. We took the season one game at a time and fought to win every series, one series at a time. We never doubted ourselves even when others started to lose faith in us."

Milt was right. The clubhouse was filled with guys whom, as Dutch Daulton said, "you wanted in your foxhole." Sitting in the Ghetto, the Phillies had one of the most effective—though most unlikely—panic suppressors in the game. John Kruk didn't panic. Krukker was a ballplayer and professional sport's most recognizable Everyman—a guy with a truck driver's body who zinged Rodney Dangerfield-type barbs to all fields, the same way he hit line drives. Kruk was a guy who jumped on pretentiousness like a hanging curve ball.

Play That Funky Music

I'm a big music buff. I may not remember to take the trash out on Mondays (or is it Tuesdays?), but I can remember the year that Springsteen's "Born to Run" came out and I can recite all the lyrics to Don McLean's "American Pie."

A lot of songs transport me back to 1993. There was a definite soundtrack for that Enchanted Season, as Philly columnist Bill Lyon calls it.

At the beginning of the season, the players collected over $3000 for the CD fund. That's CD as in compact disc, not certificate of deposit. Whenever they lost what they considered a good-luck song, it was almost as big a crisis as running out of beer. *Almost.*

One of the clubhouse attendants had to rush out, buy a new one, and have it ready to spin when the Phillies came off the field after the game. We went through about six copies of the Spin Doctors' "Pocket Full of Kryptonite." Guys would sneak them home for themselves or leave them in road locker rooms, and we'd need replacements. Tower Records loved the Phillies that year.

"Spin Doctors was our group," funkmaster Larry Andersen recollects. "After every win, we'd put on 'Two Princes' and play it over and over."

This gang of Phillies liked their music loud—so loud they blew out four boom boxes by midseason. Maybe that explains why Mitch couldn't hear any boos. Mitch and Curt finally put an end to the technical difficulties by purchasing a state-of-the-art Bose speaker system that was permanently mounted to the ceiling of the clubhouse. It's still there. They also bought a portable sound system that they packed for road trips. That system put out enough sound to drive a headbangers crowd out of the Vet.

"If we forgot to pack that sound system for a road trip, there would be hell to pay," says Phil Sheridan, a clubhouse attendant. When he wasn't making food and CD runs, Phil and some of the other clubbies took private dance lessons in the clubhouse from Mariano Duncan. When Mariano wasn't playing Jon Secada music, he was firing up the song "Here Come the Hotsteppers," an obscure number that barely dented the charts that year. By the end of the season, Mariano had everybody in the clubhouse doing the Hotsteppers line dance (as gracefully as a chorus line of Frankensteins dancing underwater in diving bells).

That '93 Phillies soundtrack also included live musical (for want of a more appropriate term) performances by Harry Kalas, who did (and continues to do) the play-by-play for the Phils in '93. Harry's mellifluous voice made him the Ford C. Frick Award recipient in the Hall of Fame. That's mellifluous *speaking* voice. A great speaking voice does not necessarily translate into a great singing voice. It might work that way for Lou Rawls and Barry White, but not for Harry. That did not stop him from unabashedly breaking into song in the clubhouse, in the charter plane, or at piano bars in every major- league city in the country—anywhere he could find a listener who had imbibed enough.

After consuming a few adult beverages, the team often joined Harry as he kicked into his personal anthem, "High Hopes." They discovered that when they sang along, they couldn't hear Harry as much. Unfortunately, however, when the team members added their voices, it made matters worse.

HARRY KALAS: "There's a funny story about that song. Well, actually, it's anything but funny. In '92, we were playing a series against the Mets and Wally Backman, and some of his friends took me out to this great little piano bar in New York. Well, I got up, grabbed the microphone, and started singing 'High Hopes' which, I guess you could say, is my theme song. I'm in the middle of the song, and some guy comes stumbling in off the street, puts a knife to his wrists, and commits suicide right there in the bar as I'm singing 'High Hopes.' One of Wally's friends was a narcotics agent, and he kind of shuttled us all out the back door. I went back to my hotel room and immediately called my wife, Eileen. I told her the whole story and then said, 'Eileen, is my singing *that* bad?'"

Note to self: Ask Harry how Eileen answered.

Note to self: Better ask Eileen instead.

That '93 soundtrack included some definitive fan favorites, too. The season's anthem was easily Tag Team's "Whoomp There It Is," a little hip-hop ditty that for some reason pumped the Philly crowd up. A group called 95 South put out a song called "Whoot There It Is" the same year. Apparently, so much musical ground was left uncovered by the Tag Team version that a second version *with the very same lyrics* was necessary, except *Whoomp* was changed to *Whoot*.

Knowing that I was putting the club's harmony at risk, I polled the team. Which version did the Phillies prefer? Or in Meat Loaf's terms: What's it gonna be, boy; whoomp or whoot? The Phils turned out to be Tag Teamers—practically a unanimous choice. Problem solved.

I've got to admit there's a certain feeling of power associated with choosing the tunes for 50,000 people. One night, Tug McGraw poked his head into the control room before a game and said, "Hey, Tom, my son just cut an album, and I was hoping you might play one or two of his songs during the game."

Tug pushed a cassette case under my nose. I took one look at it and spotted Tim McGraw wearing a cowboy hat. Country music ... yuck!

"S-u-u-u-re, Tug, I'll see what I can do," I lied.

When Tug left I showed the tape to the guys in the booth. "Tug's son is singing country music ... what a joke!"

I wasted no time throwing the cassette into the "Never Play It" heap. What an idiot! If I had been in Memphis in the fifties, I would have been the guy telling Elvis, "Go back to truck driving, Kid. You'll never make it as a singer." Of course, it would have been a different story if Tim's wife, Faith Hill, with or without a cowboy hat, had been on the cassette cover. Yeah, put this one over there with those Lynne Austin photos.

The Krukker

"You could wake John Kruk up at 3 a.m. and he could hit a 95 mph fastball, although that's misleading. You normally didn't have to wake Kruk up at 3 a.m.—9 a.m., yeah, but not 3."
— *Lee Thomas, 1993 Phils General Manager*

See ball, hit ball. That was John Kruk's strength as a hitter. Actually, it's his strength as a person too. John Kruk keeps life simple, same as hitting. The Krukker never set out to set the world on fire, so he doesn't waste his life in a frenzied, all-consuming search for kindling. John would rather just sit by a modest fire and smell the roses—or maybe the hops. He is a master of taking each day as it comes, of accepting himself for what he is, and of not taking himself too seriously.

Sometimes those kinds of phrases attach to the world-weary, or the downtrodden, or the mediocre. John Kruk is none of the above. John was the ideal representation, the lasting Everyman and icon of the '93 team. He was utterly absorbed with one short-term objective—win a baseball game today. Baseball and society in general have shelved that baby-step approach to success. It's old-fashioned. Kids nowadays obsess about getting the BMW and swimming pool right out of high school. John Kruk wanted neither. In high school it's possible he didn't know what a BMW was, and although he didn't call a swimming pool a "see-ment pond," owning one was probably not on his radar screen—not that Kruk gave much thought to radar screens either.

JOHN KRUK: "I grew up in New Creek, West Virginia, which had a population of about 500 people. I graduated from Keyser High School in 1979 and ended up going to Allegheny Junior College. I hated school. I wanted to play baseball. A scout watched us and offered me $500 to sign with San Diego. I asked him, "Where the hell is San Diego?" So I signed, and they gave me a plane ticket to a place called Walla Walla, Washington. I got there and walked into my room. My roommate was already there. He stood up, we talked for a couple minutes, and he said, 'You haven't seen many black people, have you?' And I said, 'Actually, I haven't, to be honest.' So he said, 'Well, my name's Tony Gwynn.' And that's how I started in professional ball."

That was in 1981. The Krukker batted .242 in 157 at-bats that season. Afterwards, he hung around the minors another four seasons, topping .300 every year and averaging .327 for his minor-league career. San Diego brought him up in 1986, and he hit .309 as a rookie. He was reunited with his old roomie,

Tony Gwynn, and the "see ball, hit ball" guy from West Virginia became a lot savvier than his image would lead you to believe.

JOHN KRUK: "Tony would go out early to the park and hit. He didn't like to take normal batting practice. He thought he couldn't see the ball as well, and he would form bad habits hitting under those conditions. Tony was a real student of hitting. He got me started watching films of pitchers and of myself hitting. As I got older, I used films more and more. When I got to the Phillies, I lived in the video room. That Video Dan is so talented—he should be doing bigger things. No matter what I asked him for, he came up with it. I'd go back and watch my last at-bat against a new pitcher coming in—I'd ask Dan to have the clip ready, and he would. I hated cages and tees. They're worthless. I needed to go out to the field and hit."

KEVIN STOCKER: "John was crafty, so much smarter than people know. And he used that to his advantage. He set pitchers up. He'd purposely miss pitches he could handle, like high fastballs, when he knew the pitcher was watching. Then he'd get it in the game and slam it."

Kruk stayed with San Diego from '86 through '89. He batted a lusty .313 in 1987 but slipped to .241 in 1988. He was batting .184 in 76 at-bats in 1989 when he was traded with Randy Ready for Chris James.

JOHN KRUK: "I was happy to come to Philadelphia. In San Diego, the atmosphere at the ballpark is totally different. The fans there don't really care that much that there's a game going on like they do in Philly. I'd find my mind wandering out there. In Philly, the fans make you concentrate. And the team we had here in '93—we were made for Philly fans. We were like hockey and football players playing baseball. That's another reason I have so much respect for Tony Gwynn—putting up the numbers he did in that quiet atmosphere—the guy's amazing."

Kruk had a renaissance in Philly right away. In '89, he raised the .184 average he had with the Padres to a seasonal average of .300 by hitting at a .313 clip in Phillie pinstripes. More importantly, the Krukker became a charter member of the "new Phillies," the throwback guys with nothing but baseball on their agenda.

JOHN KRUK: "When I came to Philly, I used to sit in the trainer's room after the game and listen to Von Hayes and Darren arguing over how to call a game and what pitches Dutch should have been calling. I sat there and thought this was a pretty good thing. You learn a lot by hashing out the game that way. It got to the point that the pitchers were afraid to come into the trainer's room to ice 'cause they knew they'd get grilled. And that was a good thing. It's like, 'Let's air it out and talk.' That's what we did here. They didn't do that in San Diego. They didn't do it in Chicago, either, when I went there in '95.

"By the time Milt and Inky and Larry Andersen arrived in '93, there was nobody on the team who wasn't a real baseball guy. Look, I'd never ask that team to rewire my house. I'd be dead. But we all knew baseball. That's all we knew."

A lot was written that year about the Krukker's unorthodox appearance. He had the clout of a slugger and the look of a sluggard. But John's appearance belies his talent and intelligence. Kruk is aware of that. Long ago, he learned to turn it to his advantage. He is often characterized, if not caricaturized, in mocking, loving, or cheeky terms—or any combination of the three. The Krukker lets unflattering words roll off his back. You get the sense that he understands that unflattering comments usually mask begrudging wonderment that a guy with his physique and appearance could pound out hits the way he did. Even the Krukker's swing was not heavy on style.

RUBEN AMARO: "Kruk would take some of the ugliest swings in the history of the game and end up with doubles. But the guy could hit, year in and year out. He had tremendous eye-hand coordination and a strong upper body, even though it wasn't obvious."

MITCH WILLIAMS: "I've watched John Kruk hit since we were both signed. He was 17 and I was 18. Krukkie signed for $500 and a gift certificate to a Waffle House, but his focus at the plate was like a gymnast's, no matter what he looked like. In fact, he could only hit fat. After '91, he went to a fat-reduction place in LA, and came back trim. And he stopped getting hits. He walked by Fregosi one time after making an out, and Fregosi told him, 'Get fat again.' So he did."

MICKEY MORANDINI: "The Krukker? Horrible body, great hitter."

The Krukker's older brothers, Joe and Tom, said their kid brother became an opposite-field hitter because their mom had a garden in right field, and whenever he pulled the ball, the ground rules said it was an out. As kids, the Kruk boys played baseball, football, and basketball all the time.

HARRY KALAS: "John was a good basketball player in high school. He was just a good athlete, and he was a tremendous entertainer. You look at him and laugh. He was the guy on the field that the fans couldn't take their eyes off— a truly unique ballplayer."

People *couldn't* take their eyes off Kruk. Once he was unwillingly thrust into the limelight, the Krukker turned out to be one of baseball's wittiest homespun philosophers and humorists. He mixed wit with wisdom and slapstick and gunned down pretentiousness like a veritable Will Rogers of the diamond. He captivated the country at the All-Star game with his comments and demeanor. He did the same thing in several Letterman appearances. Kruk was the Rodney Dangerfield of the clubhouse, zinging everyone with his one-liners and claiming he got no respect. Even his manager told the press, "The thing that disgusts me is he's my two-year-old's favorite ballplayer."

What was refreshing about Kruk was that his appearance was not a statement. He came across as baseball's most ingenuous personality since Mark Fidrych. Kruk's appearance was slovenly not because he was contemptuous, not because he was trying to flaunt convention, not because he was trying to gain attention, but simply because appearance wasn't important to him. "Look" and "image" meant nothing. In the heyday of Garrison Keilor's Lake Woebegone, Keilor regaled how liberating and redemptive it was that the people in Lake Woebegone didn't have to bother with having a lifestyle. Such was the case with Kruk. His lifestyle was simple: go to the ballpark win a game. See ball, hit ball.

During the National League Championship Series, Kruk told the press, "I'd like to get a haircut and shave, but guys like Hollins and Daulton won't let me. They say, 'We'll kill you if you get a haircut. You can't shave or get a haircut as long as we stay in first place.' Hey, when guys that big tell you that, you'd better do it."

John Kruk was simply a ballplayer, a humble guy who downplayed himself into the hearts of fans everywhere. David Letterman was fascinated with Krukker as a guest, and Chris Farley, cast as John Kruk, along with the rest of the *SNL* troupe, spoofed the '93 squad on *Saturday Night Live*. Kruk was flabbergasted at his own celebrity.

JOHN KRUK: "I know Chris Farley's brothers—one's fat like he was, and the other is thin. They told me Chris loved me. I can never figure that out. I'm always kind of intimidated with big-name people, actors and the like. I was at an event once with David Wells, and he knows everybody, goes right up to the celebrities. I kind of hang back. I'm always amazed when somebody famous comes over to me and tells me they're thrilled to meet me. Why? And, as for the Letterman show, the first time I was on, Leigh Tobin (Phils publicity manager in '93), came down and told me Letterman called. It was an off day for us, and I said I didn't want to go all the way up to New York, but they talked me into it. David Letterman came down to my dressing room beforehand. Everybody there told me he was a real fan and anxious to meet me. They said it was unusual for him to visit like that."

PAUL HAGAN: "John never wanted to do Letterman! Vuke had to take him aside and tell him to go on. Of course, once he was on the show, Krukkie was a natural—just a great guest. But John never considered himself important enough to be taken seriously."

DARREN DAULTON: "The truth is, John Kruk considered himself a ballplayer. He was out to win ballgames, not for endorsements. He could have made a lot more than he did. We all could have. But he didn't care. He only cared about doing his job."

There's an arcane notion from the archives of old-fashioned America. How many members of the corporate world watch a parade of pretenders whisk through their departments, promoted to jobs they know nothing about and care about less? How many managers use their jobs merely as a stepping stone, a springboard to something bigger, at the expense of their current performance? Kruk is portrayed as the hero of the truck driver, the slow-pitch softball player, and the Everyman out-of-shape wannabe because of his physique and slovenliness. But subconsciously, people connect with the ingenuous nature of this guy—his blunt candor, his comfort, rather than frustration and rage, at his own humanity and limitations. In a sophisticated age of infinite data—often more confusing than convincing—John Kruk chooses to keep things simple. And he succeeds because he seems to have the instinct and wherewithal to hone in on the relevant data.

John Kruk is, in the words of Jim Fregosi, "the worst card player ever." And in 1993, life dealt John a bad hand. Right after the season ended, the Krukker was diagnosed with testicular cancer. Ever since, he has played his cards courageously and wisely. When he showed up in the clubhouse on opening day 1994, his teammates "Krukked" him. They all wore T-shirts that had John's face on the front with an inscription underneath: "If I can't play, I'm taking my ball and going home!" The Krukker was introduced to a sellout crowd to thunderous applause that day, and then, in Hollywood fashion, he pounded out a hit in his first at-bat, followed by another one a few innings later. But the disease abbreviated his career, though his statistics don't indicate it. He hit .302 that season. The following year he was with the White Sox, and in midseason at age 34, he decided to call it a career. As he had done 1169 times before, Kruk stepped to the plate and lashed out a safety before walking away from the game he couldn't believe they paid him to play. He retired with a .300 career batting average.

The Krukker is still the Krukker. He's got a lovely new wife, Melissa, and a new son Kyle now. He's in good health. He's given up smoking and drinking, but he's safeguarded his quirky personality, his outlook, and his insight. Once John realized the situation, that he had to make some lifestyle adjustments, he made them. He understood what he had to do. He did it, and he's a happy man. See ball, hit ball.

The Sensitivity Trainer

John Kruk was an admitted slob. He was Oscar Madison, Pig Pen, and Oscar the Grouch all rolled into one. Hey, don't get me wrong, the Phanatic is no Felix Unger either, but the Krukker took slovenliness to new heights. The dapper Mariano Duncan—he of the designer suits and tailored threads—used to watch John walk by and shake his head. "That guy Kruk, he's got to be buying his clothes from K-Mart." Kruk's locker had the look of a trailer park after a Category 5 tornado came ripping through it. Clubbie Phil Sheridan used to find half-eaten sandwiches, old newspapers, dirty laundry, and other "goodies" scattered by and in his locker. One day, Phil found $2,500 lying around Krukker's locker. John didn't know where it came from.

FRANK COPPENBARGER: "John Kruk was an equipment manager's worst nightmare. You needed a bulldozer to find stuff in his locker. He used to get undressed on the way to the shower, just dropping his clothes in a trail along the way. He'd break bats constantly during batting practice if he wasn't swinging the bat real well. One day Fregosi came up to me and said, 'Hey, Frank, John said he's out of bats and you didn't order him any more.' And I said, 'I just ordered him a box of bats, but he keeps breaking them on the dugout steps and tossing them into the stands during BP!' Kruk rode me hard. We're friends now, but back then, there were times I wasn't sure if I was going to go back to the clubhouse the next day for work. If I didn't have a wife and a family to support, who knows ... "

PETE INCAVIGLIA: "Johnny used to walk into the clubhouse and scream at the top of his lungs, 'FRANK!' It used to drive Frank nuts. I remember one day, I really thought Frank was going to have a nervous breakdown. Me and Dutch had to go into to Frank's room and calm him down."

JOHN KRUK: "Yeah, I was pretty rough on Frank. I used to complain about everything. I don't think Frank and I talked for seven years. I remember Darren taking me aside and telling me to lighten up on Frank. Darren said, 'John, you don't understand, he really can't take it!' It just never occurred to me that people could be sensitive."

Night Owls

"I remember Lenny saying to Dutch one night, 'I'm gonna be the lead story on Sports Center *tonight.' Dutch said, 'Yeah? You feel that good, huh?' Lenny looked at him and said, 'I think I'm gonna have a heart attack.' That's the way we were. We ran hard on and off the field. I'm surprised one of us didn't have a heart attack that year. We had a lot of fun playing good hard baseball and competing on the field, but we had just as much fun as friends off the field. You could ask a lot of bellmen around the league at the hotels where we stayed. They'd tell you when the Phillies came to town, we never really got to our rooms till probably 5 or 6 in the morning anyways. There were a lot more sunrises than sunsets as far as getting into the hotel room. But that's the kind of club we were. We played hard on the field and off."*
— Terry Mulholland

Lightning in a bottle. That's the explanation a lot of people give for that 1993 pennant. By that reasoning, up and down the roster, the Phillies players all must have had "career years." Everything all came together for one brief shining moment, for some inexplicable reason, or so the argument goes. And it's a credible argument; however, the data supporting the argument is far from compelling.

A few members of the 1993 Phillies *did* have career years—a very few. However, most did not, so ... well, consider the following and you be the judge.

If you compare the squad's individual 1993 numbers to their career stats, about six different categories emerge.

1) Guys who actually did have career years.

A "career year," as we'll take the liberty of defining it, means that, in 1993, someone put up numbers that he never approached any other season. Kevin Stocker, David West, and Kim Batiste fall squarely into this category. But that's it.

After reporting to the Phillies from the minors in early July, Kevin Stocker hit .324 and fielded his position superbly. He never hit anywhere near .324 again. Although he reached a lofty .299 with Tampa Bay in 1999, the best he could do any other season was .273, which, itself, far exceeded his career average of .254

David West posted his career-best winning percentage (.600) in 1993, which far exceed his career winning percentage of .449. David's 2.92 ERA in '93 was well under his career ERA of 4.66. Westie appeared in 76 games in '93. In a ten-year career, he never appeared in more than 31 games in any one season. In fact, in a major-league career that spanned ten years, David made 37 percent of his mound appearances in 1993.

Kim Batiste played five years in the majors. He played 251 games and batted .234. In '93, he averaged .282 and hit 5 home runs (half his lifetime total). Kim had a career year, getting some huge hits and supplying plenty of pop as a role player.

2) Guys who had their best year in a good career.

Lenny Dykstra had a sensational year, his best ever for hits, doubles, triples, and home runs. Let's not forget, however, that Lenny's career and talent merits him the number 44 spot among all the center fielders who ever played the game in the *New Bill James Historical Abstract*. Agree with the ranking or not (isn't that what baseball is all about?), Lenny is listed ahead of guys like Hall of Famer Lloyd Waner, Garry Maddox, Mickey Rivers, Bill Bruton, Paul Blair, and Brady Anderson, to name a few. Admittedly, the Dude reached some heights that season that he barely approached any other year. He worked 129 bases on balls, which led the league. His next best season for walks was 89 in 1990, and in a 12-year major-league career, he never drew more than 68 walks in any other season. His 19 home runs in 1993 almost doubled his next best effort (10 in 1987). His 143 runs led the majors in '93. In only one other season did he top the century figure. However, before coming to Philly, Lenny was platooned in New York, which severely lowered his stats, and after 1993, injuries hampered his production. Nonetheless, Lenny had enjoyed considerable success before 1993. He had been named a starter on the 1990 All-Star squad—a year he finished with a glittery .325 batting average. That average dwarfed his .305 in 1993. Yes, his best season was 1993, but no one would argue that the Dude was a flash in the pan, or that he could never again match his '93 numbers if injuries hadn't plagued him.

Pete Incaviglia matched or topped the 24 round-trippers he whacked in 1993 in three other campaigns. His '93 batting average of .274 was a career best. Without question, '93 was Inky's most productive year insofar as home runs per at-bat. He homered every 15.33 at-bats in 1993. His next best season in that department was his rookie year, when he hit 30 homers, one out every 18 at-bats. Had he hit home runs in his rookie season with the same frequency as in '93, his total would have been 35 instead of 30—not an earth-shattering leap. Furthermore, in a 12-year career, Inky blasted 206 round-trippers for an average of about 17 per year. Those 24 in 1993 were hardly an outlier.

3) Guys who had a better-than-average year but had other equally good years.

Dave Hollins's numbers in 1992 and 1993 were practically identical. In fact, they *were* identical in runs scored (104), triples (4), and RBIs (93). He actually hit far more home runs (50 percent more) in 1992 (27) than in 1993 (18), but he worked a few more walks in 1993 (85 versus 76 in 1992) and hit a couple more doubles (30 versus 28) in '93. His batting average both years was effectively the same (.270 in 1993 and .273 in 1992). If you examine Dave's career *in toto*, 1992 and 1993 combine for 40 percent of his lifetime home runs. But again, Hollins was injury-plagued. A healthy Dave Hollins was capable of duplicating his 1993 performance. He had done it the previous year, which *was*, in fact, his career year.

Tommy Greene notched his career-best winning percentage in 1993. However, like Hollins, his overall numbers were almost identical to 1991, when Jethro (Tommy's nickname) was 13-7 on a team with a losing record, with a 3.38 ERA in 207 innings pitched. In 1993, he was 16-4, with a 3.42 ERA in 200 innings pitched. Like Hollins, injuries hampered Tommy's promising career.

Dutch Daulton's most productive stretch occurred within the 1992-1995 time frame. Dutch had spent several years prior to 1992 battling career-threatening injuries. He had a breakout season that year, leading the National League in RBIs with 109 and batting .270. His production in 1993 fell off slightly to 105 RBIs with a .257 batting average. Dutch even chipped in with 11 stolen bases in '93 despite banged-up knees and other hurts (actually, Dutch was 50 out of 60 lifetime as a base stealer, which is *the fifth best stolen base percentage in baseball history*). In 1994, the strike-curtailed season, Dutch hit .300, hammered 15 round-trippers and drove in 56 in only 257 at-bats. He again started the All-Star game in 1995, but his homers declined to 9 and his RBIs to 55. By the end of 1997, Dutch had called it quits.

Wes Chamberlain's career was short. He played only 385 games and batted only 1,262 times. Wes hit 12 home runs in 1993 with 45 RBIs, but he had hit 13 homers in 1991, with 50 RBIs. Those two years combine for 58 percent of his lifetime production. Wes never reached his full potential, but he was certainly capable of putting up the numbers he did in '91 and '93.

4) Guys who had a good year among many good years.

John Kruk, Mariano Duncan, and Jim Eisenreich all had solid seasons — seasons that were right in line with the balance of their careers. Kruk hit .316 in 1993, on the heels of .323 the year before. He closed his 10-year career with a .300 average. He hit 14 homers in 1993, well below his top power seasons. The Krukker twice reached the 20-home run mark.

Mariano Duncan hit a clutch .282 in '93, but he hit .306 for Cincinnati in 1990 when he led the league with 11 triples. He hit a whopping .340 for the Yankees in 1996. For Eisey, 1993, when he batted .318, was the first of four consecutive .300 seasons. In 1996, he soared to .361. In a 15-year career, Eisey swung for a .290 batting average, so 1993 was hardly a career season.

Ricky Jordan performed his backup role exceptionally, but his .289 average in 1993 was in the same neighborhood as his .281 career average.

Curt Schilling had a good year in 1993. His stats from the previous year were far more impressive, however. In the postseason, Schil established himself as one of the game's premier pitchers. He put together several seasons from the late nineties into the new century that far surpass what he did in 1993.

Mitch Williams ended 1993 with a 3.34 ERA, which is comparable to his lifetime 3.65 ERA. In Mitch's 1989 All-Star season as a Cub, his ERA was 2.76. In 1991, Mitch was 12-5 with a 2.34 ERA. He had seven more saves in '93 than in any other season; however, his setup men and the Phillies' potent offense had a lot to do with that.

Terry Mulholland had one of his better years, but '93 wasn't out of sync with the rest of his career. Terry won 16, 13, and 12 games respectively in 1991, 1992, and 1993. His ERA in 1993 was 3.25, which is comparable to the three preceding years (3.34, 3.61, and 3.81, respectively).

5) Guys who had subpar years.

Mickey Morandini hit only .247. He followed the '93 campaign with .292 in '94 and .283 (and a berth on the All-Star squad) in '95 , .295 in '97, and .296 in '98. His '93 batting average was his *lowest* in seven complete seasons as a Phil.

Milt Thompson's .262 average in '93 was sandwiched between .307 in '91, .293 in '92, and .274 in '94. Milt hit .300 three different times in a 13-year career in which he averaged .274.

Ben Rivera ended his career with a 23-17 log and a 4.52 ERA. In 1993, he was 13-9 with a 5.02 ERA. In '92, Ben was 7-4 with a 3.07 ERA—he gave up two fewer runs per game in 1992 than in 1993. His final year was 1994 when he pitched only 38 innings.

6) The "I can't believe those guys had a year like that left in them" contingent.

Danny Jackson actually had two great years left in him. After his brilliant 23-8 season with Cincinnati in 1988, Danny hit hard times due to injuries. From 1989-1992, DJ was 25-35. Most thought he was washed up, but DJ came through with a 12-11 record in 1993 followed by 14-6, and an All-Star slot, in 1994.

Larry Andersen's numbers were not declining prior to 1993; nor was his age. LA turned forty in May of 1993, thus many were set to write him off prematurely—rather than immaturely, as Larry would prefer. In 1991 and 1992, with Houston, LA was 3-4 and 1-1 respectively, with ERAs of 2.30 and 3.34. However, nobody expected him to own the '93 staff's lowest ERA. LA did call it quits after 1994, when his ERA jumped to 4.41, well above his 3.15 career ERA.

No, saying the Phillies all had career years in 1993 is too facile an explanation for what was going on in Philadelphia that year. The more interesting question to pose is: why did it *seem* as though everyone had a career year? Or, if you insist that they all had career years, then *why* so?

DARREN DAULTON: "I never learned so much about the game as I did that year from my teammates. We played intelligently. We worked everything to our advantage, set other teams up, intimidated them. Those kinds of things won lots of ballgames."

JIM EISENREICH: "I never learned how to be patient at the plate till I came to this team. I changed my approach to hitting. That's why I had my best years here. I wasn't patient in Minnesota or Kansas City. I'd see three pitches in three at-bats. But I studied Lenny and Dutch and Krukker here. I saw how they worked pitchers and made pitchers come to them. I saw how that helped everyone in the lineup. I learned the fine points of the game by constantly talking game situations and rehashing games. That clubhouse environment really helped players improve."

Fregosi encouraged his "clubhouse rats" to hang around, to discuss baseball, to air out differences, to find out what made each other tick, and to come together as a team. As Fregosi told us, mouthing each word in measured staccato, *"They – were – a – team."*

The Clubhouse Hilton

None of us can complain about not having the opportunity to savor 1993. With all the extra-inning games, all the rain delays, Dykstra, Kruk, Hollins, and Daulton working long counts every at-bat, and Mitch's late-inning high-wire acts, our games were l-o-o-o-o-o-o-o-o-ng. Up in the control room, my cronies and I could occasionally get a little stir crazy. To pass the time, the Phanavision camera guys would scan the crowd, searching for the prettiest girls. Or they'd film cockroaches racing along the Astroturf, and we'd bet on them. We'd put phony "Welcome" messages up on the scoreboard. One night, I asked Joanne Hudson, one of our 1993 scoreboard operators, to put a special welcome on the board. My parents' church group was at the game, and I wanted to do something special for them. Joanne typed in "Welcome Mary, Mother of the Redeemer" and forgot to put the word "Church" at the end. Our director, Anthony Fanticola, looked up and said, "Wow, Mary, Mother of the Redeemer is here!" We were going to follow that up with a "Welcome Joseph T. Carpenter," where T. stood for The. But we didn't want to seem sacrilegious.

On some of those long nights when the game ended late, after we drank a few beers in the press club, no sooner did I get home than it was time to come back to the ball park again.

John Kruk had the right idea. Just like my kids, the Krukker seemed to like sleepovers. Every Saturday night, John made the Phillies' clubhouse his home, and he made the couch in Video Dan's room his bed.

VIDEO DAN STEPHENSON: "I'd come in every Sunday morning and I'd find the Krukker sprawled out on my couch asleep. I'd come in and wake John up. Then he'd make a beeline for the clubhouse and walk back in with three hot dogs and a couple of doughnuts at 9 o'clock in the morning.

"One morning, after I woke Krukkie up, he tells me he's not playing that day. He says Fregosi's giving him the day off and Ricky Jordan is getting the start. A few minutes later, he sneaks back into my room looking pale. I ask, 'What's up, John?' He squints and says, 'Ricky Jordan's got a pulled muscle. He can't go today.' I ask, 'So, what's the problem with that?' Krukker says, 'The problem is that I was in the clubhouse playing wiffle ball until 6:30 in the morning with the clubbies. *I pitched 97 innings last night* and now I can't even lift my arm above my shoulder.' I know it sounds like one of those *yeah-right* baseball tales, but John went three for four that day."

JOHN KRUK: "And one of those hits was a home run. I think what happened was that I was so tired that I couldn't even think. I just went out and played. It was like when Michael Jordan had the flu in that playoff game against the Utah Jazz and he was throwing up at halftime and he still scored like 40-something points. The only difference was he really *did* have the flu. I had the Budweiser flu."

The whole club rode Kruk about his personal Clubhouse Hilton, particularly since the team won so many games on Sundays. But Kruk took his Hilton gig on the road one time too. In San Francisco, after a 14-inning win against the Giants on July 23, Larry Andersen and Tee the Greene joined him for a slumber party in the visitor's locker room at Candlestick Park.

LARRY ANDERSEN: "I wanted to see what it'd be like rooming with Krukkie. Plus, we were playing a day game after a night game. We thought we could save at least an hour because we were supposed to catch an early bus back to the park the next morning. Anyway, we slept on the trainer's tables, which are vinyl and hardly have any cushion. Krukkie took the only blanket we had, so I didn't have a blanket or a sheet or nothing. Everytime I moved, my skin sort of stuck to the vinyl. At one point, Krukkie and I both woke up 'cause we heard something outside the trainer's room. It was Greenie fixing himself a midnight snack. When we got up that morning, we weren't a very pretty sight. Krukkie looked at me and said, 'My breath feels as ugly as you are old.' When the team started trickling in, they had a lot to say, things that weren't what you could call positive. Dutch said, 'Andy, now I know where the term 'death warmed over' comes from.'"

And I get the feeling LA won't room with Kruk again till hell freezes over.

Corporations use the term "synergy" when they talk about their corporate teams. Essentially, synergy means getting more production out of a team than the sum total of that team's parts. Synergy doesn't mean working harder. "Work smarter, not harder" is the corporate cliché. Synergy is about the team's being on the same page. On an assembly line, synergy means balancing the outputs at various stations, working like a team. It really doesn't matter if a guy at one station along the line is pushing out a hundred widgets a minute if one of his teammates only pushes out twenty.

When that happens, bad teams point fingers, get defensive, take sides, and spiral downward in productivity and morale. Good teams confront those problems. They separate personality from performance. They come up with solutions. *Rare* teams do those things with little or no management intervention. Fregosi set up that kind of model in his team's clubhouse. He called for his veteran guys to step up, analyze problems, confront them, and solve them for team benefit. He sponsored them when they counseled or admonished teammates on team issues and performance. "You shouldn't be swinging 3 and 0 in that situation," "You've got to hit the cutoff man on a play like that." The Phillies' atmosphere, their openness, their receptivity—and ultimately their trust and respect for each other—allowed messages to be delivered and received with no fallout or negative repercussions.

Like a good assembly line that adjusts and corrects problems at pinch points, the '93 Phillies could pick up for each other when one part of their "line" faltered. They didn't collectively hang their heads and give a game up because one part of their team's production failed. If the pitching stunk, the hitters took up the slack—and vice versa. They kept fighting together. They didn't point fingers. They kept creating chances and chasing them, till eventually, someone, somehow, came through—a new king for a day stepped up.

And they had so damn much infectious fun doing it. No Grinch could steal their Christmas. When they lost, they were still cutting up, still joking, still pie-ing, never ceasing to plot the next day's win together.

LARRY BOWA: "The personalities on that team didn't dwell on negatives. That's so important. A lot of teams never 'get it.' Those '93 guys loved baseball. They knew how and when to have fun, and they knew when to be serious.

"They didn't have the talent of our 1980 club. We had Rose, Schmidt, and Carlton in 1980. They had a different kind of air about them—those guys were Hall of Famers. That '93 team was like the Rocky story. They were a blue-collar, hard-working group with no limits. If you go position by position, they were good, but they weren't great. I could argue that our 1980 team was better than the 1993 team at *every* position, but the '93 guys hung together, and when the chips were down, they were always together and they usually came up big."

No, the guys on the '93 squad did not have career years. *It just seemed that way* because they came up big in so many critical situations. Each guy did at one point or another. Sure, they failed a lot, too. But they learned to survive on their second chances. If you let the Phillies hang around in a game, you were eventually going to get hurt. With that dynamic constantly at play, it's easy to think guys like Milt Thompson and Mickey Morandini had career years, when in fact, statistically, they had subpar years. But each member found ways to add value and picked an opportune moment to shine.

The '93 Phils were about teamwork and synergy. Fill an open, cohesive, fun atmosphere with people thirsting to improve, contribute, and succeed—and willing to sacrifice to help their teammates do the same—and you've got a system that any organization in the world would envy. These guys happen to be baseball players, but with their organizational dynamics in '93, they could have succeeded if they were punching out widgets in a factory instead of base hits in major-league ballpark.

The Phillies returned to the friendly confines of the Vet on Friday, July 2 to kick off a crucial four-game series with the Padres. Still reeling from the stinging losses in St. Louis, Darren Daulton called for a team meeting.

LARRY ANDERSEN: "I remember Dutch saying he didn't want to see guys hanging their heads. He said, 'I'll do anything for anybody in this room. If we're going to win this pennant, we can only do it together. And if we go down, we go down together too.' Schil spoke up and talked about the game he pitched in St. Louis. He said, 'Look, I embarrassed myself and I really embarrassed this ball club and it won't happen again.' Dude talked about how the team wasn't going out with the same intensity and intimidating people. I followed that up by saying the pitchers weren't pitching inside. We were letting hitters get comfortable. It was the most significant meeting all season."

And the beginning of the longest day. Before the meeting, the Phillies found out that popular reliever Mark Davis had been released and that Mike Williams had been called up from the minors.

The doubleheader that evening became a Philly version of *American Graffiti* —one long episodic night with thousands of follow-up yarns that stretch credibility and make for great barroom tales.

It was a dark and rainy night as Terry Mulholland took the hill for the Phils in the opener. The previous year, Mulholland had led the NL by stopping losing streaks twelve times. His magic was not working this particular evening, as the Pads bested the Phillies 5-2 in a soggy, rain-delayed match.

The Longest Day Begins

I remember how July 2—the longest day—started for me.

In '93, I used to travel to all the radio stations around Philadelphia and give away tickets and Phillies merchandise to promote the team. It was a great job, and the DJs loved the free stuff I gave them. Every Friday morning, I'd make the rounds with our two ball girls and talk on the air about the weekend's promotions at the park.

That morning, after I made my last radio stop, I drove to Independence Mall, where they happened to be taping the *Today Show*. TV lights were set up everywhere. Huge television trucks were strewn all around the lawn in front of Independence Hall. I could see Bryant Gumble and his cohost, Sara James, lounging in director's chairs on a platform just behind the pavilion where the Liberty Bell is displayed.

Live *national* TV ... How could the Phillie Phanatic pass up an opportunity like this?

I double-parked next to one of the production trucks, hopped in the back of the van, and stuffed myself into the Phanatic costume. I had a TV in the back of the van which I watched as Mayor Rendell chatted it up with Bryant live from about 50 yards from where I was parked. I strapped my head on tight, grabbed a couple of Phillies caps, and jumped out of the van like Superman out of a phone booth.

When the bystanders saw me, they started to cheer (like I need the encouragement).

I went over to where the Philly Pops was seated. Renowned maestro Peter Nero directed the Pops, and they're great! I bustled over and yanked the baton out of Peter Nero's hand and started directing the Pops myself, spazzing and waving my arms around. *Late Night with David Letterman* producer Biff Henderson heard the commotion and rushed over.

"Hey, man, we're doing a live show here," Biff said. "So why don't you make like a tree and get out of here." (just a little joke for all you Biff and Marty McFly fans). But he was smiling, so I knew something was up. As I was handing the baton over to Biff, Bryant Gumble, coming out of a commercial break, says, "You know, somebody just arrived who *always* makes me laugh. He's over there with the Philly Pops, and maybe he'll come over here if we ask him nicely. Hey, Phanatic, c'mon over here."

The camera panned over, and I mimed the old "Who, me?" act before jogging over and joining Bryant for a five-minute interview. Since the Phanatic doesn't talk, I had to act my answers out. First I bowed to Bryant, the king of morning television in those days. He asked about Lasorda and I thrust out my belly. He asked if the St. Louis Cardinals were going to catch our first-place Phillies and I flicked my tongue in his face. I tried to get up from the director's chair I was sitting in but got my bulbous butt wedged in. I struggled (for real) to pry the chair from my backside. The whole thing was done on the fly, and I wound up being on the air longer than the mayor. But then, I'm so much better looking.

It's Fo' In The Morning

I could feel it comin' in the air that night.
Not only did we have a doubleheader scheduled,
but we were also supposed to light up the skies with our annual fireworks display after the game. Philadelphians love fireworks. Even if the Phils are playing poorly, huge crowds pack the Vet on Fireworks Night, and 1993 was no exception. A throng of 54,617 jammed the Vet under threatening skies. The first game was scheduled for a 4:35 p.m. start.

Oops. The rains started just as the first pitch was scheduled to be thrown. The first pitch was eventually delivered at 5:45 p.m. after an hour and ten-minute rain delay.

Rain delay number 2 struck in the bottom of the fourth at 6:29 p.m. It lasted almost two hours. Up in the Phanavision control room, we were running thin on things to show on the big screen. Plus, the rain was pounding down so hard, we were afraid the bulbs on the oversized screen were going to explode. We shut Phanavision down and killed the time spinning discs.

At 8:25 p.m., play resumed. But not for long. At the bottom of the fifth (*inning*, that is—although some people may have been at the bottom of a different kind of fifth), the monsoon hit. I wandered out the door of the Phanavision control room and noticed that the press box was turned into a wading pool. Writers and broadcasters scrambled with their laptops and recorders while waves of water cascaded into the press box from the drains above. The wind and rain were so fierce you could barely see the outfield fence.

Chris Pohl, one of our (demented) scoreboard operators, flashed a special "Welcome to Noah" on the side scoreboards.

I was rapidly running out of music, so I popped in a CD that was gathering dust at the bottom of the CD drawer. Sorry, Tug, but Tim's music didn't make the playlist that night either. (I know. I'm an idiot.) Before long, fans were dancing in the puddles to the *Brady Bunch* theme and various other obscure and forgettable themes from sixties TV shows.

As time passed, it became more and more apparent that the fireworks were not going to happen, and at 10:30 p.m., the fireworks show was officially rescheduled for Monday night. Fans heard the announcement and started jamming the already-mobbed sheltered concourse to redeem their ticket stubs for the next night.

After a two-hour and forty-eight-minute rain delay, with the PA system blaring out the theme from the TV show *SWAT*, the Phillies took the field for the top of the sixth inning, *game one*. The time was 11:54 p.m. Six minutes later, stadium organist Paul Richardson played twelve chimes on the organ to mark the stroke of midnight. *Both* people in the stands applauded. Just kidding. Amazingly, several diehards were still hanging around.

Finally at 1:03 in the morning, the first game ended in a 5-2 Phillie loss. By that time, I almost didn't care. I was happy the night was over—or so I thought. Minutes after the game ended, the phone in the control room rang. Executive vice president and part-time meteorologist David Montgomery spoke: "Tell Danny [PA announcer Dan Baker] to make the announcement that game two starts in 20 minutes."

As the announcement boomed out, an incredulous Richie Ashburn kidded his broadcast partner, Harry Kalas. "Harry, I'm expecting a great game out of you tonight. This is the shank of the evening for you. You're usually just getting started at this hour."

The hours ticked away, with organist Paul Richardson ringing the chimes for each. In the fifth inning, the Phanatic appeared in his pajamas and nightcap, pretending to sleepwalk behind the Phillies dugout and at various places in the stands. Between innings, I played Ray Charles's version of "Still Crazy After All These Years," with Ray belting out the lyrics: *"It's fo' in the morning, tapped out, yawning, longing my life away..."* for the remaining crowd. Oh yeah, the crowd.

Sometime around 2:00 a.m., the crowd, which had thinned out earlier, started to get bigger. After last call in area bars, the pub crawlers headed to the Vet. Some buddies of mine who had been crawling around the city that night telephoned me in the control room at 2 a.m. They were forty-five minutes away but made the drive anyway. They wound up catching two hours of fun baseball!

The game went into extra innings. How could it not have? And how could it not have ended the way it did—with Mitch Williams stroking the winning hit in the tenth inning?

And twelve hours and five minutes after game one was supposed to have begun, with the stadium clock reading 4:41 a.m., the night ended. Thank God, because my music stack was down to the *Best of the Osmonds.*

Though the Phillies were notorious night owls, they didn't look like it at the start of Game 2, falling behind 5-0 by the top of the third against starter Andy Benes. Since Benes had the lowest ERA in the NL at the time, things were not looking good for the hometowners in the wee small hours.

JIM EISENREICH: "I thought we'd win. Our guys were used to watching the sun come up. If they weren't out here at the park, they'd have been watching it come up anyway, just from some other part of the city."

Phillies relievers shut down the Padres the rest of the way, while the Phillies battled back to tie in the eighth. Larry Andersen entered the game at 3:34 a.m. for a scoreless eighth-inning stint, telling first base umpire Wally Bell on his way to the mound, "I'm usually a little indisposed at this hour, so I don't know what this is going to be like."

After the Padres failed to score in the ninth, the Fightins rallied. Mariano Duncan doubled down the right-field line off hard-throwing Trevor Hoffman. In a surprise move, Tommy Greene pinch ran for Mariano and advanced to third on a wild pitch. Hoffman uncorked a second wild pitch, and Greene made a mad dash for the plate but was erased on a marvelous tag by Hoffman for the third out.

TOMMY GREENE: "I wish I was a faster runner, or I'd have made it safe. What a night! When I was on second base, I got a chance to watch one of the best fights I ever saw out there in the upper deck. The Vet was crazy that night."

After the Padres failed to score, Inky walked to open the bottom of the tenth. He went to second on an Eisenreich single to right. Mitch Williams was slated to bat, and Fregosi's cupboard was bare. He was out of pitchers, so Mitch stepped up and banged out a single. At 4:41 a.m., Inky scored, and the Phillies celebrated the earliest morning victory in baseball history: Phils 6, Padres 5.

MITCH: "Trevor Hoffman had a wicked forkball, and I didn't want any part of it. I looked back at the Padres' catcher—I think it was Kevin Higgins—and said, 'I'll wrap this bat around you if you call for the forkball.' I think I started swinging when Hoffman was looking in for the sign. I sure do love to swing a bat, though sometimes it's better to look lazy than bad. I figure a swinging bat is a dangerous thing, so I always swung hard in case I hit the ball."

INKY: "Oh, yeah, Mitch—I had mixed emotions about whether I even *wanted* him to get a hit. Sure it was late. Sure I was tired and I wanted to go home, but I knew if Mitch got a hit, we'd never hear the end of it. Before he singled, he hit a foul, and when I rounded third, I told Bowa: 'Just watch. That little *SOB's* gonna get a hit. Then we're *never* gonna hear the end of it!' Damned if he didn't and damned if we didn't!"

MITCH: "Don't pay any attention to Inky. He knows who the real hitters were on that team. And he looked like a three-year-old kid with that big grin when he crossed the plate. For me, one of the greatest parts about that night happened on my ride home. I guess, since I was so tired, I was, let's say, rapidly putting distance between the Vet and me. A cop pulled me over on the Betsy Ross Bridge, and I thought I was in trouble. But the cop recognized my pickup. He just wanted to thank me for winning the game. Then he wanted to talk about the game and the team and the season—and I said, 'Man, I gotta go get some sleep.' That's something we didn't say that too often on that team."

MILT: "I think I was the happiest guy for Mitch. I was on deck when he got the hit. I'd have felt bad if I didn't end it when I got up. Mitch saved me all that pressure, and I could go home and sleep."

KRUK: "Can you believe we played that game until 4:41 in the morning? It was another one of those crazy games that, of course, Mitch was in the middle

Let's get ready to rumble! WWF bouts routinely broke out during batting practice. Here, Danny Jackson and John Kruk stage a heavyweight match on the turf of the Vet.
(Photo by Rosemary Rahn)

The Phillie Phanatic has been shooting cooked hot dogs into the seats at the Vet since 1996. Here he is feeding the masses at the 1996 All-Star Game.
(Photo by Rosemary Rahn)

Dave Hollins's intensity was legendary. He laid down the gauntlet that year and told the Phillies pitchers that if they didn't retaliate after a Phillie got hit by a pitch, they'd have to deal with him.
(Photo by Rosemary Rahn)

Each member of the maveric[k] 1993 Phillies rotation won at least 12 games. Pictured are (from left) Tommy Greene, Cu[rt] Schilling, Danny Jackson, Ter[ry] Mulholland and Ben Rivera. (Photo courtesy of Al Teilman[n])

The Phanatic bows down and kisses the feet of Bryant Gumb[el] on the set of the *Today Show*, while cohost Sara James look[s] on. The popular morning sho[w] was in town for Fourth of Jul[y] festivities. (Photo courtesy of Liz Wuillermin)

Pete Incaviglia reminded Philly fans of Greg "The Bull" Luzinski with his tape-measure home runs. On July 31, Inky belted two homers against the Pirates and then hit one home run in each of the next three games. (Photo by Rosemary Rahn)

When it came to throwing targets, no one was safe. Not even the general manager. Here is Lee Thomas wiping shaving cream out of his ear after a Curt Schilling attack. Clubbies made easy money that year watching the backs of players during interviews.
(Photo by Rosemary Rahn)

Milt Thompson (left), sitting with Kim Batiste, belted three hits and made a spectacular game-saving catch of a potential grand slam against the Padres on April 29 in San Diego. (Photo by Rosemary Rahn)

Even though Curt Schilling was all business between the white lines, he was one of the team's leading pranksters. Just ask the Phanatic.
(Photo by Rosemary Rahn)

After shortstop Kevin Stocker (left) came up from the minors, he and second baseman Mickey Morandini (right) formed a formidable double-play combination. (Photos by Rosemary Rahn)

The Lasorda feud raged on even after Dave Raymond left the Phanatic costume. Here the new Phanatic, Tom Burgoyne, gets ready to "goose" the fake Tommy, Phillies employee Mike "Snuffy" Boyce. (Photo by Rosemary Rahn)

Outfielder Wes Chamberlain caused a stir on Opening Day by oversleeping and arriving three hours late. He later apologized to the team but had to endure the wrath of the Phanatic the next day. (Photo by Rosemary Rahn)

Larry Andersen helped keep the clubhouse rocking after Phillies wins with tunes from the Spin Doctors. Legendary rocker Alice Cooper (pictured with LA) came to visit the Phils in 1994. (Photo by Rosemary Rahn)

Besides being a big eater, David West was a big-time player in 1993, leading the Phillies' bullpen in wins (6), appearances (76), innings pitched (86.1) and strikeouts (87). (Photo by Rosemary Rahn)

"Video" Dan Stephenson's room was a favorite hangout for players that year. Here is Dan with the "Norm Peterson" of that room, Larry Andersen. (Photo by Rosemary Rahn)

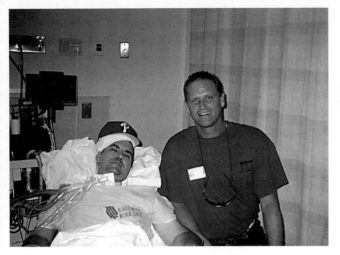

In August of 1993, Larry Andersen began to visit Officer John Marynowitz (left), a policeman who received gunshot wounds to the head and chest in June while trying to prevent a robbery. (Photo by Mindy Marynowitz)

Down 4-3 heading into the seventh inning in Pittsburgh, Mariano Duncan caps a comeback by hitting his second grand slam of the season to win the division. (Photo by Rosemary Rahn)

From left, Kevin Conrad, Kevin Steinhour, Frank Coppenbarger, Phil Sheridan and Joe Dunn comprised the overworked clubhouse staff in 1993. Here they are blowing off steam after clinching the division in Pittsburgh. (Photo by Rosemary Rahn)

Embarrassing himself was part of Tom's job description in 1993. Here he is dressed as a lowly Braves fan, until the Phanatic comes along and has different ideas. (Photo by Heddy Bergsman)

Lenny Dykstra told Curt Schilling in the dugout that if Braves reliever Mark Wohlers ran the count full, he'd take him out of the park. After slamming the game-winning home run in the tenth inning off Wohlers, The Dude rounded third base screaming, "Didn't I?! Didn't I?!" (Photo by Rosemary Rahn)

From left, Lee Thomas, Jim Fregosi and Bill Giles take a victory lap on the Veterans Stadium field with a prized possession—the Warren C. Giles Trophy. (Photo by Rosemary Rahn)

Jim Eisenreich breaks the game wide open in the third inning of Game 2 with a three-run blast. The Phillies hold on to win 6-4, tying the Series at one game apiece. (Photo by Rosemary Rahn)

Joe Carter walloped the Phanati with the dummy in his first tri back to Philadelphia after his infamous home run. Thanks t interleague play and spring training games, Joe and the Phanatic had a number of run ins after his gallop around the bases at the World Series. (Phot by Rosemary Rahn)

A happy ending after all—To and Jennifer tied the knot in November, 1993. (Photo by Sister Maryann Burgoyne)

of. Mitch getting that hit wasn't that big of a surprise. You know, Mitch was a great athlete, a terrible pitcher, but a great athlete. He was upset that they didn't rule that hit a double. He kept saying after the game, 'I could have kept on runnin'.' What I remember from that night was going into the trainer's room around 5:00 a.m. to ice down and have a few beers, you know, the usual thing. And Fregosi comes walking in and says he's gonna fine us for drinking on a game day. Can you believe that?"

MARIANO DUNCAN: "My wife and I were going through some things that year. She wasn't real happy with the hours I was keeping hanging out in the clubhouse after the games. I got home at six o'clock, and my wife started asking me where I had been. And I said, 'I was playing in a game until 4:45 in the morning. We just got finished playing the game.' She didn't believe me."

DANNY JACKSON: "I was home in bed when that second game ended. I was the starter the next day, so Fregosi let me leave "early"—at 1:00 a.m.! I didn't hear about Mitch's hit till the next day on the radio." (Then he heard about it for the rest of the season.)

Jim Fregosi summed up after the game: "I only saw one other game as crazy as that one. That was the debut of my TV commentator's job, the Phillies versus Mets in '91. There were *24* walks in 10 innings. The game was so messed up the only guy who threw strikes that night was Mitch."

"The True Hit Men of 1993"

PHANATIC PHILE

The following fact is little known outside the inner sanctum of the 1993 Phillies, although the information *is* available to the general public. The subject, due to its humiliating content, is discussed only in hushed tones because it demoralizes every major-leaguer who ever swung a bat in anger and every member of the '93 squad save two.

The top hitters in Phillie red in 1993 were Mitch Williams and Larry Andersen. Each of these "sluggers" batted 1.000.

Question: What did Larry Andersen and Mitch Williams do as hitters that Henry Aaron, Babe Ruth, Ty Cobb, Barry Bonds, Willie Mays, and many more, never did?

Answer: Williams and Andersen each batted 1.000 for an entire season. (Note: Other acceptable answers include (1) they made baseball bats appear less lethal than fly swatters or (2) they generated less bat speed than a sundial or (3) they could convince spectators that flubber was an actual substance.)

With all due respect to each of these great relievers—and I know they'll take this observation like the mature men that they're struggling not to become—having these two guys as the top hitters on a team—any team—is like having Wayne and Garth as the premier soloists in the Philadelphia Orchestra. It's like having Jake and Elwood as Lagersfeld's top runway models. It's like having Robert Downey Jr. and Charlie Sheen as crack, er, top, drug counselors. It's like having Ike and Tina as marriage counselors.

Whenever the '93 Phils get together, both LA and Wild Thing stay clear of that subject. It might be difficult. Neither guy tends to be quiet and shy. But they're both aware that their *achievement* is a source of embarrassment for the serious batsmen on the team, particularly guys like Pete Incaviglia who can still bench press the equivalent weight of the annual pasta consumption of a small Sicilian village.

The Phillies didn't turn it all around, get out of their funk, and live happily ever after once their 4:41 a.m. victory was in the record book. Danny Jackson took a 6-4 loss the following night. Mariano Duncan wound up on the disabled list after straining his right hamstring, and Larry Andersen ended his 12-game skein of 13 1/3 scoreless innings. He yielded an unearned run in the ninth. Larry, incidentally, still holds the Phillie post-1920 record for consecutive scoreless innings, with 33 in 1984.

Padres relief pitcher Roger Mason became a Phillie after the Night Owl game. He switched dugouts the morning after the night of—or, more accurately, the afternoon after the morning of.

ROGER MASON: "I was traded to the Phillies after that 4:41 a.m. game. We played each other later that same day. Since I had pitched both games of that long doubleheader for San Diego—*against* the Phillies—I had a once-in-a-lifetime opportunity to pitch *for and against* the same team on the same calendar day. I really wanted to pitch against the Padres my first day as a Phil since no one's ever done that before. But the Phils thought I was too tired. That showed me right away that as zany as these guys seemed, they were serious about winning baseball games, not individual stuff."

The Phillies won 8-4 next day, when Mason's chance came around. Milt Thompson fell a home run short of hitting for the cycle. Next, the Dodgers came to town and split the first two. On July 6, the Phillies purchased the contract of 23-year old shortstop Kevin Stocker from the Reading Phils, their farm club.

PAUL HAGAN, *Philadelphia Daily News*: "Lee Thomas decided to bring up Kevin Stocker when he watched two ground balls roll past Kim Batiste for hits in the fifth inning of that loss to the Dodgers. When the game ended, Thomas bolted into Fregosi's office and said, 'You're getting a new shortstop. Look, I'm the guy who made the decision, so give me all the grief if it doesn't work out.'"

JIM FREGOSI: "Here's the funny thing. All season long, Bowa is running up to me every day: 'Bring that kid Stocker up, bring Stocker up.' So after Lee left, I went over to Larry and told him Stocker was coming up. Larry looks at me and says, in that high- pitched voice of his, 'Do you think he can play? Do you think he can play?'"

Stocker proved quickly that he could play. The young shortstop was brought up simply for his glove, to solidify the weak underbelly of the team's defense. However, the polite young rookie exceeded all expectations with the stick.

JIM FREGOSI: "We told him not to worry about hitting. The guy went out and hit, what, .324 or so? Without Stocker doing the job he did, we don't win that pennant that year."

Stocker debuted on another night-owl night. The hometowners carried a 5-3 lead into the ninth when Mitch came in to preserve the victory. The Wild Thing walked the first batter, Lenny Webster. He then surrendered a weak hit to Brett Butler. Jose Offerman walked on four pitches to load the bases. When Mitch walked the next batter, Cory Snyder, to close the gap to 5-4, skipper Fregosi yanked Mitch and gave home-plate umpire Jim Quick an earful on his way back to the dugout. So did Mitch. Quick tossed them both—an interesting move since the Wild Thing was ineligible to play anyway—and Williams headed to Video's room. Larry Andersen came in to face Eric Karros, who hit a weak one-hopper to the mound that LA mishandled to tie the game. Then the new kid earned his stripes. Stocker backhanded a sharp grounder off the bat of Mike Piazza and nailed Jose Offerman with a perfect strike to the plate.

LARRY ANDERSEN: "If my high school coach doesn't move me from shortstop to the outfield when I was a junior, I make that play on Karros's hit back to the mound. I also wouldn't have the problem in the back of my head, or the psychological problem of not being able to field."

David West and Jose De Leon held down the fort until the recently called up Mike Williams entered the game in the top of the fifteenth. Williams blanked the Dodgers for five innings before yielding a lone run in the twentieth. In the Phillies half of that frame, however, the Dude came up with the bases loaded and lofted a long fly against the wall in left to plate two and notch a hard-fought win.

For his yeoman effort, Mike Williams was carried into the clubhouse by his teammates after the game.

LARRY ANDERSEN: "The night before Stocker got called up, we were in the trainer's room saying that we had to encourage the kid and tell him just to go out and play his game and not worry about anything else. We agreed we couldn't come down hard on him or bust his chops like we did with the other rookies. Of course, once we saw how tough he was, we had to have a *little* fun with him. Two weeks later, on a flight to San Diego, I told Stock that he had to wear a smock and serve everybody just like a flight attendant. His name was Colleen for the flight. Stock did a better job than most of the flight attendants we had. Irish Mike, who enjoyed tipping a complimentary drink or two on our flights, nudged Fregosi and said in all seriousness, 'You know, that stewardess looks a lot like Stocker.' To this day I believe that if Stock were looking for a job after baseball, he has a promising career awaiting in airline travel. I don't think he's real comfortable using the intercom and doing the seatbelt demo yet, but that'll come in time."

KEVIN STOCKER: "Those veterans were wonderful to me from the minute I arrived. I was accepted immediately. I guess the scariest part was the bat I used. I didn't have my bats, so the closest one I found to my style was Dave Hollins's. I didn't know how touchy Dave was and how superstitious all those guys were. Dave was genuinely concerned that I was stealing his hits."

LARRY ANDERSEN: "After that 20-inning game against the Dodgers, when Lenny got the big hit for the win, we went nuts in Video's room. There were a bunch of us in there by the twentieth inning. We were all jumping around on the couch with beer and pretzels flying everywhere. I ran out on the field to hug Lenny in my underwear. Video had left the room for a few minutes. When he got back, the place was trashed. He goes, 'What the hell happened here?' And I'm like, 'Video, you missed it. We were all going crazy.' So he asked us to reenact it so he could shoot it for the yearly highlight film. Video pops in the tape of the game, and when the Dude gets the big hit, Westy takes a full pitcher of beer and launches it across the room and hits one of the pinup girls hanging on the wall. Perfect strike. Video just shook his head." From all accounts, Westie's toss had more *hops* on it than any he ever threw.

R.I.P. Mitch?

Usually the Phanatic's night is over after the eighth inning. However, when a game goes into extra innings, the Phanatic generally goes to his dressing room and watches the game. He takes his head off and keeps the costume on halfway, in case the Fightin' Phils mount a rally. That way, when the winning run scores, the Phanatic can strap the head on and run out onto the field to celebrate with the team.

"When the Phillies won that 20-inning game against the Dodgers, I was in the tunnel behind home plate watching the game," recalls '93 Phanatic Dave Raymond. "Here we were coming off that 4:41 a.m. game a week before, and now we were stuck in *another* marathon. The thing I remember most about that night was that after Mitch had blown the save, John Kruk was standing out at first base yelling to no one in particular, 'I'm gonna kill Mitch! We're gonna miss last call! I'm gonna kill him!'"

Mitch had entered the game in the ninth with the score 5-3 and lost the lead, but the Phillies finally pulled out another heart-stopper in the twentieth inning.

After the game, Krukkie *still* wasn't a happy camper, spouting. "I wanna kill Mitch, but they tell me that's illegal. Honest to God, some people think we make too much money! Somebody must really hate us. I can think of about 50 guys right now who want to kill Mitch."

Krukker had some justification for his rant. After Mitch was knocked out of the game, he went back to Video Dan's room, where, while watching the game since he had been ejected, he downed a couple of brews. Actually, in a 20-inning game, it was more than a couple. Mitch was running down to the dugout during the marathon singing the praises of the postgame brewski, while his teammates were deadlocked in a tiring battle lasting into the wee small hours of the morning.

JOHN KRUK: "After blowing the save, Mitch is up in Video's room, drinking beers and eating pizza. Then he'd come running down the tunnel in his underwear yelling, 'Come on, guys, you can do it!' And I said to him, 'Look, Mitch, if you had done it, we'd be out of here by now and we'd be drinking with you.'"

So the Krukker and his teammates were—well—upset. When Mitch joked afterwards, "Twenty innings! If I'd have known it would go that long, I'd have tried harder!" it didn't help matters.

LARRY ANDERSEN: "Let's put it this way. I came into the clubhouse the next day and I figured by the time I got there, Krukkie or Dutch would have killed Mitch. The first thing I did was go to my locker to see if there was a black patch sewn on my sleeve with the number '99' [Mitch's uniform number] on it."

It was another marathon, but it was another *winning* marathon. After the 20-inning endurance test, the Fightins were 8-2 in extra-inning games, 15-6 in one-run games and 10-8 in two-run games. In contrast, in 1992 they only managed 5-7, 21-31 and 9-15 respectively in those categories.

San Francisco strutted into town right before All-Star break. They proceeded to dismantle the Phillies, who struggled through their worst series of the season. The Phils played like a team in need of a break. The Giants plated 46 runs in four games while the Phillies managed only 15. Only Tommy Greene, whose record climbed to 11-2, could manage a victory. The Phillies were showing some wear and tear from their recent night-owl marathons. The team that ate up coming to the park was now hungry for a hiatus. Despite their recent slump, they limped out of the first half with a 57-32 record, good for a five-game lead over the second-place Cards. When asked if the team was panicking, Terry Mulholland said, "No. Panic would be like if this was the movie *Groundhog Day* and we'd have to go through those two days with the Giants over and over again and keep getting our brains beat out. That would be my definition of panic, but that's not going to happen."

Walk Softly And Carry A Big Sticky Bun

A clubbie's work is never done. In '93, it seemed that every time I pulled into the parking lot for a game, one of the clubbies was jumping into a car and pulling out, heading on an emergency food run.

PHIL SHERIDAN, 1993 CLUBHOUSE ATTENDANT: "On any given night, there'd be over $100 worth of McDonald's food on the clubhouse table. We would make at least two to three runs for food a night. Mitch had us call Domino's Pizza every night and order pizzas with double cheese, double pepperoni, and tomatoes on top—had to be that way. I was always making trips to the KFC. Each guy always tried to outdo the next guy. But cheesesteaks were their favorite. Kruk would call into the clubhouse from his car while driving to the park and order a two-foot-long cheesesteak everyday. He tried to time it so he and the cheesesteaks arrived at the ballpark at the same time. And all this stuff was in addition to the spread we'd have out for them after each game."

One guy who circled that spread with more ill intent than Jaws circling the *Orca* was David West. A hungry Westie was a threat to eat the table if all the goodies were gone.

MITCH WILLIAMS: "Westie ate all the time. I remember in New York. The relief pitchers used to kind of make ourselves scarce—some might say hide—in what we relief pitchers called "the Cave," a secret hideaway by the visitor's clubhouse at Shea. It was a great little spot, and no one, especially the coaches, knew about it. There was lots of stimulating 'reading material' in there, and we had a TV too. I remember Westie eating a four-foot-long hoagie one night when we were supposed to be doing pregame stretching. David was lying on his back, shoving that four-foot-long monster into his mouth. It was like watching a tree going into a chipper."

One Sunday morning as David was circling in on the brunch spread, Terry Mulholland yelled out, "Do you know what Westie's motto is? It's 'Walk softly and carry a big sticky bun.'"

LARRY ANDERSEN: "When we were on the road, Westie and I usually went out after the game to some local establishment, being that most museums and art galleries were closed at that hour of the morning. By the time we got back to the hotel, it tended to be just a *little* past curfew, and I'd be falling asleep. Not Westie. Like usual, he'd be ready to eat. I'd be in bed, almost asleep, when I'd hear Westie on the phone: 'Hello, room service? Yeah, this room 709, are you still serving food? Great! Give me a bowl of soup. Hey

Larry, do you want some soup?'

"No, not now, I'm going to sleep," I'd yell, kind of dozing off. Then I'd hear Westie say, 'Yeah, make that two bowls of clam chowder.'

"Then I'd hear Westie say, 'Give me some mozzarella sticks with that. LA, do you want any mozzarella sticks?'

"No thanks," I'd yell, and Westie'd continue, 'Yeah, make that two orders of mozzarella sticks. Oh, uh-huh, yeah, it sounds good! You sold me. I'll take the baked cod, too! How 'bout you, LA, up for some baked cod?'

"No, David. Go to sleep," I'm yelling, and Westie's going on, 'I'm getting sweet potatoes as a side. Waddya say, LA?' and I'm yelling, *'I say I think I'm gonna kill you tomorrow when I wake up.'*

"Half hour later, I'm sound asleep, and here's Westie waking me up, 'LA, food's here. I got you some apple pie, too.'

Gee, LA, kind of a shame to waste all that food.

LARRY ANDERSEN: "Waste? I never could pass up on apple pie."

Break Dance

"That year was the only time I ever got a call from George Steinbrenner.
George called one day and said, 'That's really an exciting team you've got
there. I'd love to have them up here in New York.'"
— *Bill Giles, Phils President*

I n Philadelphia, life does not imitate sport. Sport imitates life—*Philly life*. Philadelphians don't care if their teams aren't in the national spotlight. What Philadelphia fans demand is that their teams be tough, that they stand tall and proud, and that, even in defeat, they kick butt. Think Rocky I and you get the picture. Even Philly's mayor in 1993, Ed Rendell, loved the rough and tumble bunch of ballplayers that took his city by storm that year. His Honor feels this band of brigands captured not only the heart, but the soul, of his city.

MAYOR ED RENDELL: "That '93 team was a microcosm of the city. I can't imagine that any other city ever had a team better matched to it. One of the things I've always loved about Philly is that our city is a living paradox. On the one hand, this city is one of the most significant cultural, historical, and artistic centers in the country and in the world. Yet on the other hand, Philly is the ultimate blue-collar town. That's the beautiful paradox that gives Philadelphia its unique and fascinating character. And those '93 Phils had to be one of the all-time blue-collar squads. I was personally happy, and I was happy for our city, that they came along when they did. Remember, in '93, I was newly elected and aggressively trying to change the image of the city. Philadelphia had always suffered from that W.C. Fields image that it was a dull place to be, with nothing to do for excitement. I wanted to bury that characterization and show the world that Philly was vibrant and alive and fun. Then these guys came along just at the right time, and that's exactly what they showed the world. They made the game of baseball fun. It was fun to watch those guys perform. The atmosphere at that ballpark was electric that year. That team, those guys, lit up the skies around Philly. They were overachievers—up and down the roster. Nobody was specially gifted, and they certainly didn't look like anything special. But the people sitting in the stands cheering for them related to that team. The '93 Phils showed up ready for work every day. They lived the blue-collar ethic this city lives and admires. Nothing scared that team. No one intimidated them. They played all out, all the time. To me, that team, that year, was lightning in a bottle. It was chemistry that will never be duplicated."

JIM FREGOSI: "Of course Philly fell in love with this team. They identified with them. There was somebody on that squad for everyone. Every guy who ate hot dogs and drank beer loved John Kruk. Every woman loved Darren Daulton. Every redneck kind of guy with a pickup and chewing tobacco in his pocket loved Lenny Dykstra. All this city ever asks of a team is to leave it all out on the field. They could see these guys did that. You had to love them, and the fans in Philly—they're like an extra coach. If they see a guy not running out a grounder, they'll boo the hell out of him. The coach doesn't have to say a thing."

BILL GILES: "The media couldn't stay away from the '93 team 'cause they looked like they were having so damn much fun playing the game. And they were! You know, that's the only time George Steinbrenner ever called. He called one day and said, 'Bill, that's really an exciting team you've got down there. I'd love to have them up here in New York.'"

LENNY DYKSTRA: "When I was traded from the Mets to the Phillies, I was happy. I knew I'd get a chance to play on that team and that I'd be one of their key guys. Philly was one of the few cities I wanted to go, mostly 'cause of the fans there. Philly fans are different. They love dirty uniforms. They love guys who play down and dirty and give everything they've got. That's the way I played, so I loved to play in front of that crowd."

Comfortable or not, the Phillies found themselves in an unusual position for Philadelphia by midseason 1993. They were smack dab in the center of the national spotlight. In a tradition-rich sport, the '93 Phillies broke a mold that was cast decades ago in the wake of World War I, when facial hair disappeared and long hair was viewed with suspicion. The '93 Phillies strutted the diamond with unkempt hair, raggy uniforms, and a devil-may-care attitude. They reflected the personality of their city by remaining reluctant media stars.

The Phils were sending more representatives to the '93 All-Star game than they had in the past eleven years. And for the first time since 1964, it was a Philadelphia Phillie who stole the show. And in typical '93 Phillie fashion, he stole the show unconventionally, in a way that was all his own.

When All-Star break 1993 rolled around, the Phillies placed three in the starting lineup, the most since 1982 when Manny Trillo, Mike Schmidt, and Pete Rose took the field. In 1993, the Krukker, by virtue of his irrepressible style and wit, was the media darling during the pregame hype. Everyone wanted to talk about the Phillies, but the focus was more on their appearance than their success. Kruk and the All-Star Phillies were true to form, true to the clubhouse code. Kruk was proud of how far his team had come in a year. "Dutch and me forgot to pack our Phillie warmup jerseys at last year's All-Star game in San Diego. So we went to the concession stands to buy some Phillie souvenir shirts. They didn't even sell them. That's when you know you stink."

One year before at the All-Star break, his Phillies were buried in last place where they remained the rest of the season. This year, if they stayed true to baseball tradition, as the first-place team at All-Star break they would go on to win the division. When Kruk was questioned about how it felt to be in last place the year before, the All-Star first sacker replied, "Put it this way, I'd rather be in a prison cell with Mike Tyson and let him beat my butt all day long than go through that again. This is much better this year, although the last week or so, we've played a lot like last year."

Kruk was never one to pass up a chance for self-deprecating humor, even if it did not ring true. When a reporter asked, "John, if I told you at the beginning of spring training that you'd be standing here, the NL first baseman, with your team in first place by five games at the All-Star break, what would you have said?" the Krukker replied, "I'd have said, 'Check in, you have a dependency problem. I'd have said you must be using something we've never heard of.'"

Kruk's witticisms were only part of the reason he drew the media like a magnet. John simply did not look the part of an athlete. His physique, more amorphous than cut, belied (no, not *bellied*) his talents as an athlete, and Kruk played off that visual disconnect. A woman once reprimanded him for smoking in public, saying he was setting a poor example as an athlete. Kruk shot back in all candor, "I ain't an athlete, lady. I'm a ballplayer" (the title of Kruk and Paul Hagan's excellent book about the Krukker). Kruk disarmed, simply by not taking himself seriously. Asked if he could see himself in a "Yesterday's Heroes" game in fifteen years, he fired, "Hell, no, I'll be dead in fifteen years. And if I'm not, they'll never find me. How'd they find all these guys, anyway [referring to the ex-ballplayers who played in the 'Yesterday's Heroes' game during the All-Star festivities]?"

The Phillies were so focused on their team's agenda in '93 that two Phillie All-Stars, Kruk and Mulholland, accepted their honor with mixed emotions.

KRUK: "I was pretty banged up at All-Star break. I had reconstructive surgery done on my shoulder in the off season prior to '93, and I was supposed to be out till May. You know, I didn't miss a single day in spring training, so I was tired by All-Star break. But the big thing was that right before the All-Star game, I slid into second and jammed my shoulder. I had an X-ray taken, and they found that I had bent one of the metal pins in my shoulder and that was causing some pain. So I could have used the time to recuperate. I didn't want to play and hurt my own team."

Terry Muholland's reluctance was of a different nature. Terry was picked as the National League starter—the first Phillie starter since Steve Carlton in 1980. However, he was going through a divorce in '93 and had promised his four-year old son, Tyler, that he would take him fishing over the All-Star break. Terry decided to play, telling the press, "Being selected is an honor. I don't think it would have done justice to my teammates, especially Lenny Dykstra, who should have been selected, if I hadn't gone."

Terry was right. Lenny Dykstra's omission was baffling. Lenny, who had been picked to start in 1990, had overcome his April funk and was rolling through a record-breaking season at the midpoint. The entire team, and the baseball world in general, conceded that Dykstra was the front-running Phillies most valuable player. However, the Dude was not selected by fan vote, and Bobby Cox did not name him to the roster—a slight that would come back to haunt him.

True to form, Mulholland didn't make a public issue about his quandary. Terry was perhaps the most laid-back, laconic ballplayer on the '93 roster. As Kruk described him, his teammate was "comatose. Terry doesn't talk. Sometimes when Darren goes to the mound, I go too, just so Darren has somebody to talk to."

Mulholland, with his 9-6 record and 2.72 ERA, was trying to halt a five-game American League win steak. His mound opponent was Mark Langston of the California Angels, who was en route to a 16-11, 3.20 ERA season. Things started well for the Nationals. Barry Bonds doubled in the first and Gary Sheffield followed with a homer to left. Terry goose-egged the American Leaguers in the bottom of the stanza. However, in the second, Kirby Puckett poled a center field home run that narrowed the margin to 2-1. In the third, Roberto Alomar led off with a circuit blast off Andy Benes, knotting the score at 2-2. The Americans put the game out of reach in the middle innings, as a group of Atlanta Braves gave the game away.

The American Leaguers had shot out to a 5-2 lead after five. Then a Barry Larkin sacrifice fly narrowed the gap to 5-3 in the top of the sixth. Brave short-stop Jeff Blauser booted a third-out ground ball with his Brave teammate Steve Avery on the hill. Avery walked Albert Belle and Devon White doubled him home. Brave John Smoltz relieved teammate Avery and unloaded a pair of wild pitches that enabled Belle and White to score. The game lost its competitive charm after that sloppy exhibition. However, the game was immortalized by the greatest comic incident in the history of the Midsummer Classic.

In the third inning, Kruk dug in—briefly—against Seattle's Randy Johnson. The Big Unit was headed for his first of four 300-strikeout seasons. His 1993 performance marked only the second time in history that a league strikeout leader topped three hundred when no other hurler could boast even *two* hundred Ks (in 1903, Philadelphia Athletic great Rube Waddell fanned 302, and the next best was Detroit's Bill Donovan at 187). Johnson was in the midst of a run where he would lead the American League in strikeouts from 1992-1995. A few years later, he three-peated again as NL leader from 1999-2001.

Johnson, the tallest man in the history of the sport, cut a menacing figure on the hill. Flinging his crackling fastball at speeds near 100 miles per hour, he excelled at riding the ball in on left-handed hitters and driving them back off the plate. Johnson plunked 16 batsmen that year.

Johnson's first offering sailed over Kruk's head at practically 100 mph. With his body bent at the waist, Kruk danced backward out of the batter's box like an apoplectic crane (either the bird or the mechanical device works for the visual) in a cyclone. A huge, unsettled grin settled on the Krukker's moon face as he stood palpitating his fist against his chest. Kruk, who went through thirty sticks of bubble gum per game, looked like he yearned to be the boy *in* the bubble at this point.

Later Kruk reported, "Well, it was a little fear. Guys were telling me Randy Johnson's a little hard to pick up the first time you face him. Randy told me later, 'It was humid out there. The ball slipped.' But when I got back in the box after that first pitch, Pudge [Ivan Rodriguez] told me, 'Just have fun with it.'"

John Kruk danced gingerly into the batter's box with the same caution people exercise walking around Dave Hollins's locker after he's had a bad game. Johnson loomed stone-faced on the mound. Krukker's tenuous smile and facial expressions delighted the crowd along with the players on the bench. As Kruk said later, "Ever do something crazy when you're young, like break into a farm, and now you're running like hell and zigzagging in case the farmer's got a gun? That's what I was doing the rest of that at-bat."

Kruk took strike one, a blazing fastball. The next pitch found the corner as Kruk swung weakly and rotated—part stand-up comedy and part stand-up break dance. The fourth and final pitch had the Krukker lurching as though he were perched on a high board. After he whiffed, Kruk, heels together, tossed the bat, made a polite bow to no one in particular, and exited stage left to thunderous cheers and laughter. Teammate Daulton later quipped; "That's Jake [Kruk]. He had everybody laughing. Jake is a born entertainer. He knew what was going on."

Amazingly, Kruk had been hit by a pitched ball only twice in his professional career up till then. When the game was over, Kruk was swarmed by the press and had this to offer: "If Randy was going to hit me, he was going to have to hit a moving target. I don't know where the first pitch was, and I didn't give a damn about the next three as long as they missed me. I was giving up the at-bat to save my life. If he struck me out, okay. I just didn't want him to kill me."

PROMISES

Terry Muholland's parents drove down to Baltimore in style to watch their son pitch. Terry's parents had a Cadillac.

"Terry bought that Cadillac for us," Pat Mulholland explained. "We had five boys, and one day we were all watching the big lottery show on TV, talking about what we'd do if we ever won. I said I'd give each boy $100,000 and keep a half-million for us." Terry promised his parents, "If I ever get a big-league contract, I'll buy you a Cadillac."

A staph infection from a football injury in high school almost stopped Terry from getting that baseball contract. He nearly had to have his leg amputated. But he averted tragedy and had an excellent high school baseball career—good enough to become San Francisco's second pick in the first round of the June draft in 1984. Terry went back and forth from the minors to San Francisco between 1986 to 1989, until he was dealt to the Phillies on Father's Day, 1989. In 1990, he started the season in the bullpen but quickly worked his way into the starting rotation. On August 15, he pitched a no-hitter at the Vet, becoming the only Phillie pitcher in the twentieth century to pitch a no-hitter in Philly. He faced the minimum 27 batters. Only a Charlie Hayes error marred a perfect game. When he finished the season 9-10, he assumed the mantle of staff ace. In 1991, Terry was 16-13, finishing third in the NL in complete games, fifth in wins, and sixth in innings pitched. In 1992, with a 13-11 record, he led the league in complete games (12) and broke the major-league record for pickoffs (16) while allowing the fewest stolen bases in the NL (2).

MAYOR ED RENDELL: "Terry was the first of the '93 Phillies I got to know. That team was good to the city with their time and money. We were trying to raise money to keep the city pools open in the summer. Terry promised to donate $1,000 per win to the Philadelphia Department of Recreation so we could keep the pools open, and he did. He gave us $13,000 that summer. Terry came over to one of the events where I jumped in the pool. Terry wanted to jump in too, but he wasn't prepared. I think he was upset he didn't have his bathing suit."

Terry's reluctance to report to the All-Star game speaks volumes about his character and commitment.

TERRY MULHOLLAND: "When I said I wasn't going to play because I was taking my son fishing, my father, Jim Fregosi, and Bobby Cox all convinced me I should go, not for myself, but for my teammates, and for the honor of being selected."

Manager Fregosi gave his lefty special dispensation for a day after the All-Star game. Terry had promised his son, Tyler, that he'd take him fishing at All-Star break. So, like the Mulholland generation before Terry, the generation after him found out that Terry Mulholland is one guy who keeps his promises.

Most fans got a kick out of Kruk's ad-libbed at-bat, thinking it added some fun to an otherwise dull, uncompetitive All-Star game. There were some dissenting opinions, however. Krukker's fun caused some controversy among baseball purists, like ex-Phillie great Tug McGraw, who had endeared himself to Phillies fans with his roguish style and clever one-liners. (When asked in 1975 how he would spend his salary, Tug said, "Ninety percent I'll spend on good times, women, and Irish whiskey. The other ten percent I'll probably waste.") It's ironic that Tug didn't find Kruk's gestures amusing or appropriate. Tug is best remembered in Philadelphia for his triumphant leap after he struck Willie Wilson out to win the 1980 World Series. Almost equally memorable, however, was what happened a moment before. Wilson scorched a liner that curved just foul. Pantomiming what a start the ball gave him, the Tugger stood on the mound thumping his heart with his fist—much as Kruk did after the Big Unit's fastball seared over his head.

In 1993, Tug was a sports reporter for Philly TV's Action News. After the game, he spoke out against Kruk's routine at the plate. The Tugger feels the same today.

TUG McGRAW: "I'm an old-school guy. I always viewed the All-Star game as the one opportunity to square off against the other league. Yeah, it's an exhibition game, but I didn't like making a joke out of a game that we tried so hard to win. I know everybody thought what John did was funny, but I didn't. I think Krukkie had the chance to step back in and say, "Put one over, and I'll show you what I can do with it.' But John didn't do that."

Tug himself appeared in only one All-Star game back in 1972 as a Met (he was selected as a Phil in 1975 but didn't get in the game). In his only All-Star appearance, Tug made the most of his big day in Atlanta's Fulton County Stadium as the National League won the first game of what would become an 11-game NL win streak. The Nationals had lost in 1971 but won the previous eight straight.

Tug came into the game in the ninth with the National League behind 3-2. In the bottom of the inning, the Nationals knotted the game at three. McGraw set the American League down in order in the tenth, and Joe Morgan won the game with an RBI single in the Nationals' half of the frame. It was the National League's seventh win in seven extra-inning All Star contests to that point. Tug picked up the win, something only two Phillies, Ken Raffensberger in 1944 and Doug Jones in 1994, have done in an All-Star contest.

Philly's All-Star Game History

W hen the thirties broke, the Quaker City was blessed with several great players from two franchises. The Phillies had Chuck Klein, Lefty O'Doul (whose restaurant-bar near Chinatown in San Francisco is one of Harry Kalas's favorite piano bars), Don Hurst, Spud Davis, and Pinky Whitney—.300 hitters all. In fact, in 1930, the Phillies' team batting average was a spectacular .315. Unfortunately, their team ERA was a record-high 6.71, and the Phillies finished last. Good pitching, at least in 1930, beats good hitting.

Across town, the A's had assembled Philadelphia's greatest team ever. Philadelphia Athletics players won the first four American League MVP Awards. Lefty Grove won the first in 1931, Jimmie Foxx won back-to-back awards the following two years, and Mickey Cochrane won the 1934 award. The great Phillie Chuck Klein won the second NL MVP in 1932. The following year, Klein won the Triple Crown but *not* the MVP, which went to Carl Hubbell. The Meal Ticket, as Hubbell was called, posted a 23-12 record with a 1.66 ERA. By the end of 1935, Philadelphia players had accounted for *half of the MVP awards ever presented.*

Baseball's All-Star Classic debuted in 1933. At that point, both Philly baseball franchises were in precipitous decline. Two members of the next to last place Phillies started for the National League: shortstop Dick Bartel and outfielder Chuck Klein. At All-Star break that year, *the top three hitters in the league were Phillies.* Klein led the league at .369, with catcher Spud Davis (.368) and outfielder Chick Fullis (.355) close behind. However, the fans voted in ex-Phil Lefty O'Doul, who was batting .270 at the break, and Paul Waner, who was batting .284.

New York, in typical fashion, overshadowed Philly in that first All-Star game. Lou Gehrig was the overwhelming fan choice at first base over the Athletics' Jimmie Foxx. Foxx had won the MVP the year before and was in the midst of his second-straight MVP campaign. By season's end in 1933, Foxx's numbers would be .356, 48 home runs, and 163 RBIs compared to .334, 32 home runs, and 139 RBIs for NY's Iron Horse. To make matters worse, Foxx was one of only three American Leaguers who did not get into the fray at all. Starter Gehrig, incidentally, dropped a pop fly for the first error in All-Star history.

The following year, the fans again voted Gehrig in at first base. In a controversial move, Foxx started at third base—not his normal position—and displaced

Pinky Higgins, who was batting .356 at All-Star break. Higgins, suffering the ignominy of losing his job to someone who didn't actually play the position, was, as you might guess, a Philadelphia Athletic himself.

Philadelphia is no stranger to All-Star snubs. In 1936, Phillie first baseman Dolph Camilli was batting .348 at the All-Star break and didn't even make the squad. Five years later, as a Dodger in 1941, Camilli won the MVP. He was, of course, overshadowed by the AL MVP winner, a Yankee. That was the year Joe DiMaggio hit in 56 straight games.

Johnnie Callison was second in MVP voting in 1964 when Cardinal third sacker Ken Boyer won the award. Yet Callison, like pitchers Jim Bunning and Chris Short, his two Phillie All-Star teammates that year, made the squad via managerial selection. Callison, of course, was not the only Phillie runner-up MVP who suffered an All-Star slight. In 1993, Lenny Dykstra finished a solid second in the MVP voting. Winner Barry Bonds received 372 votes, followed by Dykstra's 267. David Justice was a distant third place with 183 votes. But Lenny didn't even make the All-Star squad that year.

Even the great Mike Schmidt had a spotty history of All-Star selections. You would expect someone of Schmidt's stature to be an automatic choice year after year. However, Ron Cey, Bill Madlock, Pedro Guerrero, Ken Reitz, and Pete Rose were all selected at one time or another to start ahead of him. Schmidt ultimately made his statement. He was overwhelmingly selected as the starting third baseman in 1989, two months after he had retired from the game.

Aside from the city of Pittsburgh, Philadelphia was the last of baseball's ten original cities to host an All-Star game. The first Philadelphia All-Star contest, played at Shibe Park on July 13, 1943, was notable in many ways. It was the first All-Star game ever played completely under the lights, and was short-waved to American fighting men throughout the world. The game had a bizarre subplot. To prove a point, AL manager Joe McCarthy purposely kept his Yankees out of the match. Six Yankees were named to the squad, but none played. Faced with the incontestable dominance of the American League in World Series and All-Star competition, NL players had been insisting for years that were it not for the Yankees, the two leagues would be at parity. Remove the Yankees, the NL reasoned, and the American League would not dominate. McCarthy, in his sixth All-Star managerial appearance, was also bristling at accusations that he favored his Yanks. In any event, to the senior circuit's embarrassment, the AL won a 5-3 victory on Bobby Doerr's second-inning three-run homer.

The game also marked the first and only time that a host city with more than one franchise failed to place a starter on the field, although the Phillies had to go out of their way to contribute to that dubious distinction. Right up till the week before the game, Phils first sacker Babe Dahlgren was slated to be the starter. However, a few weeks before the All-Star game, Dahlgren, who had been leading the NL in hitting for most of the season, spun into a terrible slump. Phillie manager Bucky Walters benched him. Billy Southwark, NL All-Star pilot, decided he couldn't start a guy who was riding the bench for a seventh-place club. So Dahlgren, despite still owning the third highest batting average in the NL, lost his starting slot.

Philly has endured some All-Star lowlights. From 1937-1946, despite having two franchises in the city, Philadelphia failed to land one starting berth in either league. The Phillies duplicated that dubious feat from 1956-1965. And between 1968 and 1973, no position players made the squad. Only pitchers were selected.

However, Philly boasts some bright All-Star moments as well. Between 1950 and 1955, a Phillie pitcher started every All-Star game. Curt Simmons started in 1952, and Robin Roberts started all the rest. Besides pitching, Philly has forged a strong tradition at third base. Beginning with Foxx in 1934 and 1935, six different Philadelphia players have started eleven different times at the hot corner. Up through 1992, including nonstarters, Philadelphia third sackers have manned the hot corner in 30 percent of all the All-Star games ever played.

Here's a brief list of the Quaker City's most memorable All-Star moments and performances—Philly's phinest hours.

1935: James Emory Foxx started at third base, a position he played only twice all season, so that Lou Gehrig could play first base. With a home run and a single, Foxx drove in three of the AL's four runs in a 4-3 AL win. Unfortunately, in the same game, Foxx's Philadelphia teammate, Indian Bob Johnson, set an All-Star record by striking out three times.

1952: Curt Simmons of the Phils pitched three scoreless innings at Connie Mack Stadium, home of both the A's and the Phils. In the bottom of the fifth, Bobby Shantz, a Pottstown native (Pottstown is a suburb of Philly) fanned Whitey Lockman, Stan Musial, and Jackie Robinson in succession. The game was washed out at that point and Shantz was denied the opportunity to extend the strikeout streak. The 5'6", 139-pound Shantz went on to win the AL MVP in 1952. His NL counterpart, Phillie Robin Roberts, was 28-7 that same year, and (inexplicably) placed second in the MVP voting to Hank Sauer of the Cubs. Sauer's stats for the fifth-place Cubs were .270, 37 home runs, and 121 RBIs.

1964: Phillie pitcher Jim Bunning made All-Star history, becoming the first pitcher ever to appear in an All-Star game in each league. Bunning got Mickey Mantle to pop out on a failed drag bunt attempt. Mantle represented Bunning's twenty-eighth consecutive out at Shea Stadium, where the slim Phillie hurler had twirled a perfect game in his previous appearance. Ironically, lead-footed Harmon Killebrew ended Bunning's string with a rare infield hit. Bunning pitched two scoreless innings and left the game poised to become the first pitcher to win an All-Star game in each league. However, his Phillie teammate, Chris Short, couldn't hold the lead. The game was tied in the ninth when Phillie John Callison stepped into the box to face Boston's Dick Radatz. Henry Aaron had just whiffed. The Monster, as Radatz was known, had already racked up five strikeouts in two and two-thirds innings. The game was one out away from extra innings when Callison drove the Monster's first pitch over the right field wall for a walk-off NL victory.

1981: On August 9, after a 10-week player strike, the umpires were threatening to walk out. At issue was the fact that the umpires were paid for only 45 days of the 50-day strike. The NL walloped four homers that night. Mike Schmidt hit the final one, a two-run blast off future Hall of Famer Rollie Fingers that proved to be the game-winner in front of 72,086 Cleveland fans, the All-Star game's largest-ever crowd. Schmidt also doubled in the game, and, uncharacteristically, made an error (Schmidt won ten Gold Gloves).

1987: The National League broke the longest scoreless deadlock in history in the top of the thirteenth. In the bottom of the frame, Phillie Steve Bedrosian, who went on to win the Cy Young Award that year, made two game-saving plays in one. With runners on second and third, Bedrosian covered first on a double-play ball. Shortstop Hubie Brooks threw wild, forcing Bedrosian to make a diving catch. Meanwhile, Dave Winfield, who started the play on second base, saw the errant throw and headed home. Bedrosian sprang to his feet and nailed Winfield at the plate. Ironically, the catcher on the hookup was Ozzie Virgil, whom the Phillies had traded for Bedrosian prior to the season.

Vuke And The Bird

I like to tease people with this bit of trivia: Which current Phillie has made seven straight All-Star Game appearances? Why, it's the Phanatic, of course!

Major League Baseball started sending all the team mascots to the host city in 1996. I didn't have to go too far that year, because the game was right here in Philadelphia. What a thrill that night was for me. I was all over the stadium, giving an army of out-of-towners a little taste of the Phanatic. I gyrated through the big dance fad at the time, the Macarena, on the dugout with some of our security and hostess staff. I blasted ballpark franks out of my new Hot Dog Launcher, a three-and-a-half-foot CO_2-powered fiberglass hot dog that attaches to the back of my Honda ATV. I danced the twist with Philadelphia-born Chubby Checker. (Trivia Question: What is Chubby Checker's real name? The answer is at the end of the Phanatic Phile.) Chubby can still shake that thing. The highlight of the Phanatic's evening, though, came in the bottom of the seventh inning, when Ozzie Smith came to bat in his final All-Star Game appearance. The crowd stood and gave Ozzie a thunderous ovation. Play was halted for a minute. Ozzie grounded out, and as he was making his way back to the dugout to more cheers, he caught me jumping up and down in the first row, acting like an idiot as usual. He stopped, wheeled around, and gave the Phanatic a high five. Look, I'm from Philly. Larry Bowa is still my favorite all-time shortstop, but after that classy move by The Wizard, Ozzie has edged up on Bobby Wine and Granny Hamner.

PHANATIC PHILE

Going to other cities for the All-Star Game is a blast. Part of the fun is catching up with other loonies who do the same thing I do for a living. We usually entertain at the stadium on Workout Day and work other events associated with the game. The mascots go on an annual Friendship Tour, visiting children's hospitals in the host city. Naturally, we're always swapping stories. My favorite is one that Bromley Lowe, the Bird down in Baltimore, tells about our third base coach John Vukovich, who is no fan of mascots, *except* for the Phanatic. The Phillies were playing an interleague game against the Orioles at Camden Yards and were in the process of being swept. In the top of the ninth, the Bird appeared on top of the visitor's dugout, waving a broom and encouraging the crowd to start hollering "sweep." Within seconds, Vuke was out of the dugout glowering up at the Bird, pointing his finger at him and screaming. When Vuke gets mad, it kind of looks like one of those demon transformations on *Buffy the Vampire Slayer*. All the veins around his neck and forehead pop out and bulge. Bromley blew the incident off cause he felt safe. He forgot the whole thing. Vuke did not.

Immediately after the Orioles won that Sunday afternoon, Bromley had taken off the costume and was relaxing in his dressing room, talking on the phone. Suddenly there was a pounding at the door, and then it swung open. It wasn't the Grim Reaper. It was worse.

"Where the hell is that bird mascot?" John bellowed, veins still popping.

Bromley froze, phone in hand, watching the eyes of this mad-man in a Phillies coach's jacket pop out of their sockets. Thinking fast, Bromley calmly replied, "Uh, sorry, you *just* missed him. He left about five minutes ago."

Vuke sneered, "You tell that guy that if I ever see him near our dugout again waving a broom, I'm gonna take that broom and stick it right up his butt!"

Vuke stormed out of the room as Bromley's life passed in front of his eyes. Bromley might be a Bird, but he's not a birdbrain.

Trivia Answer: Earnest Evans, born October 3, 1941 in Philadelphia

Nailing It Down

*"Nobody ever let anything sit on that team. We would air out our
differences and ten minutes later be pulling a joke on someone. And if you
went after one of us, you went after all of us. You might as well fight a
blender."*
– *Mitch Williams*

*"They had a little team here in the sixties and they blew a lead, and when
you're in first place all year long, that's all we heard. They forgot about '80,
they forgot about '83. They always went back to that, and that was one of
the things we had to fight. They kept everything in the clubhouse."*
— *Jim Fregosi*

T he Ghetto could be a mean street. Sure, the locker room was one
part *Our Gang* clubhouse, one part *Three Stooges* backlot, and
one part *Animal House*, and the '93 Phillies loved to party, but their
parties were by invitation only. The guys in the Ghetto could make it an uncomfortable place to the uninvited, the unwanted, or outsiders in general. At times,
outsiders included the rest of the world.

JOHN KRUK: "One time, Dave Hollins's old roommate from the minors
had just been called up. He walked over to the batting cage to see Dave. Headley
looked at the guy, all serious, and said, 'You're the enemy. You don't belong here.'
Head did the same thing to Danny Jackson after DJ was traded and came back
to the clubhouse to see us. Head told him he didn't belong in the clubhouse and
told him to go."

The Ghetto could be an especially tough neighborhood for a rookie. The
team that took such pride in intimidating the opposition sometimes ate its own
young.

FREGOSI: "When I came to Philadelphia, one of the first things I did was
to bring Mickey Morandini up from the minors. I always thought Mickey could
be a full-time big-leaguer, because Mickey was tough. I knew if he was gonna
make it, he had to be tough enough to break into our own clubhouse. Wally
Backman and Lenny Dykstra were teammates at the time. Those two guys were
tight, and here's this little punk Morandini getting to play. But Mickey handled
whatever they dished out. Mickey proved himself to those guys and made himself a very good player on a good club."

The toughness that glued that team was born of a sense of desperation.

JOHN KRUK: "Yeah, we knew if we stunk it up and didn't win in '93, we'd all be gone anyway. So if we wanted to stay together, we had to win that year. We didn't want to be split up. We didn't want to play anywhere else. Staying together meant a lot to us."

The hard core, the Ghetto, fostered the good times, the grab-ass, and the fun. They worked at keeping their workplace fun and trouble-free.

TERRY MULHOLLAND: "That clubhouse was our sanctuary. No matter what anyone's problems were outside of the stadium, or at home, or if you had a horse-bleep drive in, or whatever, that was *our* clubhouse and we policed it like it was our clubhouse. There were times when we had reporters coming in trying to drum up some bullcrap, maybe pit one guy against the other, or get us to say something horse-bleep about the coaching staff, or whatever, and it was like, 'Hey, *you* don't understand. You're in *our* clubhouse, and we don't have to take that crap.' And there were times when our guys would get in the face of sports writers and say, 'Take a hike. I got no use for this. This has nothing to do with what we're doing on the field. You're just trying to stir crap. We don't need some visitor coming in here trying to disrupt what we've got going on.' So we were very careful about looking out for each other, making sure the level of BS in that clubhouse was *our* BS, not somebody else's."

JAYSON STARK: "It could be real intimidating to walk into that clubhouse for a writer. Those guys knew this was their chance in 1993, and they weren't going to let it pass. They weren't going to let anything or anyone outside that clubhouse come between them. The fact that they hung out together all those hours after games and talked baseball spells out what they were. They were *baseball animals*. They were more than guys playing baseball and picking up their paychecks."

As the season progressed, the Phillies became their persona more and more.

TERRY MULHOLLAND: We weren't only ballplayers. We were *hard ballplayers*. We were guys that physically wanted to beat you, not only in the runs column. We wanted to beat you physically, like taking you out at second base, like knocking you down at the plate to make you feel uncomfortable. We had a goal of winning the game every day no matter what, and during the season, you can go down the lineup. You'll find everyone on that team contributed a lot."

Whether we admit it or not, most of us like our nostalgia simple and slick, in bite-sized doses, and, if possible, sugar-coated so it goes down easily. There was a menacing edge to the Ghetto, and sometimes that came out unpleasantly. But as the second half of the Enchanted Season began, more than ever, the Phillies were determined to finish the job they started in Clearwater, though they didn't start like a team on a mission. Against the lowly Padres, who went on to lose 101 games in '93, the Phillies lost three in a row immediately after the All-Star break. Coupled with their loss to the Giants before All-Star break, their string of losses stretched to four for the first and only time all season. Their lead dwindled to three games over the second-place Cards. On Sunday, July 18, Schilling picked up his first W since June 11, stopping the Phillies skid and halting his personal losing streak at five. Mitch came on in the ninth for save number 24.

The Phillies moved on to L.A. The series got off to an inauspicious start when John Vukovich, pitching batting practice, hit starting pitcher Ben Rivera on the finger. Rivera had won five of his last six decisions. Mike Williams pitched effectively in Big Ben's place, and the Phillies triumphed. The Fightins followed up with two more wins for their fifth series sweep of the season. The Phillies cleaned up on the Dodgers in '93, going 10-2 for the year.

Forty-five minutes after the final game of the Dodger series, two buses and a truck pulled through the center-field fence at Dodger Stadium, circled the field, and halted in front of the first base dugout. The Phillies boarded the buses, loaded their baggage on the trucks, and went directly to Los Angeles International Airport. They boarded a charter flight and zoomed off to San Francisco, arriving at 3 a.m. for a day game a few hours later. They continued to have troubles with the Giants, who took three of four in a series that drew 173,929 fans. The Phils managed to eke out a lone victory, a 14-inning, 2-1 nail-biter. Schilling went for a complete game in the ninth, clinging to a narrow 1-0 margin. However, Barry Bonds homered to knot the score. In the fourteenth, the Phillies tallied one on an error and two sacrifices. Mitch came on for his twenty-sixth save.

Bonds

JOHN KRUK: I remember when Barry played for the Pirates, he hit one out and seemed to stand at the plate watching it forever. After the game, Mitch was fumin' in the clubhouse. 'He's goin' down! I'm gonna drill that son of a bitch. Who the hell does he think he is?' So the next game, Mitch throws a fastball right at him and nails him on the arm. Bonds steams down to first, and when he gets there he's jabbering, 'What the hell was that all about?' I said, 'I don't know, maybe he don't like the way you look.' Then Bonds starts grumbling to me, 'I'm gonna kill that son of a bitch,' just keeps repeating it. Finally I heard enough and said, 'Well, go ahead. I ain't gonna stop you. You'd be doing us all a favor.'

"Bonds started wearing that forearm protector the next day. We found out later that Bonds stood and watched that home run the day before because it was his 200th career homer and he was savoring the moment."

Well, not exactly, John ...

Bonds didn't hit his 200th homer till the following year, when he jacked one out on the Phillies' Jose DeLeon on July 8. Milestone or no milestone, Bonds makes himself a target for Philly boobirds by admiring his own shots till they land before he budges from the box. Major League Baseball is trying to speed up the game. They even cut down the time for *my* routines between innings. Here's a suggestion: limit the time Bonds stands in the batter's box. The guy has hit about 600 homers. That'll cut significant time.

Barry Bonds didn't score many points with other hurlers on the '93 staff either.

LARRY ANDERSEN: "That first home series against the Giants was rough. First they beat us 13-2. It was the night after that long 20-inning game. The bullpen was shot from the night before, and Jose was out there trying to eat up some innings. Bonds hit his home run and watched it pretty good. Fregosi took the Dude, Dutch and Krukkie out of the game.

"The next night, the Giants batted around in the first and second inning and had us down 11-0 after two. After three innings it was 13-0 and they already had 14 hits. [Giants pitcher] Mike Jackson came into the game and threw a pitch right at Pete Incaviglia's head. The benches emptied, but no punches were thrown. I was scheduled to pitch the next inning, and I knew that something had to be done. I walked up the tunnel a bit with Dutch, and he goes, 'I know what you're planning to do, and don't worry, nobody's gonna get to you.'

"I asked Terry Muholland what I should throw at Royce Clayton, their first batter that inning. He told me to throw the fastball. I wasn't too sure about that since I don't have much control of the fastball. Anyway, I went out there and threw two fastballs at him and missed. Then, on the third pitch, I threw a fastball *behind* him. The umpire immediately ejected Fregosi and me. I tried to tell him that it slipped, but he wasn't buying it."

The Phils were in San Francisco a week later. Neither Bonds nor his teammates had forgiven or forgotten.

LARRY ANDERSEN: "Bonds comes up and hits one off me and stands there watching it again. When the inning ended I told him I didn't appreciate him standing there watching it. He said, 'I'll hit 'em any way I like.' He told reporters later that he stood and watched that one to show me up since I tried hitting Clayton the week before. Anyway, that was the last time I ever faced Barry."

The problem with Barry's explanation is that he stands and watches just about every homer he hits. With all the homers he's hit, at this point, Barry must have evened the score for every pitcher whoever threw at any of his teammates all the way back to Little League—or whoever set the ball up wrong in tee-ball.

On July 27, the Phillies scampered home from the City by the Bay to the more congenial digs in Veterans Stadium. They had reached the hundred-game milestone with a record of 62-38. With the second-place Cards coming to town five games behind them, the three-game set shaped up as the key series of the season. As Larry Andersen mused, "We pretty much have to go back home and find out what we're made of."

The Cards provided the Phillies with extra motivation. Philadelphia was convinced that Mark Whiten, the Cards' right fielder, had slurred them on ESPN. Milt Thompson told reporters, "He [Whiten] said, 'It's nice to sit back and watch the Phils fall flat on their face.' But that doesn't bother us. The Cardinals are the ones that are popping off. They can talk all they want. The game is played between those lines, as the old adage goes." Whiten denied making the comments. (Whiten, who later played for the Phillies, had a peculiar career. His best season was 1993, when he slammed 25 home runs. In his first 11 years, he tallied only 105 homers, yet on September 7, 1993, he became one of only nine major-leaguers ever to hit four homers in a nine-inning game.)

Whiten's outburst was something that didn't happen on the Phillies. Despite their reputation as bad boys, they were not trash talkers.

TERRY MULHOLLAND: "Before anyone went out to talk to a reporter, Dutch would say, 'Let sleeping dogs lie. Don't say anything stupid to the press that's gonna make these guys [opponents] want to kick our butts tomorrow.' A lot of times when things were going bad, we just let Dutch go out and talk for all of us."

Wes Chamberlain shaved his head for good luck as the series commenced. Fortunately, he and his Phillie teammates kept their heads and beat up on the Cards. In the first game, Kruk went five for five against five different hurlers. The Phillies jumped off to a 7-1 second-inning lead and hung on for a 10-7 win. Tommy Greene was forced to leave the game after 2 2/3 innings with a strained groin. He would remain on the disabled list until August 12. In the second game of the series, Todd Zeile rocketed a first-inning grand slam off Terry Mulholland. The Phillies roared back as Daulton answered with his fifth career grand slam to tie the game in the third. Dutch picked up two additional RBIs and Mulholland picked up his tenth win for an easy 14-6 Phillie win.

Less than a month earlier, Daulton had grilled his team, especially pitchers Schilling and Greene, for their embarrassing 14-5 loss to these same Cards. Now, on the heels of a shaky showing in San Francisco, the Phillies muscled up on their macho and took it right to St. Louis. Daulton led the way to perhaps the key win of the season, turning the tables on their main competition. To be sure, the Phillies were not playing Spalding Guide baseball. Dave Hollins, playing hurt most of the year, had made six errors in the last eleven games—five on throws. As Kruk put it, "Dave Hollins is going to make errors. But he's going to drive in runs, too. In this game, he didn't let any in and drove in three. Helluva game, I'd say."

In the final game of the series, a Business Person's Special that drew 55,884, the Phillies won again, this time 6-4. The win sealed the Phils' second sweep of St. Louis that year. It also capped off a perfect record at home against the Cards

—the first time in franchise history that Philadelphia had swept St. Louis at home for an entire season. The three-game set drew 147,613 spectators. Again, Dutch shined—not in spectacular fashion, but by doing the little things that win games. After Kevin Stocker was intentionally walked in the eighth inning of the third contest, Dutch worked a walk that brought in the winning run. The Dude followed with a single for a two-run cushion. The Cards left the Quaker City with their tails between their legs, trailing by seven. St. Louis was never again a factor in the pennant race that season.

Oh! The Humanity

Dan Goroff's job is not glamorous. Dan spends each game holed up in his office on the second floor of the Vet, handling anything and everything that has to do with tickets. Dan and his ticket department had no chance to catch their breaths that season. Heading into 1993, the Phillies' season ticket base hovered around 15,000 tickets per game. That comes out to 1,200,000 tickets per season. From February to September that season, the Phillies sold another 2,000,000 tickets to individuals buying tickets by phone, through the mail, and in person at the ticket windows.

"When people ask me to put that number in perspective, I tell them to count to 2,000,000 by 4 [the average number of tickets per order] and then get back to me," Dan said. "That was the most exhausting year of my life. The phones never stopped ringing. We have a phone center set up to take ticket orders, but we had to put in more phone lines and hire more people that year. We hired people for the sole purpose of mailing out tickets to our customers."

The Phillies drew 3,137,674 fans in '93, a whopping *362,663* fans more than the *second* highest highest total (in 1979) in Philadelphia history. Attendance figures have been kept since 1901, and that 362,663 differential between best and second best years for attendance exceeds the *full-year* attendance figures for *every year but six* from 1901 through 1945 (for those who think baseball has lost popularity).

There were eight sellouts in '93, sixteen dates where attendance exceeded 50,000, and a 20-game streak where attendance exceeded 40,000 each game. The Phillies also established a club record for attendance on the road, averaging almost 33,000 fans a game. The entire country was smitten with this squad.

As curator of the hottest ticket in town, Dan wielded a bit of clout in those days.

"The mayor had his own box for games, but that year, he always needed extra tickets. I remember returning a call to the mayor's office one day. Normally, I spoke with a clerk, but obviously they needed extra tickets badly. David Cohen, the mayor's chief of staff and right-hand man, got on the line. I said, 'David, you're the second most powerful man in this city; what are you doing answering my call?' He said, 'Dan, right now, *you're* the second most powerful man in this city.'"

When the playoffs came, the ticket office went into overdrive.

"After taking care of our season ticket people and all of MLB's [Major League Baseball] ticket requests, only 30,000 tickets were available for each game," recalls Dan. "We decided to hold a lottery to determine who would get the remaining tickets. We received over 300,000 postcards in the mail. We sent out the first announcement to 4,000 winners of NLCS tickets right after we clinched the division in Pittsburgh. We told them they had four days to redeem their tickets at the Phillies ticket window or else they would forfeit their tickets. That first Monday, when we opened up the ticket windows, there were more than 5,000 people in line. The line wrapped around the stadium. People waited over five hours to get to the ticket window, but everyone stayed calm and in good spirits. Most people made friends with the people in line around them. The most amazing thing was the number of people who asked to be seated with people they had just met in line. Phillies fans are the greatest."

The Phillies finished out their home stand by taking two of three from Pittsburgh before going on the road and taking two of three from Atlanta and Florida. Inky kicked into a torrid power streak, hitting homers on four consecutive days. He started the streak with two round-trippers in one game against the Pirates on July 31, and continued by hitting single home runs in the next three games.

In the final game of the series against Pittsburgh on August 1, Pirate hurler Steve Cooke plunked Inky, who had words with the pitcher on his way to first. Mariano Duncan then got into a verbal exchange with Jay Bell, the Pirates' fiery shortstop, while Inky was called back to the batter's box. Umpire Jeff Kellogg ruled that the ball had hit Inky's bat. The benches cleared, and Fregosi got ejected. On the first pitch next inning, Phils pitcher Roger Mason backed Lloyd McClendon off the plate. McClendon and catcher Todd Pratt got into it and the benches cleared again. Mason, a deeply religious person, apparently chose to follow the Headley's Choice doctrine rather than turning the other cheek. Roger himself had been reborn as a pitcher since coming to the Phillies from the Padres the evening of the 4:41 game. He had been 0-7 as a Padre, but against the Pirates, he chalked up his third straight Phillie win. After the game, Inky growled, "I don't mind people throwing inside. I don't even mind getting hit from the shoulders down. That's a part of the game. But throw at my face on an 0-2 count? I won't stand for that. That's the law. If I get hit in the coconut, it would end my career. And if somebody tries to end my career, I'm going to end theirs."

Nostalgia Day

We had over 46,000 in attendance that final game of the home stand on August 1 against Pittsburgh. The game had some edge because the Pirates and the Phils were jawing at each other the entire game. It was Nostalgia Day. The "Turn Back the Clock" concept was a new fad that a lot of the teams were trying. The teams wore uniforms from whatever decade they turned the clocks back to. The concession stands rolled back food prices to that same decade. That afternoon, the Phils and Pirates squeezed into 1933-style uniforms. Transporting Veterans Stadium back sixty years was a challenge. Video scoreboards, mascots and Astroturf weren't part of the scene when Chuck Klein, Chick Fullis, and Spud Davis were patrolling Baker Bowl. But our promotions staff gave it a good shot anyway. In an elaborate pregame show, we transformed the field into a speakeasy at the corner of Broad and Lehigh Avenue where Baker Bowl once stood. For all of you youngsters out there, Baker Bowl was home to the Phillies until July 4, 1938 when they moved to Shibe Park (later renamed Connie Mack Stadium). The scene was packed with flappers, G-men, and bootleggers. There were guest appearances from impersonators playing President Franklin D. Roosevelt and Phillies great Chuck Klein. Employees dressed in 1930s garb, and music from the era blared over the loudspeakers all day. The Phanavision video board in the outfield showed only black and white, no color.

The fans enjoyed the extravaganza, which played to mixed reviews with the players.

WES CHAMBERLAIN: "I think those uniforms were supposed to be worn kind of baggy. But I remember not being able to fit into them. I had to try on about three different pairs before I could find a pair that fit. And even then, they were too tight. Everybody was making jokes that my butt was too big."

LARRY ANDERSEN: "I came into the game in the seventh, gave up three hits and was yanked in the eighth. I walked into the clubhouse and ripped that old style uniform to shreds. Some guy in the stands kept yelling, 'Hey, Andersen, how's it feel to be in your old uniform?' No, I wasn't a big fan of Nostalgia Day."

Todd Pratt was a big fan of Nostalgia Day. The Phils backup catcher hit two home runs and banged out a career-high three hits in the winning effort. Pratt was a solid backup for Daulton, batting

.287 overall and a lofty .340 in day games.

In Atlanta, the Phillies split the first two games of the Braves series. In the rubber game, Daulton was ejected for arguing balls and strikes with home plate umpire, Randy Marsh. The Braves had jumped on Ben Rivera for four runs in the first, with Maddux on the hill for Atlanta. With the bases loaded and one out, several banks of lights went out. The game was halted for fifteen minutes. When play resumed, pinch hitter Sid Bream grounded into a double play, and the whole complexion of the game changed. Led by Dave Hollins's three hits, the Phillies came back to win the game going away, 10-4. It was the first time in thirty opportunities that Maddux had lost a four-run lead.

The Phillies returned home on August 10 for a six-game home stand where they took five of six, sweeping three from Montreal and besting the Mets two of three. In the opener of the home stand, Schilling tossed his sixth complete game to join Tommy Greene, Terry Mulholland, and Ben Rivera in the ten-or-more-wins club, marking the first time since 1978 the Phils had four pitchers in double figures in wins. Before the game, the Phillies traded Jose DeLeon to the White Sox for Bobby Thigpen, who won in his first appearance in the opener of the Mets series on August 13. The Phillies trailed 5-4 in the ninth when Kim Batiste iced the game with his first career grand slam. It was the Phils' seventh salami of the season, tying the club record set initially in 1925 and equaled in 1929 and 1976. Two days later, Batiste repeated his heroics when he knocked in the winning run in the rubber game. Trailing 4-1 in the home eighth, Kruk nailed a two-run homer followed by two-out RBI singles by Wes Chamberlain and Batiste.

The Phillies were rolling again. Their lead swelled to nine games on August 15 as Tommy Greene came back off the disabled list. Schilling was pitching like a machine. Dykstra was scoring runs at a record clip. Mitch was saving games at a record clip. Incaviglia was on a power surge.

The club went on the road on August 17 and took the first two games of a three-game set against the Rockies. In the second game of three, Phils attendance soared over the two million mark on the road as Kruk slammed two homers for the second time that year, Stocker drove in three, and Mitch picked up his thirty-fourth save. When the Phillies moved on to Houston, they broke their club road attendance record of 2,061,384, set in 1987. The Phillies remained baseball's big story and most entertaining highlight film.

Returning to the Vet after going 3-3 in Colorado and Houston, Philadelphia lost to the Rockies 3-2 in thirteen innings. The next night, however, DJ won his tenth of the year, marking the first time since 1932 that the Phillies had five starters with ten or more wins. The Wild Thing earned his thirty-sixth save for the season and his ninety-fifth as a Phil, placing him second on the club's all-time list. The following night, August 25, Schil tied his career high with nine strikeouts en route to an 8-5 victory that swelled the Phillies' lead to eleven games. That lead would be the peak for the rest of the season.

Ben Rivera spun a 7-0 masterpiece to end the month of August in Chicago. Rivera scattered four singles and fanned nine to tie his career high. The Phillies were 16-11 for August. They entered September with a nine-game lead, making the 1993 team the only one in club history to spend the first day of each month in first place. The Cards, who had been vainly chasing the Phillies all season long, dropped into third place, overtaken by the surging Montreal Expos, as September broke. The Cards dealt their ace closer Lee Smith to the Yankees—a move that many viewed as conceding the division.

MIDDLE RELIEF

Larry Andersen achieved something in '93 that perhaps no other player in the history of the game has achieved. He led his team in both batting average and ERA in the same year. Perhaps some other player accomplished that same feat somewhere back in the nineteenth century. If so, then Larry was probably the only one who ever accomplished it on a pennant-winning team. And if that still doesn't wash, then he must be the only 40-year old to have done it on a pennant-winner.

His major contribution, however, was as a reliable middle reliever, the table-setter, along with leftie David West, for closer Mitch Williams. LA and Westie tied for the lowest ERA (2.92) on the staff. Both hurlers had been question marks prior to the season—Larry because of age (he would "celebrate"—a term used more for convention than description—his fortieth birthday during the season) and West because his career stats prior to 1993 were 16-20, 5.45. In '93, however, both relief artists had great seasons. Both strung together 13 1/3-inning scoreless streaks. West's streak lasted from April 14 to May 15; Andy's from June 1 to July 3.

The rest of the 'pen got the job done, too. Roger Mason pitched 49 2/3 innings and recorded five wins after coming over to the Phillies on July 3. Bobby Thigpen, acquired on August 11 for Jose DeLeon, went 3-1 as a Phil. Donnie Pall, acquired from the White Sox on September 1, twirled only 17 2/3 innings but allowed only 5 earned runs for a 2.55 ERA and a 1-0 record. Mark Davis was the single disappointment. Brought over from the Braves on April 13, Doc, as he was called, was released on July 2.

All in all, the middle relievers far surpassed expectations in 1993 and became a vital cog in the Phillies' attack.

CHRIS WHEELER, PHILLIE ANNOUNCER: "Middle relievers turned in the kind of season that allowed Fregosi to manage the 'pen the way he needed. Fregosi's philosophy was for the middle relief corps to get him to the ninth and set up a save situation for Mitch. Fregosi didn't want Mitch in before the ninth, and he didn't want to bring Mitch in with anyone on. For the most part, those middle relievers did just that all season. Their good setup work had a lot to do with Mitch getting those 43 saves."

Following Rivera's masterpiece, the Phillies starters tossed a couple more complete games. On September 1, Muholland threw his league-leading seventh CG in a 4-1 victory over the Cubs, followed on Friday by Tommy Greene, who threw his sixth while striking out a career-high eleven. Tee the Greene also blasted his second home run of the season in a 14-2 shellacking of the Reds. In Greenie's game, the Phillies also tied the record for most consecutive games (150) without being shut out, set by the 1924-25 Pirates. The next night they broke the record but lost the game 6-5, when a four-run ninth-inning rally fell one run short.

Schil put the team on the winning track again the following night with a 5-3 decision over Cincinnati, as Mitch added another save.

As the month of September broke, the Phillies, who had remained relatively healthy for most of the year, suddenly were besieged with injuries. On September 1, Mulholland had to leave the game after facing just three batters. The All-Star lefty had a strained hip flexor (the *sartorius* muscle that runs from the front of the hip to the knee), and he would be out of action till September 30. Larry Andersen had been suffering from a bad back for about three weeks. Though he didn't miss action, the injury inhibited his performance. On September 8, against the Cubs, Inky sprained his left knee going after a fly ball in the eighth and was forced to miss a few games. On September 10, Schilling had to leave the game in the eighth when Ed Taubensee lined a shot back through the box that rocked his shin.

MARIANO'S STREAKS

It was a bad scene on September 9 at the Vet. In the first inning, Cubs starter Jose Bautista brushed Mariano Duncan back after Lenny Dykstra's leadoff home run. En route to a five-RBI, three-run day, the Dude homered again in the third to give the Phils a 9-2 advantage. This time, it was Frank Castillo who brushed Mariano back. Castillo was immediately heaved from the game, but Mariano streaked to the mound anyway. Both benches erupted. In the melee, Castillo hurt his left hand. He was taken to Methodist Hospital and treated for laceration between the third and fourth fingers. Castillo later returned to the stadium and challenged Duncan to meet him under the stands. To maintain order, two cops were stationed in the basement hall that separates the home and visitor's clubhouses. Mariano was personally escorted to his car by a security guard.

Castillo was suspended three days and fined $500. In a strange twist, the fiery pitcher was sent home by the Cubs for insubordination. It seems that when the Cubs left Philadelphia for New York, Castillo, without bothering to inform the Cubs, took a limousine instead of the team bus. To tick his employers off more, he was caught playing catch twice after being ordered by the Cubs not to do so because of the possibility of reinjuring his hand.

Mariano was also suspended three days and fined $500. He immediately appealed the fine but dropped the appeal so he could play in the all-important series against the Expos. The Phillie second baseman was on a tear at the time. His hit streak hit 18 games on the final day of the Montreal series—Mariano's last day prior to his suspension. When he came back to action, Mariano immediately lost his streak. Reflecting after the game on his ill-fated streak to the mound that led to his suspension: "Now that I think about it, I shouldn't have charged the mound."

J-E-L-L-O

Larry Andersen has been a big help writing this book. When we discussed September, though, Larry shook his head. "The clubhouse was in a slump. All of a sudden, we didn't have the same enthusiasm or drive, and we weren't having the same fun that we had all season. It's just that everybody was tired, and when the minor-leaguers were called up, it seemed like the veterans were acting a little differently—you know, that chemistry thing was just a little disturbed."

I responded, "Fine, Larry, but we can't have a slump in our book. So tell me about the *greatest prank of all,* the best one you ever pulled off."

LARRY ANDERSEN: "That would be the Jello Prank, or Jellogate, as it was sometimes called. The year was 1982, and I was playing with the Mariners. We were on the road, staying in a hotel in Chicago, when a couple of teammates of mine, Joe Simpson and Richie Zisk, and I decided to have a little fun at the expense of Rene Lachemann, who was our manager at the time. We conned the traveling secretary into giving us Lach's hotel room key while Lach was out. We consumed a few beverages, went out and bought sixteen boxes of Jello, and stormed into Lach's room, kind of making it look like Hurricane Andrew had hit it. We took the mattress and all of the bedding and put it in one of the bathrooms. He had two bathrooms in the suite, so there was plenty of room left to stuff the rest of his furniture into the bathrooms. We took all the lights out of the fixtures. We changed the time on his clock. We took the mouthpiece out of his phone. We took the toilet paper and papered his whole room. The place was so trashed, it was unrecognizable.

"Then came the best part. We put eight boxes of cherry Jello in each toilet and went down the hall and got a couple of buckets of ice so it jelled.

"Well, when Lach got back to the hotel and opened the door, he nearly hit the roof. I mean he was pissed. He couldn't use the toilets because if you tried to go to the bathroom— well, I'm sure you can figure it out. He tried to use the phone and couldn't understand why he could hear but nobody could hear him! It was beautiful!

"Anyway, the next day at the park, Lach is still screaming and cursing and threatening to call the FBI to have the place dusted for fingerprints. But it didn't end there. For the rest of the year, we would have room service deliver Jello to his room without him knowing who ordered it. We even broke into the little refrigerator in the manager's office and poked a hole in the bottoms of the beer cans. We drained the beer out and poured in the Jello mixture through the little holes. Then we put them back in his refrigerator. He'd go to pull a beer out after the game, open it, and discover it was a can of Jello! The best part was that he never knew who the culprits were. Ten years later, we had some hats made up that read "Mr. Jello—10-Year Anniversary." The front was done up like a box of Jello. Lach is probably not a big fan of Jello at this point in his life."

The minor injuries and the wear and tear of the season were taking their toll. The Phillies suffered through their worst home stand of the year, a seven-game debacle starting on Labor Day, where they managed but two wins and watched their lead wither from nine to five with but nineteen games to go.

Greene and Schilling kept their ship afloat during that swoon. From September 10 through September 20, Schilling won three and Greene won two, while the rest of the staff lost five. Two of those five losses came against Montreal, who was coming on strong at the end of the season.

The Phillies-Expos three-game series drew 136,242 fans to Olympic Stadium—the highest three-game total since August 1982. Expo fans were pumped about their team. Montreal had gone 20-3 since August 20. The Phillies were 11-13 in the same period. During that time frame, the Expos whittled the Phillies' lead down from 14 games to four. The specter of 1964 hovered over the '93 squad.

In the first game of the Montreal-Philadelphia faceoff, the Phillies fell behind 3-0 after five innings before surging ahead 7-4 with a seven-run sixth-inning burst. The bullpen yielded three more runs the next inning as Montreal tied. The score remained knotted at seven from the eighth through the eleventh. Then in the twelfth, Mitch gave up the winning run and took the loss.

The next day, Tommy Greene was working on a two-hitter before yielding a three-run homer in the eighth that brought the Expos to within one. This time,

Mitch came on for the save, his thirty-ninth of the season, and the Phillies' ninetieth win. Next day, however, the Wild Thing was back in trouble, taking the loss in the rubber game. The score was knotted at five when Mitch appeared in the bottom of the ninth. He surrendered two and lost. A blown call at first base by umpire Charlie Williams led to his demise.

Mitch had already let the tying run cross the plate when Larry Walker hit a grounder to Kruk. The Wild Thing covered first and appeared to have beaten Walker to the bag with Kruk's toss in hand for the out. However, umpire Charlie Williams called Walker safe. Sean Berry followed Walker with a popup, but Will Cordero drove in the deciding score.

After the game, Mitch fumed, "There's no way in the *friggin'* world he was safe. It was a stupid call. There's no way he could have missed it if he was doing his job. It wasn't even a bang-bang play. Impact umpire. Brutal."

JOHN KRUK: "I bobbled that ball that Walker hit. But the most surprising thing about that play was that Mitch was actually covering first base. He never covered first base! I was shocked to see him over there."

Philadelphia—the entire city—was apprehensive as the Phillies returned to the Vet. Larry Andersen and Mitch tried to defuse the crowd. Before the game, the two bullpen stalwarts switched jerseys. Actually, Andersen balked about wearing Mitch's jersey. "I was afraid of snipers," reasoned LA. Mitch walked down left field to the 'pen with "Andersen" written across the back of his jersey. Mitch still had to listen to the boos that Santa, the Easter Bunny, and scores of other Philly players heard before him.

Writing Glove Letters In The Sand

Watching Mitch make his way to the bullpen in Larry Andersen's jersey after he had blown those two games in Montreal reminded me of 1985. Mike Schmidt had ripped the Philly boobirds in an April interview with a writer from the *Montreal Gazette*. Eventually the article found its way back to the Philadelphia media.

LARRY ANDERSEN: "Schmitty knew that he was going to hear it from the fans as soon as he stepped on to the field. He acted like he didn't care about getting booed, but I think he *did* care. I grabbed this brown, long-haired wig and told Schmitty, 'Put this on. The fans are just waiting to bury you right now, so you might as well have fun. It can't get much worse.' So he put the wig on, put his hat on and put on a pair of sunglasses and ran out to first base to take infield practice. The crowd, which was ready to boo him, stood up and gave him a standing ovation instead."

> Dick Allen was another lightning rod for boos. But whereas Mitch and Schmitty used humor to make fun of themselves, Dick used it to incite the crowd even more.
>
> BILL CONLIN: "There was always controversy surrounding Allen, and 1969 was no different. Standing at first base, Allen would scribble words into the dirt. He wrote the words, 'Mom,' 'Coke,' 'Boo,' 'Why' and 'October 2,' which was the last day of the season. The Phils finished the season in New York that year, and Allen told the New York media before the game that the Mets needed him next year. He went out and hit three huge home runs. It was the only three-home run game of his career. After the game he told the media, 'See, I told you so.'"
>
> Maybe Dick should have tried a wig. He ended up not in New York, not in Philly, but in St. Louis the following year.

Schilling's win on the first night of the home stand on September 20 silenced the 1964 prophets of doom. It was Schil's seventh complete game of the season, his seventh straight win, and his fifteenth victory overall. The game set the tone for a three-game sweep over the Marlins, which grew the lead back to five games by the end of the Marlins series. In the second game against the Marlins, late season acquisition Donnie Pall checked in with his first victory as a Phil, and the Phillies' magic number to clinch the division dropped to seven. The following night, the magic number dropped to six, when Roger Mason won his fifth game of the season.

The Braves came to town on Friday, September 24, to close out the home season at the Vet. Tommy Greene and Mitch combined in the opener for a nifty three-hit shutout. Mitch struck out the last two Braves to stamp a big exclamation point on his forty-first save of the season, a new Phillie record.

The Phillies dropped the next two—the final home games of the year—in front of sellout crowds of 57,176 and 57,588. In the home finale, which was Fan Appreciation Day, Curt Schilling lost his only game since the All-Star break. Larry Andersen provided some laughs at the affair. In a pretaped segment shown on Phanavision between innings, players took turns thanking the Phillies faithful for their support. Larry's message was: "I'd like to thank you, the fans. You people have made us what we are this year. But I also don't want you to forget that you made us what we were last year, too."

On Monday, September 27, the Phillies trekked to Pittsburgh where Ben Rivera won his thirteenth, 6-4, lowering the magic number to one. The next night, trailing 4-3 in the top of the seventh, Mariano Duncan reprised his Mother's Day act when he launched his second grand slam of the season to seal the Phillies' forty-sixth comeback win of the season. Mariano's slam was the team's eighth of the year, setting a club record. As fate would have it, ten years earlier the Phillies had clinched their last title on the same date.

The day after the clinch, the Phillies lost 9-1. Dykstra sat out for the first time all season. The following evening, the Phillies were shut out by Tim Wakefield, who became only the second pitcher all year to complete a game against them. Their remarkable streak of 174 consecutive games without being shut out began and ended in Pittsburgh.

JOHN VUKOVICH: "Losing that streak shows the character of that team. Records like that meant nothing to them. Just like they didn't care about all the national attention they got, they didn't care about records. They only cared about wins. A lot of teams claimed to be that way. These guys really were."

The team moved on to St. Louis for a meaningless series to close out the season. Schilling won the opener for his all-time best sixteenth victory, as Mitch notched his all-time best forty-third save.

Party Time!

Tuesday, September 28 ... the team that had earned its reputation, brew by brew, as the biggest party animals that baseball has seen in decades, was busting to party on.

FRANK COPPENBARGER: "A win that night, and we clinched. Every locker had a roll of plastic above it, set to be rolled down so the beer and champagne didn't splash all over the lockers. We had boxes of hats and T-shirts that said "National League East Champions." We had 144 bottles of champagne and ten cases of beer on ice. TV lights were set up for postclinch locker room interviews. I remember Curt Schilling walking in, all excited, saying, 'So, Frank, what's gonna happen when we win it? What's gonna happen?' Curt was like a kid on Christmas Eve."

When Mariano hit the big grand slam to ice the game, Frank pulled down the plastic in front of the lockers, pulled out the booze, and ripped open the boxes containing the T-shirts and hats. After the fat lady sang, the boys rolled in and the party started.

WES CHAMBERLAIN: "I grabbed Todd Pratt out on the field and just started singing 'Whoomp There It Is' over and over. Just screaming it at the top of our lungs."

When the team returned to the clubhouse, they ripped into the booze, the hats and the T-shirts. The clubhouse was awash in champagne. As Milt Thompson explained, "I'm kind of numb. I'm standing here drinking champagne ... and I don't even drink."

John Kruk drinks. Krukkie was standing in the middle of the locker room with a beer can in one hand and a champagne bottle in the other. After a few sips of champagne, America's consummate beer drinker put down the champagne and said, "Too sweet. I'm going with the beer," adding, "I know it hasn't sunk in yet. It won't

PHANATIC PHILE

sink in till tomorrow morning when I wake up and feel like hell. Then I'll know that something happened here."

LARRY ANDERSEN: "What a night! Harry the K led the team in "High Hopes" in the trainer's room. Schil pied Bill Giles and was worried later when he heard he was traded to the Mariners for a couple of balls and a fungo bat. Westie's biggest concern was wondering where the spread was. Coach Mel Roberts, (who grew up in Abington, PA, outside of Philly) one of the nicest guys you ever want to meet, had a headlock on a giant magnum of champagne and he wasn't letting go. In fact, he went into one of the bathroom stalls, locked the door, and drank it. 'I've waited 30 years for this,' he was yelling out. We helped Mel out of the clubhouse that night.

"There was a joke going around the clubhouse that you better not drink too much champagne because Dahmer was lurking, and if you passed out in the clubhouse, you might wake up in the morning short an arm or a leg."

MEL ROBERTS, '93 COACH: "I don't drink! And I never will again. I started and quit the same day."

Phillies broadcaster Chris Wheeler had the unenviable job of trying to interview the partiers.

CHRIS WHEELER: "After Schil pied Giles, some of the players were grabbing huge handfuls of the pie and stuffing it down my pants while I was doing the interviews live. Then they started pouring beer and champagne down my pants and goosing me while I'm on camera. I was freezing. Irish Mike Ryan saw me and said to Vuke, 'Look at Wheels, he's shrinking.' The TV director at the time was Ray Tipton. He was back in the TV truck shouting into my earpiece, 'We got to keep going, this is great stuff.' And I said, 'No, Tip, we got to wrap it up soon, because my earpiece keeps slipping out, and I have beer, champagne, chocolate cake and ice running down my back and down my pants!'"

In true 1993 fashion, the party boys ran out of beer. They wound up pooling a ton of money together and sending the clubbies to nearby Clark's Bar to buy five more cases.

LARRY ANDERSEN: "The next day my hair hurt. Mickey played that night after we clinched, and before the game he said, 'Listen, if I get a base hit and I round first and trip and then puke, I don't want anyone to laugh.' It's like he was psychic. His first at-bat, he hit a gapper to left center for a sure double. As he rounded first he went down like a sniper shot him—face first into the dirt. When he got up, he wasn't sure which way to go. He tried to make it to second, but he got thrown out. An inning later he ate the turf trying to make a play in the field. Mickey had a long night."

That Phillie celebration became a moveable feast.

ERIC GREGG, 1993 UMPIRE: "They partied right up until the last series of the season. I remember on the second to last day of the season, they played a day game in St. Louis, and I was umpiring second base. I called Lenny out, trying to steal second base. He was out by a mile, not even close. The Dude gets up and starts arguing with me. He had been partying the night before and all week, and he was dying for me to toss him out so he could have the rest of the day off. I said to him, 'Lenny, I know what you're trying to do and it ain't gonna work. If I have to be out here working, then so do you.' Fregosi came out to make a pitching change a couple of innings later. He looked over at me and said, 'Thanks for not tossing Lenny.' Lenny was so mad that I *didn't* eject him that he didn't talk to me all spring training the following year."

Schil

"Look, Schil's a pitcher. Sometimes pitchers have to be selfish. But if I had to pick one pitcher to pitch a big game, in all of baseball, he's the guy I'd pick."
— *John Kruk*

When Curt Schilling posted a 14-11 record and a dazzling 2.35 ERA in 1992, he proved he had talent. When he punched out five consecutive batters in the NLCS and hurled a '93 World Series shutout, he proved he had guts and grit. When he stood front and center in the media circus that attends baseball's fall classic, he proved he had star power. Schil liked the camera. He liked the interviews. He liked the hoopla—all qualities that made him enigmatic, and sometimes perplexing, to his teammates.

Curt was well respected, albeit out of kilter in a few respects with some members of the '93 squad. Whereas, in the main, team members eschewed the limelight and preferred chilling inconspicuously in the shadows, Curt Schilling was in a perpetual New York state of mind, media-ready and media-friendly.

JIM FREGOSI: "Part of the unwritten clubhouse code of conduct was not to admit to enjoying the media attention. Curt Schilling said he had fun when he was out and about. The rest of the guys had a circle-the-wagons mentality. Whatever happened in the clubhouse stayed in the clubhouse. They weren't free and easy with the media. So Schil acted different that way—and he was the only one, so he heard about it."

ANGELO CATALDI, WIP SPORTS RADIO: "Curt Schilling was on hold every day at 6:00 a.m., waiting to go on the air with us at WIP. People thought it was prearranged, but honest to God, it wasn't. And he'd stay on the air as long as possible. We tried to figure out why Curt did it. Hey, we were happy he did! It was good for us. But none of the other Phillies ever bothered. In fact, they hated us, considered us chicken bleep."

JAYSON STARK: "I think Schil was shaped by the way he grew up in Alaska [Curt was born in Alaska], because he was so remote up there and lived so far away from where the game was actually being played. Curt devoured baseball news. That's how he learned the game as a kid—from the media—from reading and watching TV. Growing up, Curt's connection with baseball was through the media. I still consider him the most media-savvy guy who ever passed through that clubhouse. When he came to the Phils in '92, he knew exactly who I was before he ever walked in, because I had some national exposure with my column. At the World Series, he was running around the field introducing himself to Dan Patrick and other national media people. Curt was in awe of those guys.

He was a media junkie as a kid, and he still is. I can understand how that kind of stuff rubbed a few of the '93 guys the wrong way, but Schil got media attention for two reasons. First, he could really pitch, and second, he could really talk. He was an excellent interview. He answered questions intelligently and he's a history buff, so he knew the historic context of numbers and records, even though his teammates didn't care about those kinds of things."

Yes, Curt Schilling does care about numbers. He's a pensive guy. As Bill Giles says with admiration, respect, and a pinch of puzzlement, "Schil is on his own island." Schil loves history, particularly the history of World War II. Numbers, dates, and details mean more to him than they do to most of his peers. Guys who focus squarely on the here and now find Schilling's drive for media attention and his zest for immortality puzzling and alien.

PAUL HAGAN, *PHILADELPHIA DAILY NEWS*: "Curt Schilling is the most complex athlete I've ever covered. He was capable of incredible acts of generosity, but he's also so self-absorbed."

That self-absorption caused a bit of a row briefly between Schil and Dutch Daulton. At All-Star time, Tommy Greene was 11-2. Curt had pitched well too, although he was slumping at All-Star break. Both pitchers felt they deserved a nod for an All-Star berth. Dutch bristled that both Tommy and Curt were focusing on their own numbers instead of the team's objective.

TERRY MULHOLLAND: "Schil and Greenie were young then. They were just trying to feel their way through the league. When an honor like the All-Star game presents itself, at their age, they felt they could go just out there and just turn it up a notch, put up numbers, and be selected for the game. But veterans know that's not the way it works. You go out there day by day and do the best you can. You try to let those numbers take care of themselves, and let the people who are supposed to make the decisions on who goes and who doesn't go make those decisions."

CURT SCHILLING: "I was immature back in '93, but I grew up a lot that year, thanks to people like Johnny Podres. I was in awe of Pods, of what he had accomplished in his career."

Pods's advice and encouragement helped in Curt Schilling's coming of age that pennant-winning season. After Schil's impressive 8-1 start, he closed out the campaign with seven straight wins before splitting his final two regular season decisions. In between those brilliant bookend streaks, however, the big hurler endured a crisis of confidence. He addresses his little funk frankly, with no sugar coating.

CURT SCHILLING: "I had just given up—what?—106 runs in three innings against the Cards [on July 1], and Darren Daulton blasted Tommy Greene and me publicly. That's the only time Dutch ever did anything like that. He said he never named names, but he didn't have to. Everybody knew who he was talking about. But the second I read that article, I knew it was exactly what I needed. Dutch could push me that way and make me better instead of getting me to withdraw. I remember getting on the plane that night and coming back to Philadelphia. I was sitting right behind Dutch. We were playing our normal card game, and he looked at me and said, 'I just want to kick your ass right now.' He was dead serious. He wasn't joking. I was embarrassed at the way I had pitched, and I told him, 'You have every right to kick my ass.' But Dutch helped me mature with that incident. I could go on forever about what that guy did for our team in the clubhouse. He was the unquestioned leader. He was the glue, but I don't want to diminish what he did on the field either—he had all those RBIs, caught all those games when he was hurt, had a great arm, played great defense ... "

DARREN DAULTON: "I used to tell Schil that he was going to be great as soon as he lost about three feet from his fastball. Then he'd be forced to use his head. Schil decided not to wait till his skills diminished. And that's when he became great. He's as well prepared for a game as any pitcher you'll ever see. He studies films of the opposing hitters, takes them home, and really has an idea of what he's going to do."

Curt Schilling is a consummate professional. He applies himself diligently to his craft. It paid off in the postseason.

CURT SCHILLING: "I studied the tapes in the NLCS all night, and everything worked. I had luck on my side, too. When I woke up the morning of the first game against the Braves, I still remember feeling something I had never felt before. And I still, to this day, don't know what it was—nervousness, anxiousness—I can't explain. I was just excited. Shonda [Curt's wife] and I were sitting at the table that morning, and our dog came in with a horseshoe he had dug up in the yard. We figured that was a sign of good luck. I got to the park, and don't remember ever feeling more pressure, but it was a blast. The place was packed, the loudest environment and most exciting environment I've ever been in. And from the first pitch, everything went right. Then, when the World Series came, I watched so much tape and studied so much that I made twelve plans for every hitter when all I needed was one good plan. That's what Vuke had told me. But for the first time all season, I didn't listen to Vuke, and I had a bad night. But I got back on the right track again in my next start."

Curt Schilling may like to talk, but he has proven himself an attentive listener as well.

CURT SCHILLING: "I listened to Lenny Dykstra talk about hitting every chance I could get. I wanted to learn pitching from the hitter's perspective as well, and the Dude was the guy to talk to. I'll bet thirty times that year he told me exactly what was going to happen when he went up to the plate. He told me exactly how the pitcher would work him, and exactly what he'd be trying to do. Lenny was also the best big-game player I ever saw. Fregosi called Lenny a 'red light' player. I never knew what a red light player was till Fregosi called me one in the World Series."

As Phils skipper Fregosi describes it, "Red light players are guys who want the bat in their hand when the game is on the line. They want to be the guy at the plate or on the mound or in the field who has to make the big play. When they see that red television light go on, they're able to go up to a level that other players can't reach."

CURT SCHILLING: "I was pumped for the NLCS, but once we reached the World Series, I remember being out on the mound, getting the ball from Dave Hollins at third when the first inning was about to start, turning around to face home plate, and thinking, 'Wow, there's a billion people watching this game. How cool is that?' But it wasn't pressure. The playoffs are pressure. Once you get to the Series, it's fun."

JAYSON STARK: "Curt told me a few years ago that the thing he likes most about being on the mound is the feeling his teammates have when he has the ball."

And that feeling is confidence—confidence that their pitcher is going to leave it all on the field and keep them in the game. Ironically, Curt's own actions when teammate Mitch Williams had the ball during the '93 postseason led to the Enchanted Season's biggest sour note. Schil began putting a towel over his head in the dugout while he white-knuckled his way through Mitch's high-wire act in the late innings. It started out as a little fun. Even Mitch told the press initially, "He's [Schilling] probably the only one who has the nerve to put a towel over his head. The rest of them watch. But they'd rather be under the towel with Schil. They ought to get a blanket. Then they could cover up the whole team. You'll see them in the ninth inning—all of them down under the tarp. I can hear it now: 'They're putting the tarp over the players in the dugout.'"

But it didn't end as fun. The incident caused a long-term schism between the two stars.

CURT SCHILLING: "The one regret I have about season is the towel incident in the postseason. I was, whatever you want to call it, stupid or naïve. I had no idea that what I was doing was offensive or disrespectful. When I found that out—Headley was the guy who brought it up to me—I was absolutely stunned, and I was ashamed, because that was against everything that '93 team was about. You know, Mitch and I didn't get along, and there are things that I said that, to this day, I regret saying. But Mitch was one of the guys who made the season. Yes, he had a brash personality, to say the least, but you can't *not* respect people that have no fear of putting it on the line every day. And Mitch took the ball every single day that Fregosi gave it to him, and he wanted it when Fregosi didn't give it to him. That was one of the strongest qualities of that whole team: a deep-seated desire to be the guy who wins the game for the team."

JAYSON STARK: "Yeah, at the time of the towel incident, Mitch *did* say he thought the whole city wanted to get under a towel. Mitch was the source of all the jokes, but basically, Schil didn't gauge that one right. But I know Curt Schilling. He's a well-intentioned guy. And I like the guy. He didn't mean harm by any of that."

JOHN KRUK: "I spoke out against Schil at the time. I thought it was disrespectful to Mitch. I mean, Mitch is the same kind of competitor as Schil. He was out there giving it everything he had. But, Schil grew up a lot after that season."

Curt grew into a superstar in the ensuing years. He's undeniably in the uppermost stratum of major-league pitchers. He now sports a championship ring that he won with Arizona in 2001. However, he still savors the Enchanted Season as a ballplayer, as a member of 1993's band of gypsies, tramps, and thieves, and as a historian.

CURT SCHILLING: "I can remember Mitch coming into Game 6 in the World Series and Vuke saying, 'This is it. Mitch is gonna wrap it up right here. Three up, three down.' And I remember thinking, 'Okay, yeah, I know he's going to do it. I just wonder *how* he's going to do it tonight.' Then I remember watching the ball off Joe Carter's bat, knowing it was a home run right away, and thinking, 'Wow! I just watched one of the greatest home runs in the history of this sport.' It didn't dawn on me immediately that we had just lost the World Series, but then it did, obviously. I was disappointed, for sure, that we lost. But I was almost immediately in awe of what we had done, where we had gone, and what we had experienced. And, really, we turned this country into Phillie fans. It was a USA-against-Canada World Series. It truly was, which was cool, because you knew that this country was behind us, no matter how badly they thought of us as being whatever—you know, we called ourselves gypsies, tramps, and thieves, which was really kind when you think of some of the vagrants that were on this team! But we were America's Team for about two weeks, and that was pretty cool."

As Paul Hagan says, yes, Schil can be self-absorbed, but he is generous and caring at the same time. He initiated "Curt's Pitch for ALS" (also known as Lou Gehrig's Disease). In 1993, he personally donated $17,440 and raised $70,000. Curt continued that effort every year he was here in Philadelphia [he left Philly in 2000]. In conjunction with his golf tournament, through 1999, he had helped to raise $1,270,000 for ALS. In 1996, he was awarded with Phi Delta Theta's Lou Gehrig Award, presented to the major-league baseball player who best exemplifies the giving character of Hall of Famer Lou Gehrig. That same year, Curt was named Baseball's Most Caring Athlete by *USA Today Weekend* magazine and the March of Dimes Phillie of the Year. He won the Phillies True Value Roberto Clemente Award in 1997 and 1998.

Complex, self-absorbed, giving and caring—no matter what, Curt Schilling, whether on the mound or speaking in front of the camera, is entertaining and at ease. No matter how Schil strikes you off the field, he can strike anyone out when he's on the hill—especially when the red light went on, as America's Team was about to find out.

America's Team Meets
America's Most Wanted Team

"Jim Fregosi was the perfect guy for that gang. He taught them that the season was 162 games long. Every game mattered. He taught the coaches about not panicking. He put people only in roles where they could succeed. He always kept everyone fresh and feeling important. Fregosi knew how to manage people."
— *John Vukovich, Phillies coach, 1993*

Jim Fregosi is an old-fashioned guy. He's hardly an academic, but most of his management techniques have a familiar business-school ring. In 1993, Fregosi put into play what most MBAs foul off when they manage in the real world. Fregosi empowered, delegated, mentored, and modeled proper behaviors. He allowed people to perform, forgave failure, and placed his charges in positions where they could win and feel good about themselves. Those words are the stuff of corporate consultants. Fregosi embraced those concepts empirically. Fregosi's world seems unsuitable as a paragon of sound management principles. After all, belch-offs, streakers, and blasting boom boxes are not the staples of most corporate meetings. But to dismiss Fregosi's management style because of these trappings is to ignore a fundamental corporate imperative: to think "out of the box"—a *cause célèbre* in corporate strategy sessions nationwide.

Fregosi was no academic, nor was he a saint. As coach John Vukovich says, "Fregosi didn't let any grass grow under his feet in his playing days." But Fregosi trusted in a few old-fashioned values, like loyalty, teamwork, responsibility, and effort. His management style allowed a diverse group to come together by being themselves. He allowed them to cultivate and animate their own workplace environment. His system was neither complex nor scholarly but as straightforward as Curly's in the movie *City Slickers*. Curly's secret was "just one thing." Fregosi's was two: (1) come to the park every day ready to win a baseball game, and (2) be on time. Fregosi believed that an employee owed his employer not only his best effort, but his loyalty.

That's the the mom and apple-pie—duh—stuff. Everybody believes in loyalty, honesty, effort, responsibility, and so on. Few know how to embed those things in the workplace culture. Fregosi did, at least with this team. In corporate lingo, Fregosi got their buy-in. He not only made those values happen, he made them drive his team.

How? Organizationally, he blurred the line between management and the players. And he did so without compromising management's authority. He and Darren Daulton were aligned and in accord. There was no *line* separating team and management. There was a *link*.

PAUL HAGAN: "Fregosi was more comfortable with veterans. The guy had been a star himself. He was a six-time All-Star, so stars and big-name guys did not intimidate him. Some managers who weren't good players themselves seem afraid to confront the big-name guys because they're in awe of them. Fregosi was not. He could play cards with a guy for two hours before a game and then, if he had to, get on that same guy's case better than anyone I ever saw. He had a strong personality. He didn't just sit back and let Dutch take care of problems. He just knew that was the *best* way to handle most problems. He knew *how* to use Dutch in the role he groomed him for."

Fregosi and Lee Thomas brought in the guys with the right attitude—guys who placed team ahead of individual. A lot of players discarded by other teams were welcomed into the Fregosi-Thomas church of the second chance.

MITCH: "I never saw a manager get so much from players. No other manager could *ever* have managed that group. Fregosi didn't make silly rules. He didn't let rules get in the way. When I went to Houston, they told me to shave. That was the worst thing to do. You shouldn't try to change someone, and Fregosi didn't."

Fregosi, in baseball terms, was a *player's manager*. He tried to make the flow of loyalty and trust across that management/employee line equal in both directions. His style let him do things a manager can't do without such a relationship. Most notably, Fregosi platooned—not one platoon, not two, but three.

FREGOSI: When you platoon, what that does is it keeps *two* guys on your roster sharp. In the National League, your bench ends up winning games for you. The guys on the bench are going to pinch hit in the late innings and you're going to make the double switch that you don't do in the American League with the designated hitter. We were able to get production out of right field and left field that was really unbelievable. All six guys that platooned stayed sharp all year long."

Ballplayers do not like to platoon because it cuts down their personal numbers. Numbers determine salary. Part-time players can't put up the big numbers the full-time guys do. Managers who platoon can expect bellyaching, bad feelings, and dissension. Consequently, many managers won't *risk* platooning, even if they think it would be effective.

But Fregosi leveraged his team's obsession with winning. He also practiced what he preached. Going into 1993, Fregosi was one of the lowest paid managers in baseball, yet he showed nothing but total commitment to his team and organization. He didn't sign his '93 contract until midseason, June 23, when the Phillies were well entrenched in first place.

JIM FREGOSI: "You don't see much loyalty these days. The guys on that '93 team were loyal. They wanted to play *here*. They turned down opportunities to play elsewhere for more money. And you could see it around the league that year. Opposing players used to come over and tell me they wanted to play with the Phillies because they could see that our guys thought of this as their *home*."

Maya Angelou describes home as "the safe place where we can go as we are and not be questioned." Fregosi let his players be who they were. He allowed— no, he encouraged—his players to make the clubhouse their home. No matter what was happening in the outside world, no matter how well or poorly the team was playing, there was a comfort and constancy within those crazy walls, and it was Fregosi who provided that atmosphere. Under his direction, a motley crew bonded. The team showed a sense of purpose, never a sense of panic. On an emotional team, in as bonkers a place as the Phillies' locker room, there was an underlying sense of home. And Jim Fregosi, drink and cigarette in hand, was like a proud papa. He was damn proud of those kids.

HEAD GAMES

DAVE HOLLINS: "I hated the Braves. Never liked them from day one. They acted like they were better than us, like we didn't belong on the same field with them. I would purposely try and crowd the plate just to try to show them I wasn't gonna back down from them."

In 1992, Dave Hollins backed away from nobody. Of the 19 times that he was hit by a pitch, four of them were thrown by Atlanta's all-time great, Greg Maddux.

JOHN KRUK: "After the '92 season, I took Dave out to Las Vegas with me for a charity event. We saw Greg Maddux and Steve Avery in one of the casinos. Dave saw Greg, walked across the room, and said, 'Listen, if you ever hit me or one of my teammates again, I'm gonna kill you.' Then he walked away.

"I saw Maddux the next day, and he asked me, 'What was up with that yesterday? Was Hollins serious?' And I said, 'Oh yeah, he's serious. He's as serious as a heart attack.'"

"He never hit Headley again. And can you blame him? I'd rather fight Mike Tyson without his medication than fight Dave Hollins."

The Opponents

The two contestants in the 1993 National League Championship Series (NLCS) took decidedly different paths to get there. Looking at the final records for each team, the paths appear flip-flopped. The Phillies, with a 95-67 mark, set a National League (NL) mark and tied a major-league mark set by the 1984 Detroit Tigers by spending 181 days in first place. To recap, the Phillies sizzled through April with a 17-5 record, and simmered through May and June at a 35-

20 pace. After that torrid first half, they slipped to a more modest 45-40 clip. They had considerable cool-downs in July and September, when they were 14-14 and 14-13 respectively. Still, the Phillies train simply built up too much early momentum to be derailed.

Atlanta, or America's Team as they were/are wont to call themselves, won 104 games. To put that in perspective, that's three more wins than the highest Phillie win total in history. Atlanta's record was the best in the NL since the Mets' glittery 108-54 standard in 1986, the most wins ever by a NL club. Yet Atlanta's season was emotionally draining, a white-knuckle ride. Bad locker room vibes didn't crack a strong foundation. A dizzying dash to the wire ended in a photo finish the last day of the season when Atlanta won by a nose—or, more accurately, San Francisco opened up its Golden Gates for Atlanta to advance.

The '93 Braves followed their standard early-nineties formula: bad first half plus overpowering second half equals divisional flag. America's Team had a habit of tantalizing its fans. The '91 Braves came from a nine and a half-game deficit to overtake the Dodgers by one game. To do so, they had to go 55-28 (.663) after the midseason break. In '92, Atlanta overcame a 20-27 start. They picked up seven games to overtake the Reds and eventually won by eight on the strength of a 49-27 (.645) second half. And in 1993, they sizzled through a 54-19 (.740) second half—the third best second-half performance in baseball history (the 1942 St. Louis Cardinals were 63-19, and the 1954 Cleveland Indians were 55-16) to again overcome a lethargic start. The Giants never faltered all year long, finishing an outstanding campaign at 103-59. *As late as July 22*, San Francisco led Atlanta by ten games.

There was reason—other than tradition—for the Braves' 1993 midseason resurgence. Atlanta acquired Fred McGriff from San Diego on July 20 for three minor-leaguers. In his first game as a Brave, Crime Dog, as he is known, watched a stadium fire consume several luxury seats while the game was halted. The fire seemed a perfect metaphor. The Braves caught fire that night—a fire that crackled the rest of the season. In the eleven games before McGriff stormed into Atlanta, the Braves were 5-6 with 29 runs scored. In the eleven games after his arrival, they were 9-2 with 88 runs scored.

The Braves had a potent attack (53-41) before the Crime Dog showed up, but their artillery was underfiring. After adding McGriff's big gun, the Braves went an astonishing 51-17. His arrival lifted everyone's performance. Terry Pendleton, 1991 NL MVP, was mired at .253, six home runs, and 38 RBIs before McGriff arrived. Post-McGriff, he was .298, 11 home runs, and 46 RBIs. David Justice upped his .253 pre-McGriff batting average to .270 by year's end, hitting .310 with Crime Dog in the lineup. Ron Gant's average prior to McGriff was .261. Post-McGriff, it rocketed to .290.

In contrast to the Phillies, the Braves had struggled through a 12-13 April. Gant hit a scrawny .198, Justice, .157, and Pendleton, .158. By April's end, America's Team was ranked thirteenth out of fourteen in team batting.

Clubhouse friction was also ripping at the Braves. On May 26, third baseman Pendleton stormed off the field when Braves pitcher (and ex-Phil) Marvin Freeman threw a strike past Reds pitcher Tim Belcher. Pendleton wanted Freeman to retaliate against Belcher for throwing at Deion Sanders the inning before. Pendleton's little pout polarized the Braves' clubhouse. Sanders had just returned to the team from a three-week holdout for more money and more playing time. That schism never fully mended all season. Nonetheless, Atlanta's house divided against itself managed to stand.

Some Predictions on the NLCS

Here's how the National League Championship Series was viewed in the neutral territory of Detroit. After painstaking analysis, columnist Mitch Albom of the *Detroit Free Press* provided his readers with this provocative, convincing summary.

Team Characteristics: The Phillies like to eat bottle caps, roll in the mud, and beat each other up.

Stadiums: The Phillies play in Veterans Stadium, where believe it or not, I used to work as a program vendor. I was thirteen. One night, I stuck a wad of gum under my seat. Last year, I went back for a visit, reached down and found the gum was still there.

Miscellaneous: the Phillies have Mitch Williams, who has his nickname, 'Wild Thing,' engraved in his bowling ball. They have Lenny Dykstra, who drools tobacco and calls everybody Dude. They have Darren Daulton, who is married to a former Penthouse Pet. They have hot pretzels, cheesesteaks, and hoagies, all of which, on a steady diet, will kill you within six months. Also they have my gum.

Advantage: Phillies.

A good analysis, except the gum he found might be the third or fourth generation occupying that particular spot.

The rest of the nation, it appeared, was hunkering down for serious battle.

Pete Rose, former member of the 1983 pennant-winning Phillies, said, "The Phillies have twenty-five guys who'll do anything to win a baseball game. They didn't have all the talent in the world, but they went out there and played the game the way it's supposed to be played. Philadelphia has four or five guys who would make the All-Madden team."

Ed Rendell: "The Phillies in six."

Philly's mayor bet Atlanta's mayor, Maynard Jackson, $1,500 in sporting equipment for youth recreation programs that the Phillies would win.

Statistics and history favored the Braves. Not only did the West hold a 14-10 lead over the East since the inception of playoff competition in 1969, but the West had also triumphed the last five years consecutively. The Braves were shooting for their third pennant in a row. Compound that with the fact that *every* active Cy Young winner for the last eight years, and *every* active NL MVP, played for a club in the NL West, and the favorites became clear.

Baseball is not played on paper, however. It's a game of matchups. Head to head in 1993, the two opponents played practically dead even. The regular season series ended 6-6. Both staffs posted *identical ERAs of 4.89* against the opposing team. The Phillies batted .264, with seven home runs and 58 RBIs, against Braves pitching. The Braves batted .260, with nine home runs and 56 RBIs, against Philadelphia pitching. Pete Incaviglia slammed four home runs in only thirty-two at-bats against the Braves. But three of those homers, accompanied by five RBIs, came against Steve Avery. Take Avery away and the Inkman's hitting was anemic against the rest of the Braves' staff. No Phil regular batted .300 against Brave pitching except for Dave Hollins at .343. West, Mason, Mulholland, and Mike Williams had been lit up by the Braves. The trio sported ERAs of 13.52, 27.00, 9.00, and 12.00 respectively. Of the starters, Ben Rivera's stats (2-2, 2.30) were the best. In the 'pen, neither Mitch, LA, nor Thigpen had surrendered a run to Atlanta, although each had worked only short stints.

On the other hand, three Brave regulars topped .300 against Phil pitching: David Justice (.344), Mark Lemke (.381), and Terry Pendleton (.326). Not surprisingly, eventual 1993 Cy Young winner, Greg Maddux, at 2-1, 2.05, was the Braves' toughest hurler against the Phils. Tommy Glavine was ineffective at 1-1, 8.27, and Smoltz was a shaky 0-1, 4.91. In the bullpen, closer Greg McMichael was 0-1, 8.53, Mike Stanton, 0-0, 5.40, and Mark Wohlers, 0-0, 6.23.

However, the Braves were heavy favorites. The city of Atlanta was confident. In a ceremony in Phoenix, Arizona, Atlanta Mayor Maynard Jackson conferred honorary Atlanta citizenship on 1993 Dodgers manager Tommy Lasorda. The mayor gave the Dodgers' loquacious, bodacious blue-blood-bleeder a plaque, a box of Georgia peaches, and a New South meal of rock shrimp pasta and black-eyed peas. Lasorda grew up near Philly. He was honored by Atlanta because Lasorda's Dodgers had beaten the Giants on the last day of the regular season, thus making a playoff between the Braves and Giants unnecessary. Tommy said, "I'm accepting because I married a girl from Greenville, South Carolina and I love the city of Atlanta." Lasorda did turn down a tomahawk when it was offered, however, possibly because it was not edible.

Tommy Lasorda

Tommy Lasorda is a Philly guy. He grew up in Norristown, Pennsylvania, a town just outside the Philadelphia city limits. Tommy is Italian (duh!). He loves his pasta and gravy. He grew up listening to Phillies games on the radio. So why is it that every time he sees the Phanatic, his blood boils and he becomes a raving lunatic?

DAVE RAYMOND: "Tommy's *love* of the Phanatic started in 1980, when I went over to Japan with a group of major-league players to play the Japanese All-Star team. The biggest baseball names of the era were there: Phil Niekro, John Candalaria, Steve Garvey, Tug McGraw. I felt pretty important, especially when the players decided to cut me in on the $1,000 *per diem* money they were getting. A thousand dollars! I couldn't believe it! I wound up spending the money on ski equipment because it was so cheap. I had to buy a second suitcase to carry all the stuff I had bought with my meal money.

"Anyway, I walked into the clubhouse one day and saw a box of balls sitting on the table for the players to sign. There was nobody around, and I thought, 'Hey, I'm one of the guys now. I'm gonna sign these balls to remind people that the Phanatic was over here in Japan.' What I didn't realize was that I signed all of the balls on the *sweet* spot, which is where the manager normally signs it. Tommy Lasorda was the manager of that team. When he walked in and saw that the Phanatic had signed the balls *in his spot*, it was like somebody mixed Welch's grape jelly in his Prego sauce—not that doing that would stop Tommy from eating it. He'd just be mad, which he was.

"Next day, there was another box of balls on the table. I started signing them again. This time, Tommy was waiting for me, like Brutus was waiting for Caesar at the Senate. He came out from the coach's room and said, 'Okay, hot shot. [Hot Shot's the name of a hockey mascot. But my unerring instinct told me this was *not* a case of mistaken identity. Tommy was speaking to *me*.] If you want to autograph balls, here are a few more for you to sign.'

"He made me sign baseballs, hundreds of them, until my hand hurt—trying to teach me a lesson and take me down a peg."

That was the start of a feud that spanned nearly two decades. The Phanatic and Lasorda—kind of like the Hatfields and McCoys, but without the banjo music.

Every time the Dodgers came to Philly, the Phanatic would stick out his belly and waddle that pigeon-toed waddle of his, trailing Lasorda and mocking his every move. Tommy used to roll out of the dugout before the game and walk along the edge of the field, waving to friends and family in the stands. The Phanatic would follow, blowing kisses to the fans and mimicking Tommy's every move. Tommy would steam visibly. What he didn't know was that his own players, who may have bled Dodger blue, had a sense of humor that was colored more like Phanatic green. The Dodgers used to egg the Phanatic on when Tommy wasn't looking.

DAVE RAYMOND: "Steve Sax helped me 'procure' Tommy's road uniform one night. Steve said, 'Dave, don't tell Lasorda! If he finds out, he'll kill me!'

"We bought a little dummy and put Lasorda's uniform on it. For years, that dummy got much more use than, let's say, Larry Andersen did as a pinch hitter. Tommy had to watch the Phanatic speed onto the field on his trusty four-wheeler, lugging Tommy the Dummy—ooh! that might be confusing— make that, lugging *Tommy's dummy* behind him. The Phanatic would start dancing with the dummy—with "LASORDA" written across the back—spin it above his head, and then slap it against the Astroturf. At this point, Tommy, not the dummy but the Dodgers manager, would start cursing at the Phanatic from the dugout. I used to think Tommy also had Tourette Syndrome, because Tommy has called the Phanatic just about every name in the book from inside that dugout. The Phanatic would toss the dummy in the air and put his arms out to catch it, only to have the dummy land with a thud, five feet behind him. True to form, Lasorda would pick up baseballs and rifle them at the Phanatic's head, at which point the Phillie Phanatic turned into Artful Dodger, ducking Lasorda's tosses. (Although none of them ever came close enough for the Phanatic to see whether Tommy had signed them on the sweet spot. Tommy's ERA as an active player was 6.48.) He gingerly set the dummy down in front of the front tires of his motor-bike. Standing over the dummy, the Phanatic would look up at the crowd, miming, 'Should I do it?' Then the Phanatic would stand on the bike, leap, and belly flop onto the dummy. As the Philly crowd roared and Tommy muttered, the Phanatic would toss the dummy on the seat of the ATV and hop back on the bike, right on top of the dummy. The fan's final glimpse was that of Tommy Lasorda being suffocated by the rather large posterior of the Phanatic, driving off into the sunset, or more appropriately, moonrise.

One time, Lasorda really snapped. He came charging out of the dugout, grabbed the dummy and whipped it across the Phanatic's green snout. The Phanatic went down like Rocky Balboa did in the first fourteen rounds of every fight he ever fought. With the Phanatic sprawled on the turf, Tommy beat him over the head repeatedly with his own dummy—perhaps another reason to rethink cloning. In a huff, the Dodgers skipper took the dummy and stormed back to the dugout, spewing curse words like a portly little Vesuvius. Then he made a fatal mistake. Instead of throwing the dummy out, Tommy left it lying on the ground in the tunnel leading to the visitor's clubhouse. One of the Phanatic's "spies" recaptured it and got it back to Dave Raymond. Tommy didn't know it, but the sequel, "Revenge of the Dummy" was coming to area ballparks soon.

DAVE RAYMOND: "At first I didn't know if he was joking or not. But then he punched me, and I thought, 'You know, maybe Tommy doesn't think this is as funny as I do.' He had about five years of frustration built up, so he was really ready to blow."

Of course, that didn't stop Dave Raymond. It wasn't long after that little incident that Tommy was tapped as the spokesperson for Slim-Fast. To the Phanatic, that news brought the same joy that Clinton's reelection brought to stand-up comics nationwide.

DAVE RAYMOND: "I couldn't pass that one up. Between innings, I would bring cans of Slim-Fast on the field and mime to Tommy that he might need to eat a *little* more Slim-Fast and a little less everything else. I'd smash the cans with the tamper we use on the basepaths. Slim-Fast dust would blow everywhere. Guys in the on-deck circle probably lost weight those nights.

"Some Slim-Fast representatives were in their private box in the 400 level in right field one night. I went into the box to schmooze them a little bit and saw that they had this life-sized cutout of Tommy holding a can of Slim-Fast. I grabbed it and dangled it out of the box, like I was going to drop it all the way down to the turf below. Tommy had a perfect view from where he was sitting. I felt like a coach, 'cause Tommy was flashing me a hand signal, but I don't think that signal was in any of their playbooks."

When I took over for Dave, the Lasorda – Phanatic pheud raged on. The first Dodgers game that I appeared at, I was on the field before the game, "Phanaticking" around with the players along the left-field foul line. The Dodger players egged me on.

"Tom, you got to come after Tommy tonight. Don't let this thing go just cause Dave's gone!" Just before the player introductions, Tony Valerio, one of our dugout security guards and a friend of Lasorda's, came over to me. "Hey, Tom, why don't you go over there and meet Mr. Lasorda? Maybe you guys can bury the hatchet." I started thinking that maybe Tommy had had enough. Maybe my taking this gig over from Dave should mark the end of the feud. Deep down, though, I didn't want it to end. I couldn't wait to pick up where Dave had left off and maybe add a few wrinkles of my own.

Tony went over to Lasorda. As he did, I started to gesture like I'm not interested in a truce. I started to flick my tongue at him and waddle around with my tummy sticking out, just the way Dave used to do. Tommy sneered the sneer of a guy who knew that even though there was a new guy in costume, it was the same old Phanatic.

That night, like usual in the fifth inning, I came out to dance in front of the visitor's dugout. As I was dancing, Phyliss Phanatic, the Phanatic's "girlfriend," came bounding out from behind the plate to flirt with the Phanatic. The love-struck Phanatic feigned surprise and turned his back on Phyliss to look up to the heavens and thank God for his good fortune. The Phanatic also sniffed his armpits, making sure he didn't offend. While the Phanatic went through all those shenanigans, Mike "Snuffy" Boyce, a guy from our Phanavision crew, came stomping out of the dugout, wearing the same Lasorda jersey that Steve Sax had stolen years before. We had stuffed three pillows down the front of his shirt and another down the back of his pants to portray Tommy in his pre- (and post-, for that matter) Slim-Fast days. Snuffy even went so far as to powder his hair white and walk that Lasorda waddle. With my back still turned on Phyliss Phanatic, Snuffy tapped the girl on the shoulder and gestured for her to scram. With the girl out of the picture and only the fake Tommy standing there with his arms crossed, I wheeled around and without looking planted a huge Phanatic kiss on the Lasorda clone. As we both spit out our kisses, the real Tommy was fuming, peppering us with every four-letter word he could think of. Where's the love?

Tommy retired in 1996. That next season, the Phillies had a Tommy Lasorda night, to honor a native son. The Phils invited some of Tommy's family and buddies from Norristown onto the field for a pregame ceremony. The last one to walk out there to wish Tommy well was me, the Phanatic. As I ran out to the field, I could see that Tommy was about as ecstatic as a wife meeting her husband's prom date at a reunion. Tommy was staring daggers at me as I handed him a Phanatic doll and gave him a big hug. Then I whispered in his ear, "It's not over."

Show biz—I love it!

In the fifth inning, I ditched my customary four-wheeler right-field entrance and walked out from behind the plate with a folding chair in my hand. I set up the chair right in front of the visitor's dugout, the scene of all those Phanatic/Lasorda battles over the years. I sat down and stared up at Phanavision. Suddenly, the lyrics blared:

Memories light the corners of my mind,
Misty water-colored memories,
Of the way we were...

Video Dan had put together a two-minute video showing some great Lasorda bits from over the years. The dummy assault, the smashing of the Slim-Fast cans, Snuffy dressed as Lasorda, and of course, Tommy cussing and pacing and heaving things out of the dugout. As Tommy buried his face in his hands, hardly able to look up from his VIP box, I sat there pretending to cry like a baby. Froggy came over and gave me a towel to wipe my tears away. When it was over, Froggy helped me up and escorted me off the field. The sight of all those classic Lasorda moments had turned the Phanatic into a sentimental blubbering mess.

Thanks for the memories, Tommy.

In Center Field – Billy Penn

The Playoffs were coming! The whole Phillies organization was humming along: mailing out playoff tickets, preparing for a deluge of international media, and building field-level seats right behind the plate for a host of special guests, including baseball's first couple, Ted Turner and Jane Fonda. Froggy wasn't happy about those special seats right in front of his Plexiglas window. They were kind of like a lunar eclipse on him, if you catch my drift.

Red, white and blue bunting was hung everywhere, scoreboard lights were changed, and every window on the press level was washed. Video Dan worked feverishly putting Phillies highlights together to show on Phanavision. I was setting up the music and helping Dave Raymond dream up special Phanatic antics.

When I drove to Phanatic appearances in my Phillies Bandwagon, all I heard were people honking horns. All I saw were Philadelphians flashing the "We're #1" sign to me. There was more red showing up on Philadelphia streets than on Enron's balance sheet (I realize that's an anachronism), or on Tug McGraw's face after a few shots of Jamison (that's *not* an anachronism). Midge Rendell, the mayor's wife, was swept up in Phillie Phever.

MAYOR RENDELL: "I couldn't go anywhere without hearing talk about the Phillies. After the Phils clinched the division in Pittsburgh, Midge turned to me and said we should put a big red Phillies cap on Billy Penn's head. I loved the idea, so I called Bill [Giles] then and there and pitched her idea to him to see if it could be done. I knew Bill would try anything."

For non-Philadelphians, a huge 37-foot-high statue of William Penn, Philadelphia's founder, has perched atop Philly's City Hall since 1894. Alexander Calder cast that sucker, and it weighs 53,348 pounds. It's the largest sculpture atop a building in the world. New York tried to upstage us with King Kong, but that didn't pan out. Up until the early 1980s, a gentlemen's agreement in Philadelphia had prohibited erecting any building higher than Billy Penn's hat. But that unwritten law was broken in 1983 when One Liberty Place was okayed. The Sixers won an NBA championship that year. But ever since 1987, when One Liberty Place was completed, Philly has suffered the Curse of Billy Penn. Not one of our professional sports teams has won a title since Billy Penn's skybox was downgraded to the cheap seats in Philly's skyline.

DAVE BUCK, PHILLIES MARKETING EXECUTIVE: "My phone rang right before the playoffs. It was Bill Giles, who was with the mayor at a cocktail reception. Bill said, 'Dave, can you find somebody to put a Phillies cap on Billy Penn?' I said, 'No problem, Bill. Great idea.' The truth is, I didn't know where to begin. I knew I couldn't just call Boyd's of Philadelphia and ask for the big and tall department. I flipped through my Rolodex. I thumbed through the Yellow Pages. Everybody I called laughed at me, especially when I said I needed it in three days."

It was the Mummers, and more specifically Dave Moscinski, who came to the rescue. Moscinski was a sheet metal worker who owned a small second-floor costume shop in the heart of Mummerland, at 2nd and Morris Streets. In Mummers' circles, Moscinski is a genius when it comes to feathers and sequins for Mummers costumes. The guy has built barns, alligators, scarecrows, and Vikings costumes. He accepted the challenge, and that Sunday morning, he ascended all 486'6" necessary for a face-to-face meeting with William Penn. This is not Spiderman stuff. You can get up there from *inside* City Hall. However, Dave had to do his work outside, including taking Billy's measurements, making preliminary sketches, and snapping photos high atop the City Hall tower.

Later that day, he set to work constructing the cap, welding the frame out of cold-rolled steel and wrapping it in chicken wire. Next he glued foam onto the chicken wire and finished by adding the bright red cap fabric onto the foam. He topped it off with a blue button for the top of the hat and used vinyl for the shiny white "P" on the front. The completed hat measured seven feet by five feet by four feet. Rumor has it that it fit either Todd Pratt or Dave Hollins. No one will tell me which one.

Moscinki proved to be a "red light" metal worker, finishing his project under enormous pressure before the playoffs began.

"This is nothing compared to New Year's Day," he told the *Philadelphia Inquirer*. "All these guys screaming, 'Where's my suit? Where's my suit?' Now, *that's* pressure. This is just one guy—one very *large* guy—who needs a hat."

Let the Games Begin

"My colleague said it best, 'Of all the improbable endings to this season, the most improbable is probably Mitch having a one-two-three inning.'"
– Tim McCarver in postgame interview with Jim Fregosi

A Little Game 1 Buildup

Bobby Cox, Braves manager, announced that Steve Avery, Greg Maddux and Tommy Glavine would start the first three games of the NLCS. Cox sent John Smoltz to the bullpen for the first two games with a tentative nod as the Game 4 starter. Smoltz smoldered, failing to show up at the team's celebration for winning the Western Division. Smoltz had always been a spectacular postseason performer. In five League Championship Series starts, his numbers were 4-0, 2.27. In four World Series games, he was 1-0, 1.95.

At age twenty-three, Steve Avery, the Atlanta Game 1 starter, was already making his ninth playoff start. Avery, a leftie, was 18-6, 2.94 overall for the season and 1-1, 3.46 against the Phillies. The Phillies' top four hitters, Kruk, Dykstra, Hollins, and Daulton, all batted left-handed. The '93 Phillies, however, not only defied opponents, they often defied logic as well. They were 31-18 in games started by left-handers. Regardless, they respected Avery, and Krukker had this pregame observation: "The guy's sixteen years old. He throws about 95 mph. Great breaking ball. Great change-up. And he throws everything for strikes. Other than that, he's nothing special. Well, I guess he's eighteen now [he was twenty-three at the time]. I don't think he shaves yet. He makes me feel old when I go out there."

Curt Schilling was tapped as the Phils' Game 1 starter. Schil had hardly torn up Atlanta in the regular season, going 0-2 with two no-decisions in four starts and a 6.65 ERA. Curt was nervous before the start. His beautiful wife, Shonda, said, "He's been very quiet. He wanted people around, but he didn't want to talk."

LARRY ANDERSEN: "I remember walking into the clubhouse that first game. It's a tribute to Fregosi's leadership. The clubhouse felt and looked the same as it did all year long, no panic. Jimmy really kept everything on an even keel. There was Fregosi playing cards with Bowa and Kruk and Mickey. Then Schil walked in. His eyes were like half-dollars, and he's all pumped, saying sarcastically, *'Yeah, like I got a lot of sleep* last night.' Schil told us he was up all night long watching the videos of the Braves' hitters."

The papers were full of rumors that John Kruk, hobbled by strained muscles in his lower back, would not start. Kruk had missed the final two games of the regular season. Before the game, Fregosi was asked about Kruk's health and scowled, "He's only at 83 percent today. At game time, he'll be 112 3/4 percent." Kruk himself resolved, "I've spent eight years up here, eight years of losing. The only thing that's going to keep me out of this game is if I'm six feet under." Asked if the ballyhoo and national media attention was exciting, the Krukker "krukked," "Exciting? There's too many people here. You can't even pass gas."

Atlanta was 11:5 favorites, according to *USA Today*. Analysts and Atlanta papers were placing a lot of emphasis on the disparity in playoff experience between the teams, regaling how the Braves had matured playing in the preceding two World Series. In contrast, the Phillies hadn't participated in the postseason jubilee since 1983. Only two Phil starters, Dykstra and Duncan, had playoff experience.

Pundits nationwide pointed to the Braves' superiority in pitching and fielding. Atlanta led the pack in pitching with a miserly 3.14 ERA, while the Phillies (3.95) ended up close to midpack. Phils hurlers, however, were very capable of cranking up exceptional performances. They led the senior circuit with 24 complete games, a whopping 25 percent more than the 18 CGs registered by the next closest staff, Atlanta.

The Phils dominated the offensive stats, with a team batting average of .274, second in the NL right behind the Giants at .276. Atlanta was below the median, ranking ninth in team batting (.262), but leading in home runs with 169. Philadelphia, with 156, was not far behind. Justice, Gant, and McGriff each hit more than 30 homers. No Phillie reached the 30-home run platform. However, the Phillies' power was distributed more evenly throughout their roster.

The Phils led the circuit in on-base percentage (OBP) by ten points. They also left more runners on base than anyone else. By far. They stranded *82* more runners than the next worst team in the category. That means that the Phillies, on average, stranded *half a runner more* per game than the next worst stranders, and a whopping *two more per game* than the most efficient team at plating base runners.

LEE THOMAS: "The most important statistic in baseball is on-base percentage. You have to get on base to score. It's that simple! We may have left some people on base, but we never stopped coming at you. We were always getting on base, always threatening to score, and always keeping the pressure on. That was the secret of our success."

Runs win games. That *is* simple. The Phillies tallied a colossal 877 runs in 1993—the most runs any team in the NL scored since Brooklyn's Boys of Summer plated 955 in 1953. The Phils' 877 surpassed the Giants' total by 69 runs—that's almost half a run more per game than the second most prolific scoring team in the NL.

But the Braves had Mo'on their side. *Mo*-mentum. Phillie bats cooled off after the All-Star game, none more precipitously than Kruk's, whose second-half average tumbled to an unimpressive .274. It wasn't only Phillie bats that cooled. The starters, after amassing a 40-14 log by June 24, went 26-29 afterwards. The Brave starters, in contrast, were 47-17 from late June till season's end.

Given all that, it was a confident group of Braves, led by Braves owner Ted Turner and his wife Jane Fonda, that checked into the Ritz-Carlton in Philly. They called the series America's Team versus America's Most Wanted Team. The Braves were all Ritz, and the Phils were all Motel Six. Except Philly wasn't about to leave the lights on for their Atlanta guests.

Dale Murphy stopped by both locker rooms prior to the first game. Murph diplomatically told the world he didn't know which team to root for. The Wild Thing gave Murph a practical reason to swing his vote over to the Phillies' side: "Root for us. Then you can boo me too."

Game 1: Wednesday, October 6, at Philadelphia

After the Phanatic and Mayor Rendell conducted the Philadelphia Orchestra in the playing of the National Anthem, Curt Schilling took the hill. He struck out the first five Braves he faced for a playoff record.

The Phillies drew first blood. To the strains of the Stones' "Start Me Up," the Dude belted a double to lead off the home first. He moved to third on Duncan's single and scored the first run of the series when Kruk grounded out to second. Schilling got a bit sloppy in the third. With two outs, pitcher Avery and Nixon hit back-to-back doubles over Inky's head in left to tie the score. Atlanta took the lead the next inning when Gant walked, moved to third on McGriff's single, and scored on Justice's sacrifice fly. Inky answered in the bottom of the fourth with a monstrous 423-foot, center-field shot—his fourth circuit blast of the season off Avery. The Phillies took the lead in the sixth when two walks helped load the bases and Kruk scurried home on an Avery wild pitch. Since Schilling's pitch count had pushed past 130, Fregosi removed him after eight innings. After the contest, Schil said, "I couldn't have argued to come out of the electric chair any harder than I argued to stay in the ballgame. You have to understand we have an Italian manager. *No* means no. You can't push him further."

Mitch entered in the ninth to preserve Schilling's 3-2 lead. The Vet, thunderous all evening, gave him a mixed reception. The Wild Thing immediately threw four straight balls and walked Bill Pecota. Mark Lemke followed, bouncing a double-play ball to Kim Batiste, defensive replacement for Dave Hollins at third. Batiste threw the ball ten feet wide of second. A Rafael Belliard sacrifice bunt and an Otis Nixon groundout to Stocker at short plated the tying run. The Wild Thing struck out the dangerous Ron Gant on a 3-2 count with two runners aboard to end the inning. After the Phillies failed to score in the bottom of the ninth, Mitch did an encore in the tenth, striking out pinch hitter Tony Tarasco with two on to escape unscathed.

In the bottom of the tenth, Batiste came to the plate with Kruk on second. Batty fell behind 1-2 before knocking the next serving to left for a base hit. Kruk scored as the Vet erupted. Batty was hoisted on the shoulders of his teammates, who carried Philly's latest hero into the locker room. In the merriment of the postgame clubhouse, Milt Thompson said, "It was just an emotional thing. We all felt so good for Kim, coming back the way he did. I just looked over, and DJ was holding him up in the air, trying to carry him by himself. And I said, 'I better give him a hand. He's got to pitch in this series.'"

Madcap and practical all at once—oh, those wacky '93 Phillies. Jayson Stark commented the following day, "It was a scene that you don't often see in this game—professional athletes staging an impromptu parade for the hero of the moment. It was a scene that epitomized exactly why the Phillies have gotten to this point." Batiste had done the same thing two months earlier. On August 15, Batty made an error against the Mets, only to redeem himself with a game-winning single in the eighth.

KIM BATISTE: "There's a certain truth in baseball. When you're on the bench for eight innings, that ball finds you as soon as you go out on the field! It found me. I was dying on that bench after that error, but the guys on that team were unbelievable. All they told me when I went up to hit was to give it all I had. I remember Schil and some guys at the end of the bench saying, 'Hey, if you don't do it, we're still going to win this thing.' And I thought about what LA had told me the day before. LA was saying that baseball's a great game 'cause sometimes you get a second chance. You don't always get a second chance in life. In baseball, you do. I kept thinking about that the whole at-bat."

After the game, Mitch confessed that Batty's error made him bear down more. "If I get the first guy out, we don't have to worry about the double-play ball. I walked the first guy. It was my fault. The last thing I want is a guy to walk off the field thinking he blew the game. I know what it feels like, so I tried my hardest so he wouldn't feel that way."

After the game, when asked about Mitch, the Krukker krukked, "What can you do? Mitch is Mitch. They won't let me bring a gun out there and shoot him. I think I'd get caught anyway. Sixty thousand people watching. Not much of an alibi there. I can see why Michael Jordan retired. This sports world is really strange."

PHILS 4-BRAWES 3

Chop This

Whenever Dave Raymond needed a Phanatic foil in 1993, there I was putting on a dress and a wig as a Phanatic girlfriend or mom, ridiculously flirting with the opposing team. On Mid-Atlantic Milk Marketing Night, I put on half of a cow costume (the front end, thank you) and was "milked" by the Phanatic during the pregame show. That wasn't the low point, though. Whenever the Mets or Braves came to town, I would dress as a Mets fan or Braves fan, jump onto the dugout and whoop it up for the visiting team. As a Braves fan, I chopped a Styrofoam tomahawk wildly at the crowd. To me, donning that Mets and Braves cap was pure sacrilege. I avoided mirrors more than Dracula or Cher on a bad-hair day (yeah, like that would stop her). Couldn't bear to see myself like that. "I'm taking one for the team," I'd tell myself over and over.

The worst part of the Braves-fan routine—downright dangerous in Philly—came in the innings leading up to the skit. In order to "sell" the fact that I was a legitimate Braves fan, I had to plant myself behind the Phillies dugout and root for the Braves and heckle the Phillies. It was tough for me to do—tougher than a bachelor saying the L-word to a girlfriend.

"Let's go, Crime Dog, this pitcher's got nothing!" The words used to stick in my throat. Inevitably, some Phillies fan sitting behind me would start kicking the back of my chair, or someone would report me to the Phils' hostess, like I was sitting in the wrong seat. So I used to have some fun with the whole scene.

"Hey, pal," I'd whisper to the guy sitting next to me. "After this inning's over I'm gonna jump onto the dugout and start doing the tomahawk chop."

The guy would say, "You're nuts. They'll throw you out for sure."

"Oh, yeah?" I'd say. Watch me!"

With that, I would jump over the railing onto the dugout and start doing my thing. "Let's go Braves! Beat the Phillies! Crime Dog for president! We love you, Greg! Go Braves!" All the while, I'm wondering how I'm going to live with myself.

Here's a tip. If you're planning to do a routine like that in Philly, alert the security staff. We overlooked that detail one time. But only one time. Fortunately, I lived to tell about it. As I was jumping up and down on top of the Braves' dugout, wearing my Atlanta T-shirt and cap and waving that freakin' tomahawk, a security guard the size of Pete Incaviglia came running over towards the dugout.

"Get the hell off that dugout right now!" he screamed. I could see he was ready to snap, so I wandered down the dugout roof, doing my best to ignore him. He was about to grab me when two of our hostesses raced over and told him I was part of a Phanatic skit. I started chopping and yelling again, "Go Braves! We're number one! I love you, Ted Turner!" That's a good thing about my job. I don't have to wait to dance the "Mummer's Strut" at a wedding to embarrass myself.

While I was in mid-"chop," the Phanatic suddenly appeared, grabbed the tomahawk and threw it into the crowd. Next he snagged the Braves cap off my head and stomped on it until it flattened like a pancake. For the big finish, he grabbed my shirt around the collar and with one clean jerk ripped it right off my back. The Phanatic then threw me a Phillies cap and T-shirt and "converted" me into a Phillies fan. With Wilson Pickett's "Land of 1000 Dances" blaring out, the Phanatic and his new convert danced to the baseball gods for the Phils.

I could never dance dressed as a Braves fan. Guilty feet ain't got no rhythm.

Game 2: Thursday, October 7, at Philadelphia

Before the game, Schilling held a bat behind his neck while he stretched and groaned the groans of a guy who had thrown 136 tension-packed pitches the night before. Mitch strutted by and asked, "What are you bitching about? I threw as many pitches as you did and I did it in two innings."

Ex-Phillie great and 1993 Phillies announcer for the cable-station PRISM Garry Maddox bounced the ceremonial first pitch to the plate. Tug McGraw later explained: "Garry's an outfielder. They're trained to throw to the plate on one bounce. Some habits die hard." Maddox won eight consecutive Gold Gloves in his playing days, earning the nickname the Secretary of Defense. Ralph Kiner once said of Maddox's defensive skills, "Two-thirds of the earth is covered by water. The other one-third is covered by Garry Maddox."

Game 2 was to be a battle between Greg Maddux and Tommy Greene. The game started bad and got abominable. Uncharacteristically, the Dude swung at Maddux's first pitch and flew out to center. In the seventh, the Dude swung and missed three times. As the Dude went, so went the '93 Phillies. And on this particular night, they went.

The game quickly lost its competitive charm when the Braves knocked Greene out of the box and jumped out to an 8-0 lead after three innings. Atlanta batted around twice and hit four homers on their way to a playoff-record 14 runs. Hollins and Dykstra countered with round-trippers, too little and far too late, as the Phillies fell embarrassingly short in a 14-3 downer.

McGriff's first-inning round-tripper was a mammoth blast, one of only seven balls in Vet history to reach the right-field upper deck. The only thing the Phillies could do was laugh about McGriff's blast after the game. Kruk: "It killed a family of four." Morandini: "Good thing it hit the upper deck. It might have killed somebody in Chicago." And Mitch, the closer: "That's one where you have to check the ball afterwards—for tears." McGriff's homer and Inky's the night before were the two longest drives in the two years that IBM had been estimating homer distances. A total of 259 homers were hit in that period, and those two headed the list.

BRAVES 14 – PHILS 3

Game 3: Saturday, October 9, at Atlanta

The Phillies' bad-boy image preceded them as the NLCS shifted to the Capital of the New South. The *Atlanta Constitution* ran a headline: "Hide the Women and Children." Ron Green of the *Charlotte Observer* observed: "The Phillies, all hairy and lumpy, look like the supporting cast in a biker movie about the softball team from a slaughterhouse. They scratch a lot and adjust their underwear on TV.

"Lenny Dykstra shifts his industrial-sized wad of chewing tobacco from side to side when he's at the plate, which makes for some yucky TV close-ups.

When he opens his mouth to maneuver his cud, women faint and men run to the bathroom.

"John Kruk chews as many as thirty pieces of bubble gum at a time, which makes his jaws puff out like the rest of him. Kruk's hair is long and shaggy and disheveled, sticking out beneath a batting helmet that has a heavy accumulation of pine tar and other stuff on it. And his body is big and puffs out in lots of places.

"Pete Incaviglia's body is also, um, large and unathletic, which he is. In game one, the Braves hit one ball over his head and one to the right of him, and his pursuit of them resembled nothing so much as a drunk chasing a bus on an icy street."

As the Series moved to Atlanta, each team sent an All-Star to the mound—with trepidation. All-Star starter Terry Mulholland's 1993 line against Atlanta read 1-1, 9.00. McGriff brought a lifetime average of .484 (15-31) to the plate against Mulholland. And the Crime Dog was not the lone Mulholland mauler on the roster. As a team, Atlanta swung for a lusty .325 average against Terry.

Atlanta was in equally bad shape. Their starter, Tom Glavine, the 1991 Cy Young Award winner (Glavine went on to win a second Cy Young in 1998) was 1-1, 8.27 against the '93 Phillies. As a team, the Phillies pummeled Glavine at a .313 clip. To make matters worse, Glavine was 0-4, 6.33 in LCS play.

Ralph Garr, who won a batting title as a Brave in 1974, threw out the first ball. For the second game in a row, the Dude's first at-bat did not bode well. Lenny whiffed on three pitches. In the fourth, Duncan and Kruk stroked back-to-back triples, the first back-to-back triples in postseason play since two Red Sox, Amos Strunk and George Whiteman, did it in the 1918 World Series. Duncan became the first player in LCS to triple twice in one game.

The Phillies went ahead 2-0, a lead they clung to till the sixth. In the span of thirteen pitches, a 2-0 lead reversed into a 4-2 deficit thanks to three singles, a walk and a two-run double by Dave Justice. An error by Mariano Duncan allowed Justice to score, and just like that, the Phillies found themselves down three runs. It got worse. An RBI single by Terry Pendleton and a three-run double by Mark Lemke one inning later led to the lopsided final, 9-4 Braves.

The Phillies' team ERA was 7.67 after three games (*sans* Schilling, it bulged to 11.12). To put that in historical perspective, the highest ERA ever in a series of five or more games up to 1993 was 6.70, set by the 1987 Tigers against the Twins. With the run-fest, Glavine managed to pick up his first playoff win.

BRAVES 9 – PHILS 4

Game 4: Sunday, October 10, at Atlanta

JIM FREGOSI: "After that third game, things weren't looking promising. Bill Giles saw me afterwards and said to me, 'We know Atlanta's tough, and you guys had a helluva season no matter what happens.' I said, 'Bill, we're *gonna* beat Atlanta.' I believed in my heart we would 'cause our guys just wouldn't quit. We were down 2-1, but these guys never thought of quitting. We needed a big game in Game 4, and Danny Jackson went out that night and pitched the game of his life."

The Phillies needed a strong showing from Danny Jackson, who had lasted only one and two-thirds innings in the previous year's NLCS as the Pirates' Game 2 starter. The Braves spanked DJ 13-5 in that game. This year was a different story. The Braves tallied one in the second. Then DJ and Mitch shut the door as the Phillies won 2-1, and DJ—or Jason, as the Phillies called him—drove in one of the runs. Danny had batted 0-11 in LCS competition till he got that RBI. Mitch was summoned in the eighth, and Milt Thompson allowed him to survive the frame by making a fabulous against-the-fence catch. Left-handed hitting Milt had stayed in the game to face Kent Mercker, a portsider, in the seventh. Thus Milt was still in left field in the eighth for that game-saving catch— a grab that Incaviglia is unlikely to have made. Before the game, Fregosi had insisted he wouldn't keep Thompson in strictly for defense. The skipper's apparent change of heart won the game.

In the ninth inning, the Wild Thing made it exciting again. After Mitch double-dribbled a bunt by Nixon, he found himself in a two-on, nobody-out situation in the ninth, with Atlanta's 2-3-4 hitters coming to bat. Jeff Blauser laid down another bunt, but this time Williams picked it cleanly, whirled and threw to third to chop down a charging Bill Pecota. Kim Batiste made a game-saving play on the Wild Thing's toss, stretching far into foul territory to spear it. Ron Gant then grounded into a game-ending twin-killing, giving Mitch the save.

Smoltz and Wohlers also pitched masterfully for the opposition, combining for 15 strikeouts. Kruk alone whiffed four times. The Phillies left 15 runners on base, batting a miserable 1-14 with runners in scoring position. Daulton walked four times to set an LCS record. However, the 15 men left on base and 15 strikeouts were also dubious playoff distinctions that now belong to the '93 Phils.

Mitch took the ball at the end, despite passing a sleepless night after a bout with food poisoning the night before. He wound up trying to catch a few winks in the clubhouse during the game. For the first time, the nation watched Curt Schilling wrap his head in a towel because he couldn't bear to watch as Mitch pitched. But the real hero of the evening was Danny Jackson.

DANNY JACKSON: "I had a ball that game. We *had* to win. I loved being the guy that the team was counting on, and I had extra incentive that night. The media kept bringing up the fact that the Braves ripped me pretty good the year before in the playoffs. They never talked about my other good pitching performances in the playoff. So basically, I wanted to stick it right up their butts that night."

PHILS 2 – BRAVES 1

Jason

I was walking through the clubhouse one morning before the players arrived. The clubhouse was empty except for Frank Coppenbarger, who was at a table in the middle of the room sewing white buttons on a Phillies jersey.

"What's up, Frank?" I asked.

"DJ," he grumbled, never looking up.

That's all he had to say. I knew Jason, the Incredible Hulk, had struck again.

LARRY ANDERSEN: "We called Danny Jackson "Jason" from the *Friday the 13th* movies. He was psychotic at times, but in a good way. You never really knew when he was going to snap."

All season long, when the team really needed to be pumped up, DJ would transform into "Jason," his version of the Incredible Hulk. He would get this look in his eyes, bend over at the waist, throw his chest out and flex every muscle in his body. The veins in his neck would pop out, and in this loud, strained voice he'd yell, 'I'm gonna pump you up!' The next thing you knew, he was ripping off his shirt and whatever else he was wearing and throwing his mates into hysterics.

DANNY JACKSON: "That whole 'pump you up' thing sort of happened by accident. I was in the weight room one night with Dave Hollins. Head was feeling a little down. So as I was leaving the weight room, I went over and said, 'Hey, Davey, I'm here to pump you up'. I started flexing right there. Well, he started laughing, and the next thing I knew, the rest of the guys heard about it and they started egging me on. We were watching WWF one night, and one of the wrestlers, I think it was Hulk Hogan, was doing the same thing. So I started doing it like Hulk—I'd start with three smaller pumps and then one big one to end it. I started ripping my clothes off as a special touch. It was really giving [equipment manager] Frank Coppenbarger headaches, because I was going through jerseys pretty good that year. At one point, instead of sewing buttons back on my uniform, he sewed on some Velcro. I never used that jersey."

So Frank became a part-time tailor. By the way, Frank, if you're feeling ambitious, the pants on my good suit need to be brought in a little.

Usually Jason would appear if the team needed a little jolt. Sometimes he'd do it after a big win. And sometimes he did it for the hell of it.

LARRY ANDERSON: "A bunch of us took some sleds [ballplayer talk for limos] to New York for a series with the Mets. We were heading up the NJ turnpike the night before the game and enjoying some cocktails. At one point, we pulled over into a rest area. In the men's room, DJ started transforming into Jason: 'I'm gonna pump you up.' We were like, 'Go for it, Jason, but we don't have an extra shirt for you to wear.' That didn't stop him, and there he was, doing his best Lou Ferrigno impersonation in the restroom. He tore his shirt to shreds. When we got to New York, Jason was walking around the Grand Hyatt with a shirt that was torn to pieces. It was beautiful."

PETE INCAVIGLIA: "Danny Jackson was probably the craziest guy on that team. I remember one time in Atlanta, we were riding in the team bus heading to the hotel. DJ stood up and started doing his pump-up thing on the bus, ripping his shirt in half. When we got to the hotel, we were all standing around in the lobby waiting for our luggage. Danny was standing there with a sport coat on and no shirt. We started yelling, 'C'mon DJ, pump us up again!' So he ripped his sport coat off and started flexing and pumping out his arms, doing it right there in the lobby of the Ritz Carlton Hotel. I'm sure the people at the hotel *loved* us."

Inky said that DJ actually suffered for his art.

PETE INCAVIGLIA: "I remember on a San Francisco trip, Jason was one of the last guys on the bus. Our lead in the division had shrunk a little, and he wanted to spark us up. That was the greatest thing about Jason, he could snap at any time—didn't matter where you were. Anyway, he got on the bus and started yelling and screaming about how we had to get our act together and screw the rest of the league and God knows what else he was ranting about. He got madder and madder the more he ranted. Then, all of a sudden, he started head-butting the luggage rack while he's still cursing and hollering. And you think the rest of us were nuts! The lights of the bus were off, but as he's yelling, I noticed his face getting darker. There was this shadow or something covering his face, but I couldn't make out what it was. I told the driver to put the light on, and there was DJ, blood all over his face gushing out everywhere! Some of the guys could hardly look, it was that bad. But DJ didn't mind. [assistant trainer] Mark Anderson had to put a butterfly on it to stop the bleeding. I felt bad for DJ, because he was hurting the next day. He looked really funny, too, because the cut was right at the hairline and he had to wear his cap way up high on his head."

The whole world eventually found out what the team already knew. Danny Jackson was a lunatic. After the division-clinching win against the Pirates, Jason made an appearance. With beer and champagne spritzing around the victorious locker room, Jason shed and shredded his shirt while the TV cameras rolled. That night, ESPN and all the major networks ran the tape of Jason pumping up the clubhouse.

I was working in the Phanavision control room during the playoffs. As a tribute to Jason, I adopted Elvis Costello's classic "Pump It Up" as one of the Phillies' unofficial theme songs for the playoffs. In every NLCS game at the Vet, I cranked up "Pump It Up" when the Phils took the field. When Mitch got the final strikeout to win Game 6, Danny Jackson capped off the celebration by going to the pitcher's mound and pumping everyone up. The picture of DJ with his veins bulging under his shredded warmup shirt was plastered on the back page of the *Daily News* the next day. Danny's wife showed their kids a "normal" photo of DJ, followed by the "Jason—Pump You Up" photo, saying, "This is your father. This is your father on drugs. Don't do drugs."

Any questions?

BULLPEN BARKS

All those extra-inning games had taken their toll on the Phillies' bullpen. By the fourth game of the NLCS, if you combined the ERAs of every Phillie reliever who was *not* named Mitch, it was a colossal 9.31. Gritty starting pitching, particularly from Schilling and Danny Jackson, was keeping the ship afloat. That formula was how the Phils started the season, with great starting pitching. At this point in October, the guys in their 'pen were, regrettably, as Fregosi says, "barking."

Between May 31 and August 17, Larry Andersen pitched in 31 games and was scored on in only 4 of them. But in 19 appearances since August 17, he was scored on 9 times. David West had issued 13 walks, six hits, and seven runs in his last six and two-thirds innings. Bobby Thigpen's ERA was 7.27 since September 9, and Roger Mason had yielded five homers and posted a 7.07 ERA since Aug 30. As for Mitch, he had not enjoyed a 1-2-3 inning since July.

Game 5: Monday, October 11, at Atlanta

Avery and Schilling met again, as they had in the opener. Again the Phillies jumped out to a first-inning score on a Duncan single and Kruk double. In the fourth, the Phillies picked up an unearned run when Ron Gant misplayed Inky's long fly to left into a three-base error. Wes Chamberlain drove him in with a sacrifice fly. In the ninth, Darren Daulton hit his first-ever postseason homer for insurance.

Curt Schilling, who had pitched masterfully, took the mound in the bottom of the ninth with a 3-0 lead. The inning started ominously when he walked leadoff batter Otis Nixon. Jeff Blauser then hit what should have been a double-play grounder to Kim Batiste, Dave Hollins's defensive replacement at third base. For the second time in five games, Paws flubbed the play. Suddenly, Schilling faced a two-on, no-out situation with the tying run at the plate.

Fregosi headed for the mound. Schilling, reluctant to relinquish the ball, entreated Daulton, "He can't take me out of this game." "I'm afraid he can," Dutch replied. Mitch came in, and Gant hit a single to drive in a run. David Justice hit a sacrifice fly to tighten the score to 3-2. Next, Terry Pendleton singled to put runners on first and third. Francisco Cabrera, who stroked an unforgettable game-winning hit in the '92 NLCS, singled for a tie, moving the potential winning run to third. In the tensest moment of the year, Mitch struck out Mark Lemke and got Bill Pecota to fly out. In the top of the tenth, Atlanta fireballer Mark Wohlers took over. Mickey Morandini, leading off, flew out. Lenny Dykstra worked a 2-2 count then watched a breaking ball whoosh uncomfortably close to the plate for ball three. With the count full, the Dude drove the next pitch almost 400 feet for a game-winning home run. In the tenth, Larry Andersen came on for his first and only save of the year.

FREGOSI: "Andy was just about barking in that fifth game. And I'll never forget the pitch he struck Gant out with to end that game. He kept shaking off signs, and I thought, 'Something's going on here.' Andy threw Gant a split-fingered fastball—a pitch that *he does not have*. He was making them up as he went along. I think Gant was in a state of shock 'cause he was looking for a slider away, and he just watched that split-finger pass him by for a strike."

JOHN KRUK: "In the clubhouse after the game I went up to Larry and said, 'What the hell kind of pitch was that?' And he said, 'It was a forkball.' I said, 'A forkball. I didn't know you had one of those.' And LA goes, 'Neither did I!' Can you believe it? The guy uses the tenth inning of the Game 5 of the NLCS to start experimenting with pitches!"

As for Dykstra, his clutch home run in the tenth was the key hit of the entire NLCS.

SCHILLING: "The Dude was the most intelligent hitter I ever saw. The Dude told me, 'If Wohlers goes to a full count, he's gonna try to bust me inside, and I'm gonna turn on it and take him deep.' That's what happened, and that's what he did. I can still see Lenny running around third base, yelling, *'Didn't I?! Didn't I?!'*"

After the game, Inky told Frank Fitzpatrick of the *Inquirer*, "Lenny thrives on big games and packed houses, those times when everybody is staring at him and the game is on the line. He always wants to be the man. He raises himself to some other level, one not a lot of players are familiar with."

The little Dude had been 0-4 till he hit his homer. It was his sixth homer in postseason play, which includes his days in the Big Apple. Seven years earlier, on the same date, Lenny had slammed a two-run homer in the ninth that won the game that put New York up 2-1 in a series they went on to win.

Facing annihilation only two days earlier, the Phillies were now one victory away from winning a pennant in a series in which their closer had blown two saves and their defensive replacement at third base had made two potentially lethal ninth-inning errors. In one of their wins, they had struck out 15 times and left 13 men on base. Bill Lyon, one of Philly's astute columnists, hit the nail on the head, writing, "Whatever the Phillies sink their teeth into—beer can, sandwich, or the other team's throat—they stay with and shake and chew and swallow until it is all gone. Then they burp and ask for seconds."

PHILLIES 4 – ATLANTA 3

Philly Aerobics

PHANATIC PHILE

It's October 13, the night the Phils can put the Braves away for good. A mascot lives for nights like that—nights when the crowd is going to be juiced and the TV cameras will be rolling. You pray you get an opportunity to send the crowd into an even wilder frenzy—or maybe Dutch Daulton would put me down as an "Impact Mascot." Anyway, for Game 6, Dave Raymond was ready to rumble.

After the Phillies were retired in the bottom of the fifth, out he came on his four-wheeler, blazing across the field in a gaudy nylon electric green-and-blue workout jumpsuit. He parked the bike right in front of Braves owner Ted Turner and wife Jane Fonda. At first, Jane had a bemused, "Oh, isn't this cute?" smile on her face. Then she looked up at Phanavision and saw herself jumping around in her own little pink leotard (Dave Raymond went out and *rented* the Jane Fonda workout video). When Jane wheeled around to look at the Phanatic again, he was jumping around ridiculously, rolling his belly, attempting scissor kicks, and generally making an idiot of himself. Jane is an accomplished actress and a good sport, but she had been *Phanaticked*! Suddenly, the screen cut to the video of Danny Jackson ripping off his shirt and doing his Incredible Hulk thing. That was a signal for the crowd to stand and clap to "Pump it Up." DJ was flexin', the Phanatic was floppin', the crowd was hootin' (as in Burt Hooten), and, in her VIP seat, Jane was slumping more than the Braves with a man in scoring position.

Jane, aside from the before- and after-workout-session cheesesteaks, this is aerobics, Philly-style!

Postscript: On October 15, 1993, on the David Letterman show, this appeared on one of David Letterman's "Top Ten Lists": "What was the surest sign that the Braves were *not* going to win the pennant?" **Answer:** "You could see Jane Fonda making out with the Phillie Phanatic."

Well, Jane, it just goes to show you ... it's always something, if it's not one thing, it's another thing ...

Game 6: Wednesday, October 13, at Philadelphia

Wes Chamberlain had taped his own version of Murphy's Law to his locker the day after he overslept for the home opener. "Nothing is as easy as it looks, take as long as you need, and if anything can go wrong, it will." It was Wes's ode to his team. At least one anonymous Phillie fan agreed, especially with the "if anything that can go wrong, it will" sentence. Before the sixth game, Fregosi received 1,000 packs of Alka-Seltzer and a case of Maalox from someone at Kennedy Memorial Hospital in Turnersville, NJ. In this series, that might be a two-inning supply.

The Braves had been down like this before in 1991. They trailed Pittsburgh 3-2 when the series moved to Pittsburgh. The Braves' hurlers responded with two consecutive shutouts to win the pennant.

Greg Maddux, the ace of the staff, was squaring off against the Phillies' Tommy Greene. Tommy's wife, Lorie, was at the Vet for the game. While she was there, Lorie said a special hello to the Braves' David Justice, who was her husband Tommy's college buddy and had fixed Tommy and Lorie up. Garry Matthews, the Phillies' 1983 NLCS MVP who had also played for the Braves from 1977-1980, threw out the first ball.

Maddux, whose only blight on a near-perfect resume was his postseason record with the '89 Cubs (0-1, 13.50), was not himself that night, thanks to Mickey Morandini. Mickey started instead of Mariano Duncan because Mickey had always hit Maddux well. The little infielder was 14-39 (.359) lifetime versus Maddux, whereas Duncan was 5-29 (.172). Fregosi's hunch proved brilliant. The second batter of the game, Mickey Morandini rocketed a ball off Maddux's shin. Braves second baseman Mark Lemke got the ricochet and threw Morandini out, but Maddux never regained his form.

JOHN KRUK: "[Braves pitching coach] Leo Mazzone told me later that that ball hurt Maddux—got him right in the calf—and he wasn't the same after that. He had a hard time pushing off with his leg. Something was wrong. You don't score six runs off Maddux."

The master control artist uncharacteristically followed with six straight balls. He even walked pitcher Tommy Greene two innings later to start the third. Later in that frame, Dutch Daulton put the Phillies ahead with a two-run double. The Braves answered with a solo run in the fifth, but Hollins hit a monster 422-foot two-run homer in the Phillies' half of the same frame.

DAVE HOLLINS: "When Mickey hit Maddux with that line drive up the middle, it took his effectiveness away. He threw me a change-up that didn't really do what he wanted. It sort of hung up there. I waited on it just long enough to give it a pretty good ride. That was the biggest home run of my life.'

In the sixth, the Braves, heeding Fregosi's assertions about the Dude's "red light" tendencies, intentionally walked Dykstra to get to Mickey Morandini. But Mickey continued his Maddux mastery and delivered the killer blow—a two-run triple that sent the 1993 Cy Young winner to an early shower. It was the most runs Maddux allowed in 94 starts and the first time he had given up six runs in a game since June 26, 1991.

The Braves added two runs in the next inning on Blauser's first-pitch homer with Otis Nixon aboard. But that was it for the evening. David West pitched a 1-2-3 eighth, and the Wild Thing sat the Braves down in order in the ninth as color commentator Tim McCarver screamed to a nationwide audience, "My colleague said it best, 'Of all the improbable endings to this season, the most improbable is probably Mitch having a one-two-three inning.'"

Phillies 4 – Atlanta 3

Team Grit had topped Team Grace. Out on the mound, DJ transformed into Jason, who stood, flexing, for all the world to see, ripping his shirt off in primal celebration. Phillies fans let out a nonstop chorus for an hour after the game. The players trickled back onto the field in their new National League Champion T-shirts and caps, clutching bottles of champagne. GM Lee Thomas, Jim Fregosi, and Bill Giles climbed aboard a red convertible with the Warren Giles Trophy (for the NL pennant winner) and drove a victory lap around the field as the crowd sang endless rounds of "Whoomp! There It Is."

The Phillies had won the NLCS with a team batting average of .227 compared to the Braves' .274 and a team ERA of 4.75 compared to the Braves' 3.15. Lenny was the only Phil who hit safely in every game. Befitting a series where statistics not only *didn't* tell the story, but *mistold* the story, Curt Schilling was the series MVP. The Phillies' super starter had zero wins to show posterity for his efforts. Mitch the maligned, in contrast, was 2-0. Curt was awarded a red Chevrolet convertible, which he donated to the ALS Foundation. And although Danny Jackson's 1.17 ERA was the lowest on the staff, in an ironic twist, Mitch and Curt shared identical gaudy 1.69 ERAs.

Washington Post columnist Thomas Boswell observed, "The Phillies don't play baseball right. They are an aesthetic abomination. They play antibaseball and revel in it. In fact, they may not even know what the rules are. Any normal baseball team rolls over and dies after such embarrassment as Games 2 and 3. And just when you think they'll quit, they spit in your eye."

America was begrudgingly starting to admire America's Most Wanted Team. Their scrappy style and refusal to say "uncle" made them irresistibly human. Even their appearance was suddenly less threatening. The Phillies were winning over their detractors. Victory was their redemption—victory and their unabashed joy for the game of baseball. Since their opponents in the World Series represented another country to the north of the USA, sentiment started shifting away from Atlanta's now-vanquished America's Team. In a week's time the Phillies morphed into Team America—Team America was taking on heavily favored Team Canada.

The players on Team Canada had watched the Phils' 2-1 win in Game 5 on Sunday in wonderment. One of their biggest stars told a reporter, "No, I would not want to be their manager with the Wild Thing. I think Jim Fregosi would just give the ball to Mitch, leave the dugout, turn off the TVs and radios, and hope to see everyone come into the clubhouse smiling." With that description, Joe Carter wrote a perfect ending to the madcap drama that was the Phillies' '93 season. Then Joe went and ruined it.

The Dude

"The Dude would be an experience even if it had nothing to do with baseball. You could meet the Dude away from the field and come away dazed and confused as to what had just happened."
— *Terry Mulholland*

"Tell us a little about the Dude." We lobbed that softball up to everyone on the '93 team. Not surprisingly, everyone took a healthy swing. The responses themselves are classics of bemused admiration. There were line shots, like Mitch Williams's "Is this book gonna be edited?" and Darren Daulton's "What's the book title? *If You Only Knew!*" There were bouncers up the middle, like Terry Mulholland's "The Dude would be an experience even if it had nothing to do with baseball. You could meet the Dude away from the field and come away dazed and confused as to what had just happened." There were wall-bangers like Pete Incaviglia's "No one ever lived the life of the professional baseball player more completely than the Dude," or Mariano Duncan's "I never met anyone like him in my whole, entire life! That guy's crazy!" But Kim Batiste hit the sweet spot when he observed, "The Dude's in a zone of his own."

Between the lines, the Dude *was* in his own zone in 1993. In 1990, he had finally punched through and achieved legitimate stardom, when he started the All-Star game in center field and batted .325, fourth best in the NL. However, the following year in early May, he smashed up his Mercedes—along with passenger Darren Daulton and himself—returning from John Kruk's bachelor party. He returned to the lineup in mid-July and hit .297. Then on August 27, he smashed into a wall and rebroke his right collarbone to wrap up his season prematurely. In '92, he hit .301 but played in only 85 games due to injuries. With Lenny in the lineup in '91 and '92, the Phillies were 76-71 (.517). They were 72-105 without him. In 1993, then Astros manager Art Howe said, "To me, Lenny Dykstra means more to the Phillies lineup than any one player means to any lineup." The '93 Phillies echoed that sentiment, and then some.

JOHN KRUK: "You take all the leadoff hitters of all time, from the beginning of baseball to right now, and I'll take Dykstra every time. There is none better. None."

JIM FREGOSI: "In '93, Lenny Dykstra had the greatest year as a leadoff hitter that anyone in baseball ever had. Lenny should have won the MVP that year hands down."

CURT SCHILLING: "One of the disappointing memories of that season is that Lenny did not win the MVP. I don't think there's any question he deserved it. Say what you want about Lenny—and I got to know him as a player about as well as anyone—he was the smartest hitter I've ever played with my whole life, hands down. He did the job of leading off better than anyone I've ever seen. I've never seen anyone do so successfully what he did that year. If we needed a home run, he'd hit one late in the game. He went to the plate knowing what he had to do, and he did it."

Lenny is smart. He recognized early that he had talent. But he also knew he was small in stature and needed to play smart in order to play with the big boys.

LENNY DYKSTRA: "People don't realize it, but I was dedicated to this game. Early on, I knew I wanted to be a baseball player. Baseball was my way to break out of the middle-class environment where I grew up. I was dedicated to playing pro ball even in high school. I didn't even go to my high school dance 'cause I was so into baseball, and I was always reading books about the game, trying to improve. I knew I needed to find an edge. In the majors, everybody's talented. At the very top of the profession, there are a few guys like Barry Bonds who simply have more ability than everybody else. So the rest of us have to do the little things to excel. So I applied myself to learning them. I had some great teachers in Philly in '93. Vuke, Bowa, and Dennis Menke really know the game. They taught me about the little things – how to work pitchers, how to be selective, and what strategy different situations called for."

Lenny was cunning. He was calculating, confident, and committed to his own game plan. He was also characterized as cocky and arrogant, particularly in Atlanta and Toronto in the postseason.

MITCH WILLIAMS: "To be a great player you need a certain amount of arrogance. Lenny had his share and two others. That's why he was so superstitious. Lenny could never bring himself to believe that *he* had struck out or made an out—'*Must be the batting gloves.* No way in hell *I* struck out!' But Lenny knew what he was doing at all times out there. Look, he was like the rest of us with most other things. I wouldn't call the Dude over to help me put a jigsaw puzzle together, but the guy was born to play baseball."

Lenny's focus on baseball and his personal "plan" was all-consuming. His plan was one part sound baseball strategy, one part old wives' tales, and one part superstition. And it was his plan—his and his alone. He was so obsessed with sticking to his program that he exasperated coaches as much as opposing pitchers.

JOHN VUKOVICH: "Lenny was my biggest test ever as a coach. He tested everybody's limits. In spring training, he didn't want to play away games. He was so superstitious he sincerely believed he only had so many base hits in him per year, and if he dipped into that tank in spring training, he'd get one less hit in the regular season. So he only wanted so many at-bats—he figured out what that number was. He also didn't want to do certain drills that everybody else did. They weren't part of his program. He'd fight with me to sit them out. And, yes, he was a red light player, as Fregosi called him. But he was also a horrible 10-2 player. What I mean is, he hated to play in a 10-2 game, whether we were ahead or behind. He'd lose focus. He only wanted to play with the game on the line all the time."

Vuke is right. In 1993, the Dude went 4-5 in the clincher against the Pirates. He then went 1-14 to close out the season—all of which were meaningless games. His average dipped from .310 to .305 in that period. But that was the Dude, the ultimate competitor, the red light player. He was always sizing up the opponent, the coach, or whomever.

JIM FREGOSI: "I'll tell you a cute story about Lenny. My wife and I were eating dinner one night in Cincinnati, and Lenny must have come in, 'cause next day, he comes walking into my office. He's got this big smirk on his face, and he says to me; 'Well, Skip, I finally caught you! Yeah, I caught you!' I said, 'What do you mean, Lenny?' He says, 'I saw you with that woman last night at that restaurant.' And I said, 'Uh-huh ...' and Lenny says, 'Nice looking woman!' Lenny's standing there with this big smile. Then I say, 'Lenny, that was *my wife*.' He comes right back, never misses a beat, 'Yeah—nice looking woman!' But that was Lenny! Always working you—but he was a sweetheart, and just a pleasure to have in that clubhouse."

CURT SCHILLING: "I don't know if Lenny ever said anything in the clubhouse I didn't laugh at. He was another one of the personalities that made the whole mix perfect on that team. He went out of his way to let me know how much he appreciated what I did. The guy always showed respect to my family and me. I know there are stories out there about things he's done and said, but, genuinely, he's one of he nicest guys I ever played with, even though he was definitely a lot different than anybody I ever played with."

Yes, there are stories about Lenny—some of them have been publicized. Others remain perpetually hidden amidst those wagons that the '93 gang circled in the clubhouse. Lenny, admittedly, lived life to the hilt, or perhaps the tilt. As Dutch Daulton says, "Lenny used to tell me, 'I'll sleep in the winter or when I'm dead.'" The Dude was never dull. He made life exhilarating and memorable for his mates.

PETE INCAVIGLIA: "The Dude was a great teammate. Every city we'd go, he always stayed at the top hotel. No matter what time we arrived, Lenny would call up one of the top chefs in that city and invite us all over to eat—all at his expense. Lenny knew everyone, everywhere. One day, we were eating in the Peninsula in Los Angeles. Well, Lenny's having a party that night, and we're sitting in the restaurant, and we overhear people behind us talking about Lenny's party. We're wondering who the hell that could be, so we turn around and there's Jack Nicholson, sitting at a table with a group of his friends. So we finish eating and head over to the Dude's party. Later, I'm standing at the door with Dave Hollins, and the doorbell rings. Dave opens the door, and I hear, '*Where's Nails?*' in that Nicholson voice. So Jack walks in with his friends."

On the field, Lenny hardly looked the part of the *bon vivant* man about town. Dirt-covered, tobacco-stained, and gritty, Lenny was the prototypical throwback. As Andy Van Slyke, Pirate center fielder, noted, "There's so much tobacco juice out there, you can get cancer just by playing center field. It's like a toxic waste dump." Unfortunately, after 1993, all Lenny's great expectorations and great expectations dried up. Back problems hindered him from achieving the greatness he seemed destined for. But off the field, Lenny never slowed down.

PETE INCAVIGLIA: "I had played over in Japan in 1995—then I came back to the Phillies in 1996. Fregosi told me, 'Keep your eye on Lenny. He's having knee and back problems. Make sure he gets his rest.' After a week, I said, 'I quit!' Lenny didn't slow down. He'll never slow down."

Nor will Lenny ever conform. He remains the Dude, the singular, most unusual personality on a team noted for its flakes. He's the guy who makes the gypsies, tramps, and thieves shake their heads. Keith Hernandez once stated, "Lenny and I played together on the Mets, who proceeded to trade him … because he's a little on the wild and crazy side. The Phillies acquired him for just that reason. There is nothing corporate about the man."

No, Lenny will never be corporate. Like his teammate Kruk, Lenny's a ballplayer. As he once said, "Everyone thinks I'm a little hoopy. At least that's the impression I must give. The public sees me as some wild type of guy, let-it-fly type person. That's not the way I am. I'm a very mental person. That's the whole key to my success. I have a plan. I know I'm not always going to be successful—because I'm a human being. But I will be successful more than not. I never considered myself a home run hitter, but I'm not your basic leadoff hitter, either. Just call me a situation player."

No, Lenny is neither a home run hitter, nor a basic leadoff hitter. The man is simply in a zone of his own. As Toronto and the world were about to see.

Team America

"It's so ironic. The Phillies beat America's Team and now they're Team
America. Everybody's pulling for them to bring the World Series
championship back from Canada."
— Dan Patrick, ESPN

Team America was right in front of our Philadelphia noses all season.
The '93 Phils were a hodgepodge, a motley group of rowdies who
had been tossed away by others—guys who weren't given a chance
elsewhere, guys who weren't granted freedom to be themselves. The outlandish
mix that wound up in Phillie pinstripes in 1993 had nothing in common with
one another other than a shared, fierce desire to build a new successful baseball
life.

This '93 group was rough around the edges. They were underestimated,
dismissed as uncivilized, awkward, and uncouth—just like the Colonials were in
the eighteenth century. They fought their battles unconventionally, just like the
Colonials. And just like the Colonials, they stood shoulder to shoulder with
those who supported their cause. They stood up against those who did not.

As a group, they were resilient and determined. Setbacks strengthened their
resolve. They lost battles, but never doubted they'd win wars. They never looked
back. They let bad things slide away into yesterday. They greeted tomorrow with
optimism. They didn't have delusions that they were better than anyone else.
They didn't brag, belittle, or browbeat their competition. They simply had faith
in themselves and in one another—faith that, working together as a team, they
could accomplish what the world told them they could not.

Now, ain't that America?

A Tale of Two Cities

"Oh, they be bad. They be bold. They be ballsy. But most of all, they be
comely as a baboon's butt. Which might be considered a compliment in that
peculiar clubhouse … They chew, they spit, they cuss, and belch. They are a
species that could be found tippling brewskies in any Legion hall, a slo-pitch
team sponsored by Billy Bob's hardware perhaps, except this particular group
of hardy 'n' lardy sportsmen has made it to the World Series"
— Toronto Star columnist Rosie DiManno.

There's a joke that goes like this: How do you get fifty Canadians out of a pool? *Answer:* You say, "Excuse me, will all of you please get out of the pool?" The answer takes on a whole 'nother character when the same question is posed about Philadelphians. Phrases like canine unit, mounted police, Philadelphia lawyers, Philadelphia boxers, "I got your pool right here," med-vacs, and Action News vans pepper the answer—with the full story at eleven.

Forget the Team Canada/Team America clash, there was and is a distinct difference between the two representative cities: Philadelphia and Toronto. Philadelphia has been described as either an elegant but jaded great lady, or as an overage and sickly spinster of American colonial cities. Toronto is a thoroughly modern showcase.

Toronto was a quiet trading post in the eighteenth century, when Philadelphia was the crown jewel of the New World, the third largest port in the English-speaking world. Toronto, then known as York and capital of the Canadian province of Ontario, consisted of twelve cottages and a military establishment. By 1834, the name York was scrapped and the city was officially incorporated as Toronto with a population of 9,000.

At the dawn of the twentieth century, Toronto's census had swelled beyond 200,000. Over the next hundred years, Toronto would morph into a megalopolis with a cosmopolitan population of four and a half million. In contrast to Philly, Toronto had the benefit of undergoing its major expansion from the 1950s through the 1970s, when the sedate provincial town that had been called "Toronto the Good" became a lively, thriving population center. Waves of European immigrants, mostly from Italy and Germany, essentially doubled the city population in those decades alone.

Meanwhile, back in Philadelphia in the fifties and sixties, population declined as old neighborhoods decayed and residents and businesses forsook the city. Crime and blight threatened urban vitality. However, Philly's heritage prevailed. The Quaker City undertook massive revitalization programs and fed off its own varied ethnicity. If people were fleeing the city in alarming numbers, there was a solid nucleus of lifetime residents who never wanted to leave. And didn't. On their shoulders, Philly rebuilt and spruced up.

Obviously, the two cities whose teams were clashing in this ninetieth World Series were shaped quite differently. Ironically, Toronto, the Canadian entry, was All-American Boy and Uptown Girl, while Philly was all down and dirty and South Street. Peter Ustinov once described Toronto as New York City run by the Swiss. Toronto people were polite and reserved. Philly people were— well ... consider this. During the NLCS, Michael Madden of the *Boston Globe* went to the JFK Plaza in center city Philadelphia for a Phillies rally staged by Philly radio station WIP. Madden placed Philadelphia fans squarely in a league of their own. "There are fans, there are fans and then there are Philadelphia fans (boooo!). They are a breed unto themselves. Philadelphia fans are (boo!), and the rest of

America are angels and choir children compared to them. There is no city like Philadelphia when it comes to sports. Cruel. Hard. Tough. Mean."

Toronto seemed aghast at Philly's unkempt ruffians invading their pristine town. The *Toronto Sun* ran a headline in bright Phillie red in its Saturday edition: "PHAT PHIL—TALENTED ... BUTT UGLY!!" The article said, "Oh, say can you see ... past their beer bellies? Yes, the City of Brotherly Love has a ball team with looks only a mother could love. Talented, butt ugly. Long-haired, slack-jawed, they'll make Blue Jays fans cringe at the sight."

The *Globe and Mail* reported, "Enough of the Phillies are round and lumpy and mangy—enough of them are crude—enough of them have nicknames like Nails and Pig Pen and Wild Thing, that in the otherwise prefabricated world of professional sports, they stand out."

Even Juan Guzman, talented Toronto hurler, said the Phillies looked like truck drivers, with one major difference—the Phillies looked wild because they wore their hair so long and were "big guys." It was an interesting observation on Juan's part, inasmuch as he wore his hair in a mohawk.

For their part, the Phils played up their image good-naturedly and with typical wit. Larry Andersen was asked, if he had a sister, would he want any of his teammates to date her? LA said, "Hell, no!" When pressed further, "Well, what about Kevin Stocker?" Andy shot back, "Give him time!" Meanwhile, Kruk was telling a Toronto reporter "Honest, we're not bad people. But you wouldn't want us in your home." After Curt Schilling had dubbed his team "America's Most Wanted Team" in the NLCS, the *America's Most Wanted* TV show shipped forty "America's Most Wanted" caps to the Phils. The caps arrived on Thursday before the Series started, and the national media focused and feasted on the Phils' workout that day when the team all wore the new caps. In the spirit of the joke, the TV show told the media, "We're not aware of any outstanding warrants, but we'll be looking very closely at tattoos."

To be sure, Toronto was not a hotbed for tattoos. Tattoos don't play well in corporate meetings, and Toronto is an international corporate center. The city prides itself on its low crime rate and a squeaky clean image. The city is modern and spiffy. Even the baseball stadium, the SkyDome, is a showcase. A 348-room hotel is built into the complex, with seventy of the rooms looking out on to the field. For the Series, those rooms cost $1,655 plus 15 percent Canadian tax. Things had gotten dicey in one of those rooms back on May 15, 1990. The rooms do *not* feature one-way glass. Two guests perhaps thought they did—or not. Perhaps they thought the new park was named Exhibitionist Stadium, an understandable misunderstanding since *Exhibition* Stadium was where the Jays had played their first twelve seasons. In any event, during the baseball game, a couple in one of the rooms decided to make whoopee with the drapes open. In the wake of that particular escapade, future guests had to sign a form agreeing not to engage in *inappropriate behavior* without closing the drapes. Inappropriate behavior ... food for thought.

THE SKYDOME

The Blue Jays' first home was Exhibition Stadium, where the team played from 1977 to 1989. SkyDome has been their home park ever since June 5, 1989. The mammoth structure features an 11,000-ton roof that can be opened or closed in twenty minutes. The widest span of the roof is 674 feet; the greatest height is 282 feet.

The park's "Jumbotron" scoreboard is the largest video display board in North America and second largest in the world (to Japan). The Jumbotron cost $17,000,000 and is 33 feet high and 110 feet wide. A hotel circumscribes part of the field. The facility has 348 rooms, of which 70 overlook the playing field. SkyDome has a 520-seat restaurant called Windows on SkyDome, as well as Sidelines, which features a 300-foot bar with all seats facing the playing field, a Bistro at the SkyDome Hotel, and a Hard Rock Café.

Attendance figures for the early nineties were: 1990, 3,885,284; 1991, 4,001,058; 1992, 4,028,318; and 1993, 4,057,947.

The Opponent

On March 26, 1976, the American League voted to award a baseball franchise to a group consisting of Imperial Trust Ltd., Labatt's Breweries, and the Canadian Imperial Bank of Commerce. Major League Baseball had arrived in Toronto. In a "Name the Team" contest, the name, Blue Jays, was selected from over 30,000 entries, in which 4,000 different names were suggested. That same year, the Blue Jays announced that Dunedin, Florida, would be their spring training site. Dunedin is located only a few Pete Incaviglia tape-measure blasts away from Clearwater, Florida. Because of the proximity of their training camps, the Phillies and Blue Jays play one another often during the preseason.

The Blue Jays made a big hit in Canada right from the start, even though they were the American League's doormat in their early years. Despite finishing 45 games back with a 54-107 record (.335) in their inaugural season, the Jays had already established a new attendance record for a first-year expansion club after *only fifty* home dates. By season's end that first year, 1,701,052 fans had made their way to Exhibition Stadium in Toronto. The Jays grew roots in the AL East cellar for the first six years of their existence. In 1983, they had a turn-around season, ascending to fourth with an 89-73 record while topping the junior circuit in team hitting with a .277 average.

In 1984, Toronto became the eighteenth major-league franchise to surpass the 2,000,000 mark (the Phillies first surpassed two million in 1976 and replicated the feat in seven of the next eight seasons). The Jays finished second in '84, 15 games behind the red-hot runaway Tigers. The following year, which was Bobby Cox's fourth and final as the Blue Jays' manager, the Jays clinched the AL East on October 5, 1985 when Doyle Alexander beat the Yankees 5-1. Toronto went on to lose a tight seven-game American League Championship Series to the Royals.

The Jays slipped to fourth in 1986 but rebounded to second in 1987, when they led the AL in attendance for the first time. They also registered the sixth highest home run total in league history with 215, including a major-league-record 10 home run game on September 14. Toronto's attendance topped off at 2,778,429 in 1987, the most ever for an AL East team. On November 17, after the season, George Bell became the first Toronto Blue Jay ever named American League Most Valuable Player.

On June 5, 1989, the club played its first game ever in its grandiose SkyDome. The team had gotten off to a skittish start that season and replaced manager Jimy Willliams with "interim manager" Cito Gaston. By May 31, however, Gaston was named the fifth manager in franchise history.

Once ensconced in the SkyDome, the team caught fire, going 17-10 in June. The Jays were still back in the pack, tied for fourth at All-Star break. Then, in early August, they picked up Lee Mazilli and Mookie Wilson, Lenny Dykstra's platoon-mate with the Mets.

With the the ex-Met duet hitting the right notes, the Jays rolled to twenty wins in August, catching up to the front-running Orioles on the final day of the month. Back-to-back wins over Baltimore on the last weekend of the season clinched the AL East title. The Athletics, however, beat the Jays four out of five for the pennant. On the final day, October 8, when the A's won the final game of the ALCS, the Blue Jays drew 50,024 fans to mark the forty-first consecutive SkyDome sellout. A new era of Blue Jays dominance had been ushered in, and that December, Ernie Whitt, the club's final link with the 1976 expansion draft, was traded to the Atlanta Braves.

In 1990, the Jays completed their first full season in the SkyDome. They finished second and set a major-league attendance record of 3,885,284. The old mark, set in 1982, belonged to the Los Angeles Dodgers. That December, Toronto made a blockbuster deal that sent Tony Fernandez and Fred McGriff to the Padres for Roberto Alomar and Joe Carter. The trade set the stage for a third AL East crown in 1991. The Jays lost to the Twins in the ALCS but became the first team in baseball history to draw more than 4,000,000 fans. Toronto also hosted the All-Star game, which the American League won 4-2, with Toronto pitcher Jimmy Key picking up the win. That winter, Dave Winfield agreed to a one-year contract and moved over to the Blue Jays from California. Besides Winfield, Toronto picked up Jack Morris, David Cone, and Alfredo Griffin.

Nineteen ninety-two was different. The Jays got past the Oakland A's in the ALCS to reach the World Series for the first time. After the Jays lost the opener to the Braves, they charged back to win three straight—two on dramatic ninth-inning comebacks. After Atlanta bounced back for a game-five victory, the Jays won Game 6 in eleven innings for the title.

Amazingly, after their World Series victory, the Blue Jays entered the 1993 season with eleven new faces. Toronto had lost more starters than any other World Series champ in history—David Cone, Jimmy Key, Jack Morris, David Wells, Tom Henke, Candy Maldonado, Kelly Gruber, Manny Lee, and Dave Winfield. The Jays had to replace an astounding *2,526 at-bats*. Since teams in that era were sending about 5,500 players to the plate per season, that figure represents an astounding 45 percent of a team's at-bats in a year. To put more teeth into that figure, only one champ, the '43 Yanks, had to replace *more than 1,700* at bats, and they dipped to third place the year afterwards. Furthermore, their huge turnover was brought about by the war.

Toronto General Manager Pat Gillick used to be called "Stand Pat" Gillick. No more. He went out and got Paul Molitor and Dave Stewart. On June 11, he reacquired ex-Blue Jay shortstop Tony Fernandez from the Mets. The team Gillick threw together that off season was the class of the American League. Seven Blue Jays (Alomar, Carter, Hentgen, Molitor, Olerud, Ward, and White) were chosen for the '93 All-Star game. Gillick still wasn't finished, however. He acquired Rickey Henderson from the A's for the stretch run.

On September 26, the Blue Jays broke their own major-league attendance record when a crowd of 50,518 upped the seasonal turnstile count to 4,057,947. Toronto had an overpowering year. Blue Jays John Olerud (.363), Paul Molitor (.332), and Roberto Alomar (.326) finished 1-2-3 in the AL batting race. That feat hadn't been accomplished for a century. Fittingly, the Phillies were the last team to do it. In 1893, Billy Hamilton, Sam Thompson, and Ed Delahanty—all three members of the Hall of Fame—finished 1-2-3 in the National League.

John Olerud was an interesting story himself. At 6'5", 210 pounds, Olerud was 15-0 as a pitcher at Washington State University. However, in January 1989, he collapsed during a workout, and doctors discovered an aneurysm at the base of his brain. Undiscovered, it probably would have ruptured and killed him. Olerud underwent a six-hour operation, with surgeons working in the vicinity of his optic nerve and frontal lobe. Once a prized prospect, he was now considered a gamble. The Jays took a chance, however, and drafted him in the third round. He wowed everyone in the Instructional League and came north with the parent club, never having played a day in the minors. His rapid development prompted the Jays to peddle McGriff to the Padres for Alomar.

After taking the '93 AL East crown, Toronto went on to defeat the White Sox in six games to advance to the World Series.

Toronto entered the ninetieth World Series as heavy favorites and as one of baseball's hottest and most successful franchises. By 1993, Toronto had strung together eleven straight winning seasons, fasahioning a 1,006-778 record during that span and appearing in the playoffs four of the previous five years.

Lucky Ties And Caps

As champagne spritzed and beer sprayed around the clubhouse in Pittsburgh, a drenched Harry Kalas slid the yellow and blue paisley tie he was wearing over his head and placed it over the head of his broadcast partner-to-be, Larry Andersen. Larry, who has a tough time even *spelling* the word necktie (but can flawlessly spell every domestic and imported brewery product on the market) accepted Harry's haberdashery and never took it off the rest of the night. When the beer kicked that night—early that morning—Larry was seen (by the few who could still see) wringing drops of some strange beer/champagne concoction from his tie and into his mouth (a longtime fraternity-house survival-skill tactic).

That same unwashed tie hung in LA's locker for the rest of the season and right into the series against the Braves.

LARRY ANDERSEN: "That tie was ugly ugly. But at the same time it was the most beautiful tie I had ever seen in my life, because Harry gave it to me. Harry toasted us after that game and said, 'Gentlemen, thank you for giving me the best year of my life.' That really touched me, because I knew Harry was sincere.

"I remember Game 3 in Atlanta. We lost 9-4, and I didn't pitch well. After the game, as I got undressed, I noticed the tie was off the hook and crumpled up in my shoe. I hung it back on the hook and we won the NLCS. It was soaked with beer and champagne again after we beat Atlanta. By the end of the night, that tie was *rank*, but I was packing it for Toronto."

Curt Schilling's lucky cap almost never made it to Toronto.

During the mayhem after the Game 6 win over Atlanta, Curt Schilling was blindsided by Pete Incaviglia as they rushed out on the field, and Curt's cap disappeared. Bruce Baskow, a euphoric fan, jumped the railing, broke through security, and stormed the field to join in the celebration. He saw the cap on the Astroturf and grabbed it as a souvenir. When he heard on WIP that it was Schilling's lucky cap and that Curt really *needed* it for good luck, Bruce Baskow wanted to return the cap.

JOE WEACHTER, PRODUCER OF THE MORNING SHOW ON WIP RADIO: "We get a lot of calls from crackpots, so we didn't believe him at first. We gave him a hard time on the air. Curt happened to be listening, and he called Angelo Cataldi [a WIP personality]. They made arrangements to deliver the cap, and the guy brought it to Curt at the Vet just as the Phillies' bus was pulling away for the airport to go to Toronto." It's a good thing Curt was listening.

THE BLUE JAYS — BLUE JAYS SERIES

The Phillies had averaged 107 losses per year from 1938 through 1942. They lived in the basement all those years. In 1943, William Cox took over the club's reigns and hired a new manager, Bucky Harris, who, shortly after, was replaced by Fred Fitzsimmons. The Phillies crawled out of the basement—not spectacularly as in 1993, but they took a baby step. Their seventh-place finish, however, helped *double* attendance (from an abysmal 230,183 to 466,975). New owner Cox, unfortunately, got into some trouble betting on baseball games, and the following year, Robert Carpenter, Jr. bought the club. He wanted to snap the club out of the torpor that gripped it (one first-division finish in the previous 26 years) by changing its name. The Phils had a contest to rename the team. They received 5,064 letters with 623 different choices. Seven people submitted "Blue Jays." To determine the winner, the Phils had a drawing, and Mrs. John L. Crooks was the lucky winner. She received a $100 War Bond and three season tickets.

Nothing goes smoothly in Philly. The Phillies' office received a letter—actually a "nasty-gram"—from Baltimore. The writer called the Phillies' name change "a reprehensible act which brought disgrace and dishonor to the good name of Johns Hopkins University." Apparently, Johns Hopkins had been calling its teams the Blue Jays for over a half century. In any event, the Phillies—make that Blue Jays—stayed the course and let Johns Hopkins deal with the ignominy.

Carpenter had no intention of dropping the official name, Phillies. However, he felt a new insignia and nickname might help. It didn't. The Phillies sank back into the basement in 1944 and again in 1945. Attendance withered back to 285,057. In 1945, as America's fighting men began returning from overseas, the Phillies climbed up to fifth place and exceeded one million in attendance for the first time ever. By that time, the name Blue Jays, for all intents and purposes, had flown the coup. Had it not, the 1993 Series would have been an all Blue Jays World Series—with, perhaps, an appearance by the Johns Hopkins marching band.

The Lone Stranger And Toronto

Bill Giles was on cloud nine. As champions of the National League, the '93 Phillies, the team he helped put together, had their name inscribed on the Warren C. Giles trophy, the coveted prize that bore his dad's name. Just as fulfilling to Bill Giles was the fact that he loved this particular team. He loved their renegade personalities and their men-at-work image that endeared them to fellow Philadelphians.

Bill loves a good party. The Series is baseball's traditional party, and since getting there is half the fun, Bill chartered a plane for the front office. The night before the Series started, we all took off for the Great White North (which looked very green that time of year) to cheer our Phils on in Games 1 and 2 of the World Series.

That was my first flight on a charter, and it spoiled me forever. When we arrived at the airport, our luggage was checked immediately, and we were bussed directly out to the runway to board the plane. Next time we saw our luggage was in our rooms at Toronto. (What? You expected me to say in St. Louis two years later?) Bill invited every employee to bring a spouse, friend, or family member. I took my oldest brother Joe, nicknamed "Philly Joe" for his fierce loyalty to Philly teams in his Canisius College days in Buffalo. Joe is so eternally indebted to me for taking him that he still brings me all my drinks at family parties. Before we were airborne, Danny Ingersoll of our merchandising department handed out official NL Champion caps to everybody on the plane. Everyone wore the cap the whole flight, which was one big party—sipping red wine, feasting on filet mignon, singing, and joking. As I said before, Bill Giles knows how to throw a party.

Speaking of parties ... There's always a lot of partying going on at the 'big dance"—from the World Series Gala the night before the Series begins, through pregame parties, postgame parties, and all the parties in between. With all the partying, none of us felt like strangers in the strange land of Toronto, though, unfortunately, the Phanatic was the lone stranger from the Phillie contingent who had to sing—well, clown—for his supper.

DAVE RAYMOND: "The Blue Jays called me and invited the Phanatic to work Game 1. That was a thrill, especially since I knew this would be my last season and last World Series. In 1980, I performed at the Series in Kansas City, and I performed at Baltimore in 1983, but it's always an honor and a thrill to be a part of the World Series, whether you're a player or a mascot.

"Toronto had its own mascot, a bird called BJ who was pretty tame and well behaved. It wasn't entirely his fault, because the Toronto organization didn't give him much freedom. When I got there, I was amazed that I could do just what I did in Philly. And I seemed to be a hit with the Toronto fans.

"I was on the field pregame. Unfortunately, the logistics were messed up. The planned festivities finished ten minutes before the game went on the air, so there was a ten-minute gap to fill. So I just kind of filled in the slack. I walked over to where the Phillie contingent was sitting. You couldn't miss them. With their white and red caps, they stood out like sore thumbs in all that Blue Jay blue. I started a cheering contest, pitting the Blue Jay fans against the Phillie fans. Then I hopped back out on the field and started harassing a uniformed police officer—"flirting" with him, giving him a big Phanatic kiss, and goosing him when he walked away. Later, the Toronto organization thanked me profusely for helping them fill the dead air."

About that goose, Dave—didn't you sign that form about "inappropriate behavior?"

The Series

"I'll tell you what October is all about. There isn't a player on the field who isn't running on fumes. Your tanks are empty and you're trying to see who can crawl across the finish line first. It all comes down to what you've learned over the years. It comes down to your physical and mental approach to the game. It all comes to a head in situations like when I faced Willie Wilson for that last out. It's your ability to tap into yourself and find where that 'extra' is inside you, to find anything you have left, and to know how to use it. You're standing on the mound and you realize that this is what you've been working for your whole life. And you're out there representing your parents and the coaches and teachers you had when you were a kid. You're representing a combination of everything that has been invested into your whole career and your whole life."
— *Tug McGraw*

Game 1: Saturday, October 16, at Toronto

The Phils awoke on Saturday morning to the *Toronto Star* headline: "'I'm Not a Slob,' Kruk Protests." The article went on to describe the Phillies as "a motley crew of hairy, beer-soused brutes who haven't a hope of beating our beloved Boys of Summer." The Phils weren't too concerned about swaying public opinion; they were more interested in reversing history. All three previous World Series under a dome had been won by the home team: in 1987, Minnesota beat St. Louis in seven games, in 1991, Minnesota beat Atlanta in seven, and in 1992, Toronto beat Atlanta in six. In fact, Atlanta's 7-2 win in Game 5 was first time an NL team ever won a Series game inside. Admittedly, dome domination probably related more to American League superiority than any form of visiting team dome-ophobia.

Curt Schilling was tapped as the starter for the World Series, just as he had been tapped to start the NLCS. His opponent, Juan Guzman, finished with a regular season record of 14-3 and an ERA of 3.99. Guzman was coming out of a blazing hot ALCS, where he went 2-0 with a 2.08 ERA. Guzman had shown himself to be a formidable postseason performer, fashioning a 5-0 postseason log and a 2.04 ERA.

The game started well for the National Leaguers. The Phils reached back for a familiar formula—effective but not spectacular—that had worked for them all year. Dykstra led off with a walk, stole second, and crossed the plate on Kruk's single. As he had done in the NLCS, Kruk again knocked in the first Phillie run in the World Series. Hollins followed with a walk, moving Kruk to second. When Daulton singled, Kruk came home for a 2-0 advantage. The lead, however, was short-lived.

After setting down the Blue Jays in order in the first, Schilling gave up three singles to Joe Carter, John Olerud and Paul Molitor, which, together with a Daulton passed ball and a force out, plated two for the Jays to tie the match. The Phillies roared back for another run in the fourth and another in the fifth. Each time, the Jays matched them. In the bottom of the sixth, however, Olerud broke the tie for good with a solo blast as the Jays surged ahead for the first time. In the seventh, after catcher Pat Borders and outfielder Rickey Henderson singled, Schilling was lifted for David West, who promptly yielded a double to Devon White and a double to Alomar. Larry Andersen was summoned to close the inning, but three runs had already scored, putting the Jays safely ahead 8-4. The Phils recouped a harmless run in the ninth on singles by Kruk and Eisenreich but wound up on the short end of the final 8-5 tally.

GAME 1 FINAL: BLUE JAYS 8 – PHILS 5

Game 2: Sunday, October 17, at Toronto

Several Philly writers detected and reported an air of smugness up north. Perhaps the prevalent mood was best captured in a banner hanging over the right-field bullpen area that mused: "Phillies? You Can't Be Serious." Mitch chirped to the press, "The way they're ripping us up here, you'd think it was a one-game series. I believe that was just Game 1, wasn't it?" To add insult to injury, before Game 2, Michael Bolton sang such an extended version of the National Anthem that many observers swore his hair grew an inch on the quavering excursion from "Oh" to "brave."

Dave Stewart faced Terry Mulholland in this contest. Mulholland leveraged his ability to hold runners, his strongest attribute, to maximum advantage and set the tone of the game early. After the Phillies went down quietly in the first, Rickey Henderson, baseball's greatest all-time base stealer, opened the bottom of the frame with a walk. Mulholland tossed the ball over to first several times to keep Rickey honest. Henderson, however, had larceny in his heart. He attempted what only six NL base runners had tried in 191 innings. Henderson tried to swipe second and was gunned out. The last base runner all year to steal successfully off Mulholland was Darren Lewis on April 27. No one even *attempted* a steal on Mulholland after June 27. Henderson's out defused the Toronto juggernaut in the first.

In the third, the Phils broke a scoreless game wide open. The crusher was a three-run Eisenreich blast that gave the visitors a 5-0 advantage. The Phils' five-run inning matched their previous best-ever World Series inning. In Game 1 of the 1980 Series, they had scored five runs against Kansas City. Their five-run blitz for the inning matched their total run production for the entire four-game series in 1950.

The Jays surged back in their half of the fourth with a Molitor single and a Joe Carter circuit blast. The homer was Carter's first extra-base hit in six ALCS games and two World Series games. Joe Carter was the most productive power hitter in the majors from 1985 through 1993. His 262 homers and 952 RBIs were tops in both categories. The Blue Jays chipped away at the Phillie lead, tacking on another score in the sixth. But the Dude dialed long distance in the seventh, smashing his second home run in as many days. Mitch entered the fray in the eighth, relieving Roger Mason after Mason had surrendered a leadoff double to Paul Molitor. Molitor stole third on Mitch and scored on Olerud's sacrifice fly. The Wild Thing followed with a five-pitch walk to Alomar. The speedy second baseman easily stole second; however, before the next pitch, Mitch alertly caught him breaking prematurely for third. Mitch flipped the ball over to Hollins, who tagged out the embarrassed Alomar for out number three. Alomar's base-running blunder was a big gaffe, but not the biggest in World Series competition. That distinction belongs to Babe Ruth. In the '26 Series, the Yankees were down one run, with two out in the ninth. The Series was tied three games apiece.

The Babe was on first with Lou Gehrig at the plate when the Bambino inexplicably broke for second and was thrown out to end the Series and hand a victory over to the Cards.

In the ninth, Mitch, *de rigeur*, issued a four-pitch free pass to the leadoff batter but got a fielder's choice groundout on another shaky throw by defensive replacement Kim Batiste. The game ended with a 6-4-3 double play.

Curt Schilling had watched Mitch's performance with a towel over his head. The image would come back to haunt the team and the fans. It was the Wild Thing's longest outing in terms of innings pitched and the second longest in number of pitches thrown in a save all season long.

The Phils, who had left 11 on base in Game 1, left nine this time around. At this point in the Series, Kruk was smoking at a .556 clip, tops for both teams. As for Lenny, the Dude contributed two great defensive plays. In the fourth, he made a wall-thumper to stymie a big inning. He also robbed Alomar by catching Roberto's screaming liner against the fence after the Carter home run. Devon White told reporters that he'd pay money to see Dykstra, but not himself—quite a tribute since White had proven himself a red light player. At this point in the Series, White was the only player in baseball history with more than 100 at-bats in postseason play who had a higher batting average than Lou Gehrig. Devon was batting .392 versus Gehrig's .361.

Heading back to Philly, the Phils were happy for a split. The city of Toronto felt relieved that the gypsies, tramps, and thieves were departing. The winner of the *Toronto Sun's* contest, "*The Phillies are so ugly that …*" contest was selected. The winner was: "the turf spits back."

Not very exciting, eh?

GAME 2 FINAL: PHILLIES 6 -BLUE JAYS 4

A Kid At Heart

Larry Andersen might be a kid at heart, but I've seen firsthand that his heart is in the right place.

In 1995, Larry was the pitching coach for the Phillies' Double A affiliate, the Reading Phillies, and they won the Eastern League Championship. Reading, PA is a Pennsylvania city that calls itself "Baseballtown." I performed as the Phanatic the night Reading won the title. After the game, I rushed into the clubhouse to join the celebration. Larry was conspicuous by his absence, simply because LA never misses a party. Larry had gone out to the field to bring in a young handicapped boy who was a huge fan of the team all season. Larry saw the boy and his family at the park frequently and befriended them over the course of the season. The youngster was ecstatic amidst all his heroes, but I wasn't sure who had the bigger smile, Larry or the boy.

Back in August 1993, in the middle of the stretch drive for the pennant, Larry started to visit a wounded Philadelphia police officer named John Marynowitz. On June 16 of that year, on a routine car stop, Officer Marynowitz received gunshot wounds to the head and chest. He was given a slim chance of survival. His partner Robert Hayes had been shot and fatally wounded in the same incident. John couldn't talk for three months after he was shot. However, Larry visited John several times, and the two became friends. Just before the start of Game 4 of the World Series, Larry helped John's wife Mindy push John out onto the field in his wheelchair with the game ball in hand. John handed the first ball to Phillies legend Robin Roberts for the ceremonial first pitch.

JOHN MARYNOWITZ: "That was a difficult year for me that Larry helped me through. I was in pretty bad shape, but Larry came anyway. Larry would talk, and I'd blink: once for yes, twice for no."

MINDY MARYNOWITZ, JOHN'S WIFE: "Larry was such a regular down-to-earth guy. When he visited, all the nurses and kids in the hospital would run in to John's room to meet Larry. He would sign pictures and chat with everybody. Then, when John came home, Larry visited us here, at our house. He used to play catch with our three-year-old son, Joey, in the yard, which is still a thrill for Joey."

JOHN: "Larry sent me a video of behind-the-scenes footage of the Phillies' NLCS celebration. Larry's looking into the camera and yelling, 'Hey John, we won this one for you!'"

Mindy told me she doesn't think that particular video is available to the general public—something about "inappropriate behavior."

Game 3: Tuesday, October 19, at Philadelphia

Since the Series had moved to the National League city, there would be no designated hitter. Before Game 3, NL pitchers were hitting .086 (9-105) since 1976 when the DH invaded the World Series. AL pitchers were hitting much worse, a pathetic .035 (4-113). However, Toronto manager Cito Gaston fretted about how to set his lineup without a DH. He thought it imperative to keep Paul Molitor's bat in the lineup although doing so meant benching either John Olerud at first or Ed Sprague at third. Molitor was 37 years old at the time. He had been the Jays' DH all year and was, at this point in his career, not a sterling gloveman, particularly at the hot corner. Gaston opted to bench Olerud, the reigning AL batting champ. Molitor consecrated Gaston's hunch by homering, tripling, and driving in three runs. In the 1992 Series, Gaston had faced a similar dilemma. He ended up benching Olerud that year also so that DH Dave Winfield's bat could remain in the lineup. Winfield ended up slamming a key two-run double in the crucial eleventh inning of Game 6.

Olerud, strangely enough, was not the only batting champion ever benched in a Series game. In 1931, the Cards' eventual Hall of Famer Chick Hafey sat out Game 7, and in 1990, Willie McGee was benched in Games 2 and 3 as an Oakland Athletic (interestingly, McGee won the *National League* batting crown that year).

The Jays arrived safe and sound, although they had a rocky welcome to the City of Brotherly Love. There was a snafu with their hotel reservations. The reservations had been mistakenly canceled, so the team wound up staying at the Marriott in West Conshohocken, outside Philadelphia, a good 40-minute drive (without traffic) from the Vet.

The game, which was supposed to start at 8:12 p.m., didn't start till 9:24 p.m. The skies, ominous all day long, finally let loose after the pregame show, causing a seventy-two-minute rain delay—the first delay at the start of a Series game since 1968.

When Mike Schmidt strolled to the mound to toss out the first pitch, the Vet crowd gave him a prolonged standing ovation. The rest of the evening was pretty much ovationless.

The starting pitchers for the game were two veterans: Pat Hentgen and Danny Jackson. DJ was only the third pitcher in history to appear in a World Series for three different teams: the '85 Royals, the '90 Reds, and the '93 Phillies (the others were Joe Bush: '13 A's, '18 Red Sox, and '22 Yankees; and Jack Morris: '84 Tigers, '91 Twins, and '92 Blue Jays). Joe Carter and DJ live near each other in Kansas City. Before the game, Carter said, "DJ's a good neighbor. We call him Jason. He'll tear up a wall, do his Lou Ferrigno pose, whatever it takes to get pumped up. That's just DJ."

Jason was pumped up before the game, but the long rain delay discombobulated him. The Jays jumped all over him to take a 3-0 lead in the first. Molitor's two-run triple was the main blow in the rally. Toronto stayed in front for good. Molitor solo-homered in the third to increase the advantage to 4-0 before Alomar ran his way to another run the next inning. Roberto stroked a single, stole two bases, and scored on a Fernandez sacrifice fly. The Phils tacked a lone run up on the board with two walks and an Eisenreich RBI single in the bottom of the fourth. However, the Jays put the game out of reach next inning when they tallied three to up the score to 8-1. Milt Thompson led off with a round-tripper in the bottom of the ninth to bring the score to 10-3, but that was all she wrote.

The game was the Phils' fourth straight World Series loss at the Vet. The Phillies stranded nine base runners this time around, swelling their three-game total in the category to 29.

GAME 3 FINAL: BLUE JAYS 10 – PHILLIES 3

Game 4: Wednesday, October 20, at Philadelphia
"Blue Jays Win on late TD."
— headline in Paul Hagan's column

The starters were Tommy Greene and Todd Stottlemyre, whose father, Mel, had started three games for the Yanks in 1964 against the Cards. The elder Stottlemyre beat Bob Gibson in Game 2, who came back to beat him in Game 7 for a Cardinal title. The Phillies had to confront some bad historical vibes in this game and the next, since no Phillie team had ever won a Game 3 or Game 4 in World Series competition. With right-hander Greene on the hill, Olerud was reinstated at first base. Molitor stayed in the lineup, displacing regular Ed Sprague at the hot corner. Thus far in the Series, Molitor was hitting an out-of-his-head .583 (by Series end, Molitor would "cool down" to an even .500) and Sprague an anemic .083.

There were a few entertaining sideshows attached to the game. Toronto starter Todd Stottlemyre was feuding with Philly mayor Ed Rendell who said he himself could hit Stottlemyre. And, across the street, Madonna was in concert.

YOU *CAN* FIGHT CITY HALL

Mayor Ed Rendell, a true-red Phillies fan, was getting a little irked at the constant chatter about Toronto's superiority. In Toronto, after the first game, he was interviewed about the possibility of a Blue Jays Series sweep. The mayor, an avid sports fan who has done postgame Eagles commentary for a few years, chimed in, "If you had the Whites Sox pitching and the Blue Jays' lineup, maybe that would have happened. But I don't think Todd Stottlemyre can beat the Phillies. I saw that 430-foot homer that Frank Thomas hit off him [in the ALCS]. I think I could hit the ball 270 feet off Stottlemyre, and that's a pretty good shot for me."

The national press was all over that one! David Letterman invited Stottlemyre on his show, fanning the flames of the Rendell comment. The Jays' pitcher flung back some zingers of his own. "I'll tell you what. When this thing is over with, I'll fly to Philly. Tell the mayor to put a uniform on, and we'll see what happens."

"How will you pitch him?" Stottlemyre was asked.

"I'll probably put the first three behind his head, then paint the outside corner," the Jays' hurler retaliated.

Rendell, undaunted, replied, "I'm happy to do it. But he's got to throw me the same hanging curve he threw Frank Thomas. He can't throw me a fastball. I don't think I could hit Todd Stottlemyre's fastball. We're going to freeze-frame that pitch for him. And if he can throw that exact pitch to me over and over again, in the same location and at the same speed, and if I don't hit one of them 270 feet, then I'll give him $250 for the charity of his choice."

The mayor was getting besieged from all sides, even for putting the Phils cap on Billy Penn ("That's the most popular thing I ever did as mayor," Hizzoner still maintains). Three city Law Department honchos pulled Rendell's leg, sending him a two-page memo titled "The Big Hat," written by Joseph Dworetzky, Abby Pozefsky and Kenneth Bashoff, all deputy city solicitors. They cited eleven different municipal regulations that were bypassed in hoisting the hat onto City Hall's tower. The violations ranged from failure to secure a zoning variance or a permit for the cap, to interference with "the established patterns of Philadelphia bird life, including, without limitation, the Eagles."

JIM FREGOSI: "What a great mayor Eddie was! And what a fan! He was kidding me up in Toronto, 'Jim, if you guys win the World Series, you won't have to pay taxes.' He called me the day after we lost and said, 'Tough one, Jim, but my auditors will be down at your office in the morning!'"

Madonna:
A Frig Of Her Own

During the game, Madonna was in concert across the street from the Vet at the Spectrum, Philly's largest indoor arena at the time. Mitch told the press, "I wouldn't walk across the street for Madonna (but you probably *would run*, wouldn't you, Wild Thing?). Now, if it was Randy Travis, yeah. But she doesn't play my kind of music."

According to newspaper accounts the day after the concert, Madonna demonstrated what a big baseball fan she was when she stopped her show that night to yell, "I understand there's some stiff competition for me across the street. Frig Toronto. Frig the Blue Jays. Frig 'em. As a matter of fact, frig any team except the Phillies. As a matter of fact, frig every city except Philly, okay? As a matter of fact, I think I did."

The Material Girl will have few dissenters on that one.

For an encore, Madonna reportedly wore a red Phillies shirt, hanging open over teeny cutoffs and fishnet stockings —not quite the same baseball look she showed us in *A League of Their Own*. Too bad we didn't get Madonna to model the 1992 Phillies uniform, but then the fans would have expected that handcuffs and whips were part of every uniform.

> As she was about to sing her song "Holiday," Madonna told the crowd she had just been in Toronto the week before. She continued, "I hated it. They're very conservative. It's not my favorite town."
>
> Then, to the cheers of "Whoomp, There It Is" (or, was it "Whoot, There It Is?"), Madonna called up some lucky guy with a Blue Jays shirt to the stage and ordered him to do 50 push-ups.
>
> The next day, a Toronto radio station was calling for the city to ban Madonna records unless she apologized. It appears she survived the snub, although I don't know that she has ever appeared at the SkyDome—something about signing an "inappropriate behavior" disclaimer.

The game had a carnival-like atmosphere all night long, or all the long night. By the end of the game, the contest was arguably the most bizarre World Series game ever played. More runs went up on the board in this game than in the entire 1983 World Series (27 runs in five games). Since the divisional playoffs began, only one team had ever scored 14 runs in a game (the '91 Braves). That's a *34-year* period, covering 415 games. On this night, *both* teams scored 14 or more. No team had ever scored more than nine runs and lost a World Series game. Inauspiciously, the 1960 Yanks who lost Game 7, 10-9, came closest. Until 1993, that was the only Series that ended with a walk-off home run. It was the longest World Series game ever, and at four hours, 14 minutes, *it was the longest 9-inning night game ever*—period. The Jays had set that record just thirty-seven days earlier! Todd Stottlemyre had been the starting pitcher in that game as well.

While Tommy Greene was warming up, pitching coach Johnny Podres assured Fregosi, "They won't touch Tommy tonight." Pods proved a poor prognosticator. Tommy, who had scrawled "Aggressive" on the underbrim of his hat for the game, didn't get much chance to read it. He was out of the breach after two and one-third innings, during which he yielded seven earned runs. He did outlast his opponent. Stottlemyre was lifted after two innings and six earned runs.

It was misting rain the entire game, but the action was never halted—nor did it ever stop. This marked the second night in a row that the elements intervened. Although Phillie officials assured Major League Baseball officials that "It never rains at the Vet," Philadelphia had been the scene of the longest period of World Series postponement. Way back in 1911, rain forced a *six-day* postponement of Game 4 between the A's and the NY Giants. They were supposed to play in Shibe Park (renamed Connie Mack Stadium in the fifties) on October 18 and didn't get the game in till October 24.

The Phillies used more pitchers (six) in this one game than the Orioles used in the entire 1966 World Series against the Dodgers. Somebody scored in every inning except the ninth. And strangest of all, in a game in which the Phillies scored 14 runs, John Kruk was hitless in five tries.

The game started with a Henderson double. Two singles and two walks later, the Phillies were down three and coming to bat. Dykstra opened with a walk. Duncan flew out, and Kruk whiffed for the second out. Then—well, you can't say lightning struck—but the Phils, almost Ghandi-esque, again used patience as a weapon. Hollins, Daulton and Eisenreich walked in succession (the Phillies swung at only *two* of Stottlemyre's first 27 pitches), forcing in Dykstra for the first run. Then Milt Thompson cleared the bases with a triple to put the Phils ahead 4-3. Milt, who collected four RBIs in the months of August and September *combined*, knocked in five in this game alone.

Greene held Toronto scoreless in the second, then singled (his ninth hit in his last nineteen at-bats) to open the Phillies' half of the frame. The Dude followed with a homer. Later, Jays pitcher Al Leiter ("Unbelievable, I only hit .257 in high school!") doubled. Thus, for the first time since 1974, two opposing pitchers got safeties in the same Series game. The next inning, Toronto used four hits and two walks for four runs. The Phillies tied them in the bottom half of the fourth and then roared ahead by five the following inning on the strength of homers by Daulton and the Dude. Going into the eighth, the Phillies held a comfortable five-run lead. Larry Andersen, who had put the Jays down 1-2-3 in the seventh, was on the hill.

Andersen retired leadoff man Alomar on a grounder to Hollins. However, a Carter single, followed by an Olerud walk and an error by Hollins led to LA's exit. It was time for the Wild Thing. Mitch came in and gave up a single and a walk before striking out pinch hitter Ed Sprague for the second out. At this point, only two runs had scored. However, a Rickey Henderson single and a Devon White triple plated four more in a 6-run inning that put the Jays ahead by one. Toronto held on the rest of the way. In the bottom of the eighth, Mike Timlin struck out the side (Stocker, Morandini, and Dykstra). The Phils also went down in order in the ninth to end the marathon.

Toronto, so concerned about not playing with a designated hitter, had scored 25 runs in the two contests played under NL rules. That total was *eight more runs* than the Jays had scored in winning the World Series the previous year.

Two Phillies emerged from the game with several postseason distinctions, though one was dubious. With the announced retirement of George Brett, Lenny Dykstra became the major leagues' active leader in career postseason home runs with ten. On the dubious side of the ledger, David West—he of the 27.00 Series ERA—became the only player who appeared in all three postseason games since 1960 in which a team scored 14 or more runs: Game 5 of '91 World Series, Game 2 of the '93 playoffs, and this one.

Larry Andersen summed up: "If we can stop crying tonight, we can start laughing tomorrow."

GAME FINAL: BLUE JAYS 15 - PHILLIES 14.

Game 5: Thursday, October 21, at Philadelphia

With Toronto one victory away from the title, the two Game 1 pitchers, Guzman and Schillling, locked horns for a rematch. While fielding questions from reporters the day after the 15-14 debacle, Schilling wore a cap with a button: "I survived watching Mitch pitch." Schil explained to onlookers, "Mitch gave the button to me."

The Phillies scored single runs in the first two frames, which accounted for all the scoring in the contest. The game was a Schilling show from start to finish. Schil threw 148 pitches in a complete game victory.

Lenny opened the first with a walk, stole second, and scurried to third when Pat Borders's throw to second trickled into center field. The Dude scampered home when Kruk grounded out. In the second, Daulton opened with a double off the wall in left center. After Eisey and Thompson made outs, Stocker doubled him home. Stocker made Toronto pay for their decision to pitch to him in that situation. First base was open, and pitcher Schilling was coming to bat.

Schilling scattered five hits and three walks in pitching a gem. Toronto never placed more than a single runner on base except in the eighth inning. Borders and Rob Butler opened that frame with singles. But Rickey Henderson bounced a hopper that Schilling batted down and nailed Willie Canate (who was pinch running for Borders) in a rundown at the plate. Schilling followed with a strikeout of the dangerous Devon White before getting Alomar to ground out to end the threat. In the Phillies' half of the eighth, Kruk and Hollins walked to start the inning, but Dutch, Eisey, and Milt all struck out swinging to put another goose egg up on the scoreboard.

CURT SCHILLING: "In my career, I look back at two innings where I gave it absolutely everything I could possible give, where I just reached inside for everything I had. That eighth inning was one of them. I battled each one of those guys—Henderson, White, and Alomar—for those outs. We weren't banging the ball around that night, so we played 'small ball.' We got that lead early, and it was up to me to hold it."

The Phillie faithful remained staunch in their support, despite the fact that their heroes were so close to elimination. Mitch got a standing ovation as he sauntered down to the bullpen in the seventh. Nonetheless, a banner flapping in the outfield, "Will Pitch Middle Relief for Food," was a stark sentinel to the club's woes. Dave Hollins was asked after the match, "How can a team bounce back from a 15-14 defeat like that?" Hollins's response captured the spirit of his team. "I'll always be here. It's never tough for me to put on the uniform and go out and play. Just coming in here and going out on the field in a big-league park is enough incentive for me."

GAME FINAL: PHILLIES 2 – BLUE JAYS 0

Game 6: Saturday, October 23, at Toronto

As the Series shifted back to Canada, the good news for the Phils was that five of the last six teams to trail the Series 3-2 won it. However, the Phillies had to do so on the road—and that made it a daunting feat. Only six teams had accomplished that in the history of the Fall Classic. As it had been in Game 2, the matchup was Dave Stewart and Terry Mulholland.

CHRIS WHEELER: "Before the game, I was talking to Fregosi in his office. Schilling came in and told Fregosi, 'I'm ready if you need me. I can go in there for you tonight.' Fregosi thanked Curt but told him he wasn't going to use him. When Curt left, Fregosi told me he wouldn't use Schilling 'cause he had thrown 150 pitches the other day, and the guy had such a great arm and bright future that he wouldn't jeopardize his career by throwing him in. When they talk about 'player's manager,' that's what they're talking about."

Again, Toronto jumped out to a first-inning 3-0 lead, using a walk, a Molitor triple, a Carter sacrifice, an Olerud double, and an Alomar single. The Phils answered with a single run in the fourth, but the Blue Jays countered with a lone run in their half of the stanza. Molitor hit a solo shot in the sixth to give the Jays a 5-1 lead after six. Stocker walked to open the seventh. Morandini followed with a single, and then the Dude cranked out his fourth home run of the Series. His blast chased starter Stewart from the contest. Danny Cox replaced him, and Mariano Duncan promptly singled, stole second, and scored on a Dave Hollins single. After Daulton walked and Eisenreich singled, Al Leiter came on. Inky hit a sacrifice fly that brought home the fifth run of the inning, giving the Phils the lead, 6-5. Stocker struck out swinging with Daulton on third to end the rally.

Middle relief, the bane of the Phillies' postseason, held Toronto at bay in the sixth, seventh, and eighth. Roger Mason relieved Mulholland in the sixth, and after yielding a single to first batter Alomar, Roger retired the next six Jays in order. In the eighth, with the Phils still clinging to a 6-5 lead, Mason erased Joe Carter on a long fly ball for the first out. West replaced Mason (Toronto was hitting .625 against him in the Series) and walked Olerud on five pitches. Andersen came in and got Alomar on a groundout. However, LA then hit Fernandez with a pitch and walked Ed Sprague before Borders popped out to end the inning.

Duane Ward relieved Leiter in the ninth and sat the Phils down in order. In the bottom of the ninth, Batiste came in for defense at third, and Mitch again took the ball for the save. The Wild Thing walked leadoff batter Henderson. White flew out to Incaviglia before Molitor singled. Joe Carter stepped to the plate, the count went to 2-2, and Joe lined a slider over the left-field wall. The curtain descended on the Series and the Enchanted Season at 11:39 p.m. as Carter and his delirious teammates celebrated at home plate.

Tug McGraw was familiar with the drama. The Tugger had pitched in that same situation and chiseled himself into Philly lore in the 1980 Series, when he came on to strike out Willie Wilson to bring Philly its first-ever World Series championship.

TUG McGRAW: "In sports, you can only guarantee the effort. You can't guarantee the results. There's a certain point in any sport where you've done all you can do. You release the ball, and that's it. You can't do any more. The difference between Mitch and me in that situation is a half-inch. Willie Wilson missed my pitch by a half-inch. Carter got Mitch's by a half-inch."

FREGOSI: "If you look at Game 6, I think the biggest problem we had was the eighth inning. Larry Andersen came off the mound at the end of the eighth and hyperventilated in my arms. Between David West and Andy, we loaded the bases, and if we had *not* done that, Mitch would not have had to face the top of the Toronto order in the ninth. To me, that's the difference in the ballgame. No, Tommy Greene was not prepared to come into the game in that situation. He was not prepared to play that kind of a role. Tommy was a starting pitcher all year. I always believed that what you did in the regular season, that's what you did in the postseason. I never believed in putting starting pitchers down in the bullpen. And just because a guy struggled recently, you still use the guys who got you there. Years ago, I was the manager on this club, and the owner called me and said, 'Don't *ever* use that guy again in that situation' and I said, 'Well, I really didn't know you went out and got Gossage for me.' I did the same thing in Game 6 in '93. I used the guys available to me. Probably the only change I'd have made going into that '93 Series is that I'd have gone with an extra pitcher. I would have included Mike Williams on the Series roster.

"But everybody was there that Series. We were all there together, and we were all pulling for Mitch. Even Schil, when he was putting the towel over his head, I don't think he really meant anything by that. Maybe Mitch didn't take it that way. I just think Schil couldn't watch it. There were a lot of games Mitch pitched that *I* couldn't watch either."

The Enchanted Season was over. Kruk said that as he was headed back to the locker room for the final time that year, a photographer growled at him, "Why don't you *friggin'* freaks get back home where you belong?" But Pete Incaviglia summed up the team's feelings best.

PETE INCAVIGLIA: "Honest, all I could think about when I watched that Carter home run go over the fence was, 'What do we do tomorrow?' All I lived for was coming to that park every day. I knew there'd never be a season like that again. I'd never have as much fun again. And I felt so bad for Mitch. Mitch leaves it all on the mound. He gave it everything he had, and sometimes that's what happens. I just felt so bad because we couldn't come back the next day. Really, I almost felt lost."

KRUK: "We got back in that clubhouse after the game and iced down and had some beers. I remember looking at [Daulton], seeing how beat up he was after a year of this, and just thinking how much we needed a rest. We were feeling down for about an hour or so, but then everybody came in, like we had all year, and we talked just like we had all year, and we didn't feel bad any more. We felt good. Hell, we *almost* did it, and we couldn't have done a damn thing more. And we had a helluva lot of fun trying."

TERRY MULHOLLAND: "I think we all mostly felt bad for Mitch, even worse than losing the Series. We got in that locker room, and the media guys just swarmed him. Mitch is such a stand-up guy. He stood there like a man answering their questions, making no excuses. After awhile, *I* couldn't take it. I went over and got Mitch and brought him into the trainer's room."

FREGOSI: "A lot of people picked us for dead last before the season. And people jumped on the bandwagon and thought we were supposed to win the World Series. I couldn't have been prouder of a group of guys. They were all stand-up guys. If they fouled up a game, they would stand up and admit it— every one of them. And they would give all they could give."

The '93 squad stayed in the locker room for long hours that night, rehashing the game, the season, and holding on, just one last time. There's no crying in baseball, but sometimes you wish there could be.

As Jim Fregosi said in the early morning Toronto chill on October 25, 1993, "We'll never have anything like this team again. God, how they fought. They fought and they fought. And it'll never be the same again. We'll never have it back, because that's the nature of baseball today. It just doesn't carry over from year to year. But God, I'm proud of these guys."

GAME FINAL: BLUE JAYS 8 - PHILLIES 6

Aftermath

"With half-closed eyes, I stared into the room where my friends and I spent many an afternoon. Ten thousand dollars at the drop of a hat, I'd give it all gladly, if things could be like that."
— *Bob Dylan*

Columnist Jayson Stark was on the field for what proved to be the '93 Phils' final workout. The Phils had just battled back from their crushing, demoralizing 15-14 loss in Game 4 of the World Series. Facing elimination the following night, Curt Schilling threw a gutsy 2-0 shutout that kept the Series and the Phillies' hopes alive. Jayson wandered around the diamond that day under the SkyDome, watching the boys at play. He was impressed at what he witnessed—no, make that *moved*, although don't use that word with the boys in Macho Row. They'd bury Jayson in embarrassment, the same way the bad boys in class would bury a buddy if they laid their hands on the secret book of verse and poetry he'd been scrawling.

The diorama Jayson described captured the essence and power of this team.

"So there they were, back up north of the border, doing the same old baseball stuff that has filled almost every day of their lives for the last eight months.

"Except it would be hard to make a case that they were doing it with feverish military precision.

"They laughed. They talked. They hit a bunch of baseballs all over SkyDome. But mostly they did what has made this season so special for this band of crazed, talented ballplayers: they savored each other's company.

"This team has spent 245 days together. And the Phillies have ended most of those days by trooping into the players' lounge or the trainer's room afterward and sitting around half the night, telling their war stories, talking about baseball, and just enjoying each other's company … That has been their life for all of these months. So every day it continues, they will enjoy it for every precious second."

Jayson Stark's column appeared in the *Philadelphia Inquirer* on October 23, 1993. At 11:39 that evening, the Enchanted Season was over. Team America was coming home. The next day, the Phillies' entourage boarded their A-300 Airbus and taxied toward the runway. Suddenly, the loudspeaker hissed and a familiar voice crackled, "This is *not* your captain speaking. This is Captain Bill." Bill Giles fought to get the words out, but his voice and emotions were failing him. "I just want to thank you all from the bottom of my heart for the great season you all have given us, particularly the players … " His thoughts trailed off into the Toronto skies.

When the plane landed in Philly, a huge throng awaited the passengers. Larry Andersen walked along holding two fingers aloft, proclaiming "We're Number Two!" The '93 bunch—hard-boiled professionals and realists—had already come to grips with their defeat.

They were setting foot one last time as a team in Rocky's city—Rocky, the underdog who went the distance with a great champ, who stood toe to toe with him, traded punches, refused to be intimidated, and wouldn't give in. These guys were Rocky's team from Rocky's own city. And when the final bell sounded, they didn't really lose. They just ran out of rounds.

FREGOSI: "I thought at the end of the '93 season that this was a one-year club. I did not think we could stay healthy enough after we were fortunate enough to stay healthy in '93. A lot of these players were older, and that '93 season, more or less, was their last hurrah. They were together, these guys—a closer knit group of guys I have never seen."

One prominent member of the team was not aboard the team's final flight. Mitch Williams flew directly to his ranch in Texas. Mitch would never again fly with the team as a Phillie player.

The rest of the team landed, emptied the collected funk of 200-plus days out of the locker room, bade their farewells, and drifted home.

JAYSON STARK: "It was hard for those guys to believe it was over. The season was one of those magic carpet rides that seemed like it would never end. It had no business happening, but it did. You had to appreciate the season for what it was, because a season like that isn't normal. You can't recreate it. Whatever the formula is, you just sit back and hold it. And the players realized it. I ran a magazine story two days after the season. Darren Daulton and Larry Andersen were in the clubhouse to clean out their lockers. They saw Video Dan working on a highlight reel of the season. Dan asked them to watch it so he could get their input on what they thought was good and what should be cut. At that point in the production, it was just one long, unedited run. But the two of them sat there with Dan and watched the whole season unfold again. Neither one wanted to leave. They knew that when they walked out the door, all those things they had just watched in Dan's video walked out with them. That whole season they just experienced, all those good times, were gone, and they wouldn't be back."

Jim Fregosi, Bill Giles, Dennis Menke, and many of the '93 Phils players talk about how other players around the league wanted to become Phillies themselves. Other players saw the camaraderie, the cutting up, and the fun this team was having. They saw spirit that was lacking in their own clubhouses—spirit that steeled into killer resolve between the lines. Pittsburgh's Andy Van Slyke summed up the way the competition remembers the club: "People talk about how goofy the Phillies are, and to some extent, that's true. But all you had to do was play them once to realize that these goofy guys would die for each other. They've got a lot of talented players there, but I think there were other reasons why they played so well all year. Things that began in their clubhouse."

That clubhouse changed subtly in 1994. Mitch and Mulholland were gone. The Krukker was battling testicular cancer. The delicate chemistry—actually the mystifying *alchemy* that transformed ordinary elements into gold—was altered irretrievably. In the *Philadelphia Inquirer's* "Baseball '94" supplement, Frank Fitzpatrick painted the new clubhouse, garish as a Jackson Pollock canvas one year earlier, now more muted and mellow. "This spring, in the compact Jack Russell Stadium clubhouse in Clearwater, Florida, there were no card games punctuated by needling and name-calling. (Danny) Jackson never tore off his shirt and 'pumped it up.' Injuries preoccupied Andersen more than belches and pranks. Players spoke quietly about serious topics such as marital problems and cancer, and there were more than a few days when no one even bothered to pop a disc into a CD player that had run nonstop in 1993."

The '93 Phils faded fast from the Philly scene but not from its heart. Over the winter, Mitch was traded to Houston for Jeff Juden and Doug Jones. In '94, John Brazer, who replaced Tom Burgoyne as the Vet's '94 music mixer, would no longer spin "Wild Thing" for the Phillie closer. Closer Doug Jones's overture was "Mr. Jones" by the Counting Crows. The Phillies traded Terry Mulholland to the Yankees in the off season, although Terry did return to Philly for a partial-season stint in 1996. The Krukker's battle with cancer curtailed his career. John played only 120 more games—75 in 1994 and 45 in 1995. Ruben Amaro was dealt to Cleveland for Heathcliff Slocumb.

A huge wave of departures and retirements hit during and after the '94 campaign. In midseason '94, "Pops," Milt Thompson, was dealt to Houston and Wes Chamberlain to Boston. Tommy Greene, plagued by injuries, won just two games in 1994. He never registered another win. Ben Rivera went 3-4 in 1994 and never pitched another major-league season. Larry Andersen retired after '94. A chronic bad back abbreviated Lenny Dykstra's career. The Dude played in only 186 games over the next three seasons. He called it quits in 1996. Inky played the strike-curtailed season of '94 before hopping to Japan in 1995. Dave Hollins, hampered by injuries in '94, played only 44 games. He was traded to Boston in 1995. Jim Eisenreich stuck around Philly a few years and became one of the town's most beloved athletes. In 1997, Eisey went to the Marlins and earned a World Championship ring. He was reunited in Florida later in that championship season with Dutch Daulton. Dutch stayed in Philly till the end of the 1996 season. Then, in an emotional parting during the 1997 campaign, Dutch joined the Marlins and helped them win a World Championship. Racked by injuries, the rock-solid backstop who had played in 145-plus games in '92 and '93, never again caught 100 games in one year.

David West, who made 76 appearances that Enchanted Season, made 31 the following year but never more than eight in any of the three seasons that remained in his career. Mariano Duncan, Kevin Stocker, Mickey Morandini, and others, including manager Jim Fregosi, had departed by '97 or '98. When Curt Schilling left for Arizona to team up with Randy Johnson in one of baseball's most powerful pitching tandems of all time, the last vestige of the '93 champs vanished. Though the glory was short-lived, the ballplayers themselves, practically to a man, consider that season the most rewarding and memorable in their professional lives.

DAVE HOLLINS: "I've played this game a long time with a lot of different teams. But when I left the Phillies, I really went through 'Phillie withdrawal.' I don't know what else to call it. I never found the same atmosphere, the same intensity about winning, never got the same pleasure playing baseball—never again. My baseball life was so good and rewarding in '93, it almost hurt me, because I knew I'd never have anything like that again."

INKY: "I played a number of years in Texas and with lots of other clubs. But when I think of myself as a ballplayer, I'm a Phillie. Practically all the guys on that club feel that way. That team, that year, those guys, the fans—everything ... I'll always be a Phillie."

The leagues realigned in 1994 into three divisions: East, Central, and West. Atlanta and Philadelphia both wound up in the eastern division. The Phillies slipped to next to last in 1994 in the realigned structure. Atlanta eased into unrelenting dominance. They won the division every year from 1994 through 2001. Until 2001, the Phils had never come within twenty games of the front-runners. But the Phillies turned it around in 2001 with a talented nucleus of youngsters who battled Atlanta down to the last week of the season. With its new stadium in 2004, the Phillies appear prepped to string a number of good seasons together again.

The '93 guys didn't string successful seasons together. But they did give the Phillies one superb season and one superb effort. Maybe Philly did catch lightning in a bottle in '93, but people all around the baseball world still remember it as one of the most entertaining light shows the grand old game has ever seen.

JIM FREGOSI: "In every city I go, even nowadays, people come up to me and say, 'Thanks for '93!'"

The New Guy

"And the Toronto Blue Jays are the World Champions ..." I sat there staring at the TV in disbelief as Joe Carter skipped giddily around the bases at SkyDome.

My soon-to-be-bride, Jennifer, and I had gone to a friend's house for one of those last-hurrah get-togethers before our big November wedding (although that little bachelor party the week before "W"-Day was *really* the last hurrah). After Carter's home run, everyone got right back into the swing of the party, chatting it up and heading for the snacks table. Not me. I couldn't stop staring at the TV.

The '93 Phils had pulled out so many wild and crazy comebacks and had won in so many weird and wonderful ways. Then we knocked off the mighty Braves, misleading me into believing the World Series was a mere formality, that we were simply destined to win.

PHANATIC PHILE

But good things were happening for me. After the wedding and the honeymoon, I had that cheese-whiz-filled meeting with Dave Raymond when he let me in on his impending departure. I had almost put that Series loss to bed. Then my little world came crashing down.

I was with some friends in a bar a week later, watching *Monday Night Football*. At halftime, local sports anchor Gary Papa, live behind his news desk, announced: "Coming up on *Action News*: after 16 years, Dave Raymond is calling it quits as the Phillie Phanatic. The Phillies are looking for a new Phanatic. Do you have what it takes? Story after the game."

My friends' jaws dropped—right after mine hit the bar.

"Yo, Tom, I thought they were grooming you for that job?" one said.

So did I. Was there something someone wasn't telling me? Were the Phillies going to hold open auditions for the mascot job, even though for the past five years I was averaging 225 appearances a year as the backup Phanatic? Maybe the club figured they could put *any*one in that costume and have it work!

Naahhhh!

Sure enough, the lead story on *Action News* after the football game was the Phanatic story. Papa, obviously elated with the scoop, showed clips of Dave doing his Jane Fonda bit in the NLCS. Then he ran interviews with people on the street, asking them if they thought they could be the Phanatic. Almost as an afterthought (see, the Phanatic is a sensitive guy), Papa mentioned that Dave had a backup who in all likelihood would be taking over for Dave.

Whewww.

The next morning our PR department hastily put out a press release. Yes, Dave Raymond has a backup whose name is Tom Burgoyne, and he will be taking over, full-time, as the Phanatic.

The press release didn't stop the story from getting botched. One TV reporter asked kids at a Philly elementary school what they thought about the Phanatic leaving. One kid, almost in tears, looked into the camera sobbing, 'I loved the Phanatic and I'm really going to miss him.' Think the "Yeller's dead" scene in *Old Yeller*, minus Fess Parker, and you've got the picture.

But I understood the confusion. I really did. The Phanatic has become so real to kids and adults alike that to hear that there are two of them is hard to comprehend. He has a defined personality that is totally Philly—passionate, obnoxious at times, but at his core, he's all heart. When you go to a Phillies games he's always there, as comfortable as your favorite baseball cap and as natural as a Harry Kalas's "Outta Here" home run call.

That's why the three months leading up to the 1994 opener were a frenzy of media attention and speculation as to how the new kid would do stepping into the large shoes vacated by Dave Raymond. *USA Today Baseball Weekly* ran a two-page cover story headlined with, "He's been phunny, phurry, phat and phriendly for phifteen years, but the Phillie Phanatic is phinished." Close—it had actually been sixteen years, but I guess the alliteration was too hard to resist. The *Philadelphia Daily News* put me on their annual list of 15 local celebrities who were "On The Spot." The question posed was: "Does the man make the costume or does the costume make the man?" with the comment, "Slapping on that humongous furry green suit sure doesn't look easy." Even the gruff Bill Conlin waxed warm and "phuzzy" with an "ode to the Phanatic" column, writing, "The best mascot in the history of a genre that includes the West Point mule, the Naval Academy goat, Bevo, the University of Texas Long-horn, and hundreds of pale imitations is hanging up the big green suit. Downwind, please." Bill admitted his love of the character and summed up: "I have seen Tom Burgoyne, the backup Phanatic perform, and he is good. No wonder the Phillies have turned down my application for the job—I figured they could save some money simply by putting me in a warmup suit and hiring a crop duster to spraypaint me green."

When opening day 1994 finally arrived, I was bouncing off the walls. Play ball! Among the sellout crowd of 58,627 was a section filled with my family and friends, all cheering me on. The *Philadelphia Inquirer* dispatched a reporter to follow my every move that day, informing readers on how the new kid performed.

At 1:41 p.m., after the Philadelphia Boys Choir had sung a medley of patriotic songs and Phanavision had shown a quick three-minute video of 1993 highlights, I roared down the truck ramp in right field for the first time, my heart thumping against my chest. The crowd let out an enthusiastic cheer that stifled my nervousness and let the Phanatic take over. I rumbled over to Bob Hamilton, conductor of the Philadelphia Boys Choir, hopped off the four-wheeler, and snatched his baton. After frantically mimicking Bob's every move, I planted a Phanatic smooch on him and started spitting the kiss out with my paper tongue. When the '94 Phillies were presented, I bowed down when Lenny Dykstra was introduced and high-fived Kevin Stocker as he ran from the dugout. When John Kruk was announced, the stadium simply erupted. John had battled testicular cancer with radiation treatment after the Enchanted Season, and the fans were letting John know they were in his corner. Philly fans are the greatest. I stayed in Phanatic-mode, dramatically kneeling down, blessing myself and looking up to heaven as if to say, "Thanks, Big Fella!"

When I ventured into the stands, a bunch of guys in the 300 level started chanting, "We want Dave! We want Dave!"

Welcome to the Big Leagues, Mr. Burgoyne!

But like Curt Schilling was ready for those Braves, I was ready for our fans. I whipped out a can of Silly String and doused the bunch of them, to the delight of the fans sitting around them. Even the hecklers were impressed. Slimed, but impressed.

The next day, the *Inquirer* ran the headline: "New Rug Wearer, Same Old Phanatic." It was a solid review of my first day at work. The transition from Phanatic One to Two was a success.

Fifteen years have passed since I put this green costume on for the first time, and I still feel like the new guy. And that's a good thing, because every day is a new experience, with new people to meet, new laughs to play for, and new memories to make. Some things grow old in life, but I pray those things, those commodities the Phanatic trades in —the laughs, the smiles, and the memories, never grow old. Every spring fills me with new hope and makes me feel like a kid again. And, you know, that's why that '93 gang meant so much to me. They'll always make me feel and act like a boy eternal. And, after all, that's my job.

Wild Thing

"He didn't do it pretty, but face it, if Mitch did it 1-2-3 that year, you guys
wouldn't be writing this book. Think about it!"
— *Darren Daulton*

The Prodigal Son Returns

It was May 27, 1994. Homecoming. The Wild Thing was coming back to the Vet wearing a Houston Astros uniform, and every fan in the packed stadium prayed that Houston's starter would stumble so that the Wild Thing would see some action. Every time an Astro coach or manager walked out to the mound, the chant of "We Want Mitch" reverberated through the stadium like a Larry Andersen locker-rattler.

I knew Mitch always made his way from the dugout to the bullpen after the fifth inning, so I grabbed my trusty Super Soaker, hopped on my ATV, and got into position to enter the field from the truck ramp in right field. Mitch popped out of the dugout right on cue and headed down to the visitor's bullpen along the left-field foul line. As I ripped across the outfield on my four-wheeler, the crowd noise was swelling. The fans in left field were all on their feet. Some cheered, some jeered. Many held signs welcoming back their fallen hero.

I jumped off my bike just behind third base and followed Mitch down the foul line while pointing my oversized water gun at his back. Mitch playfully raised both hands over his head, looking the part of the '93 Prison Squad. Good-naturedly, he let me squirt him in his back as he marched. Everyone cheered, even the people who were there to boo Mitch. Of course, I'm sure there were some who were disappointed it was only a water gun.

Joe Carter also returned to the Vet in June of 1997 in the first interleague game between the Phillies and the Blue Jays. Joe knew that the Philadelphia boobirds would let the boos fly. Joe was the grinch who stole Philly's title and parade.

During the player warmups before the game, I started pointing at Joe Carter, pantomiming that the Phanatic hadn't forgotten what he did to the Phillies in '93. I even stepped out of character, because this was an extraordinary circumstance, like a Hatfield dropping in for noon tea at a McCoy's. I yelled out, "Hey, Joe, I'm coming after you in the fifth inning tonight.'

Joe smiled and returned fire. "Bring it on, Phanatic."

When the fifth inning ended, I came blazing across the field on the Phanatic four-wheeler, carrying the old Lasorda dummy. But this time, I dressed it in a Joe Carter jersey and Blue Jays cap. As the song "Whoomp! There It Is" played, I tossed the Carter dummy around, threw it up in the air, and repeatedly did belly flops onto it. Midway through all of the shenanigans, Joe came flying out of the dugout, grabbed the dummy, and started beating me with it. It was like Mount Lasorda erupting all over again! Except that Joe is a lot bigger! He stormed into the dugout after he had beaten me soundly, and I started to wonder if maybe he really was mad that I had denigrated the sacred Toronto Blue Jays uniform. But as everyone high-fived Joe in the dugout, a big grin spread across his face.

Still, I didn't take any chances. The next night, I eased up on the Joe Carter bashing. I didn't want Joe stalking me or hunting me down to let me know what he really thought of me. Then, before the third game of the set, Joe spotted me walking through the visitor's clubhouse and chided me. "Yo, Phanatic, where were you yesterday? You gotta come after me. That's what the fans come to see—me and you mixing it up. I'm going after your four-wheeler today."

"Bring it on, Joe," I said.

That day, before the game and after the National Anthem, Joe came running out of the dugout, flipped the bike over on its side and ran out behind third base pointing and laughing at me. The Phanatic was outraged. I put the water gun that I was holding down on the ground, rolled up my sleeves and marched out in a huff to where Joe was standing. This was war. *Mano-a-mascot*. We circled each other like two Sumo wrestlers and then lunged at each other like Rocky and Clubber Lang. The fur was flying as we rolled into the outfield. The Phillies were introduced and were taking the field as the Phanatic and the "villain" from '93 were settling things like men. Well, okay, like boys.

He started it.

You make us feel so young. That's what Philly's band of boys did for us in 1993. As Mayor Rendell observed, they supplied the jolt that electrified a lethargic city giant. The Phillies were a Marx Brothers show where nothing seemed planned, nothing looked rehearsed, and Groucho, aka Mitch Williams, was the central figure, deadpanning amidst the crumbling chaos of his own making. Yes, Mitch was the perfect Groucho, right in the middle of every imbroglio, exasperating friend and foe alike, pouting, spouting one-liners, and baffling everyone by dodging devastation that seemed forever imminent. As Jim Fregosi muttered, "Mitch doesn't have an ulcer himself. But he's a carrier."

TERRY MULHOLLAND: "Mitch was not your conventional closer. He'd come into a game, and it became a high-wire act. *Sports Illustrated* asked me once what it was like to have Mitch come into the game. I said it's like hiring a stunt pilot for an airline. He'll do a couple of loop-the-loops and thrill the passengers, but then he'll probably put that thing down on the ground pretty soft, nine out of ten times."

Yes, Mitch was Groucho, stunt pilot, and gambler—living to flirt with disaster and tempt fate. Bringing Mitch into a game was like pouring red wine into a glass while standing on a white carpet.

DUTCH DAULTON: "Face it, if Mitch had gotten them out 1-2-3 that year, you guys wouldn't be writing this book! He was a big kid. He wanted the ball all the time, and he'd throw a fit if he didn't get the ball. A lot of guys get timid. If they don't have their best stuff, they want to sit out. Not Mitch. He didn't do it pretty, but he was there pitching his heart out whenever you called. Fregosi would bring him in and head for the tunnel, smoking one heater after another. Then Mitch would walk a couple, give up a hit, load up the bases—and I'd go out to the mound and say, 'Okay, Poo [they called the Wild Thing "Mitchie-Poo" also] are you done now? You gonna get serious?'"

Yes, those Mitchie mound conferences … put them on a CD or a video, and everyone from Robin Williams to Jay Leno would be taking notes for their next stand-up routine.

PAUL HAGAN: "Mitch was as funny as any player I've ever met. He was just a big kid. The guys were telling me one day about a conference at the mound with Kruk, Dutch, Stocker, Mitch and Mickey. Mitch keeps saying, 'Let's try a pickoff at second.' The rest of them just blow him off, pay him no attention. Mitch keeps repeating it. Finally, Dutch says, 'No, Mitch,' and Mitch whines, 'See. Nobody *ever* wants to do what I want!'"

KRUK: "I said things to Mitch I wouldn't say to a dog out there at the mound. That was just Mitch. He knew I didn't mean anything by it. We played a lot of long games that year, and we'd be tired by the ninth. Then Mitch would come in and walk somebody. Guys on other teams would get on first base and tell me, 'I couldn't take this if Mitch was on my team.' Well, I got used to it. I knew when Mitch came in, I'd have someone to talk to at first base. I just hoped the guy who led off the inning was a nice guy to talk to."

If it's better to be talked about than not talked about, then Mitch was in better shape than anyone on the Phils. Darren Daulton is correct. Take Mitch

Williams off that team, and the epic loses the edge. The '93 Phils story becomes *The Three Musketeers* without d'Artagnan, *Taxi* without Louie, *Friends* without Joey. Most of all, it becomes *Major League* without Rick Vaughn (Charlie Sheen), the Wild Thing. The Phils skipped through that '93 season like a hurricane, and Mitch was the eye.

CURT SCHILLING: "No matter what you think about Mitch, you've got to realize two things: (1) we would not have gotten to the World Series without him. Say what you want about the stress, but the guy did the job, and (2) Mitch wanted the ball every single day. He made no excuses. He was always ready."

It's the rest of us who weren't ready. The Phils' 1993 announcer, Andy Musser, missed Game 3 of the World Series. Andy needed emergency surgery for a detached retina. He had first noticed the problem during the NLCS. Crony Richie Ashburn chuckled, "A doctor said it could be the result of stress. I guess Andy's just another victim of Mitch."

HARRY KALAS: "Stressful? Yes, Mitchie-Poo was stressful, but entertaining. I walked into Fregosi's office in San Diego one day and saw four packs of cigarettes on his desk. I said, 'Jim, you're not going to smoke all of them today, are you?' And Fregosi said, 'Not if Mitch doesn't pitch.'"

Mitch *was* entertaining. In Philly, during the Series, West Coast Video's rentals were off 30 - 40 percent, according to Steven Apple, their VP of communications at the time. United Artists lamented a slow weekend. *42nd Street* opened at the Merriam and had to offer half-price tickets on days when the Series was in Philadelphia. Mark Russell sold out his afternoon performance at the Keswick on Sunday, but was only partially full that evening when the Series was on. And Comedy Cabarets from Philly to Delaware took a big hit, owing, to a great extent, to Mitch's comedy-dramas on the mound.

ANDY SCARPATI, OWNER/OPERATOR OF THE COMEDY CABARET CHAIN: "The Phillies were so entertaining that postseason, they hurt the comedy business around here. Nobody wanted to leave home and miss the action on TV. With Mitch out there on the mound at the end of those games, our comedians couldn't compete. Business was down about 30 percent. Of course, Mitch put about 30 percent more people on the basepaths, so they might account for our empty seats."

ANGELO CATALDI, WIP PERSONALITY: "Mitch was astonishingly funny. I did a show for a while with Mitch and Kruk. The Krukker was funny, too. They never had a mean edge to their humor. But the thing about Mitch, even more than the humor, was the effect he had on the city. It was amazing. Everyone had a strong opinion about Mitch. Look what the guy went through with the death threats and the eggings to his house. Mitch brought out such passion in people around here! Literally! We had one caller on that show, an older woman. She called in and told Mitch, 'I'm glad you guys won that pennant, cause when you came into all those games, my husband and I had the best sex we ever had.' Well, Kruk, Mitch, and I laughed and thought—well, I don't know what we thought. But then she called again and thanked Mitch for turning her sex life around."

While Mitch specialized in all things topsy-turvy, he was also considerate and generous to a fault.

HARRY KALAS: "Mitch would give you the shirt off his back. He took me, LA, and DJ—about five of us in all—to Reno one off day. Mitch flew us all out there, paid for the whole thing. He bought us all some expensive ostrich leather boots. I think he ended up buying them for just about everybody after that."

MITCH: "Yeah, I bought them for Inky 'cause he complained that I hadn't given him a pair. Seeing Inky in those things was like seeing earrings on a pig."

Mitch liked ostrich boots. Think big kid here. He liked pickup trucks, and he liked watching videos of himself pitching—at least he said that in one of his early big-league interviews. Mitch might have enjoyed watching those videos, but he didn't necessarily consider them instructional. Mitch didn't want to change a lot. He walked into the majors as a Wild Thing, a hard thrower. And that's the way he was bent on leaving.

In his early years, Bobby Valentine of the Rangers had sent Mitch to a hypnotist to try to cure him of his wildness. As Mitch recalled, "They wanted to control my emotions. I pitch on emotions. It didn't work."

When Mitch came to Philly, Tug McGraw didn't have much luck getting into Mitch's head either.

TUG McGRAW: "I tried to talk to Mitch once and he made it clear to me: 'Nice try, Tug. I appreciate your help, but here's the truth. Ever since I've been old enough to throw a baseball, I've always done it this way. It's always worked, and when it stops working, I'm gonna walk away from this game and you can kiss my ass goodbye.'

"I liked Mitch. He's a straight-up, honest guy. He respected me, what I had accomplished, and I respected him. It was just a matter of a difference in style. The difference between Mitch and me is that I liked working out. I liked working on different things, designing new pitches. Mitch didn't like working out. He liked to throw hard. That's two different styles. It's not to say that one style is better than the other, but I felt, in crunch time, I needed those extra resources. I needed to be able to change speeds and hit spots with pitches. Mitch just threw it. And it worked for him. He had a lot of success."

MITCH WILLIAMS: "Look, I wasn't great. I was decent. I only wanted to be remembered as a guy who went out there and busted his butt."

Mitch is consistent. He could forget a loss like he could savor a win. He could dish out jokes and he could take them. Mitch was the brunt of so many gags and jokes about his wildness, his escape acts, and his pitching style. Mitch's pitching style was basically no style—just rear back and heave it. He flailed in his follow-through like a figure skater gyrating into a full axel or a gymnast launching into a cartwheel. As Larry Bowa noted, "Most guys have a toe plate on their landing shoe. Mitch has one on his glove."

Mitch was about action and motion, not technique. During the World Series, he told the press, "I was bored by baseball as a kid. I liked football. I just liked to go out there and let it all hang out, but I'd pay to watch *us* (the '93 Phils), because we're exciting."

And that's exactly what Mitch did. He let it all hang out all season long. When the postseason rolled in, the biggest kid on the squad answered the bell and tried to take out his opponent. But he had no punch left, only heart. When he let it all hang out this time, Joe Carter blasted the two of them into history—partnered eternally in the sport's lore, right there with Thomson and Branca.

As Tug says, there's got to be a winner and a loser in a contest. Mitch lost. And Mitch's take on the episode is this: "If it had to happen, I'm just glad it was Joe Carter who hit that home run. He's one of the finest people in the game, a real gentleman."

Mitch doesn't look back now. However, at 1:00 a.m. following the evening of October 23, he was still reliving that moment. As he was leaving the visitor's locker room in Toronto, the Wild Thing walked into Fregosi's office in jeans and a sweater and said, "Jimmy, I just want to thank you for never giving up on me this year. I'm sorry I let you and the team down tonight." The paternal pilot studied his harried reliever. Even then, Fregosi knew Mitch was taking his final walk out of a locker room as a Phillie. "You didn't let anybody down," Fregosi assured his big kid. "If it wasn't for you, we're not even in this *friggin'* thing. If it wasn't for you, we're watching this *bleeper* on TV. Hey, go home, Mitch, and rest up. Thanks for a great year."

Life Goes On

"You need two things to be a closer: no mind and a short memory. I'm a genius when it comes to the 'no mind' stuff."
— Mitch Williams

The scene: February, 2002. Clearwater, Florida, Phillies Phantasy Camp 2002. Phillies announcer Scott Graham is the emcee. Scott is introducing several ex-Phillie stars to a packed house at a casual evening event. Milt Thompson, John Denny, Bobby Wine, Del Unser, and others are seated at the dais. After Scott Graham presents Greg Luzinski, "The man known as the Bull, who hit 307 lifetime homers, was second in MVP voting in 1977, knocked in 1128 RBIs, and was famous for his Bull blasts," Scott spins toward Mitch, seated to his left, and begins his introduction. "And this is the man they called the Wild Thing, wh—o-o ..." Scott never finishes. Mitch reaches over, yanks the microphone from the startled emcee's hand, and announces, **"It was a low inside fastball, I suck, and I'm sorry."**

Mitch brings down the house. Groucho rides again. You bet your life.

In October 1993, crazed fans, as in fanatics, *were* trying to bring down Mitch's house in New Jersey. Fortunately they didn't. The worst thing that happened was that his house was "egged." The big yoke—sorry, joke—around Philly was, "Hey, they found the guy who threw the eggs at Mitch's house? Yeah, it was *Mitch*. He was trying to hit his neighbor's house."

After the World Series, Mitch headed directly down to his farm in Hico, Texas, "The 3 & 2 Ranch." Yes, the Series was a nightmare for Mitch, with his 20.25 ERA and his 0-2 record, and, of course, Carter's walk-off home run. However, there *were* some reasonable excuses for his funk. For one thing, he had scrapped his normal delivery and gone to a slide step in an effort to slow down the Blue Jays on the basepaths. Mitch had never pitched with that slide step, and he pitched as if he hadn't. Another thing, until Game 4 of the NLCS, Mitch had made 78 straight appearances over two seasons without once entering a game in the eighth inning in a save situation. However, he appeared in the eighth twice in the postseason—once in the playoffs and again in Game 2 of the Series. The bullpen, as Fregosi said, was barking, but Mitch never let out a yelp.

FREGOSI: "Right after that sixth game, Mitch stood up and said he made a bad pitch and Carter hit it. He made no excuses. I was very proud of him for that. And the best part of it was that, mentally, it didn't affect him, it didn't ruin his life. I think that speaks more for the individual than anything.

TERRY MULHOLLAND: "The only thing I felt bad about when we lost that Series was Mitch. We gave it everything we had, and just lost. We have nothing to be ashamed of. Neither does Mitch. Mitch made no excuses. He stood up to the world and said he made a bad pitch."

ANGELO CATALDI: "What Mitch went through—well, it's something that stays with you the rest of your life. But if it had to happen to anybody, I'm glad it happened to Mitch. He can handle it."

TUG McGRAW: "Mitch has a great perspective. If you only understand winning, then you'll be a miserable SOB. You have to be able to take a hit every once in a while. Mitch understands that."

Mitch wasn't long for Philadelphia after the Enchanted Season, though he never wanted to leave. He was traded to Houston later in the same year. Even then, the one-liners at Mitch's expense flew. Astros GM Bob Watson said, "Our concessionaires will love Mitch. Nobody will leave the park early. But manager Terry Collins and I will have to invest in Maalox and Grecian Formula."

Mitch's dunk in the choppy waters of immortality did not drown him as they would a lesser spirit. Mitch not only managed to keep his head above the waves, he also learned how to swim against the current, because, astoundingly, in a town noted for cruelty to its athletes, Philly has embraced the Wild Thing. Mitch gets cheers, not boos, in front of Philly's tough crowds.

How did that happen? Maybe it's because Mitch never once hung his head in shame or embarrassment. Or maybe Mitch left out the most important ingredient for any closer, on or off the diamond. Yes, a short memory and no brain help. But really, despite everything Mitch has gone through, he's just a kid who believes in happy endings.

> *"Out of the night that covers me,*
> *Black is the pitch from pole to pole*
> *I thank whatever gods may be*
> *For my unconquerable soul.*
> *In the fell clutch of circumstance*
> *I have not winced nor cried aloud*
> *Under the bludgeonings of chance,*
> *My head is bloody but unbowed."*
> — *William Ernest Henley*

Where Are They Now?

Larry Anderson

Nickname: "LA," "Grandpa," "Viejo Cabrió" (Means 'old goat' in Spanish)
Date of Birth: May 6, 1953
Place of Birth: Portland, OR
High School: 1971 graduate of Interlake High School (Seattle, WA)
How Obtained: Signed by Phillies as a free agent, 12/8/92
Baseball Career After 1993: Larry lasted one more season in the big leagues, retiring as a Phillie after the '94 campaign. He made stops in Reading and Scranton as a Phillies minor-league pitching coach.
What He's Doing These Days: Larry joined the Phillies broadcasting team in 1998. He resides just outside Philadelphia in Lafayette Hills, Pennsylvania.

Kim Batiste

Nickname: "Batty," "Paws" (Because of his large hands)
Date of Birth: March 15, 1968
Place of Birth: New Orleans, LA
High School: 1986 graduate of St. Amant High School (LA)
How Obtained: Phillies' third pick in June 1987
Baseball Career After 1993: Kim played one more season with the Phillies and then signed with the Giants in 1996. He was released after the '96 campaign.
What He's Doing These Days: Batty's still getting hits and making plays for the Nashua Pride in the Atlantic League. He goes home to Louisiana in the off season to be with family and friends.

Wes Chamberlain

Nickname: "Chili," "Chili World"
Date of Birth: April 13, 1966
Place of Birth: Chicago, IL
High School: 1984 graduate of Simeon High School
How Obtained: Acquired from Pittsburgh Pirates with Julio Peguero and a player to be named later (Tony Longmire) for Carmelo Martinez, 8/30/90
Baseball Career After 1993: Wes was traded to Boston during the '94 season and then spent time with Kansas City and Toronto before playing professional baseball in Japan. When he returned at the end of 1997, he jumped around to various organizations, including the Pirates, Mets, Cardinals and Rangers.
What He's Doing These Days: Wes is still roving the outfield and playing first base for the Newark Bears of the Atlantic League.

Darren Daulton

Nickname: "Dutch," "Bubba"
Date of Birth: January 3, 1962
Place of Birth: Arkansas City, KS
High School: 1980 graduate of Arkansas City (KS) High School
College: Attended Cowley County (KS) Community College
How Obtained: Phillies' 25th pick in the June, 1980 draft
Baseball Career After 1993: Darren batted .300 in a strike-shortened '94 campaign. He stayed with the Phils, struggling with injuries until July 21, 1997, when he was traded to the Florida Marlins for outfielder Billy McMillon. Darren won the championship ring he wanted so much that season and announced his retirement the following year in Philadelphia.
What He's Doing These Days: Darren resides outside of Tampa, Florida with his wife Nicole and their three children. He had a brief stint as the bullpen coach for the Devil Rays in 2001. He remains one of Philly's favorite athletes.

Mariano Duncan

Nickname: "Dunky"
Date of Birth: March 13, 1963
Place of Birth: San Pedro de Macoris, Dominican Republic
How Obtained: Signed as a free agent, 12/10/91
Baseball Career after 1993: Mariano followed his gutsy '93 performance by being named to the All-Star Game in '94. He was claimed off waivers by the Reds in August of '95 and signed by the Yankees before the '96 season. Mariano posted a .340 batting average that year, helping the Yanks to a World Championship over the Atlanta Braves.
What He's Doing These Days: Mariano splits time between Miami and Dominican Republic, where he is heavily involved with youth baseball programs in his home country.

Lenny Dykstra

Nickname: "Dude," "Nails"
Date of Birth: February 10, 1963
Place of Birth: Santa Ana, CA
High School: 1981 graduate of Garden Grove (CA) High School
How Obtained: Acquired from NY Mets with Roger McDowell and Tom Edens for Juan Samuel, 6/18/89
Baseball Career After 1993: Lenny was ravaged with injuries after his stellar postseason in '93. In 1994, he spent June and July on the DL and then missed the entire second half of the '95 season due to back problems. He did make up for his '93 All-Star Game snub by making the All Star team in '95. On May 19, 1996 the Dude was placed on the disabled list one last time, marking the end of his career.
What He's Doing These Days: Lenny lives outside of Los Angeles and owns a successful chain of car washes.

Jim Eisenreich

Nickname: "Eisey," "Dahmer," (Kruk's affectionate nickname for Jim)
Date of Birth: April 18, 1959
Place of Birth: St. Cloud, MN
High School: 1977 graduate of St. Cloud (MN) Technical High School
College: Attended St. Cloud State College (MN)
How Obtained: Signed by the Phillies as a free agent, 1/19/93
Baseball Career After 1993: Eisey continued to hit after the 1993 season. He posted batting averages of .300, .316 and .361 in the next three years as a Phil. He signed as a free agent with the Florida Marlins in 1997 and won a World Championship that year with Dutch. In May 1998, he and Gary Sheffield were part of a blockbuster deal that sent Mike Piazza and Todd Zeile to the Marlins. Eisey retired after the 1998 campaign, sporting a lifetime .290 batting average.
What He's Doing These Days: Jim continues to be a national spokesperson for Tourette Syndrome. He travels around the country speaking to children and educating them about Tourette Syndrome. In 1997, the Phillies recognized Eisey with a special award to commemorate his many contributions in the community.

Tommy Greene

Nickname: "Jethro" (He's from the sticks in North Carolina, and "Jethro" is his license plate), "Tee the Greene" (Harry Kalas's name for Tommy)
Date of Birth: April 6, 1967
Place of Birth: Lumberton, NC
High School: 1985 graduate of Whiteville (NC) High School
How Obtained: Acquired from Atlanta Braves with Dale Murphy for Jeff Parrett, Jim Vatcher and Victor Rosario, 8/3/90
Baseball Career After 1993: Tommy posted only two more victories after the 1993 season. Injuries plagued him throughout the '94, '95 and '96 seasons. He signed with the Houston Astros in 1997 but was released after only two appearances.
What He's Doing These Days: Tee the Greene is still talkin' baseball and whatever else is on his mind as a pitching coach for the Lincoln Saltdogs of the Northern League.

Dave Hollins

Nickname: "Headley" (Like Todd Pratt, he's got a big head), "Mikey" (Dave's self-proclaimed alter ego)
Date of Birth: May 25, 1966
Place of Birth: Buffalo, NY
High School: 1984 graduate of Orchid Park (NY) High School
College: Attended University of South Carolina and University of Buffalo
How Obtained: Selected by he Phillies in 1989 annual major-league winter draft
Baseball Career After 1993: Headley was traded to the Boston Red Sox on July 24, 1995 for outfielder Mark Whiten. He then made stops in Minnesota, Seattle, Anaheim and Toronto before returning to the Phillies in the spring of 2002.
What He's Doing These Days: Dave is still running like a linebacker for the Fightin' Phils and travels north to Buffalo, his hometown, in the off season.

Pete Incaviglia

Nickname: "Inky," "Load" (Mitch's pet name for Inky)
Date of Birth: April 2, 1962
Place of Birth: Pebble Beach, CA
High School: 1982 graduate of Monterey High School (CA)
College: Oklahoma State
How Obtained: Signed as a free agent, 12/8/92
Baseball Career After 1993: Inky was granted free agency after the '94 season and signed with the Chiba Lotte Marines of the Japan Pacific League. Pete came back to Philadelphia in 1996, bashing 16 home runs in 99 games, before being shipped to Baltimore with Todd Zeile for pitchers Calvin Maduro and Garrett Stephenson. Then it was off to the Yankees, Detroit, Houston, Arizona and then back to Houston in 2000.
What He's Doing These Days: Pete attempted a comeback in 2002 with the San Diego but did not remain with the club after spring training. He is living happily with his family in his adopted state of Texas.

Danny Jackson

Nickname: "DJ," "Jason" (*From Friday the 13th*)
Date of Birth: January 5, 1962
Place of Birth: San Antonio, TX
High School: 1980 graduate of Central High School (Aurora, CO)
College: Attended Trinidad State Junior College (CO) and University of Oklahoma
How Obtained: Acquired from Florida Marlins for Matt Whisenant and Joel Adamson, 11/17/92
Baseball Career After 1993: Danny made it to the All-Star Game in 1994, posting 14 wins in a strike-shortened season. He signed as a free agent with the Cardinals in 1995 and battled injuries until he was traded to the Padres in June of 1997. Two months later he announced his retirement.
What He's Doing These Days: DJ and his wife are living in the same town in Kansas where they first met. They have opened an 8,000 square-foot Fan Entertainment Center, which includes a 40-lane bowling alley, arcade and miniature golf course. His business is doing well; at least, he's not losing his shirt (sorry!).

Ricky Jordan

Nickname: "Cool Papa" (Ricky was real smooth out on the field)
Date of Birth: May 26, 1965
Place of Birth: Richmond, CA
High School: 1983 graduate of Grant (Sacramento, CA) High School
How Obtained: Phillies' first pick in June, 1983 draft
Baseball Career After 1993: Ricky signed as a free agent with the Angels in 1995, but injuries kept him from playing with the big club the entire season. The Seattle Mariners bought Ricky's contract in 1996, but shoulder injuries forced him to miss most of the season. Ricky retired midway through the 1997 season playing for the Pittsburgh Pirates' Double A team, the Carolina Mudcats.
What He's Doing These Days: Ricky was always a numbers guy and has applied those skills in his career after baseball. Ricky and his stepfather own and operate a tile marble and granite business, with Ricky doing most of the numbers-crunching. He's also enjoying coaching his two children's Little League teams.

John Kruk

Nickname: "Krukker," "Krukkie," "Jake" (From *Jake and the Fatman* TV show)
Date of Birth: February 9, 1961
Place of Birth: Charleston, WV
High School: 1979 graduate of Keyser High School
College: Attended Allegheny Community College
How Obtained: Acquired from San Diego with Randy Ready, June 3, 1989 for Chris James
Baseball Career After 1993: John recovered from testicular cancer in the off season and was in a Phillies uniform pounding out three hits and one RBI in the home opener in 1994. He batted .302 in 75 games before the strike and then was signed as a free agent in 1995 by the Chicago White Sox. On July 30, 1995, after only 159 plate appearances, the Krukker hit a single and walked away from the game. He ended his career with a perfect .300 batting average.
What He's Doing These Days: John and his wife Melissa announced the birth of a bouncing baby boy, Kyle, in 2002. The happy dad hosts *The Best Damn Sports Show Period* in Los Angeles for Fox Sports.

Tony Longmire

Date of Birth: August 12, 1968
Place of Birth: Vallejo, CA
High School: 1986 graduate of Hogan High School in Vallejo, CA
How Obtained: Acquired from the Pirates as the player to be named later along with Wes Chamberlain and Julio Peguero in a trade for Carmelo Martinez on 8/30/90
Baseball Career After 1993: Tony played two more seasons with the Phils, posting a .356 average in 104 at-bats in 1995, his final season in the majors.

Roger Mason

Nickname: "Mase"
Date of Birth: September 18, 1958
Place of Birth: Bellaire, MI
High School: 1976 graduate of Bellaire (MI) High School
College: Attended Saginaw Valley State College
How Obtained: Acquired from San Diego, 7/3/93 for Tim Mauser
Baseball Career After 1993: Roger went to the Mets in 1994, ending the year with a 3.75 ERA in 60 innings pitched. He had surgery on his right arm that off season and never fully recovered after two years of rehab.
What He's Doing These Days: Roger opened a restaurant called "Big League Pizza" in his hometown of Bellaire, Michigan.

Mickey Morandini

Nickname: "Mickey Mo," "Beaker" (He looks like the Muppets character)
Date of Birth: April 22, 1966
Place of Birth: Valparaiso, IN
High School: 1984 graduate of Leechburg Area (PA) High School
College: Attended Indiana University
How Obtained: Phillies' fifth pick, June 1988 free agent draft

Baseball Career After 1993: Mickey earned a spot on the All-Star team in 1995 and was always a Philly fan favorite. In 1998, he was traded in a deal that sent him to the Cubs for outfielder Doug Glanville. That year, Mickey helped lead the Cubs to a post-season berth, though they lost to the Braves in three games. Mickey came back to Philadelphia for a brief stint in 2000 but was dealt to Toronto towards the end of the season. He finished out his career in Toronto.

What He's Doing These Days: Mickey and family are back in their home state of Indiana, where Mickey is coaching Little League and assisting his wife, Peg, in opening a card shop.

Terry Mulholland

Nickname: "Mo"
Date of Birth: March 9, 1963
Place of Birth: Uniontown, PA
High School: 1981 graduate of Laurel Highlands High School (Uniontown, PA)
College: Marietta (OH) College
How Obtained: Acquired from San Francisco with Dennis Cook and Charlie Hayes, 6/18/89 for Steve Bedrosian and a player to be named later (Rick Parker)
Baseball Career After 1993: Terry's career has mirrored that of the Energizer Bunny—he just keeps going and going. In 1994, he was traded to the Yankees (with Jeff Patterson) in exchange for pitchers Bobby Munoz and Ryan Karp and infielder Kevin Jordan. He signed as a free agent back with the Phils in 1996 but was dealt later that year to Seattle for shortstop Desi Relaford. He has since played for the Giants, Cubs, Braves, Dodgers and Indians.

What He's Doing These Days: Terry is still pitching for the Indians and has earned the reputation of being a steady and gutsy pitcher, doing anything that the team asks him to do.

Todd Pratt

Nickname: "Tank," "Tankhead" (Todd's got a large cranium)
Date of Birth: February 9, 1967
Place of Birth: Bellevue, NE
High School: 1985 graduate of Hilltop High School (CA)
How Obtained: Selected by the Phillies in 1991 annual major-league winter draft, 12/9/91
Baseball Career After 1993: Todd was traded to the Cubs in '95 and then spent four seasons with the Mets. In 1999, Todd hit a solo home run in the bottom of the tenth inning of Game 4 of the NLDS to beat the Diamondbacks 4-3. It was only the fourth postseason series-clinching walk-off HR in baseball history.

What He's Doing These Days: Tank made his return to the Phillies for the 2001 season and is still providing leadership to young catchers in the organization.

Ben Rivera

Nickname: "Big Ben"
Date of Birth: January 11, 1968
Place of Birth: San Pedro de Macoris, Dominican Republic
High School: Graduate of San Jose High School (San Pedro de Macoris)
How Obtained: Acquired from the Atlanta Braves, 5/28/92 for RHP Donnie Elliott

Baseball Career After 1993: Ben finished his major-league career the following year and has pitched for various teams in the independent minor-league system.

Curt Schilling
Nickname: "Schil" "Uncle Fester" (He had a bad haircut in spring training. Larry Andersen put a light bulb in Curt's mouth and he looked just like the *Addams Family* star—well, if you ask Larry, anyway.)
Date of Birth: November 14, 1966
Place of Birth: Anchorage, AK
High School: 1985 graduate of Shadow Mountain High in Arizona
College: Yavapai Junior College in Arizona
How Obtained: Acquired 4/2/92 from the Houston Astros for Jason Grimsley
Baseball Career After 1993: No question about it, 1993 was Curt's coming-out party. Although sometimes plagued with arm injuries, Schilling sprinkled in dominant years for the Phillies, including back-to-back years of 300 strikeouts or more (1997 and 1998). He led the league in complete games in '96 and '98 with 8 and 15 respectively. He was sent to Arizona in a blockbuster deal that brought pitchers Omar Daal, Nelson Figueroa, Vicente Padilla, and first baseman Travis Lee to the Phillies.
What He's Doing These Days: Curt help lead the Diamondbacks to a World Championship in 2001 and continued his red light postseason play, splitting MVP honors with teammate Randy Johnson in the World Series.

Kevin Stocker
Nickname: "Stock"
Date of Birth: February 13, 1970
Place of Birth: Spokane, WA
High School: 1988 graduate of Central Valley High School in Spokane, WA
College: Attended the University of Washington
How Obtained: Phillies' second pick in June, 1991 draft
Baseball Career After 1993: Kevin teamed up with Mickey Morandini to become a solid double-play combination for four years after '93. He was traded to the Tampa Bay Devil Rays for outfielder Bobby Abreu after the expansion draft of 1997. He finished out his playing career in 2000 with the Angels.
What He's Doing These Days: Kevin is still adjusting to "retired" life with his wife Brooke and three children.

Bobby Thigpen
Nickname: "Thiggy"
Date of Birth: July 17, 1963
Place of Birth: Tallahassee, FL
High School: Aucilla Christian Academy in Monticello, Florida
College: Attended Mississippi State College
How Obtained: Acquired from the Chicago White Sox for Jose Deleon, 8/10/93
Baseball Career After 1993: Bobby signed with the Seattle Mariners in 1994 where he ended his career the same season.

Milt Thompson

Nickname: "Papa Thompson," "Uncle Milty," "Scooter" (Because of his speed—he can really scoot)
Date of Birth: January 5, 1959
Place of Birth: Washington, D.C.
High School: 1977 graduate of Zadok Magruder High in Washington, D.C.
College: Attended Howard University
How Obtained: Signed as a free agent, 12/9/92
Baseball Career After 1993: Milt went on to play in Houston, Los Angeles and Colorado before retiring after the 1996 season.
What He's Doing These Days: Milt was always a fan favorite. He has been a familiar presence in the Phillies' minor-league system since his playing days ended in '96. He is currently a minor-league roving hitting instructor and a friendly face at the Phillies Phantasy camp in Clearwater, Florida every year.

David West

Nickname: "Westy," "Big Bird" (Because of the way he walks)
Date of Birth: September 1, 1964
Place of Birth: Memphis, TN
High School: 1983 graduate of Craigmont High School (TN)
How Obtained: Acquired from the Minnesota Twins, 12/5/92, for Mike Hartley
Baseball Career After 1993: Due to injuries, David never duplicated his stellar 1993 performance. He missed most of the 1996 season and all of 1997. He retired after trying to make a comeback with the Red Sox in 1998.

Mitch Williams

Nickname: "Wild Thing," "Mitchie-poo," (Harry Kalas called him Mitchie-Poo over the air at 4:41 a.m., when Mitch knocked in the winning run) "Dumb Dumb" (Inky's pet name for Mitch)
Date of Birth: November 17, 1964
Place of Birth: Santa Ana, CA
High School: 1982 graduate of West Linn (OR) High School
How Obtained: Acquired from the Chicago Cubs for Chuck McElroy and Bob Scanlan, 4/7/91
Baseball Career After 1993: On December 2, 1994, amid much fanfare, Mitch was traded to the Houston Astros for pitchers Doug Jones and Jeff Juden. He spent 1995 with the Angels and part of 1996 with the Royals before walking away from the game for good.
What He's Doing These Days: Mitch has been seen all over the Delaware Valley since retiring in 1996. He opened up a restaurant inside the Vet with John Kruk and had a short-lived local TV show with the Krukker. He is currently the manager for the Atlantic City Surf of the Northern League, and, yes, Mitch is one of the most heartily cheered in old-timer's games and get-togethers.

Jim Fregosi – Manager

Nickname: "Skip"
Date of Birth: April 4, 1942

Place of Birth: San Francisco, CA

Playing Career: Jim hit .265 during his 18-year major-league career which included stints in Los Angeles (AL), California, Texas, New York (NL) and Pittsburgh. He became the Phillies' skipper on April 23, 1991, replacing Nick Leyva.

Baseball Career After 1993: Jim ended his managerial career with the Phillies in 1996, posting a record of 431-463 with the Phils. He spent 1997 and 1998 with the San Francisco Giants in their scouting department.

What He's Doing These Days: Jim is currently the special assistant to the general manager and is a major-league scout for the team he knocked out of the World Series in 1993—the Atlanta Braves.

Larry Bowa – Third Base Coach

Nickname: "Bo," "Pee Wee"

Date of Birth: December 6, 1945

Place of Birth: Sacramento, CA

High School: Graduate of McCatchy High School (Sacramento, CA)

College: Attended Sacramento City College

Playing Career: Played 20 years of pro baseball, signing with the Phillies in 1965. Larry was posted the highest career fielding percentage in league history (.980) at shortstop.

Baseball Career After 1993: Larry continued to coach third for the Phils through the 1996 season. He went on to join the coaching staff in Anaheim for three years and spent the 2000 season with the Mariners.

What He's Doing These Days: Larry still bleeds Phillies red. He became the Phils 49th manager on November 1, 2000. In his first season as skipper of the Phils, he was named NL Manager of the Year by the Baseball Writers Association of America, *The Sporting News, USA Today Baseball Weekly,* and *ESPN the Magazine.*

Denis Menke – Hitting Instructor

Nickname: "Menk," "Tomato Face" (LA's special name for Dennis)

Date of Birth: July 21, 1940

Place of Birth: Bancroft, IA

High School: 1958 graduate of St. John's High School (Bancroft, IA)

Playing Career: 17 year pro with 13 years in the major leagues with Milwaukee, Atlanta, Houston and Cincinnati. Dennis was a sure-handed shortstop and also played the other infield positions and a few games in the outfield.

Baseball Career After 1993: Dennis's last year in Philadelphia was 1996. He joined the Cincinnati Reds coaching staff in 1997. He split his duties between bench coach and hitting instructor and retired after the 2000 season.

What He's Doing These Days: Denis is enjoying the retired life, spending most of his time golfing and babysitting his grandchildren.

Johnny Podres – Pitching Coach

Nickname: "Pods"

Date of Birth: September 30, 1932

Place of Birth: Witherbee, NY

High School: Graduate of Mineville High School

Playing Career: Spent 15 seasons in the major leagues as a member of the Dodgers

(1953-55, 1957-66), Tigers (1966-67), and Padres (1969). Johnny's probably best remembered for his dominating performance in the 1955 World Series as he posted two wins, including a 2-0 shutout of the Yankees in Game 7.

Baseball Career After 1993: Pods still offered words of encouragement to Phillies pitching staffs through the 1995 season.

What He's Doing These Days: Pods is enjoying the retired life and living in New York.

Mel Roberts – First Base Coach

Nickname: Just "Mel"
Date of Birth: January 18, 1943
Place of Birth: Abington, PA
High School: Graduate of Abington High School (PA)
College: Attended Temple University and Spartanburg Tech
Playing Career: Originally signed by the Dodgers, Mel played nine years of professional baseball (1962-1970) as an outfielder. Mel was a loyal Phillies minor-league coach and instructor when he was called up in 1991 as the team's first base coach
Baseball Career After 1993: Mel joined the Atlanta Braves organization in 1996, coaching the Greenville Braves in the southern League. He also spent two years with the Richmond Braves, Atlanta's Double A affiliate.
What He's Doing These Days: Mel is back coaching Greenville, which is closer to his home in Spartanburg, South Carolina. Mel is so committed to the youth in Spartanburg that a scholarship was established in his name. On July 26, 1993, the mayor of Spartanburg proclaimed the day Mel Roberts Day in the community.

Mike Ryan – Bullpen Coach

Nickname: "Irish"
Date of Birth: November 25, 1941
Place of Birth: Haverhill, MA
High School: Graduate of St. James (Haverhill, MA) High School
Playing Career: "Irish" Mike played 11 years in the major leagues with the Red Sox (1964-67), Phillies (1968-73) and Pirates (1974).
Baseball Career After 1993: Mike continued coaching in the bullpen and retired with his pal Johnny Podres after the 1995 season.
What He's Doing These Days: Irish is enjoying retirement in New Hampshire, floating on his lake and refurbishing old houses. He's found peace knowing that he won't have to catch a baseball out of a helicopter ever again.

John Vukovich – Dugout Assistant

Nickname: "Vuke"
Date of Birth: July 31, 1947
Place of Birth: Sacramento, CA
High School: Graduate of Amador County High School (Sutter Creek, CA)
College: Graduate of American River College (Sacramento)
Playing Career: Played 16 years of pro baseball including parts of 10 seasons in the major leagues with the Phillies, Brewers and Reds. John was a member of the Phillies' 1980 championship team, backing up a certain third baseman named Mike Schmidt.
What He's Doing These Days: "Vuke" has stood shoulder to shoulder with five different Phillies managers including his friend Larry Bowa, and he remains one of the best bench coaches in the game.